THE KENNEDY HEIRS

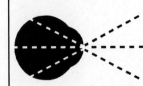

This Large Print Book carries the
Seal of Approval of N.A.V.H.

THE KENNEDY HEIRS

JOHN, CAROLINE, AND THE NEW GENERATION — A LEGACY OF TRIUMPH AND TRAGEDY

J. RANDY TARABORRELLI

THORNDIKE PRESS
A part of Gale, a Cengage Company

GALE
A Cengage Company

Farmington Hills, Mich • San Francisco • New York • Waterville, Maine
Meriden, Conn • Mason, Ohio • Chicago

GALE
A Cengage Company

Copyright © 2019 by Rose Books, Inc.
Thorndike Press, a part of Gale, a Cengage Company.

ALL RIGHTS RESERVED
Thorndike Press® Large Print Nonfiction.
The text of this Large Print edition is unabridged.
Other aspects of the book may vary from the original edition.
Set in 16 pt. Plantin.

LIBRARY OF CONGRESS CIP DATA ON FILE.
CATALOGUING IN PUBLICATION FOR THIS BOOK
IS AVAILABLE FROM THE LIBRARY OF CONGRESS

ISBN-13: 978-1-4328-6676-1 (hardcover alk. paper)

Published in 2019 by arrangement with Macmillan Publishing Group,
LLC/St. Martin's Press

Printed in Mexico
1 2 3 4 5 6 7 23 22 21 20 19

For my sister, Roz,
a sister, a friend, a survivor
whose love for life, for family
inspires all who know her
to shine on

CONTENTS

INTRODUCTION 11

BOOK I

Part One: Son of Camelot 21
Prologue: The Tide of Events 23
Part Two: The Senator's Family 107
Part Three: Being Kennedy 163
Part Four: Family Secrets 209
Part Five: The Caretakers 271
Part Six: A Tale of Two Brothers . . . 301
Part Seven: The Reckoning 387
Part Eight: The In-Laws 467
Part Nine: Running Out of Time . . . 485

BOOK II

Part One: Daughter of Camelot . . . 531
Prologue: Pinkie Swear 533
Part Two: The Politics of Marriage . . 571
Part Three: "The Kennedy Curse
    Ends Here" 591

Part Four: The Shriver Way 617
Part Five: Family at War and Peace . . 665
Part Six: A Political Gamble 739
Part Seven: Betrayal of the Heart . . . 789
Part Eight: A Miraculous Life 815
Part Nine: Demons 831
Part Ten: The Family Endures 853
Epilogue: American Promise 892
Postscript: Permission to Speak
    Freely 905

AUTHOR'S NOTE. 913
RESEARCH 921
SOURCES AND OTHER
    NOTES 929
PERSONAL
    ACKNOWLEDGMENTS . . . 965

And even in our sleep, pain which cannot
forget falls drop by drop upon the heart
until in our own despair, against our will,
comes wisdom through the awful
grace of God.

— AESCHYLUS

INTRODUCTION

For our purposes with *The Kennedy Heirs,* I ask that you consider the first generation of Kennedys to be the one that includes those children born to Joseph Patrick Kennedy Sr. (born 1888) and his wife, Rose Elizabeth Fitzgerald Kennedy (born 1890). Their first child was Joseph Patrick Jr. (born 1915). The rest followed quickly: John Fitzgerald (born 1917), Rose Marie (born 1918), Kathleen Agnes (born 1920), Eunice Mary (born 1921), Patricia Helen (born 1924), Robert Francis (born 1925), Jean Ann (born 1928), and Edward Moore (born 1932).

The second generation are the surviving children of Joseph and Rose, and their spouses: John and Jacqueline Bouvier (born 1929), Eunice and Sargent Shriver (born 1915), Pat and Peter Lawford (born 1923), Bobby and Ethel Skakel (born 1928), Jean and Stephen Smith (born 1927), and Ted and Virginia Joan Bennett (born 1936) and, later, Victoria Reggie (born 1954).

11

The third generation — the primary subject of this work — comprises the progeny of the second, and there were many, twenty-nine in all.

John and Jackie were the parents of Caroline Bouvier (born 1957) and John Fitzgerald Jr. (born 1960).

Eunice and Sargent were the parents of Robert Sargent III (born 1954), Maria Owings (born 1955), Timothy Perry (born 1959), Mark Kennedy (born 1964), and Anthony Paul (born 1965).

Pat and Peter Lawford were the parents of Christopher Kennedy (born 1955), Sydney Maleia (born 1956), Victoria Francis (born 1958), and Robin Elizabeth (born 1961).

Bobby and Ethel were the parents of Kathleen Hartington (born 1951), Joseph Patrick II (born 1952), Robert Francis Jr. (born 1954), David Anthony (born 1955), Mary Courtney (born 1956), Michael LeMoyne (born 1958), Mary Kerry (born 1959), Christopher George (born 1963), Matthew Maxwell Taylor (born 1965), Douglas Harriman (born 1967), and Rory Elizabeth (born 1968).

Jean and Stephen were the parents of Stephen Edward Jr. (born 1957), William Kennedy (born 1960), Amanda Mary (born 1967), and Kym Maria (born 1972).

Edward (Ted) and Joan were the parents of Kara Anne (born 1960), Edward Moore Jr.

(born 1961), and Patrick Joseph (born 1967). The fourth generation, then, would be the many children of the third, some of whom are also considered for this work, such as Joseph Patrick III (son of Joseph II and Sheila Rauch, born 1980), John Conor (son of Robert II and Mary Richardson, born 1994), and John "Jack" Bouvier Kennedy (son of Caroline Kennedy and Edwin Arthur Schlossberg, born 1993).

My mandate with this volume was not to write about every Kennedy of the third generation who ever drew breath. Admittedly, as I was doing my research, some held my fascination more than others. In the end, I sought to tell what I think are the stories that best explored the truth of who these people were in one another's lives and that also revealed their true selves, warts and all, as well as their many contributions to our society. After all, this is a generation that was ubiquitous in our culture in the 1960s, '70s, '80s, into the '90s, and beyond, and, as you will read on these pages, even today. Maybe *Life* once put it best when the magazine reported of them: "They were America's children. Born at a time when the nation itself seemed reborn, the grandchildren of Joseph and Rose Kennedy became a compelling symbol of the future for people hungry for change. And we couldn't get enough of them. Americans probably saw more of the Kennedys on television and in photographs than they saw of their own families. At a time when the American family was said to be falling apart, the Kennedy family seemed of biblical strength."

A myth I think worth dispelling from the outset is that these particular Kennedys did little to nothing of any great significance in our culture. In fact, they were all raised to have a strong sense of noblesse oblige. Of course, when one considers the global ramifications of what President Kennedy did with his time in office, maybe not much can compare. The same holds true of the great work of Bobby and Ted, not to mention Sargent and Eunice. "They're all competing with icons and legends," political consultant David Axelrod, who has advised several of them, noted of the younger Kennedys. However, as you will read, so many of them have contributed a great deal to the world, if not in elected office, then as activists. Ethel's daughters Rory and Kerry make films about poverty and travel the world as warriors for social justice, for instance; Eunice's son Tim Shriver runs his mother's Special Olympics; Jackie's daughter, Caroline Kennedy, works tirelessly to raise funds for education. "If such causes appear modest next to staring down the Russians, integrating the South or going to the moon, they are not," *Time* once observed.

"They are simply of their time." Some would change the world in small ways in the private sector, others in a much bigger manner while in public office. The number of legislation, for instance, either sponsored or cosponsored by Ted's son Patrick Kennedy during his many years in government amounts to 3,156. Put it this way: There aren't many who do nothing with their lives. Not in that family.

What I have also learned over the years as a Kennedy historian is that, despite the complexities of their lives, personal and political, it's really not that difficult to understand them. Of course, some of their experiences have been amplified tenfold because of money, power, and prestige. Also, fame does tend to twist everything. However, at the heart of their stories are the kinds of choices and decisions similar, at least I think, to those we may have made in our own lives as we've attempted to navigate the sometimes rocky terrain of getting along with parents, siblings, and children. I believe we can relate to the Kennedys on a deep, visceral level that has to do with a thing so basic and so uncomplicated: our shared humanity. To my mind, this is why the Kennedys' story continues to resonate. Plus, of course, the many tragedies of their lives have reached out to us over the years, causing our hearts to ache unbearably for them.

At a symposium on the legacy of the Kennedy women at the John Fitzgerald Kennedy Presidential Library and Museum, Kerry Kennedy told me, "It's difficult when your most private moments are also your most public moments, but it's interesting, too, because we have never really felt alone in any of it. We have always felt at one with the American public, and I think they have felt the same dynamic with us. There's this special, symbiotic relationship Americans have with my family going all the way back to my grandparents, to President Kennedy and my aunt Jackie, to my father, my mom . . . Uncle Teddy, Aunt Joan . . . my late brother David . . . and while I think a lot of it has to do with basic empathy, I also think it has to do with a collective human experience. All people have troubles in their lives. If understanding how we have dealt with our own problems can in some way help people cope with their own, well, then I think that's good. In fact, I think that's very good, and I know my family members would agree."

Senator Ted Kennedy put it this way in addressing the question of how the Kennedys dealt with tragedy. "Yes, we have had some hard knocks," he told me. "But we have survived because we have heart. And heart matters."

Here's a hard truth, though: The name "Kennedy" can inflame as much as inspire; there are people for whom the very name stirs

16

up anger and resentment. Their critics believe the Kennedys, especially those of the third and fourth generations, to be an entitled and spoiled lot used to getting away with bad behavior and never suffering true consequences because of it. Maybe *Newsweek* put it best in 1998 when describing what it called "the duality of the Kennedy experience in the popular imagination — sin and service." There have certainly been times of great disgrace — many of which have to do with self-inflicted tragedies — that remain an integral part of family history and, as such, are closely examined in these pages. However, I hope you'll agree that even those parents, sons, or daughters of this American dynasty who've at times been perhaps not so deserving of our admiration still have certain traits instantly recognizable not only in people we know and love, but maybe in ourselves, too.

"Family is family," John Kennedy Jr. told me when I had a chance to interview him after the press conference for the unveiling of his *George* magazine in September 1995. "You can pick the Kennedys apart, and I'm sure you will," he said with a nod at what he knew I did for a living, "but at the end of the day, we're just people trying to understand each other as we share this incredible life we've all been blessed with. It's nothing more than just that, if you really want to know the truth."

BOOK I

PART I
SON OF CAMELOT

PROLOGUE

THE TIDE OF EVENTS
July 1999

John Kennedy didn't want to have this fight again, but he also knew there was no way around it. He and his wife, Carolyn Bessette-Kennedy, had been invited to his cousin Rory's wedding at the family's private compound in Hyannis Port. "And . . . here we go again," he told his personal assistant, Rose-Marie Terenzio. He cursed under his breath, dreading the argument he knew was in the offing with his wife over it.

The problem John faced was that from the first time Carolyn ever set foot on the family's property some four years earlier, she didn't feel that she fit in with his family. While he and his relatives always felt insulated against the world at the compound, cocooned within its familiar, pleasant surroundings, she just felt exposed, as if her deepest insecurities were on display. On some level, he understood that only a person who'd actually been

23

raised a Kennedy could truly fathom the complex machinations of the family's culture — the competitive nature of their sportsmanship, the constant and not-so-gentle ribbing of one another, their unique camaraderie and secret language, not to mention their constant obsession over the family business: politics, of course. The Kennedys had always existed in an exclusive world, and even John had to admit that sometimes they weren't welcoming to outsiders.

In truth, Carolyn wasn't really that close to Rory, the late Senator Robert F. Kennedy's daughter. Was she really expected to be friends with every one of John's twenty-seven cousins and their spouses and other partners, as well as all his aunts and uncles? That wasn't the primary reason for Carolyn's trepidation, however. Nor did it have to do with the feelings of inadequacy that somehow always washed over her whenever she was around the Kennedys. She'd dealt with it all in the past and had managed to get through many uncomfortable visits. The truth about this upcoming wedding was that she had a sinking intuition, maybe even a premonition about it. Whatever it was, it was telling her not to go.

To John, Carolyn's reasoning seemed pretty weak. *"You just don't want to?"* After four years of tolerating his relatives, he didn't understand why she couldn't just endure one more party. So John went ahead and sent back the RSVP for two. It was a family obligation, he decided, and Carolyn would just have to sort through her emotions about it and attend. She was a Kennedy by marriage, and sometimes Kennedys had to do what they didn't want to do for the sake of the greater good. The storm would pass.

John was wrong; Carolyn wouldn't let the storm blow over. In fact, it just grew in intensity. "They had a pretty big argument about it," said a very good friend of Carolyn's. "What was at stake for her was more than just getting her way. It had to do with respect, with being visible in her marriage, with being recognized . . . *acknowledged.* In a family full of loud voices, one thing Carolyn had learned about being around the Kennedys was that she had to speak up if she ever wanted to be heard."

The irony of this marital dispute would not have eluded anyone aware of John's personal history. He and Carolyn were actually of the same mind, at least in some important respects. Especially in recent years, John had been battling preconceived notions of how he was supposed to act as the namesake and only son of America's thirty-fifth President, John Fitzgerald Kennedy, and First Lady Jacqueline Bouvier Kennedy Onassis. Like Carolyn, he didn't like being told what to do either, and he roundly rejected the cookie-cutter version of how a Kennedy of his generation was *supposed* to act. If he squinted at the equation hard enough, he probably would have been able to identify with Carolyn's side of it. However, as often happens when a person is in the middle of a big fight, he could only see his side. "Carolyn's not going," he glumly told RoseMarie Terenzio a few days before the Saturday wedding. "I just have to accept that I'm going alone."

"But John, that's only asking for trouble," RoseMarie said.

"Well, I'm not going to fight her on it anymore," John said, seeming fed up with it all.

"It's just not good, John," she said. Not only did RoseMarie feel Carolyn should be present as John's spouse, she worried that her absence would send a message to the world about the state of their union. It would definitely spark a firestorm of rumors, she felt, which, as usual, she would then be responsible for containing. After all, John was a special case in the Kennedy family. Any of them could show up without their partners and it wouldn't have mattered much to the press. It's not as if Ethel's son Bobby Jr. or Ted's son Teddy Jr. would have caused a media sensation by going stag to a cousin's wedding. However, as the most popular member of the new generation, all eyes were

26

always on John — and even more so in recent years since taking Carolyn as his wife. His being alone would be noticed, and the following week would find RoseMarie inundated with queries — all of which could be avoided if Carolyn just went to the doggone wedding. Therefore, without being asked to do so by John, she slipped into his office and called Carolyn herself.

RoseMarie, a New York Italian American, was known to be a straight shooter, forthright and blunt. "Carolyn, are you fucking kidding me?" she asked, getting right to the point. "What are you doing? You're smarter than this. You don't want to put John in a position where he has to explain where you are, and you don't want to put yourself in a position of being judged. You get enough of that." Somehow RoseMarie was able to convince Carolyn that her judgment was being crippled by emotion. Eventually, Carolyn agreed to accompany John to the wedding.

Of course, when Carolyn told John she'd changed her mind, he was elated. He promised that this would be the last time he'd ever insist that she go with him to this kind of family event at the Kennedy compound. "I'll owe you one" is how he put it. He would fly them both up to Hyannis Port in his Piper Saratoga, he said. They'd attend the wedding, spend the night, and leave the very next day. She wouldn't regret it. "Just wait and see," he assured her. "Things are going to be great." Then he flashed his dazzling smile, usually her cue to melt into his arms. What she didn't do, though, was tell him how she *really* felt. That deep sadness she'd been trying to shake for longer than she cared to admit somehow now felt even more acute.

"She told me she felt manipulated and compromised," said Carolyn's trusted friend, "as if she had no authority over her own life. She said she was putting John on probation. 'I'm going to give it three more months and see how I feel,' she said. 'Are you sure you're not just pissed off because you don't like being told what to do?' I asked her. She admitted that this might be the case. She felt she needed a cooling-off period and that in a few months she'd have more clarity. They'd been having a lot of marital problems lately, she said, and she was worn down by them."

Was she thinking divorce? "Who divorces *John Kennedy Jr.?*" she asked. "You'd have to be insane, or at least that's what people will think." However, she said that if she decided on it she would steel herself for a serious fight and get through it as best she could. Even though she was thrown by events from time to time, Carolyn had demonstrated a new kind of focus and determination ever since she married John. Maybe in that respect she was becoming a little more "Kennedy" than even she knew. Whatever the case, Carolyn said she actually felt better about things because at least now she had a plan. She just needed more time.

As for John, there wasn't as much joy in his victory as Carolyn believed. He knew she felt bullied. "This same fight you keep having with her about being with your relatives, it has to stop," his good friend John Perry Barlow told him. "It's not good, John. Not for you. Not for her. Definitely not for your marriage."

John had to agree. He'd set it all straight after Rory's wedding, he decided. Like Carolyn, he, too, just needed a little more time, not to figure out how he felt, but instead how to fix things with the woman he truly loved. Who knows? Perhaps John, a real student of history when it came to his father's administration, could hear the words of President Kennedy echoing in his head: "The hour of decision has arrived. We cannot afford to wait and see what happens, while the tide of events sweeps over and beyond us. We must use time as a tool . . . We must carve out our own destiny."

John knew what his destiny held, and it was to be with Carolyn. He wanted to make it right with her.

He was thirty-eight. She was only thirty-three. They had all the time in the world.

CHOSEN ONE

Five Years Earlier: May 19, 1994

Thirty-three-year-old John Kennedy Jr. stood next to the telescope he had so loved as a child, still in the exact same place it had been when he was growing up — in the corner of a large square drawing room with high ceilings, wide windows, and French doors facing an exquisite view of the city, north, south, and west all the way to the reservoir. On either side of the telescope, falling with grace onto polished hardwood floors, were red-and-gold silk drapes. Around it were multiple stacks of books and magazines on shelves, on tables, on the floor. "Orderly chaos," is how John's mother, Jacqueline Kennedy Onassis, once put it, having lived among it for almost thirty years.

"Always loved this thing," John told his uncle Yusha Auchincloss as he slid his fingers across the telescope. "Mummy bought this for me when I was a kid," he added as he bent down and peered into the tube at the

31

iridescent New York vista.

"It's a beaut, all right," said Yusha. Yusha, the stepbrother of John's mother, then recalled to John the day Jackie first showed him the telescope in a Manhattan store window. She said she wanted to buy it for her boy on the occasion of his seventh birthday. He remembered it as being "typical" of his stepsister to purchase a present she felt could be used as a learning tool.

Just an hour earlier, John and Yusha had wept while their beloved Jackie took her last breath. As the two men spoke, John's aunt Ethel Kennedy puttered around in the kitchen, preparing tea for those who'd stayed behind after saying their final goodbyes, including John's uncle Ted Kennedy and his wife, Vicki.

It had all happened so quickly. Jackie had just been diagnosed with non-Hodgkin's lymphoma a few months earlier, in January. After the diagnosis, a priority for her was the spending of quality time with her longtime companion, the financier Maurice Tempelsman; her children, John and Caroline; and her grandchildren by Caroline — Rose, Tatiana, and John, better known as Jack.

Taking a step back from the telescope, John rose to his full six-foot-one height. Somehow he always seemed taller, though. Maybe it was his self-confidence that gave him the appearance of greater stature; his body was lean and trimly built like that of a dedicated athlete. He was arguably the best-looking of the Kennedys of his generation, with his square-jawed, lean, and angular features, his shock of thick black hair, the deep brown eyes and gleaming smile. The moment a person shook his hand, John made a deep impression. It wasn't just the firm grip, it was also the laser-focused eye contact — friendly, curious, intense, all at the same time.

Like his mother, John had mastered the art of making anyone with whom he was engaged feel as if he were the only person of relevance in that moment. His sister, Caroline, didn't possess quite the same gift. Not always comfortable with direct eye contact from people, especially reporters, she'd make it clear that she didn't welcome intrusion. Caroline was like Jackie; both could shut a person down if he had the temerity to ask an intrusive question. John was more like his father; he didn't avoid invasive inquiries, he addressed them eagerly, almost like a politician, but without the slickness that comes with a hidden agenda.

Again, much like a person in politics, John could also command a room. He had an innate ability to communicate ideas with eloquence and passion, qualities a lot of people felt were genetic. However, not every Kennedy was blessed with them. For instance, John's cousin Patrick — Ted's son —

was less authoritative. Even though he'd been in government since he was just twenty-one — elected to the Rhode Island House of Representatives in 1988 as the youngest member of the family to ever hold office — Patrick had to work hard at, as he once put it, "being *that* guy, when, actually, I'm *this* guy." *Time* noted, "Speechmaking so terrified Patrick that colleagues recalled seeing his hands shake from across the chamber." Patrick, of course, proved himself over time because he put in the work to do so. However, it definitely wasn't a fait accompli that just because a person was born a Kennedy he or she would be a natural communicator; Patrick's uncle Bobby Kennedy Sr. was also a clumsy speaker at first; he, too, had to really work at it. However, when John Kennedy Jr. addressed the Democratic National Convention in July 1988 to introduce his uncle Teddy, he somehow seemed to have *it* naturally, whatever *it* is:

Over a quarter century ago my father stood before you to accept the nomination for the presidency of the United States. So many of you came into public service because of him. In a very real sense because of you he is with us still, and for that I'm grateful to all of you. I owe a special debt to the man his nephews and nieces call Teddy, not just because of what he means to me personally but because of the causes he's carried on. He has shown that an unwavering commitment to the poor, to the elderly, to those without hope, regardless of fashion or convention, is the greatest reward of public service. I'm not a political leader, but I can speak for those of my age who have been inspired by Teddy to give their energy and their ideas to their community . . . He has shown that our hope is not lost idealism but a realistic possibility.

It wasn't much, but it was enough to convince a lot of people that John could very well be the heir apparent to the Kennedy throne. A two-minute standing ovation for the twenty-seven-year-old Kennedy scion said it all.

When *People* magazine named him "Sexiest Man Alive" that same year, John took it in stride and accepted as par for the course the gentle ribbing from friends and relatives that went along with such silliness. He didn't surround himself with sycophants. It didn't matter who a person was, John showed that person respect if he was engaged by him. One observer of his life aptly noted, "he had the ability to spend twenty seconds with you and leave you feeling as if the sun had just shone on you and you alone." For example, once at Hickory Hill — the home owned by Ethel Kennedy, where his cousins had been raised

— John was having a conversation with Fina Harvin about politics. She was smart and engaging, even if she was "only" the daughter of Ethel's governess. As they spoke, a beautiful and sophisticated young woman approached and began hitting on John, completely ignoring Fina. Maybe the interloper even wondered what such a plain-clothed, "ordinary" girl could possibly mean to him. John looked at the gorgeous stranger and said, "excuse me, but I'm talking to *this* young lady right now." Then he turned his back on the other person and continued his conversation with Fina.

Another interesting component to his personality was his temper. John had a short fuse. He could take a lot, but there would come a point when he would just explode. When that happened he could unleash a fury that was surprising considering his generally amiable personality. Madonna, when she dated him back in 1985, used to complain about it to her friends. At the time, she was separated from her husband, Sean Penn, also known for his volatile temper. She told one person that John was "slightly more frightening." Whereas Sean would act out, perhaps give a photographer a body shot just to vent, somehow John's way seemed more personal. Madonna said he would get up in her face, maybe an inch away, and scream at her at the top of his lungs when they were in a fight.

That romance lasted just six months. All the women with whom John would become romantically involved would eventually feel the brunt of his fury, and none would ever forget it.

One of the problems John Kennedy faced was that most of his relatives viewed him as a sort of "chosen one" since he was the son and namesake of the family's only President. His father had gotten an early start in politics. At twenty-nine, John Fitzgerald Kennedy was elected to Congress. At thirty-four, his son told a reporter, "I've never really been a long horizon type person."

These days, most of John's cousins were invested in political and philanthropic activities, while he toiled away at a boring nine-to-five in the Manhattan district attorney's office. When, at twenty-six, Representative Patrick Kennedy was asked if he wanted to one day be President, he didn't even hesitate. "Yes. Absolutely," he said. Another cousin, Joe — Ethel's eldest son — had started a company, Citizens Energy, to provide oil to the underprivileged. He abandoned that enterprise in 1986 to become a Massachusetts congressman (in the same seat John's father had held from 1947 to 1953). At that time, Joe turned Citizens over to his brother Michael, who was now doing an admirable job with it. Yet another cousin, Kathleen — Ethel's oldest — also had her eye on politics;

she would become lieutenant governor of Maryland in just a year's time. Her brother Bobby was an environmental activist and an attorney for Hudson Riverkeeper, dedicated to keeping the Hudson River and its shores clean. Many of John's other relatives of his generation were charting similar paths.

"It wasn't as if John had never fulfilled the family's long-standing mandate to be of service," noted Senator George Smathers in a 1999 interview; he was one of JFK's best friends in the Senate and had been an usher at his wedding to Jackie. "I remember that when he was fifteen, he and his cousin Tim [Shriver] went to Guatemala to assist earthquake survivors. When he was in his twenties, he worked on a program to help the disabled in New York City. I know he dabbled in an organization to assist in youth drug prevention. Nothing really stuck, though."

More recently, John had founded Reaching up, a foundation he designed specifically to care for the mentally ill. He was also on the board of the Robin Hood Foundation, a retinue founded by Wall Street millionaires devoted to programs benefiting New York's poor children. Though he was obviously trying — and a lot of people thought he was doing well with philanthropy — John still couldn't shake the feeling that he wasn't making much of an impression, at least not like many of his Kennedy cousins. "You are what you do," his aunt Ethel had told him. "But how do you compete with *those* people?" John later asked, speaking of Ethel's children, as well as Ted's and Eunice's, in particular. It didn't help that some of his cousins rubbed his nose in their overachieving ways. During a particularly virulent argument, one cousin who had always been competitive with John said, "When I stack my value to society against yours, I win. I win by a lot, and you know it." John never got over the criticism.

John's sister, Caroline, had a more clear-eyed vision of how she wanted things to unfold in her life. She sailed through school with mostly good grades, traveled a great deal, and had a lot of friends. Though she became a lawyer, she wasn't practicing because she'd decided to focus on her husband and children. Like her mother, she was devoted to family. She also had a wide range of charities in which she was passionately involved. Whereas John felt he was just killing time in the DA's office, his sister's days were full of scheduled activity. John would sometimes complain to her that he'd been at a crossroads for most of his life, trying to determine the best way forward in terms of keeping up with the other Kennedys. This would always cause Caroline to lose patience with him. She couldn't have cared less about keeping up with the other Kennedys.

The Kennedy siblings were different in

other ways, too, such as in the way they handled the burden of their family responsibility to legacy, as evidenced by a wide-ranging discussion between brother and sister about funeral preparation the night their mother died.

"Caroline said she didn't want any mention of Aristotle Onassis during the service," Yusha Auchincloss would recall in a 1999 interview. "But John didn't want to ignore Onassis's place in their mother's life. 'After all, she's Jacqueline Kennedy *Onassis,*' he said. 'How can we not mention that she was married to Ari?' After Ari's death back in 1975, Jackie could have dropped the 'Onassis' surname and reverted to 'Kennedy' or even 'Bouvier.' She didn't. Caroline's mind was made up about it, though. In terms of Jackie's place in American history, she reasoned, she should only be remembered as a former First Lady who'd been married to an assassinated President. The Onassis years were a private matter for family, Caroline said, not something my stepsister ever meant to be played out in public. It was only the press who had made it such a spectacle."

John didn't agree. He reasoned that even though Jackie knew full well when she married Ari that the world would not approve, she'd had the courage of her convictions to do so anyway. In his mind, marrying Ari had been a brave move, one that should be lauded

40

during the funeral service, not ignored. He felt that Caroline's targeting of the press in the Onassis matter was disingenuous; the real truth was that she simply didn't want the man's name mentioned because she just hadn't liked him.

While John had gotten along with the Greek tycoon, Caroline never warmed to him. He could never replace her father, not that he ever tried. However, John took Ari at his word when he said he wasn't trying to be his father; he just wanted to take him to baseball games or out on his yacht where he would teach him how to fish. John didn't have high expectations of Ari. He could see, even as a kid, that what mattered most was that Ari made his mother happy, or as Jackie once put it, "Aristotle Onassis rescued me at a time when my life was engulfed in shadows."

"What should I call your mom when I meet her?" John's friends would often ask him. "Call her 'Mrs. Onassis,' unless she tells you otherwise" would be his quick answer. In the matter of Onassis's placement at Jackie's service, though, Caroline would prevail. The Greek tycoon's name would not be mentioned, nor would any of his relatives or friends who knew Jackie be invited to the funeral.

Then there was a debate about Jackie's sister, Lee. Should she be allowed to speak? The two hadn't been close in recent years; it was only in the final months of Jackie's life that Lee emerged as a supportive presence. Caroline was angry at her aunt and didn't want her to have a significant place in the service. John was torn; Lee's son, Anthony, was not only his cousin but his best friend. He pled his case but, in the end, Caroline again had her way.

That conversation was followed by another having to do with the scope of the funeral. Ted Kennedy wanted it to be big and ceremonial for public consumption, with cameras in the church. John agreed. However, Caroline was against it. She wanted the service to be more private, no cameras. Again, she would have her way; Jackie's service would end up being a private one at St. Ignatius Loyola Church, where she had been baptized and confirmed, and with no cameras, just a public address system to the crowds gathered on the streets in front of the church.

In the end, Caroline had won all three debates. This dynamic had always prevailed in the siblings' relationship, though. One of the problems John faced was that as forthcoming as he was with others, he was reticent about expressing himself to his own sister. He never wanted to argue with her. Jackie had raised them to be there for each other, always. John loved his older sibling, trusted her implicitly, and simply didn't want to fight with her. Of course, this sometimes meant that he would bottle up his feelings, which would sometimes result in those infamous flashes of anger toward others.

"At the end of the day, as always, Caroline had her way with the arrangements," John later complained to his friend John Perry Barlow. Barlow was a former Grateful Dead lyricist who went on to become an internet rights pioneer and human rights activist. He and John had been close friends for years, ever since Jackie made arrangements for her son to be a wrangler on Bar Cross Ranch near Pinedale, Wyoming (where Barlow grew up), for a couple of months back when John was seventeen.

"Why don't you, for once in your life, stand up to your sister?" Barlow asked. "No, that's not how we are," John said. "She's usually right, anyway," he added.

"But it's not good, John," Barlow told him. "She walks all over you." Sounding defeated, John said he understood that but it's just the way it had always been with them. "Well, change it," Barlow exclaimed. John said he would, "one day soon."

A few days later, following the funeral Mass, members of the family and a few close friends boarded a chartered plane at LaGuardia that would also take Jackie's body to Washington, D.C. She was then to be laid to rest next to John Fitzgerald Kennedy, the thirty-fifth President of the United States, at

Arlington National Cemetery. Fewer than a hundred people would then gather on a hillside before the same eternal flame that was first lit years earlier by Jackie in honor of her martyred husband.

"Guess we're orphans now, me and Caroline," John told Gustavo Paredes after Jackie was buried. Gustavo, who was five years older than John, had spent most of his youth and then early adult life in the company of the Kennedys. He was the son of Providencia Paredes — "Provi" — from the Dominican Republic, Jackie's assistant at the White House who then transitioned into a new role as a close friend of the former First Lady's. When he was about seven, Gustavo used to have such admiration for President Kennedy's well-tailored suits. "Sure wish *I* could have a suit like that," he would tell him. Jack would promise that once he was out of office, he would give him a couple suits as souvenirs by which to remember his administration. Shortly after he made that vow, second grader Gustavo was being picked up by Secret Service men at his Catholic school for his own protection because the President had been shot. He then attended JFK's funeral. Now, all these years later, he was at John's side as Jack's widow was also being laid to rest. "You get to this place in life, and you think, now what?" John told him. "Who are you? Are you a grown-up now? At some

44

point, all of us face this existential crisis, don't we?"

Gustavo wasn't sure how to respond. He said that the John Kennedy he knew just lived his life in the moment "and avoids questions to which there are no easy answers."

John nodded. "But maybe it's time I challenged myself," he said, all this according to Gustavo's memory as the two men walked back to their car after the service. Gustavo agreed with John, but also reminded him that he had his whole life ahead of him. "Just don't forget what your mother used to say," he cautioned him: " 'Whatever you do, don't end up being some old Kennedy living on a hill with lots of money and lots of people kissing your ass, none of whom expect much from you because . . .' "

" '. . . they know you don't expect much of yourself,' " John said, finishing the thought with a smile.

By June 1994, a month had passed since the the death of John's mother. "Sorry, man," he apologized as he slid his lanky frame into a restaurant booth at one of his favorite Italian restaurants, Ecco in Tribeca. He was meeting his childhood friend Stephen Styles-Cooper, with whom he had gone to school.

John was exactly fifteen minutes late, just as he was for almost every appointment, which, for him, happened to be right on time.

45

It was his employment of what he called "the system." He'd learned a long time ago that he could never arrive in a restaurant before a friend because, if so, he would have to sit alone and field questions from strangers, sign autographs, and be for them who they so desperately wanted him to be. If he showed up late, at least there would probably be someone at the table waiting for him who could then run interference. If his dinner companion was later than he was, he'd just have to circle the block until that person showed up. Then he'd give that friend hell. "You can't be late," he'd insist. "Because if you are, it totally screws with the system." After John settled in, the two friends quickly ordered their food. It was difficult for Stephen to ignore the stares of other diners as the room began to buzz. During a wide-ranging conversation typical of friends catching up, the subject turned to John's love life.

For almost six years, John had been dating the actress Daryl Hannah. Something about it never seemed right, though. Was it because Jackie never approved of her? She tried, and at some points along the way actually got along with her, but John knew that his mother always had reservations. John had measured most of the women in his life by Jackie's opinion of them. If his mother approved, as she did of a girlfriend named Christina Haag, John would decide he wasn't sure how he felt about her. He usually ended up pulling away from her. However, if Jackie disapproved, as she did of Daryl Hannah, John became even more attached. Was it because he didn't want to give his mother the satisfaction of being right?

"Daryl should have been over long ago," John admitted. He said she was still attached to her previous boyfriend, the musician Jackson Browne, and that he was tired of trying to figure out why. Besides, a new woman had just entered the picture, someone his mother had not had the chance to meet. John probably would have introduced them had Jackie not suddenly become so ill. Maybe it was a blessing in disguise, though. Without his mother's view, any relationship that unfolded with this newcomer would have to either succeed or fail strictly on its own merits, and perhaps that was a good thing.

"Her name is Carolyn," John told Stephen Styles-Cooper as they got ready to leave the restaurant. "And what about Daryl?" Stephen wondered. John shook his head. "To every thing there is a season, I guess," he said as he threw twenty bucks onto the table. "*Ahhh,* yes, Ecclesiastes," Stephen concluded with a nod. "um . . . no," John said, grinning. "The Byrds."

THE GIRL FOR JOHN

Carolyn Jean Bessette-Kennedy was born on January 7, 1966, in White Plains, New York, the youngest child of William and Ann Bessette. She had two siblings, twins Lauren and Lisa, born in 1964. William, an architectural engineer, and Ann, who was a schoolteacher and later an administrator in the Chappaqua public school system, divorced around 1970. After Ann married Richard Freeman, an orthopedic surgeon with three children of his own, the blended family relocated to Old Greenwich, Connecticut. Carolyn never really reconciled her parents' divorce and, some of her relatives have said, on a deep level felt abandoned by her natural father even though they did have a relationship. "He wasn't there for her in the way she would have liked, and she often questioned her mother as to why the couple made the decision to divorce," said her good friend from Old Greenwich Stewart Price. "It troubled her. She was raised Roman Catholic and used to say she would never divorce. 'It just will never happen,' she told me. 'I have these weird daddy issues,' she said, 'and I would never want to do that to a child of my own.' "

Carolyn attended Juniper Hill elementary School and then St. Mary's High School before going off to Boston University School of Education, from which she graduated in 1988. "Sometimes she seemed a little stand-offish, that is until you got to know her," said Stewart Price. "Then, when you were some-one she trusted, she was affectionate, the kind of woman who would touch you when she talked to you, connected to you. She was a real hugger, and not just quick hugs but the best, warmest kind."

Carolyn was tall, about five foot ten, thin, and held herself like a high-fashion model, with golden-blond hair — her stylist once described her natural color as "pale brown" — an aquiline nose, and wide-set, cornflower-blue eyes under artfully designed brows. She was stunning. While she considered becom-ing a model, she ultimately found herself working as a saleswoman at the Calvin Klein store in Boston's Chestnut Hill Mall and then as a rep handling Klein's celebrity clientele.

During her seven years at Calvin Klein, Carolyn would rise up the ranks from celeb-rity sales to director of PR at the flagship store in Manhattan and the head of "show production," putting in long hours casting models for shows and scouting nightclubs for new faces. That's when she met John, at a function hosted by Calvin Klein.

"She was exactly the kind of girl I imagined would date someone like John Kennedy Jr. — and she intimidated the hell out of me," recalled his personal assistant, RoseMarie Terenzio, of Carolyn in her book, *Fairy Tale Interrupted.* "Wearing a Calvin Klein pencil skirt, a white T-shirt, stiletto heels, and blue nail polish, she looked like a model, effortlessly perfect in an unstudied yet elegant outfit. When John introduced us, I felt like I'd gained ten pounds and shrunk three inches. But after he left her with me in the reception area, I could tell Carolyn was different from the typical gorgeous girls you see around Manhattan. She wasn't trying too hard. She wasn't trying at all."

"The downloading of John-John history," as one of Carolyn's friends put it (though he would never refer to himself that way) happened quickly and effortlessly. Over a series of what he later described as "intense dates," John opened up to Carolyn about a wide range of personal subjects. For instance, he talked about starting his private schooling at St. David's on Manhattan's East Side before being transferred to Collegiate for third grade. He explained that his mother thought the second school was more understanding of youngsters who couldn't catch on. He confided that he had trouble because of his ADD, which, combined with dyslexia, compromised his learning ability to the point where Jackie often found herself pleading with his instructors for leniency. He also opened up about the trauma of dealing with the assassination of a father he barely remembered.

It was only because of his loving and understanding mother, he said, that his youth hadn't just spun completely out of control, especially after his uncle was also murdered. For instance, she did everything possible to make sure an overprotective Secret Service didn't interfere with his being able to have as normal a childhood as possible. It was amazing, John noted, that Jackie had been able to devote herself to him and his sister, considering her own personal problems. He talked about the PTSD — post-traumatic stress disorder — she experienced after having witnessed the killing of her husband and the courage she then displayed in finding ways to live life on her own terms. He said he felt the least he could do in return was to be, as he put it, "a good son" and try to live up to her expectations even if he didn't always agree with them. In particular, he hated letting her down with his continuing bad grades. As a young man, he would fail the bar exam twice, which would be especially difficult on his mother given the attention these failures

51

generated in the media.

Carolyn had a mixed reaction to John. First of all, her heart went out to him. He'd obviously not had an easy life, and the way he opened up to her about it endeared him to her. Having her feel sorry for him wasn't his intention, though, and she sensed as much. She realized that his only goal was to have her know him as something more than President Kennedy's son, arguably the most famous Kennedy of his generation. His life was what it was, the good and the bad. It was an extraordinary story, epic really, with iconic characters as diverse as Bobby Kennedy and Aristotle Onassis in major roles. She knew he hoped that in explaining some of it to her she might understand him on a level deeper than what she'd maybe heard or read about in the past. Carolyn was also impressed by John's love for his mother. To have such respect for the woman who raised him spoke well of him; Carolyn felt the same way about her own mother, who'd always been there for her without fail.

Also adding to Carolyn's overall impression of John was — as much as she tried to hide it — her complete disbelief that *the* John F. Kennedy Jr. was not only sitting across from her, but that he was being so vulnerable with her. She was quite conscious of the fact that this person had been a pop culture icon since the age of three when he stood next to his grieving mother and sister and stole America's heart by saluting his father's coffin. She'd been hearing about him most of her life, and especially after she got to New York, where he was a constant fixture, a local as well as national celebrity. Many women had been swept away by this gorgeous man, and, though she wouldn't have wanted him to know it during their first dates, certainly Carolyn was now one of them. She later said, "He's staggeringly handsome. I don't know how else to put it. *Who looks like that?*" She once described getting to know John as an "out of body" experience. In other words, she could barely believe he was even in her presence. "I kept having to say, 'Snap out of it, he's just a guy,' " is how she put it to her friend Carole DiFalco (who would soon marry John's cousin Anthony Radziwill in August 1994). The first time he kissed her, she would later recall, was a real revelation. He leaned in and caressed her lips with his own. When he finally pulled away, she stared at him with wonderment. She was only able to manage two words: *"Holy shit."*

The fascination was reciprocal. John found it easy to be candid with Carolyn for one reason: he sensed from the outset that she was someone who'd be special to him for many years to come. Maybe it was love at first sight, or at least it felt that way to John. It was as if he'd known her all his life, as if they already had a history together. "You know how you always hear about meeting a girl and knowing instantly that she's the one, and you think, nah . . . that kind of instant connection doesn't happen in real life," he told Gustavo Paredes after meeting Carolyn. "Well, that happened to me." Another of his friends, Rob Littell, noted, "She had an aura that pulled him in. So taken was he by her, he couldn't wait for the Kennedys to meet her. This was unusual. 'We're sort of a tribe,' he would say. 'I don't want to scare a woman off.' "

John knew, though, the greatest challenge for Carolyn would probably be as it had been for many others he'd dated: meeting the senior women of the family. It had always been tough for his girlfriends to meet Jackie for the first time, of course. Now that she was gone, meeting Ethel Kennedy was the loaded proposition.

John told Carolyn that Ethel was the family's matriarch now that his grandmother Rose was so infirm. It wasn't Eunice, Jean, or Pat — the other senior women in the immediate family — or Joan, who had married into it by taking Ted as her husband. Because of the power of her personality and her utter devotion to all the Kennedys, if someone wanted to fit in with the family these days, that person would have to work hard to please

one woman and one woman alone: Bobby's
widow, Ethel.

55

The Matriarch

Ethel Skakel Kennedy was born on April 11, 1928, to Ann Brannack and George Skakel in Chicago, Illinois, the sixth child of seven: three sons and four daughters. The entrepreneurial George was a self-made man. Though he didn't finish grade school, he became wealthy thanks to his business, Great Lakes Carbon. His company eventually became a multibillion-dollar, high-tech manufacturer of graphite and carbon used as substitutes for coal in domestic heating. The family lived in an enormous mansion, waited on hand and foot by a legion of dutiful maids, butlers, and other household functionaries. The Skakels always treated their household employees with old-world formality, a manner Ethel would one day adopt with her own staff at her homes in Virginia and Massachusetts.

Ethel's mother, Ann, was a real character. Called "Big Ann" because she weighed more than 250 pounds, she was deeply religious and strict but also had a wild sense of humor.

She was notoriously cheap, and clever about it, too. For instance, she had business cards printed up that identified her in different ways — "Ann B. Skakel's Hardware & Tools" or "Ann B. Skakel's Garage Parts and Accessories" — and would extract from her purse the one that might get a shopkeeper to believe she had her own business and deserved some sort of discount on whatever goods she desired. Saving a buck really made her day.

The Skakels moved to New York when Ethel was about about four. An avid sports enthusiast, she was always adventurous and fun-loving. She attended the all-girls Greenwich Academy in Connecticut as well as the Convent of the Sacred Heart and then the parochial Manhattanville College in New York. She wasn't a good student and, always one to flaunt the rules, was often in trouble. Or as she jokingly once told her daughter Rory, "I wasn't a deep thinker, like I am now." Her son Christopher put it this way: "Mummy is a Skakel, and as a Skakel she inherited a healthy disregard for authority in all its forms."

When her friend from Manhattanville College Jean Kennedy introduced Ethel to her older brother Robert Kennedy — Bobby — in the winter of their freshman year of 1945, the two seemed perfect for each other: he appreciated her sense of humor; she was attracted to his intelligence and his desire to be of service to others, which, as she would learn, was how he'd been raised. Somehow, though, Bobby ended up dating Ethel's older sister Pat — and he did so for two years. With a smile, Ethel now refers to this period in her life as a "dark time." Finally, Bobby saw the light, and he and Ethel had a three-year courtship and then married on June 17, 1950, at St. Mary's Roman Catholic Church in Greenwich. She and Bobby went on to have eleven children: Kathleen, Joseph, Robert Jr., David, Courtney, Michael, Kerry, Christopher, Max, Douglas, and, after Bobby's death, Rory, whom she was expecting when he was assassinated. She was pregnant an astonishing ninety-nine months over roughly a seventeen-year period.

In the spring of 1957, Ethel purchased a new family home, the sprawling estate known as Hickory Hill at 1147 Chain Bridge Road in McLean, Virginia. Bobby Kennedy Jr. recalled, "The antebellum estate was formerly home to Robert E. Lee's father, 'Light Horse Harry' Lee, a Revolutionary War hero, and later to general George McClellan, the Union Army's supreme commander during the early years of the Civil War. Supreme Court Justice Robert H. Jackson, who presided over the trials of the Nazis at Nuremberg, later acquired the house and sold it to uncle Jack and Jackie. When they opted for a smaller Georgetown residence, my mother bought Hickory Hill."

Note that Bobby is clear that Ethel purchased the property, not she and Bobby. In fact, she bought the estate with her own money from her family's great wealth.

In years to come, Ethel would remain focused on raising her family and on Bobby's ascension to political power, while clinging to devout Roman Catholic values. Meanwhile, she had big dreams of her own, especially after her brother-in-law Jack was elected President and Bobby became his attorney general (the youngest, at thirty-five, since 1814). When Bobby decided to run for President in 1968, Ethel felt sure she was destined for the White House, following Jackie Kennedy as First Lady. Most people agreed she would be a different kind of First Lady than her sister-in-law but also a very good one. Those dreams were dashed when Bobby was assassinated by Sirhan Sirhan in June 1968.

At the time of Bobby's death, Ethel was just forty and pregnant with Rory. The country was touched by her tremendous courage as she tried to put her life back together and raise her children as the single mother of a very private public family. "The only way to deal with eleven children, with their friends, and with their first cousins is with structure, discipline, routine, and organization," said her son Christopher. "And Mummy brought structure, discipline, routine, and organization to every aspect of our lives."

"She sent the older kids to places and countries around the world so we could understand and live with different cultures," added Kerry. "So Kathleen went and lived on an Indian reservation. Joe lived with a family in Spain. Bobby lived with a group of people in Africa. Courtney and I worked on a farm in Utah. David worked with Cesar Chavez." Some people took a somewhat dimmer view of Ethel's sending the children away, though. They felt Ethel really just wanted distance from them. After all, when they were around, things weren't exactly peaceful. The boys, especially, would feel the brunt of her frustration and, at times, rage, at the way things had turned out for her. She would often become physically abusive, slapping or hitting them.

Sometimes she would walk up to one of her offspring and, standing within just inches of the child, raise her hands and clap loudly three times in order to get their attention, chastise them, or demand silence. "She's like some kind of crazy person," is how one of her sons once put it. *Who does that?* It was one thing to do it to a child, but Ethel would sometimes do the same thing to the adults in her life! Ethel's brother Jim Skakel once explained that she got the habit from their mother, Ann. "She did the same thing," he said, "but it was usually three claps followed by two pretty good slaps right across the face."

"My mother and I would take the boys to the park to get them out of Mrs. Kennedy's hair," recalled Fina Harvin, the daughter of Ethel's governess, Ena Bernard; both lived at Hickory Hill. "People would come up to us and say, 'My goodness. Who do all these wild kids belong to?' My mother would say, 'We don't know. We have no idea. We just take care of them. Mind your own business. Go away.' We could never say they were Kennedy children because we were just so afraid of people doing them harm."

Perhaps as a consequence of the way Ethel treated her sons, they would all grow up with blatantly sexist attitudes. Maybe it made sense. After all, they'd spent their youths living with an angry mother and feeling the brunt of her rage. Perhaps it's not so surprising that the boys would grow up with conflicted feelings and a lack of respect for the opposite sex.

Misogyny wasn't unusual in the Kennedy family, even before the third generation. With the possible exception of Bobby, the Kennedy men of the second generation had cheated on their wives, as had the patriarch, Joseph Kennedy I. Their generation of women worried that this behavior would be passed on to their children. For instance, Jackie's biggest problem with Ethel's sons wasn't their drug taking and rabble-rousing, as has been widely reported over the years. It was the way they mistreated the women in their lives. That just wasn't the way she wanted to raise John. As a result, he really was different from his cousins when it came to the way he viewed the opposite sex.

Joseph F. Gargan, the son of Rose Kennedy's sister, had worked on JFK's 1960 run and chaired RFK's presidential campaign; he also worked for Ted and was one of those who dove into the lake looking for Mary Jo Kopechne's body after the senator's accident at Chappaquiddick. He once remembered, "Ethel's sons Michael, Bobby, and Joe were with John at the Kennedy compound one afternoon for a barbecue while their girlfriends — whoever they were at the time, I can't remember — were in the kitchen talking to Ethel. The women appeared to be intensely involved in their conversation with Ethel. 'Looks like they're brainstorming about something major,' John said, bemused. 'I can promise you it won't be much of a storm,' Joe said, chuckling. 'In other words, don't expect much rain from *that* bunch.' His brothers thought the quip was hilarious; 'That's pretty good,' said Bobby. 'I'm gonna write that one down and use it later.' John looked at the two of them and said, 'Man. You guys disgust me.' Another time, I remember their brother Michael was talking about Kathleen and, in trying to pay her a compliment, said, 'Look, fact is, she's as good as *any* female politician.' Again, John couldn't believe his ears. 'Unbelievable,' he muttered as he walked away. He wasn't raised the same way as the others."

By 1994, more than twenty-five years had passed since Ethel Kennedy had become a widow. She was still considered a national treasure, a beloved figure from the so-called "Camelot" era. With philanthropy always foremost on her mind, "she became a force of nature in her own right," said her daughter Courtney, "and was questioning authority and calling congressmen and governors and senators to say, why aren't things being made better?" She also traveled the world on charitable missions. "Seeing our mother walk in his [Bobby's] absence along that same path really impacted all of us," her son Max said.

One thing she didn't do, though, was take a chance on another romantic relationship. "In many ways, the house was a shrine to RFK," Noelle Bombardier, who was the estate manager of Hickory Hill, recalled. "You couldn't walk into a room, even the bathrooms, without seeing his smiling, handsome face. The walls of Mrs. Kennedy's bedroom and the tops of bureaus were also covered with framed photographs of him. It was important to her that every picture be in its rightful place. Each spring when we were getting ready to relocate to Hyannis Port for the season, it was my job to gather up all of the photographs and take them to the compound. I would then place the pictures in the exact spots in that bedroom as they had been in her McLean bedroom. She wanted both rooms to look exactly alike. I think it was a statement of control in her shifting world. However, it made me feel very sad. I would find myself sitting on the bed, trying to compose myself and not cry. The more I got to know and care about Mrs. Kennedy, the harder it was to accept that she was always in such sorrow, that she never reconciled her husband's murder . . . that there was something broken on the inside."

"It's been so many years, why didn't you marry after Bobby?" the singer Andy Williams once asked her. He and Ethel dated in the 1970s and into the '80s. When he would visit her at Hickory Hill, he would sleep in the same room with her, sometimes even in the same bed, yet they were never intimate. In a 2010 interview, he said he never tried to make a move on her, waiting for some sign before he'd ever take it upon himself. It never came. "Why, Ethel?" he finally asked her. "We could have something great here, you know?"

"Oh, Andy, you know me," she answered, embarrassed.

When Andy prodded her, Ethel explained,

"Being with Bobby and the kids was such a beautiful time in my life; when he was taken from me it almost killed me." She didn't think she would ever survive it, she said. "I loved him so much," she recalled, "I never wanted to feel that kind of pain again. So," she concluded sadly, "I guess, well . . . I guess I just stopped loving."

DINNER AT MRS. KENNEDY'S

"So, what's she like?" Carolyn asked John in the company of his friend John Perry Barlow. "I don't know," John answered. "I mean, she's just . . . *Aunt Ethel.*"

Carolyn frowned and bit her lip. "What do I call her? 'Aunt Ethel'?"

John winced. "Um . . . no," he said, winking at Barlow. "If I were you, I think I'd probably go with 'Mrs. Kennedy.' "

Later, Carolyn circled the day in her little red day planner. "Dinner at Mrs. Kennedy's," she then wrote in the calendar in perfect cursive penmanship.

"I'm so excited about this thing," she exclaimed to Stewart Price as the two walked to Bergdorf's to purchase a silk scarf she'd seen earlier and felt would be perfect for the occasion. Stewart was surprised at Carolyn's girlish enthusiasm. She was usually so collected, certainly not the kind of woman prone to giddiness. Today, though, she seemed like an excited schoolgirl who'd just learned that her folks planned a trip to Disneyland for her.

According to pictures taken on the day, Carolyn looked to be maybe ten pounds heavier than she would in later photographs. Her hair was wilder, too, and seemed wind-blown, even indoors; it was streaked with highlights but much darker than her later trademark blond look. She was still gorgeously put together, in a slightly haphazard way: her white blouse was oversized with only the middle two buttons fastened, her worn jeans seemed somehow too short with shredded holes in the knees, but she definitely could pull it off. She had on leather sandals; her toenails were painted black. A large leather Kate Spade backpack was casually slung over one shoulder.

Stewart asked Carolyn where "the big event" was being held. "The White House?" he asked, bemused. Carolyn frowned. "The White House?" she asked, surprised. "You think the Kennedys live in the White House?" He shrugged resignedly and said, "Of course not," though he actually had no idea where they lived. Carolyn then excitedly explained that they "summered at the Kennedy compound in Hyannis." She added that she'd been hearing about the place her entire life, reading about it in books and magazines, seeing footage of it in television documentaries. The dinner would be at Ethel Kennedy's home, she said, and she also noted that when she told her parents about it they begged to come along. Both said they'd always wanted to meet Bobby Kennedy's widow. Stewart was surprised. "Really?" he asked. He could certainly understand wanting to meet Jackie, but Ethel? "I'm not even sure I know what she looks like," he noted.

Carolyn stopped walking and turned to face her friend. *"Get out,"* she exclaimed in disbelief. She pushed him hard, almost knocking him off his feet. *"It's Ethel Kennedy,"* she said. Then, checking herself, she giggled and covered her face with her hands. "I've really gone off the deep end with this thing, haven't I?" she asked.

"I'll say," Stewart agreed.

Carolyn Bessette didn't meet "Mrs. Kennedy" during her first full day in Hyannis Port, which fell on the fourth of September. "Don't worry. You'll meet her soon enough," John kept telling her. It wouldn't be until that night, though, when she and John would join many of Ethel's children and their spouses and some of their children for dinner in Ethel's dining room at sundown.

Carolyn would later recall that as everyone took his or her seat, she noticed that the Kennedys were smartly dressed. No T-shirts or swimsuits; everyone was in chic summer wear. There were a lot of them, too, and they all sort of resembled one another: each had an abundance of hair and polished teeth, all were slim and athletic-looking, the women were tanned, the men swarthy. The seat at the head of the table was noticeably vacant. Everyone chatted noisily. She would recall Joe Kennedy asking her, "First time at my mother's table?" She would answer, "Yes. It is." He shared a secret look with his brother Bobby and said, "Hmmm. Okay, well, good luck, then."

Five minutes or so later, there was a bit of a rustle as someone walked into the room. Everyone rose. Seeming taken aback by the sudden formality, Carolyn also quickly stood up, but she did so at an embarrassing beat behind the others.

It was Ethel, sixty-six years old and instantly a real presence. Once she was properly seated, everyone also sat down and gazed at her with respect and admiration.

Though she was a petite woman, Ethel always seemed to take up the whole room. Her face was etched with deep lines, especially around the eyes. She looked as if she'd lived a challenging life and had earned every one of the creases. Her hair was dyed blond and styled in a randomly short fashion; it appeared to be thinning, but somehow she didn't seem like the kind of woman who would care. According to photos taken on the day, she was wearing white linen pants and a matching short-sleeved blouse; she had pearls around her neck and a fine emerald pin on her shoulder. She gazed around the table with brown eyes that seemed full of enormous power. Then she turned to her oldest son. "Joe?" He bowed his head, as did everyone else, and slowly intoned: "Bless us, O lord, and these thy gifts, which we are about to receive from thy bounty, through Christ our Lord. Amen."

After everyone made the sign of the cross, Ethel picked up a small bell and rang it. On command, three servants appeared. As Ethel looked on with approval, each member of her kitchen staff began serving helpings of the family's favorite Cape Cod clam chowder out of antique tureens and into the guests' bowls. That night, the meal consisted of cold roast tenderloin of beef with potato salad and asparagus along with cranberry-nut bread, a favorite of Ethel's. There was also a copious supply of French fries. Carolyn would learn that there were almost always French fries at the dinner table. She was told that Ethel and Bobby had enjoyed them every evening during their honeymoon in Hawaii and, thusly, French fries were a staple of nearly every meal Ethel hosted during the summer months at the compound. The iced tea served that evening? Also a recipe she and Bobby had brought back from their honeymoon. For dessert: key lime pie, known to have been one of Rose Kennedy's favorites, as well as Irish bread pudding. Ethel said that she had asked the chef to prepare a Grand Marnier soufflé but that somehow "the poor man totally botched it. It's still in the kitchen if anyone wants a good laugh." She said the chef was so upset about it, she poured a nice mug of Grand Marnier for him and one for herself and suggested they make the best of a bad situation and have a little taste. Then, apparently, they had another. Finally, she recalled, "He had to carry me out of the kitchen." She was funny. One might not expect humor from her at first since she came across as imperious, but she really was quite charming.

Ethel then led the conversation with questions about current events such as: "Now, Joe, do you think the evidence against O. J. Simpson is strong enough for a conviction?" or "Bobby, what do you make of Clinton wanting to ban federal assault weapons? Do you think it will have a real impact on crime?" and "John, how do you feel about a possible invasion of Haiti?" This was a tradition that had been handed down from Joe and Rose, both of whom had always stressed to their children a sense of engagement with world affairs. If one was seated at their table, he or she had better have a valid opinion or idea. It could get heated sometimes, too, the debates often becoming harsh.

One had to know what he or she was talking about, or risk embarrassment because of their inability to argue or defend. Back in the old days, Joe actually used to give his kids complex research assignments before dinner and then quiz them over the meal. "Being American implies the obligation to both know and understand history," Rose used to say. These days, the Kennedys were just expected to keep up on events on their own, that is, if they knew what was good for them.

Eventually, Ethel looked down to the far end of the table and realized that John had brought a guest. When she asked him who the newcomer was, he introduced her as his new friend, Carolyn. Carolyn sputtered out something along the lines of "Very pleased to meet you, Mrs. Kennedy." Everyone stopped chattering as Ethel studied the guest for a moment. And then it happened. The question: "So, do you think a federal assault weapons ban will impact crime in our country, dear?" she asked. Carolyn looked stunned. "I . . . um . . . I . . . uh . . . I think it will?" she answered. It was more a query than an opinion; she was clearly out of her depth. Ethel peered at her, then glanced at John . . . and then back at Carolyn. "Indeed," she said. "I'm sure you do, dear. But you may want to read up on it. It's quite important." Noticeably, John squeezed Carolyn's hand. Meanwhile, she sank into her chair and flushed pink under Ethel's fixed scrutiny.

Apparently, according to the story handed down in the family by those who were present, things got even more tense when Ethel noticed that Carolyn was wearing a long silk scarf around her neck, which hung casually over her shoulders. The one she'd bought at Bergdorf's for the occasion, it was bubble-gum pink, a nice contrast to the mauve blouse she was wearing with a white silk skirt. If it was chic she was going after, it worked. However, Ethel couldn't help but find it a little odd. She suggested that maybe it was too warm for such neckware and added that she was actually starting to feel flush just looking at her. Shifting in her seat, Carolyn smiled self-consciously, nodded, and took off the scarf.

Later, Carolyn wanted to know why John hadn't warned her that she needed to study for dinner at Ethel's as if she were about to take a civics test. He laughed and said he didn't want to worry her. He told her that, next time, he'd be sure to sit her closer to his aunt. Why? Because the closer you were seated to her, he explained, the easier the questions; they got more difficult as the conversation wore on and so therefore people at the farthest end of the table usually had it a lot tougher. However, he also told her not to worry too much about any of it; she'd actually done quite well. "Aunt Ethel loved you," he said. Carolyn didn't think so, though. She told John she thought the meal had been a real disaster.

John was surprised by how undone Carolyn was by her first experience at Ethel's table. Her unexpected, unequivocal nervousness couldn't be overlooked. In the short time he'd known her, she had seemed so self-confident, a woman of the world even — and John had certainly known plenty of them. He found it interesting that one meal with his family could make her feel so insecure. In some ways, it was endearing and made her seem more vulnerable. "You never know a person until you *know* a person," he later told Gustavo Parades. "No one's what they seem to be, I guess." Her insecurity was also just a tad concerning to John, though. After all, he knew his family. "We don't do insecurity very well," he said. "That's definitely not on the Kennedy menu."

You missed breakfast, kiddo. Did you sleep in?" Ethel asked her. "For what?" Carolyn

Home, BOO AT breakfast, and Are you At Breakfast."

right before," said Beth Mason, who had started out with Ethel as a kitchen worker

UNDERSTANDING THE FAMILY

On September 5, 1994, the Kennedys would celebrate Labor Day at the compound, just as they did every year. "We all get up 'round here early and have breakfast at my house," said Ethel Kennedy to Carolyn Bessette that morning as she stood at the sink and washed dishes. Of course, Ethel always had plenty of help, but still she sometimes liked to chip in a little when it came to running her kitchen. She was anything but handy, though, and she knew it. Once, she fried bananas in petroleum oil for dessert; it sounded like a good idea at the time. Back in 1958, the Home Fashion League of Washington had chosen her as the Outstanding Homemaker of the Year and awarded her with a silver bowl. Ethel thought it was hilarious; she had six kids at the time and her household was pure chaos. All these years later, she still had the bowl in the entryway and would use it to throw her keys into so she'd know where to find them.

It was nine o'clock; Carolyn had slept in.

"You missed breakfast, kiddo. Did you sign up?" Ethel asked her. "For what?" Carolyn wondered. Ethel pointed to a chalkboard on the wall that was neatly divided into two sections: "6:00 AM Breakfast" and "7:30 AM Breakfast."

"Ethel then told Carolyn that she was supposed to sign up for one of the two shifts the night before," said Leah Mason, who had started out with Ethel as a kitchen worker but was lately working as one of her assistants. "It didn't matter, though; the poor dear had missed both shifts," she recalled. "Carolyn then looked at the sign-up sheet and saw John's name on the seven-thirty roster; he'd signed up but neglected to do so for her. You could see that she was sort of crushed. I told her he probably figured she would sleep in. It was always better to not be on the list at all than to be on it and then not show up at the reserved time. 'He sort of loses his mind when he's here, doesn't he?' she asked me. I said yes, that was true."

Carolyn could now fix her own breakfast if she wanted, Ethel told her. No, Carolyn decided; she'd just wait for lunch. "Better sign up, then," Ethel said as she pointed to a blackboard on another wall; lunch was being served at Eunice and Sarge's at twelve-thirty and two o'clock.

Carolyn couldn't help but note the difference between the Ethel of that morning and the one from the previous night. Yesterday's Ethel had seemed nothing short of imperious in her linen pants and matching blouse. Today she looked like a completely different woman in red shorts and a matching white-and-blue T-shirt that said GO SOX (referencing the Boston Red Sox). She had on a pink baseball cap — and wore it backward. Flip-flops completed the ensemble. "That was Mrs. Kennedy," Noelle Bombardier would say. "Royal one day, down-home the next. Generally, the rule of thumb was that during the day she was casual and at night, for dinner, more formal."

It was to be a busy holiday. The plan was for John, Carolyn, Anthony Radziwill (John and Caroline's cousin; his mother was Jackie's sister, Lee), and Anthony's new wife, Carole, as well as Ethel's sons Bobby and Michael, and Ted's sons, Patrick and Teddy, to all go sailing on one of the family's boats during the morning hours. Gustavo Paredes would join them. "Kennedys and all of us who were considered a part of them grew up on the water," Paredes would explain. "You had to know how to sail, how to handle yourself in a boat, all of the little ins and outs of being on the water, fishing, whatever . . . all water all the time, that was the Kennedys. They had a real intense relationship with the sea, and if you were going to be with them you also had to know how to handle yourself out there."

"The ocean," Ethel's daughter Kerry has said, "gives people a reverence for life and an understanding of the cycles of life. You live and die and come back again — a sense of renewal. 'You have salt water in your blood,' our parents used to tell us, 'so you should never be afraid of the sea.' " Ethel taught her kids how to swim by putting them into the bathtub, turning them on their stomachs, and telling them to kick their feet. All of them could swim by the age of three.

After sailing, everyone would meet up for the two lunch shifts at Eunice and Sarge's. Then the gang would all go down to the beach for more sun and fun — or touch football in front of the Big House or maybe some baseball on the field behind the President's House, once owned by Jack and Jackie. Then it was back up to Ted and Vicki's for cocktails.

At night, the big event of the weekend would unfold: Ted's clambake. "At least four times a year, the senator hosted a clambake at the compound, usually attended by about 150 people," Hugh Sidey from *Time* once recalled. "If you were lucky enough to get invited, this was a big deal. The tradition really started with the old man [Joseph]. There would be all of the Kennedys, sure, but also you got to meet their close friends, all of whom were political bigwigs. Don't think you were going to take pictures, though.

That was frowned upon. I saw Ethel snatch a camera out of the hands of many guests, Ted, too. They tried to keep it a private affair. There'd be reporters like me invited, just a smattering of us who tried to stay out of the way lest we not get invited back. It was always fun."

It was Ethel who had outlined all the events for Carolyn while the two were in the kitchen. "I know you're the newbie around here," she told her. "But don't worry, you'll get the hang of it. Never a dull moment, kiddo," she said, handing Carolyn a dish towel.

Once Ethel left the room, Carolyn, lowering her voice, turned to Fina Harvin. "Should I be writing all of this down?" she asked.

"No," Fina said. "You'll just feel a tide moving, and when a whole bunch of them start going in one direction, you follow. Then, as they move in another direction, you follow. Don't think about it too much. It'll drive you crazy if you do."

"But I was hoping to have some time to go over a few fashion magazines I brought with me," Carolyn said.

"Oh, well, *that's* not gonna happen," said Fina.

"Can I ask you a question?" Carolyn said.

"Sure."

"What's a clambake?"

Fina just gave her a look.

"It was a perfect Kennedy-like holiday,"

79

recalled Leah Mason, "with sports games, sailing, and other challenges. Carolyn did her best to keep up by making a real effort to fit into this mad Kennedy scene, but she was really struggling. 'I can't remember all of the names,' I heard her tell John. 'I'm scared I'll mistake Patrick for Joe, or call Teddy Bobby. There are just so many of you.' John wrapped his arms around her and kissed her on the neck. 'It doesn't matter what name you use,' he said, ' 'cause when you call one of us, we all come running, anyway.'

"I remember at one point, the cousins got involved in a typically raucous game of touch football, and John kept hollering out for Carolyn to join them. Rory was out there, as well as Kathleen, Maria, and Kara — Ethel's, Eunice's and Ted's daughters — and a whole bunch of *their* little kids. Carolyn was so clumsy. Someone threw her a football, and when it came at her, she ducked, and it sailed right over her head. 'See, now, the goal is to actually *catch* the ball,' Kara said. Carolyn wasn't laughing, though. My heart went out to her. I could see that she was a little humiliated. It just reminded me that not everyone could do it, fit into the Kennedy family right away. It took work, actually."

The Kennedys were obviously testing Carolyn to see if she could keep up, which is what the family always did to newcomers. They probably thought she was failing miserably.

Not everyone could rise to the challenge of Kennedy compound culture, though. "I remember being at the compound once, early on in my friendship with Maria Shriver," Oprah Winfrey remembered. "As an outsider, I thought, God, I'm actually here on the lawn with all the Kennedy cousins. But the games never ended. I'll never forget being in the house and someone saying, 'Where is she? Oprah, we're starting another game!' And I ran into a closet and closed the door and hid in there because I'd already done three games. *Enough!* It was all very intense."

Someone else who once fell short in similar athletic tests was Jacqueline Bouvier, who, when a football came sailing her way back in the 1950s, asked in a panic, "If I catch it, which way shall I run?" Of course, she ended up, well . . . *Jackie.* So there was still hope for Carolyn, even if she didn't feel that way in the moment and even if, like Jackie, she found some of the aesthetics at the compound a little out of the ordinary.

For instance, at midday, Ena the governess asked Carolyn if she needed anything. Carolyn said she might like some hot tea. Ten minutes later, Ena reappeared with the steaming tea . . . in a mug. "I've never had tea this way," Carolyn said. Ena just gave her a side-eyed glance and walked away. Carolyn would later recall that, at dinner, none of the servants had spoken to the Kennedys other than to maybe ask how much of a serving of food was desired. When she tried to engage one of the helpers, John shot her a look and shook his head. It was clear that the servants knew their place and that the Kennedys had a certain way with them — which was to keep them at a distance, certainly not unusual in the homes of the wealthy with live-in help. "It's just the way it is," John would later explain. "Nothing against them. It's just how things work."

Five minutes after Ena departed, Ethel approached Carolyn with a small silver tray, a cup, and a pot of hot tea. She placed it in front of her, smiled, didn't say a word, and then took her leave. Carolyn was surprised. Ethel was obviously aware of every little thing that was going on at the compound every second of the day and wanted to make sure all was in perfect order for her guests. She'd learned as much from the original matriarch, Rose Kennedy. Often, Ethel would talk about her first time visiting Rose and Joe, almost fifty years earlier, in October 1945. That's when her college friend Jean Kennedy introduced her to the Kennedys. Ethel was just seventeen. "I remember arriving at the Cape and going to Jean's room and thinking how everything was so well-thought-out for the happiness of guests and their children. There were fresh flowers, there were interesting books on the bedside table, the food was served so well, and everything was just so. All those niceties that can make life so worth living, Rose Kennedy had thought of them. Nothing went on without her being aware; it was as if she had eyes in the back of her head. Even with all our help, things were a lot less . . . organized in my household. I was so young at the time, but I thought, Yes, now, this is how I would want to be, this is how a hostess should be. I never imagined, of course, that I would one day be that hostess. Funny how things work out."

Unfortunately for Carolyn, as much as Ethel might have wanted to make her feel relaxed, even the moment when she presented her with tea was shaded with uncertainty.

Carolyn had noticed earlier that when Ethel Kennedy walked into a room, everyone jumped to their feet out of respect. She didn't know if this was required protocol or not. So when Ethel approached her with the tea, she didn't rise. John later told her it was a good idea to stand whenever any of the senior family members entered a room. After that instruction, whenever Ethel walked into a room, Carolyn would jump up from her chair. However, Ethel would then tell her it wasn't necessary and motion for her to be seated. Carolyn just wanted to be clear about the rules. When she again questioned John, he lost patience with her and told her she was making too big a deal out of it.

Toward the end of Carolyn's second day, a gaggle of Kennedy cousins were sitting at the table in Ethel's kitchen as the matriarch stood at the sink and helped one of the cooks shuck corn for the clambake. There must have been a dozen workers preparing the food, including governess Ena Bernard; her daughter, Fina Harvin; assistant Leah Mason; and many others. It was a real scene with uniformed people coming and going, each doing his or her job while chattering among themselves. It didn't matter what one's station was in the household, it was always all hands on deck whenever the time came to start preparing for the senator's clambake. In some homes on the Cape, such as Eunice Kennedy Shriver's, the help was so quietly efficient one would barely notice their presence. For some reason, at Ethel's house, they were always quite noisy, though they actually appeared to be more content in their jobs.

Carolyn was sitting on John's lap while Carole Radziwill sat on her husband, Anthony's. Carole had gotten close to Carolyn quickly; the two were like sisters already. When she jokingly mentioned that Carolyn's motto relating to men was "Date 'em. Train 'em. Drop 'em," everyone laughed — including some of the help. Ethel glanced over at Carolyn and raised a disapproving eyebrow. "But that's not true, Carole," Carolyn said, her face turning red. "Oh, yeah, it is," Carole remarked with a peck to her friend's cheek. Carolyn winced, embarrassed.

Everyone laughed, but it was clear that they'd witnessed yet another bad moment for Carolyn, who seemed to have had quite a few since first setting foot on hallowed Kennedy ground. Ethel was more curious about Carolyn's reaction to her friend's anecdote than she was about the story itself. Later, she would tell her oldest son, Joe, "I'm afraid Carolyn isn't everything she portrays herself as being." When asked to elaborate, she explained, "Look, I've raised four daughters. If there's one thing I know, it's girls. Trust me, that one is all smoke and mirrors."

KENNEDY STRONG

"We're goin' *old school* with this clambake," John Kennedy Jr. was saying as he and his cousins Anthony, Bobby Jr., Michael, and Patrick shoveled away sand from a pit they were digging into the beach. "It only has to be six feet square and two feet deep," John added, his bare chest and sinewy muscles glistening in the late-afternoon sun, "but with the sand being so wet and all," he concluded with a loud grunt, "this can be a real pain in the ass." Annoyed, Anthony said that he was well aware of how to dig for a clambake. This wasn't his first, after all. John told him to just keep digging, then, "and stop your bellyaching." A wink took any sting from the moment.

"Carolyn, wearing a white sarong, her hair braided down her back, watched with sort of a bemused expression," recalled Gustavo Paredes. " 'What's so funny?' John asked her. 'This place,' she said. 'I mean, it's just so . . . unbelievable. This is like . . . *heaven*, I guess.' Michael nudged Bobby Jr. and then motioned over at Carolyn. 'Newbies are always so impressionable,' he said.

"After the pit was dug, me and Anthony arranged large stones with firewood for the baking of the food — 'old school' style," Paredes continued. "We would have to light the fire at least two hours ahead of time. Then, when the stones were as hot as they could be, we would cover them with lots of seaweed, which provided the steam. The whole thing was then covered with a tarp to trap the heat for cooking. It was an arduous process, to say the least."

Neil Connolly — preparer of major meal events who held the title "Chef" — had pioneered what was probably a more efficient way of doing a clambake than the traditional ditch-digging process. He usually utilized two steel pans — seven feet wide and four feet deep — which he'd had specially made by a local welder. He would stack them on the sand, the bottom pan being used as a heat source and the top one for cooking. It was quicker and easier. However, the cousins preferred the conventional way, which they'd been taught by their uncle Ted when they were kids. Even though it was a lot more work, nothing bonded them more than preparing for a clambake the old-fashioned way.

As Michael and Bobby Jr. helped John dig the pit, Ted's sons, Patrick and Teddy, dragged a large wooden rowboat down to the beach. Teddy had carved and constructed this boat by hand years earlier. The brothers proudly hoisted it up off the ground on a large mound of sand. They then filled it with seaweed to balance it and covered it with a tarp. Thusly, Teddy's creation would serve as a "buffet table" upon which would be placed the hot and sizzling food fresh from the baking pit, including lobsters, soft-shell clams (steamers), ears of corn, potatoes, and knockwurst, all dripping in butter and served with coleslaw and warm corn bread.

Tonight, as always, the guests arrived just before sunset, meeting first at Ted and his wife Vicki's for cocktails. Vicki was always the perfect hostess, looking gorgeous this evening — at least according to photographs taken of the night — in a blue-and-white-striped silk caftan, her dark hair pulled into a tight chignon. After drinks, the guests walked across the lawn to a rickety wooden staircase that led down to the beach, where soft music — a favorite, of course, being Patti Page's classic, "Old Cape Cod" — played through a public address system. Before them were two enormous rectangular tents. One, the largest, was for the guests. A dozen or so round tables with six chairs to each could be found in this tent, all positioned on the sand about ten feet from the shoreline. The other tent was reserved for the chefs and waitstaff. Colorful flags from different countries were strung across the tops of both tents. "The flaps on the larger tent would always be up on all sides," said Neil Connolly, "so people could wander easily across the sand, grab a mug of clam chowder while waiting for the main courses, and see the extraordinary sights from every angle. As with all the decorations in the tents and on the beach — antique gas lanterns on the tables, colored flags strung across the tents — the theme was, of course, nautical."

Neil, wearing his white chef's uniform with a cap that said KENNEDY 94 on it, designed for friends and family to commemorate Teddy's latest run for the Senate seat he had held since 1962, ran a tight ship with more than fifty staff members assisting him. One, Theresa Lichtman, had begun working for the Kennedys as a housemaid in Ethel's kitchen two years earlier. This was her fourth clambake.

"What I recall most about that Labor Day weekend was the decision to even celebrate it," she said. "After all, the family was still mourning Mrs. Onassis. Everyone was incredibly sad. Just maybe six months earlier, Mrs. Onassis had become godmother to Mrs. Kennedy's grandson Max Jr. (born to Ethel's son Max and his wife, Victoria). Typical of the Kennedys and the way they felt about the help, their longtime governess, Ena Bernard, was co-godparent with Mrs. Onassis. We'd had such a nice celebration at the compound that day. Now we didn't know how to act now with Mrs. Onassis gone. It was Mrs. Kennedy — Ethel — who said, 'Look, no one liked a good clambake more than Jackie. We have to continue on, just as she would want us to.'

"John was thrilled when his sister, Caroline, showed up, along with her husband, Ed Schlossberg, and their three kids. I understood that Caroline rarely came to these kinds of things, so it was sort of a big deal. There were moments I would catch the siblings talking quietly, or walking hand in hand."

The Schlossbergs had just bought a new summer home in Sagaponack, Long Island, for which they'd paid almost a million dollars. It was a new construction, a two-story, five-bedroom, five-bathroom shingled home sitting on a little more than three acres including a tennis court and swimming pool. Caroline was spending a lot of time decorating it; she'd put almost sixty thousand dollars into it already and had just begun. She said the task was keeping her busy after her mother's death, a good distraction. She and Ed also had a sprawling apartment on Park Avenue.

"As I watched them, I imagined that John and Caroline were talking about their mom and how much they missed her," said Theresa Lichtman. "After spending time with his sister, John came over and handed me a drink. I told him it was my job to hand *him* a drink. He shook his head no and then said, 'This is the life, huh? Wow. I never get tired of this place.'

"One other interesting thing that comes to mind: I remember handing him an ear of corn, and he asked for the salt. When I handed him the saltshaker, he said, 'No, you should place it on the table and I'll pick it up.' I asked why, and he said, 'Ari once told me that when a person hands you salt, it means you are going to have an argument. And I don't want to argue with you.' He smiled at me. To hear him remember Onassis was just so interesting to me. He was so humble, you forgot that this sort of legendary figure was real in his life."

As always, there was no shortage of Kennedys, Shrivers, Smiths, and Lawfords at the clambake. "These were always large-scale undertakings with many various elements that needed to come together in a way that appeared effortless to the guests," recalled Neil Connolly. "On nights when the moon was full, the Kennedy clambakes had a special luminescent quality, as though the beach were a Hollywood stage set lit by a master technician. But even when the moon was just a brilliant sliver in the distant sapphire sky, these were special occasions. I was always happy to take credit for the menu and the presentation, but it was the dazzling pink-and-purple sunsets, the starry skies, and the smells of the sea and the seafood steaming to perfection that made the evenings so memorable . . . being on Cape Cod and the beach just as the sun was going down . . . the smell from the bake with the steamed clams, lobsters, and corn on the cob, and the chowder cooking on a portable burner. It was magical."

Toward the end of the evening, Neil Connolly was speaking to a gaggle of people when Carolyn Bessette sauntered over to them. Someone introduced them. "Mr. Connolly, you should be congratulated on such a wonderful evening," Carolyn said. At just that moment, Ethel happened by and overheard the compliment. "Why, thank you, dear," she said to Carolyn in a clipped tone. *"I believe that he is."* Her eyes held an expression neither Carolyn nor Neil fully understood. Finally, Ethel just walked away, Neil went back to his conversation, and Carolyn was left feeling as if she'd done something wrong. Had she somehow insulted the hostess?

Later in the evening, the male Kennedy cousins gathered around a firepit to talk about their lives and catch up on who was doing what, when, and where. "The older generation — Ted, Ethel, Vicki, Sargent, Eunice, Pat, and the rest — all went to bed, leaving us out on the beach with a roaring bonfire," Christopher Lawford recalled. "It was just the fellows; the women also retired for the evening. John, Anthony, Joe, Bobby, Patrick, Michael, Teddy, and Timmy [Shriver] and maybe one or two more. Everyone said he was busy in government or philanthropy, typical of the family dynamic. When Joe asked John what he was up to, John said, 'Same ol'.' Joe frowned. 'Find a way to serve, cousin,' he said. 'You're not getting any younger, you know?' John glanced at him with a pissed-off expression."

Getting personal, John talked a little about Carolyn and wondered how everyone felt about her. They all agreed that she was "a looker," but that was about it; it's not as if these were supposed to be moments of deep introspection. Someone also asked how John's sister felt about the new girl; he cringed and said he didn't know for sure and wanted to wait to find out.

Finally, after the passing of a couple of hours and the tossing of many bottles of beer into the nearby trash can, John held up the last bottle — which he called "the last soldier" — of the evening. "To us," he said, in a toast to all of them who'd grown up together on these sandy shores. "Kennedy strong," he added as he stood up on wobbly legs. Everyone else rose. All the guys then clinked bottles. "Kennedy strong," Joe repeated. *"Kennedy strong,"* the rest proudly agreed.

A LEGACY OF COURAGE

As is well known by now, the Kennedys have always been a family of dreamers. Long-standing prejudices against the Irish combined with anti-Catholic sentiment had imbued them with great strength and resiliency and also a desire to seek justice for others. The members of the third generation have memories of their grandparents, Joseph and Rose, talking about discrimination against the Irish and showing them newspaper clippings from the Boston press where the letters *NINA* ("No Irish Need Apply") were splashed on want ads for job opportunities. These young Kennedys came to understand that when Grandpa Joe was appointed ambassador to England back in 1938, it had been a real victory considering it had been just two generations since the family was of Irish peasantry. The way Grandpa had advanced in society while carving out his fortune in the Manhattan banking industry, on Wall Street, in politics, and, later, even in

Hollywood would always inspire them.

Born of a political family in Boston whose parents had emigrated from Ireland during the famine in 1848, Grandpa — and that would be Joseph Patrick Kennedy — was also the first to have his eye on the presidency. Throwing a shadow over his ambitions, though, was his opposition of President Franklin Delano Roosevelt over the United States' intervention in World War II. Kennedy was concerned that if the British went to war, the States would end up in it, as well. He believed it should be avoided at all costs. He actually thought a deal could be brokered with Hitler. However, Roosevelt wanted to fight, not placate, and he didn't need his ambassador acting as an appeaser, either. Given his approach, Joseph would find himself on the wrong side of history; he was soon viewed as a Nazi sympathizer, even though this wasn't the case. Then, when war began to break out despite his protestations, he sent his family home from England lest his sons become involved in it, for which he was then labeled a coward. He returned to the States after his ambassadorship to find his political career in tatters. He was despondent . . . but not for long. Typical of Joe, he pulled himself together and dedicated himself to moving forward with his life and his businesses, now in America.

In 1914, Joseph had married the redoubtable Rose Fitzgerald — daughter of John Francis "Honey Fitz" Fitzgerald, Boston's first Irish mayor. The first of many family misfortunes was that of Rose Marie "Rosemary" Kennedy, their third child. The story of how Joe authorized a frontal lobotomy performed on her in 1941 is well known. Rosemary, who had suffered learning disabilities and an unpredictable and often volatile temperament, came out of the surgery severely handicapped. Her sister Eunice would then spend the rest of her life dedicated to the cause of helping those who were intellectually challenged and disabled in other ways, much of her work being the catalyst for her signature accomplishment, the Special Olympics.

Once or twice a year, Rosemary visited the family at Rose and Joe's enormous eighteen-room home on the Nantucket Sound shoreline in Hyannis Port called "the Big House," which they'd purchased in the 1920s. (This large clapboard house eventually became the centerpiece of the so-called Kennedy compound, comprised of surrounding properties owned by Bobby and Ethel, John and Jackie, Ted and Joan, and Eunice and her husband, Sargent. Other Kennedys of the next generation would also buy property in this area.) Rosemary was always considered a part of the family, someone for whom her siblings cared deeply, until her death in 2005.

When it became clear that Joe wouldn't be occupying the White House, he looked to his namesake, Joe Jr., to be his successor. However, those dreams would be tragically dashed when, during the war in 1944, Joe was killed in a secret Navy mission while flying a Liberator bomber that exploded over the English Channel. He was only twenty-nine.

Similar aviation disasters would haunt the Kennedy family for years.

Joe and Rose's daughter Kathleen — known as "Kick" — lost her husband, Billy Cavendish (heir to the title of Duke of Devonshire) as a casualty of war less than a month after her brother Joe. Tragically, she, too, would become the victim of a plane crash in France in 1948, when she was twenty-eight. There was even comparable tragedy in the extended family; the parents of Ethel Kennedy were both killed in a plane crash in 1955 at the age of sixty-three, as was her brother George Jr. in 1966 at forty-four. Later, in 1964, Ted Kennedy would also be in a plane crash that took the life of the pilot. Ted broke his back and was almost paralyzed.

With his namesake now gone, the question remained as to who would carry the standard for the family. The grieving patriarch then turned his attention to Joe's younger brother Jack. Though Jack Kennedy — JFK — was less polished and articulate than Joe, his heart was in the right place and he had good ideas.

Of course, he wanted to serve. Much to his father's delight, Jack would go on to the Senate and then, in 1960, be elected President of the United States. Making it even more rewarding for the family, Ethel's husband, Bobby, would be named attorney general while Bobby's little brother, Ted, would go on to become a senator.

President Kennedy's time in office would be brief, as we all know; he was cut down by an assassin's bullet in 1963. Now, according to Joe's dynastic ambitions for the family, Jack's younger brother Bobby would be next in the line of succession. "He inspired a country that was deeply grieving not only JFK's death but Martin Luther King's with idealistic notions of how to best serve in the midst of civil unrest the likes of which America had never before experienced" is how his former press secretary Frank Mankiewicz encapsulated Bobby's appeal in a 1998 interview. Of course, Bobby's campaign for high office ended in 1968 when he, too, was killed in the same way as his brother, with a bullet to the head.

At that point, it fell to the youngest son, Ted, to carry the torch and, hopefully, return the family to the White House. That is, until tragedy struck again. In 1969, Ted's chances to be President were all but ruined when, impaired by alcohol, he drove off a bridge on Chappaquiddick Island in Massachusetts, killing his passenger, Mary Jo Kopechne. Though a majority of his constituency encouraged him to continue his Senate career, he would never be able to escape the specter of this scandal.

Later in 1969, Joseph P. Kennedy died, his dynastic dream for the family at least partly realized. However, the family's mandate having to do with who would be next in line for high office certainly didn't end with his passing. Now the next generation — the third — would be tasked with the responsibility of public service. By the seventies, though, times were different; America's youth wasn't the same thanks to a war abroad, civil unrest at home, a rampant drug culture, and societal mores that were so very different than those of days gone by.

As the boys of the third generation huddled in corners and eavesdropped on hushed conversations relating to who might be next in line for the golden ring, they began to understand and even fear that it was now their destiny to become a new generation of Kennedy torchbearers. "We were all, every one of us, raised to be President" is how the late Christopher Lawford — one of Pat Kennedy's sons — put it. "In what other family," Kathleen Kennedy Townsend noted, "did each boy fully expect to realize America's promise that any child can grow up to be President?"

Immersed in wealth and privilege, famous from the time of their births, most of the progeny of the second generation — boys and girls alike — couldn't help but begin to think of themselves as princes and princesses of an entitled, royal family. Without Grandpa in their lives and with Jack and Bobby now gone and Ted overwhelmed, things would definitely go off the rails for this new generation. As teenagers, many would misbehave in surprising ways. Some felt privilege was "due" them simply because of their birthright as Kennedys. They weren't yet able to appreciate the responsibility that came with power and influence. Maybe it made sense. "How does a youngster come to terms with all of this while growing up in a large family, especially one like ours where a premium was always placed on competition and on winning?" Teddy Kennedy Jr., Ted's oldest son, once wondered. "And to do it all under the glare of public scrutiny? That's asking a lot."

"There are a lot of expectations," added Eunice's son Mark. "If you think about it, there was a presidential race that the family was involved in from 1956 until 1980. That's twenty-four years where somebody's running to be the head of the most powerful country in the world or Vice President, and that's not even counting Senate races."

Further complicating matters for all twenty-nine Kennedys of the third generation was that their parents suffered incalculably from the grief and heartbreak associated with the murders of Jack and Bobby and even Ted's close call with death. Very little effort was made to help their children cope. "It wasn't a family big on outward grieving or allowing you to grieve," Eunice and Sarge's daughter, Maria, confirmed. "I don't think any of those kids ever grieved properly, grieved openly, or were allowed to grieve. They all walked around with a lot of grief, and a lot of sadness, which would pop out in different ways, as emotion or rage."

"The Kennedys of the older generation had relied on prayer to get through the hard times," says Sister Pauline Joseph, a Franciscan nun who was stationed at the St. Coletta School for Exceptional Children in Wisconsin — where the family had sent Rosemary after her lobotomy — today known simply as St. Coletta's. She would become close to Ethel, who had once considered becoming a nun herself. "They would have Mass said every Sunday at the compound," she said, "sometimes more than that, often three or four times a week a priest would visit and say Mass. Though the young ones were raised with God in mind, they definitely became, shall we say, distracted."*

"Many of us turned to drugs and other ad-

* Sister Pauline Joseph is a pseudonym for this

101

dictions," admitted Patrick Kennedy. In fact, it would be difficult to list all the Kennedys of Patrick's generation with addictions that nearly ruined some lives and entirely decimated others. Ethel's son Christopher once famously noted that it was easier in the 1990s to get an AA meeting together in Hyannis Port than a game of touch football. "I think we Kennedys did the best we could with the cards we were dealt, with the parents we had, the times in which they were raised and then in which we were raised," Patrick said. "There was that old saying, 'Kennedys don't cry.' I can't even remember how it started, but we heard it all our lives. As a kid, I used to think . . . yeah, Kennedys don't cry — in public. Privately, Kennedys *do* cry. Boy, do they ever."

As much as they have felt at one with the public, the Kennedys have also sometimes felt at odds with those who scrutinize their problems. "I've come to believe that it's not what has happened to our family that has been cursed as much as it's the fact that we've never been able to deal with it privately," concluded Eunice Shriver. "There's little dignity found in living your life in so public a fashion, and that's especially true of

---

Catholic nun, who has asked not to be identified in this text.

our children. However, this burden is one we Kennedys have carried for generations. If there's a curse," she concluded, "surely it's that."

CAROLYN'S DISILLUSIONMENT

With her visit to the fabled Kennedy compound, Carolyn Bessette had been granted an insider's view of what it was like to be a Kennedy, entrée that, doubtless, many people would have envied considering the family's long and storied history. As often happens, though, a person's idea of what it might be like rubbing elbows with the rich and famous can sometimes clash with the reality of the situation. Carolyn, as it would turn out, was deeply disappointed by her first time at the Kennedy compound.

"She called me as soon as she got back," said Stewart Price, "and I was waiting for her call because she'd been so excited about the trip. I was dying to hear about it. Much to my surprise, she sounded pretty sad. 'It was awful,' she told me. I asked how that was possible. She said, 'I didn't fit in. They're all so athletic and there are so many of them, and they all know each other so well and have this unspoken language between them, as if each always knows what the other is thinking. They looked at me like I was from another planet. Everything I said and everything I did was wrong. I didn't stand a chance.'

"This amazed me in some ways, but maybe not in others. Carolyn always had a streak of insecurity in her that she was able to hide very well. The weekend with all of those outgoing, über-confident Kennedys struck a nerve in her. 'So, what is it about these people that makes you feel so insecure?' I asked her, trying to get to the bottom of it. Carolyn said it was a mystery to her. She said she just felt she didn't belong, 'and that didn't feel good.' "

"What was Ethel Kennedy like?" Stewart asked, knowing how filled with anticipation Carolyn had been to meet her. There was a long pause. Carolyn then answered that Ethel had made her feel "pretty stupid." She said she didn't wish to get into it, but she sounded crushed. Stewart then asked her if she had told John how she felt. No, Carolyn said. She explained that it was so obvious to her that John loved his relatives — she recalled that he'd stated without reservation, "there's nothing more important than family" — and she didn't want to say anything that would upset him or, worse yet, maybe ruin things between them. Stewart then suggested that perhaps the next time she went to the compound, she could make certain adjustments in the way she looked at things and have a better time. Carolyn didn't hesitate responding. "Oh, there won't be a next time," she said with great assurance. "I'm not going back there. Are you kidding me? That's never going to happen."

"Never?"

"Never."

■ ■ ■ ■

Part II
The Senator's
Family

■ ■ ■ ■

KEEPER OF THE CASTLE

On Good Friday, March 29, 1991, Senator Edward Moore Kennedy sat in an overstuffed patio chair by the side of the glistening pool of the Kennedys' Palm Beach estate. He'd never looked worse. He was many pounds overweight, seeming sloppy in his ivory golf shirt and matching shorts, his abundant frame slumped into the chair with a tumbler of Chivas scotch in his hand. His face was paunchy with red splotches, his nose big and spongy, his eyes rimmed with red. He'd definitely seen better days.

Born on February 22, 1932, Ted was fifty-nine. He'd been serving in the United States Senate for almost three decades, having won his seat when, at just thirty, he filled the seat previously held by his brother Jack, who'd just become President, and had held on to it all these years. "He had done such great and important work in the Senate, sponsoring hundreds of bills which had been enacted into law having to do with economic and social justice, amongst them the Immigration Act of 1965, the COBRA health insurance provision, and the Americans with Disabilities Act of 1990," outlined his former chief of staff, David Burke, in a 1999 interview. "Most importantly, though, Teddy had landed on the ideal of universal health care as the cause of his life and would be dedicated to its passing for most of his career. 'If I can just make a difference in this arena,' he told me, 'my life would really have purpose.' "

Ted also championed his Civil Rights Act of 1991, which broadened the rights of employees in workplace discrimination disputes. "It was yet another political victory for a man who truly did care with everything in him, who was invested in public service like few before or after him," said K. Dun Gifford — known as Dun — who had been his legislative aide, in a 2005 interview. "He was certainly revered and respected for all he'd done for the country; like him or not, people always knew Senator Ted Kennedy was someone who could reach across the aisle and get things done. He also had his hands full with responsibilities as a surrogate father to Jack's two children and Bobby's eleven. People didn't realize, though, that he was also committed to the Shriver, Lawford, and Smith children."

"He was a big part of my life in many ways," Maria Shriver said of her uncle Teddy.

"He came to my graduations. He *showed up* in my life all the way through, and would check in on me. He was a great source of humor, of family stories, family lore, family trips and outings, and really worked hard at keeping the family together."

"Everything sort of trickled down from Ted," Ethel Kennedy once also stated. "We, as a family, would not have made it without him after Jack and Bobby were gone. He was the one who kept us all together. I guess you could say he was the keeper of the castle."

Privately, though, Ted was in a lot of trouble. The PTSD he still suffered not only as a result of the murders of two siblings but his own near-drowning at Chappaquiddick had caused him to be erratic, unpredictable, and, in his abuse of alcohol and drugs, bordering on shameless. To add to his troubles, Ted's brother-in-law Stephen Smith had recently died of cancer at sixty-three. Smith, the chief controller of the Kennedys' finances, was considered invaluable to the overseeing of its political aspirations.

Ted was as bereft about the loss of Stephen as his sister, Smith's widow, Jean. Though she'd had a difficult marriage, Jean had two children with Stephen and had adopted two more. Finding purpose other than in her relationship to her husband, she went on to establish her own successful charity in the 1970s — Very Special Arts, dedicated to handicapped children and, in a sense, continuing Eunice's life's work. (In about two years' time, President Bill Clinton would name her ambassador to Ireland, giving her an exciting third act in her life as a widow, aged sixty-five. Continuing a diplomatic family tradition, she would later help to broker the Northern Ireland peace agreement, ending eight hundred years of conflict between England and Ireland. She would serve until 1998.)

Now, on this starry night in Palm Beach, Ted, Jean, and a few of their friends reminisced about their illustrious yet tragic lives and about those they'd lost along the way. Over the course of almost two hours of boozy nostalgia, the Kennedy siblings and their friends tossed back one cocktail after another while trying to hash it all out. By the time they decided to call it a night, Ted had fallen into a deep state of melancholy and self-pity. When his sister finally went to bed, he found himself still restless. That night, he wandered the large estate, room by room, until he found his son Patrick and Jean's, Willie. "Say, do you guys want to get out for a drink?" he asked. Of course they did.

If only they'd stayed home.

Though he would find himself in the center of a storm, prior to this time William Kennedy Smith hadn't really been a bad kid. At thirty, he was in his final year at Georgetown

112

Medical School after graduating with good grades from Duke. Like most of the next generation of Kennedys, he, too, struggled in search of identity. Only for Willie, it was maybe more complex. Of course, he was a Kennedy by maternal birth, but he was never really viewed as one by the public. The Shrivers were barely thought of as Kennedys, which was fine with them. The Smiths? In the eyes of not only the Kennedys but much of the public, they truly *were* pretenders to the throne. Most people didn't even know their names. Amanda Mary Smith, Willie's sister, for instance, was all but unheard-of by even the most diehard of Kennedy aficionados. For the most part, the Smiths weren't raised with their cousins; their parents, Jean and Steve, had built a summer home on the east end of Long Island ostensibly to give them distance from the turmoil and trouble of the compound. However, the Smith kids — William and his brother, Stephen, and his adopted sisters, Amanda and Kym, the latter from Vietnam — loved being around their cousins and always concocted ways to spend time with them at the Cape, their mother carefully parsing out such visits while keeping a close eye on things.

Willie's life changed that fateful night in March 1991 when he, Ted, and Patrick went out for a drink. Later Willie showed up at the manse with a young woman named Patricia

Bowman. Eventually the two ended up on the beach, where, she alleged, he raped her. The next day, she filed charges. In the end, Willie would be found not guilty. However, a lot of people were outraged by the verdict, feeling that Willie had the best defense money could buy and that Bowman hadn't stood a chance. Still, he was a free man.

After the trial, Willie would return to obscurity. Little would ever be heard about him again other than the occasional mention of his work as an activist opposing land mines. It would be his uncle Ted who would take the biggest fall for that dreadful night. He became the butt of jokes on late-night television, and the press was even less kind. *Newsweek* called him "the living symbol of the family flaws." *Time* dubbed him a "Palm Beach boozer, lout and tabloid grotesque." After the case, his approval rating sank with more than half of Massachusetts voters now believing him unfit for office.

It had been bad for Ted before 1991; certainly what happened at Chappaquiddick had not amounted to his finest hour. However, he'd never before sunk this low in the eyes of his constituency — nor in those of his own children.

LITTLE SOLDIERS

The children of Senator Ted Kennedy — Kara, Teddy, and Patrick — were always perceived differently by the public and media than those of his brothers Jack and Bobby. Jack's two children seemed preordained for greatness just by virtue of their parents' distinguished place in history. Bobby's offspring always appeared to be troubled, so much so that even the ones who weren't prone to misbehavior — like the girls, Kathleen, Kerry, Courtney, and Rory — suffered in the public's opinion simply because of their relationship with their troublesome brothers. Ted's children had a much lower profile. It was as if they'd made a decision as kids to just keep their heads down, forge ahead, and make the best of the difficult circumstances posed by being raised by alcoholic parents. Occasionally, they would show up in photo spreads with their father, so tall and handsome and maybe the best-looking of the three brothers, and their mother, the ever-glamorous and perpetually blond Joan with the faraway, sad look in her eyes.

In 1958, Ted married Virginia Joan Bennett, who had been born on September 2, 1936, to Henry Bennett and Virginia Stead Bennett. Kara was born in 1960, Edward Jr. (Teddy) in 1961, and Patrick in 1967. For more than twenty years, Joan would grapple with the disappointment and humiliation of Ted's infidelities. In 1983, she finally found the courage to divorce him. By that time, she'd been in and out of many rehabilitation centers. Though she was mostly sober during the 1990s and into 2000s, unfortunately, as is often the case with alcoholism, milestones reached were not always milestones held. Within a year, Joan's disease would take hold again.

The fact that their mother was emotionally unavailable and their father so preoccupied with work usually meant that Kara, Teddy, and Patrick were left to fend for themselves. "Knowing that our dad was doing important work made it even harder," Patrick would later admit. "How dare we feel anything but pride considering the historic marks he was making? Dad used to say of us, 'They're tough, my little soldiers.' I don't know how tough we were, though."

"Throughout the seventies, there was always a sense of foreboding in the household, the specter of Jack's and Bobby's assassinations casting a dark shadow over almost everything," recalled Dun Gifford. "Ted said, 'There is no safety in hiding.' While he wanted to continue his work, he also didn't want his kids to be traumatized by what had happened. Of course, that was impossible to avoid."

"It has taken me a long time to even begin to understand how we were affected by it," Patrick observed. "I knew there was huge suffering going on in my family. But it was never spoken of. My father went on in silent desperation for much of his life, self-medicating and unwittingly passing his unprocessed trauma on to my sister, brother, and me."

"The one thing his kids knew about Ted was that, whatever his faults, he was a father who could always be counted on during times of crisis," observed Ted Sorensen, one of JFK's speechwriters and advisers, in 2008. At no time was that more evident than when little Teddy, at twelve, was diagnosed with a bone cancer so aggressive that few at that time survived it. It was thought that he'd likely die before he was fifteen. After Ted got past the shock, he spent many hours conferring with doctors, trying to figure out the best possible treatment plans. Always, whenever any of his children were in medical trouble, Ted's choices would be precise and well-informed.

As it happened, young Teddy had his leg amputated. While the operation was a success, the follow-up, eighteen months of chemo, was brutal. "Having a child with cancer reaches to the very depths of your soul," Ted Kennedy said many years later when speaking of the ordeal. "We were fortunate to have access to good health care and insurance. Many of the parents I met at the hospital had children who were taking a similar treatment. Some parents sold their houses to pay for it. Some could only afford twelve or fourteen months. They were asking the doctors: 'What percentage does that reduce my child's chances of being able to survive?' So you ask me why I'm for health care?" he continued. "That's why."

Somehow young Teddy got through it all and went on to live a good life, for which he would always thank his father. He got his law degree from the University of Connecticut School of Law. Three weeks later, he quietly checked into the Institute of Living rehab center in Hartford. The media reported he was suffering from "suicidal depression and alcohol dependency," but he denied wanting to end his life. He completed his treatment and became devoted to the twelve-step program. Par for the course, he would have one or two slip-ups along the way. However, as of about 1992, he has been sober. He then specialized in litigation having to do with disability issues, first at the New Haven law firm Wiggin & Dana before cofounding the Marwood Group, which advises corporations about health care and financial services.

Teddy's only sister, Kara, would chart her own path. "Growing up in my family, public service was part of our everyday life," she recalled. "My father taught me and my siblings that we had a special obligation to help people because we were so fortunate. It was a value he inherited from his parents and which animated his extraordinary life of service."

In the 1980s, after getting her degree from Tufts University, Kara had a brief stint as a television producer for the *Evening Magazine* television program in Boston. In 1990, she married architect and real estate developer Michael Allen. Immediately thereafter, she dropped her middle name, Anne, and replaced it with Kennedy, officially making her Kara Kennedy Allen.

It was always a little odd that as devoted a surrogate father as Ted was to the many children of his siblings, he didn't seem to be able to be more generous of spirit to his youngest son, Patrick. "Pat's father didn't have much patience with him," said Thomas Franken, who knew Patrick when the two were Boston teenagers. "I once heard him complain, 'Goddamn. Even Teddy is better at football than Patrick, and he's only got one leg.' Another time, Patrick was trying to play baseball and was kind of stumbling for third base, confused as to whether to take the base or go back to second. He had this peculiar look on his face as he nervously shuffled back and forth. I heard Ted tell Joan, 'Damn. That kid looks just like a confused dog.' "

"I was born a fragile person," Patrick explained. "I wasn't strong, I had severe asthma. I remember feeling awkward, anxious, separate, like a loser. But my asthma attacks were the one time I could get the nurturing and undivided attention I craved from the person who was most important to me: my dad."

In 1988, Patrick was twenty and a sophomore at Providence College when he had a benign tumor removed from his spine. He fought hard, recovered, and was eventually cancer-free. By this time, though, he'd already been treated for cocaine abuse. "At around this same time, Patrick entered a phase during which he sought to finally make his father truly proud, and he says that this desire is probably the primary reason he ended up becoming a politician," Dun Gifford noted. "I believe he'd lived in Rhode Island just a year and was only a college sophomore when he decided to take on a ten-year incumbent for the state legislature in 1988. 'Who the hell is Patrick Kennedy?' Jack Skeffington, his primary opponent, asked. 'Is he a big deal?' I know that gave Ted and Patrick a good laugh."

Ted was ebullient about Patrick's life choice, especially since it was now clear that Kara and Teddy weren't going into politics. If he could have just one child in government, he'd be happy. Amazingly, it was Patrick, the one he thought least likely. Once he realized his youngest had the desire, though, Ted was all in, totally committed to the new venture. "Pat thinks this world is worth fixing," he said, "and that's good enough for me."

Patrick's platform had to do with protecting the rights of senior citizens, legal immigrants, and the underprivileged. "He's idealistic, like his father," said his mother, Joan, who went out of her way to campaign for him. When asked the difference between stumping for her son as opposed to the years she spent doing the same thing for her husband, Joan smiled and said, "Well, for one thing, Patrick says thank you."

Fully invested in seeing his son become a political success, Ted sent one of his top staff members out to campaign with him and was then on the phone with Patrick every day urging him to work harder and suggesting talking points for speeches. Patrick knocked on more than three thousand doors trying to solicit votes; the Kennedys spent a staggering — and at the time unheard of — $93,000 (which *Time* calculated was $73 for every vote that eventually came Patrick's way) in order to win this position, which paid only about $300 a year. "On Election Day, Ted and Joan pulled out the big gun and recruited John Jr. to take Polaroid pictures with voters at polling stations," recalled Ted's former aide Richard Burke. "Then Joe came down to shake hands. Bobby Jr. posed with admirers. The Shriver cousins were also there to lend a helping hand. It was definitely an all-hands-on-deck kind of thing."

"We had always evaluated ourselves, and others evaluated us, on how Jack and Bobby and my father were and what was going on with the Kennedys in the sixties," Patrick explained at the time. "Here we were, growing up, but our mind-set was turned backward. And this [his first foray into politics] was the first time we were starting to look forward and deciding what we could do as a family."

Maybe Jack Skeffington didn't know who Patrick Kennedy was when he entered the race, but a lot of other people eventually did; Patrick was elected in a landslide, holding the distinction of being the youngest member of the Kennedy family, at twenty-one, to ever hold office. On election night, Ted telephoned Jackie and Rose and told them both it was his "happiest and proudest election."

After serving two terms in the Rhode Island

House of Representatives, representing the Ninth District in Providence, Patrick — still single — chose not to run for a third term. Instead, he ran to serve the First Congressional District of Rhode Island, a seat he won in 1994. In the House, then, Patrick would serve on the Armed Services and Natural Resources Committees before being appointed to the Appropriations Committee. At twenty-seven, he would now be the youngest member of Congress, another incredible feat.

Patrick Kennedy would be reelected seven times, serving from January 3, 1995, to January 3, 2011, winning more elections than any other Kennedy, ever. As earlier stated, he would also pass more than three thousand bills during his years in Congress, most often spearheading legislation having to do with health care concerns, which was what his father had championed for much of his life, and mental health care, which was always an enduring family interest. His big moment, though, the one that would most define him in the public eye, happened on February 29, 2000. That was the day he appeared in Woonsocket, Rhode Island, at a senior center with Tipper Gore, wife of then–Vice President Al Gore. It had started out as just another run-of-the-mill appearance in front of senior citizens, during which Gore intended to talk about mental-health issues. She had recently disclosed that she suffered from depression.

For years, Patrick had tried to keep secret his own addictions. However, he now felt a need to unburden himself. One reason was that having his mother at his side so inspired him. Joan had agreed to accompany him on this trip, which was a plus in that the senior citizens had so much respect for her. As he gazed lovingly at her, what crossed Patrick's mind was that her many secrets as a Kennedy wife had contributed so much to her problems and were real triggers to her addictions. The same held true for his father. He felt it was now time to break the pattern. Also, as he later explained it, it dawned on him that he could do more valuable work in Congress if he prioritized mental illness and addiction concerns. The only way for him to support those causes and not worry about his own secrets relating to them was to just, once and for all, disclose them.

"I myself have suffered from depression," Patrick told the stunned audience. "I have been treated by psychiatrists. I'm here to tell you, thank God I got treatment, because I wouldn't be as strong as I am today if I didn't get that treatment."

Though Patrick was also suffering from bipolar disorder, he didn't discuss that diagnosis at that time. Still, this bold statement marked a seminal moment in his life, the true beginning of his work as an advocate for reform. In the years to come, he would continue to do his work in Congress, now with even more urgency when it came to issues having to do with mental health care.

WHEN THE RIGHT ONE COMES ALONG

Though she was a tall, stunning brunette with hazel eyes and a dazzling smile, a big mistake was to underestimate her, because her beauty was the least of her attributes. At thirty-eight, Victoria Anne Reggie — known as Vicki — was a powerful woman: engaging, smart, and determined. She was of Lebanese Catholic descent, born on February 26, 1954, and raised in Crowley, Louisiana. A law school graduate, she'd worked as a partner in a Washington firm. In 1980 she married Grier C. Raclin, a telecommunications attorney; the couple had two children, Curran in 1982 and Caroline in 1985. They were just recently divorced, in 1990. She hailed from a strongly Democratic family; Vicki's father, retired judge Edmund Reggie, had known and supported the Kennedys for years, having run primary campaigns for Jack, Bobby, and Ted in his state. Reggie had also been a special envoy to the Middle East for President Kennedy.

126

Vicki came into Ted Kennedy's life on June 17, 1991, though she'd actually interned for him back in the seventies. The occasion was the fortieth-anniversary party of her parents. During that gathering, Vicki had an immediate connection with Ted. "You know what the problem with you is?" she asked him after a few dates. "It's that you're so insulated. No one ever tells you the truth. You can't live like that. You need honesty in your life, not all of these bootlickers."

Vicki was right. Ted did have his coterie of flatterers, most of them in government, who showed him unquestioning deference. Many of these sycophants were single. This gang, some in his own family, became Ted's band of merry men as they went out carousing for women and making bad decisions, such as those that led to the circumstances surrounding his nephew's rape trial. By this time, despite Ted's significant advances in the Senate, the respect of many of his colleagues as well as his constituents had continued to decline due to personal behavior they found abhorrent.

What a shame, Vicki thought. Here was a man who was almost sixty and who'd dedicated half his life to his country, a person who had truly been of service just as required of all those in his family. Yet he was widely viewed as being morally bankrupt. His troubled marriage to Joan, his high-profile womanizing, his alcoholic binges — it had been just one thing after another for many years. The cumulative effect was that Senator Edward Moore Kennedy had a serious image problem.

In a sense, Vicki felt it wasn't fair. In her opinion, Ted was grossly undervalued. "I think that some of the clichéd and easy perceptions about him, as just being fun, good-time Teddy and not serious and all that, were wrong," she would say. "He certainly did have a kind of fun — we'll call it fun — side of his life, and he had enough tabloid fodder in there, but you can't look at his life and not see these incredibly serious and focused moments as well. He was very complex — that's what made him so interesting. Hard work and discipline were very much a part of who he was."

Vicki could detect that Ted's many years of misadventures had taken a personal toll on him. He was unhealthy, and he looked it. He seemed sad and alone, even in a room full of people. He always appeared to be depressed. Deep down, though, Ted had a big heart. He *really* cared; it wasn't just a political act for him. In a short time, she had seen so many moments of his reaching out to the disadvantaged, trying to find ways that the government might lend a helping hand. It was as if every one of his days was filled by thoughts of legislation he wanted to spearhead that would help in the day-to-day lives of the disenfranchised. In his private world, though, she felt he was a man crying out for help.

"Within months of meeting her, Ted seemed to have a different outlook on life," observed Dun Gifford in 2005. "He and Vicki spent hours talking about his life, trying to figure out where it had gone wrong and what they, as a team, could do about it. She was an influential person, a smart woman who could see things in maybe a different way than Ted. He told me she helped him realize he'd made certain mistakes over the years. She came into his life at just the right time and ended up being a catalyst for great change. Influenced by her, Ted decided that one way to move forward was to publicly apologize, to admit that he was guilty of bad choices and, while he wouldn't come out and mention it, his involvement in the William Kennedy Smith business was maybe one of those missteps. I thought it was great. I was proud of him for the decision."

In October 1991, Ted gave what amounted to a mea culpa speech at Harvard's John F. Kennedy School of Government:

I recognize my shortcomings — the faults in my conduct of my private life. I realize that I am alone responsible for them, and I am the one who must confront them. Unlike my brothers, I have been given the length of years and time, and as I approach my sixtieth birthday, I am determined to give all that I have to advance the causes for which I have stood for almost a third of a century.

Many of Ted's critics were impressed. His speech seemed genuine. But did he really mean it? He wasn't going to change overnight, was he? However, the fact that he was at least trying to be a better man mattered to Vicki; the effort was admirable and made her feel even more warmly toward him. His children didn't buy it, though. They knew that Ted had been privately raging about recent public condemnation relating to his part in the William Kennedy Smith debacle. In one sense, he felt he maybe deserved the criticism, but on another even deeper level he believed he was not only misunderstood but completely unappreciated for all he'd done for his country.

While his children felt the basic sentiment behind the speech was genuine, they sensed a begrudging aspect to it and, likely, a secret motive. They knew their father well. Ted was a politician to his very core and pretty much everything he ever said or did was done with an eye toward how it would play in the court of public opinion. He actually did have a hidden agenda with his speech. He hoped that after delivering it the general consensus might be that he was being too hard on himself.

Maybe he would come out looking more sympathetic. Much to his chagrin, the response was just the opposite; it was along the lines of "What took you so long?" Ted wasn't happy with that reaction. In other words, he didn't feel liberated by the speech, he actually felt victimized by it.

As far as Kara, thirty-one, Teddy, thirty, and Patrick, twenty-four, were concerned, their father could save the public theatrics and do something privately that would have an even greater impact on his life: He could just stop drinking.

For as long as most people in the family could remember, Ted drank too much. Though many of those of the younger generation felt they'd no choice but to accept Ted's disease — and, as they grew older, they better understood the reasons behind it — after the trial, many of his nieces and nephews felt the problem needed to be addressed and that Ted's kids should be the ones to do it.

Everyone knew that forcing Ted to address his demons would be no easy feat. After all, his nieces and nephews had always viewed him through the prism of great history, even in their most private moments with him. He was "the Senator," after all — that's what almost everyone in the family called him except for his three children, who usually called him "Dad." He was the family patriarch, and his mere presence in a room could

INTERVENTION

"Drink up," Ted liked to say when he had friends over to the house for happy hour. "That's what men do." He would then toss a couple of ice cubes into a tumbler for each person, splash in some of the best scotch money could buy — usually a Macallan that cost about $1,500 a bottle — and then get good and liquored up with his friends. Sometimes Patrick would come by and use the opportunity to bond with his father. When they were both a little tipsy, things somehow seemed better between them. They were able to talk more freely, anyway. Patrick always felt guilty about it, though. He didn't want to encourage his father in his overindulgences. He felt it was wrong and agreed with his siblings that something should be done to address Ted's drinking. Therefore, after much deliberation, he, along with Kara and Teddy, decided it was time to confront their father. The date was set: Monday, December 30, 1991.

Talking to Ted about his drinking presented a frightening prospect to his children. They realized they would have to break convention and be truly candid with their father and, in the process, actually be critical of him. This kind of totally honest dynamic was not the norm in their relationship. They loved, honored, and respected their father; they'd never before challenged him. They also had no idea how to express a genuine feeling to him or be hurt or vulnerable with him. It just wasn't the way they were with one another. Joan Kennedy recalled, "Our kids were all used to a certain kind of formality with their father, which they viewed as respect, but which was actually, if you really want to know the truth about it, fear. Plain and simple fear. We were all scared of Ted. I don't know that it was his fault as much as it was just the history and the legend and all of the Kennedy crap that, I guess, always stood in the way of true intimacy."

Patrick was especially nervous since he had his own secret addictions. He was taking prescription medication to excess as well as drinking. It was easy to get away with it; he was single and there was no one to monitor him. He was also young and figured he had time to address his issues, whereas his father maybe didn't have that same luxury. Still, talking to Ted about his vices while knowing he had his own — and maybe his were even worse — wasn't going to be easy. As soon as it was decided that the difficult conversation was going to happen, Patrick started to take copious notes on index cards of what he wanted to say. He practiced different variations of commentary as if he were about to appear on *Meet the Press.* He would later confess he was more afraid of facing his father than he'd ever been of anything else he'd done.

The three Kennedys asked to see Ted at his home in McLean, Virginia. Upon arriving, they were led across a huge entryway and through the parlor by a butler, who showed them into the study. "He will be with you shortly," the servant intoned before bowing and retreating. Patrick described the study this way: ". . . big comfortable couches; books everywhere; windows overlooking the Potomac; a high ceiling with an original harpoon from whaling days hanging from it; a scrimshaw coffee table made from planks from the USS *Massachusetts;* and a fireplace with a picture of my grandfather above it."

Ted sat down on one side of the room, his children on the other. Teddy began by saying how much he and his siblings loved their father and then tentatively broached the subject of his drinking. He said they were worried about it, and about him. Kara and Patrick agreed with their brother that they wished Ted would just stop. They also said they felt his habit was ripping the family apart. They wanted a more satisfying relationship with him, and they believed that his drinking was standing in the way of it. Then . . . the three of them just burst into tears. Apparently, it was too much for them; facing the father for whom they felt so much respect and concern was more upsetting than they'd even imagined. The way the scene has been described doesn't sound as much like an intervention as it does maybe group therapy without professional guidance. "You *matter* to us, Dad," Kara said in finishing. "We love you."

Ted sat with an implacable expression. "Are you finished yet?" he asked.

"Yes."

Then, in a controlled voice, Ted said he had actually been consulting a doctor about his drinking, though he wasn't specific. Also, he claimed to have been talking to a priest. "If you had bothered to *ask* me instead of just *accusing* me, maybe you would have known that," he said. Then, without another word of explanation, he rose and walked out of the room.

The Kennedy siblings looked at one another with disbelief, a feeling of dread sweeping over them. Maybe Patrick put it best: *"Oh, shit."*

After the "intervention," Ted couldn't make

136

up his mind as to which emotion he felt more deeply: regret or rage. In his mind, he had given his children a wonderful, entitled life; they had no right to criticize him. "Kids don't get to talk to their parents that way," he said, making clear his old-school way of parenting. "I think it's very traitorous."

The next day, Ted sent each "traitor" a long letter, lambasting them for the audacity they showed in their meeting with him and telling them that he'd gotten the message loud and clear, or as he wrote to Patrick, "the point had been made." What bothered him most, Ted wrote, was when they told him his drinking had affected the family. "What in heaven's sake does anyone think has been on my mind day and night," he wrote to Patrick, "in restless dreams and sleepless nights — My God, Our family — my sisters and the cousins and the brutality of treatment to John and Bobby and I wonder how much I am to blame for all of this . . ." He finished his note to Patrick by saying he had written it not in anger but "with great disappointment and enormous sadness."

It was clear that Ted was in pain. He certainly had valid reasons for it. However, he also had no insight into his illness. For too long, he had deluded himself into believing that it was not a serious issue in his life or in the lives of his children, and there seemed to be no getting through to him. Also, it bears noting that Ted knew how to manipulate his family. Guilt was his weapon of choice, and it worked, piercing the hearts of his children, who were already so wounded. They could see through it, too. "Typical filibuster from the Senator," is how one of them described the letter. In the end, Ted told them that they should stay with one another for the foreseeable future when wanting to get together as a family. Considering what had happened, he said, he felt it best if he not host them at his home.

In February, Ted would turn sixty. Less than two months had passed, and already he missed his kids. After he'd had a little time to think about it, he began to regret the way he'd acted, especially after talking to Vicki about it. Vicki didn't know a lot about the Kennedys yet, but she'd been around long enough to know that it had probably taken everything in them for Ted's children to intervene as they had with their father. "Do you know how much courage it took for them to be able to do that?" she asked him. "Poor Patrick? Confronting you? Do you know what that must have been like for him?"

Ted knew Vicki was right. Things had gone too far, he decided. He certainly couldn't turn sixty without his sons and daughter at his side. Therefore, he wrote to all three again and invited them to his parties — not just one, but the many that would be held in honor of his milestone birthday. He didn't apologize to them, though. That wasn't Ted's way. "I don't apologize," he'd often say. "Ever." "He liked to think of himself as unapologetic," Joan Kennedy once said. " 'People in power don't say they're sorry,' he once told me, 'because that's a sure sign of weakness.' You actually could get an apology out of Ted if you really worked at it, but it was pretty rare and often not worth the trouble."

Patrick and Teddy both responded saying they would be happy to attend, but only if Ted promised not to drink. Patrick, in particular, said he realized these sorts of parties "were always particularly well lubricated." To Ted, this request smacked of emotional blackmail; he would most certainly make no such promise. "How about this?" he angrily proposed, according to one account. "You take care of *your* business, and I'll take care of *mine.*" Fine, decided his sons; they weren't in any kind of party mood anyway and definitely wouldn't be going.

Kara decided not to push her father; always a pragmatist, she felt they'd lost the battle and could maybe try again once the dust settled. Therefore, when Ted asked her not only to attend but to help with the planning of the parties, she readily agreed. She also pleaded with her brothers to reconsider. It wasn't going to happen, though. Therefore,

Joan's Voice of Experience

In January 1992, just six months after their first date, Ted asked Vicki to marry him. "I want you to be a part of my life in every way," he told her, according to her memory. He added that he didn't want to come home and report back to her about a trip he'd just taken. Rather, he wanted her to be with him. "He didn't want a separate life," she recalled. "He wanted a partnership for the first time in his life. He had enough of loneliness and separateness. He wanted togetherness."

Vicki was an accomplished woman, a well-respected attorney and someone to be taken seriously; "I've always been a substantive lawyer who helped devise strategies for resolving complex legal problems," she's said. Still, stories of the Kennedys' initial response to her have become the stuff of legend handed down in the family and, maybe not surprisingly, are specific to gender. The Kennedy men didn't quite know what to think of her. She was articulate, elegant, and refined.

She was stunning, too . . . which was maybe the problem.

There were a lot of snickers among Ethel's sons about "what a looker" their old uncle Ted had somehow managed to reel in, especially after he announced his engagement to her. Some of them crassly wondered aloud what she was like in bed. They talked among themselves, saying that if Ted couldn't satisfy her, maybe they could give him a helping hand. In other words, they were Kennedy men through and through.

"I also heard that a male attorney who'd been around the family for years said of Vicki, 'Wow, what a vamp. I haven't seen anything like *that* come down the pike since Jackie Bouvier,' " Dun Gifford once recalled. "Ethel overheard the remark and smacked the guy right across the chest," he recounted with a chuckle. ' "Don't you dare be disrespectful of women in my house,' she said. She hated that kind of thing. She was raising four daughters. If you think she liked that kind of talk, you'd be wrong."

Ethel's only hesitation about Vicki had to do with her age; Kathleen was three years older. Joe was two years older and Bobby Jr. the same age. Still, she said she was going to reserve her opinion of Vicki until she got to know her better.

Most certainly, one person who could best testify to some of the challenges of being a woman in the Kennedy family was Ted's ex-wife, Joan. Vicki had heard that Ted hadn't told Joan about his plans to marry her, and that she had to hear about it from a reporter from *The Boston Globe* calling for comment. Joan was so upset — at least this is what Vicki had heard — so much so that her sons had to rush to her side to comfort her. Was this true? When Vicki confronted Ted about it, he said yes, that was exactly what had happened. He had no problem with it, though. Why, he asked, should *Joan Kennedy,* "of all people," have to know everything that was going on in his life? He didn't feel the least bit compelled to run his personal agenda by her. Vicki was put off by his response. It was so utterly disrespectful to the mother of his children, she couldn't believe the words had come from his mouth; she made a mental note of it. "Look, you're coming in at the ninth inning of a long baseball game," he told Vicki, according to one source. "Don't try to figure out my relationship with my ex-wife, and maybe just keep your distance from her."

As fate would have it, though, Vicki would accidentally meet Joan one day on an airplane to Nantucket. She didn't know what to expect when she saw her sitting at a window seat. "No, no, no, come here and sit next to me," Joan immediately said when she saw Vicki.

Vicki sat down with some hesitation. She

then broke the ice by noting how wonderful Joan's children were and what a good job she and Ted had done in raising them. "You should be very proud of yourself and of your family," Vicki said, "and I'm so proud to become a part of it." Joan smiled her gratitude. It was a nice way to start a conversation; only another mother would have known how to best lighten the mood. Even though it was only to be an hour's flight, what Joan then had to say was definitely enlightening. She asked if she could give Vicki some advice; Vicki said she would welcome it.

"You know, I used to be beautiful once, too," Joan began. It was a sad self-evaluation that had to have been difficult for Vicki to hear. However, Joan, who was now fifty-six, did have a sort of faded blond beauty; her face was deeply lined, and maybe she'd had a tad too much cosmetic surgery. It looked like perhaps she was trying to hang on to the past a little too hard. She told Vicki that she should watch out for the Kennedy men, that the way they viewed women was "revolting." She also said she didn't think Vicki knew what she was signing up for, that it was "a real men's club over there."

Joan had a good foundation for her opinion. "Back in the fifties, she came into the family as one of the most gorgeous women to ever marry into it," recalled her former personal assistant Marcia Chellis. "She was blonde,

144

blue-eyed, and had a great figure. She'd been a model and knew how to make the best of her assets. However, every time she had a viewpoint, she was either shot down or dismissed. They didn't take her seriously simply because of her appearance. They couldn't imagine that a woman who looked as she did could also have a brain. All of those dinners at Joe and Rose's where everyone was supposed to chime in with an informed opinion? Each time Joan tried to do so, they snickered at her, shot her down, and moved on to another subject."

On their plane ride together, Joan told Vicki that even after she proved her mettle by stumping for Ted when he broke his back in that plane crash in 1965, she still felt blatant sexism from the men in the family who dismissed her as empty-headed and just a pretty face. She said that the men used to call her "the dish," as if she should be flattered. She did *not* consider it a compliment. Joan also recalled that Ethel used to tell her to not allow herself to be referred to that way because "she always knew I was a lot more than just . . . *this,*" she said, waving her hand in front of her face. Had it not been for her work on Ted's behalf, Joan said — and history does show that this is true — he would have lost his Senate seat. She got no credit for it, though. Now, years later, she warned Vicki that she would have her work cut out for her if she ever hoped to gain true respect in the Kennedy family. "Those men do not respect women," Joan concluded. *"Period."*

After that little talk, Vicki couldn't help but admire Joan. Certainly, all she'd heard about her from Ted was that she drank too much, which in and of itself seemed to prove Joan's point. Actually, Joan was a smart woman who, even if she did have her problems, seemed to be working on them. At the end of the year, she would even become an author; her book, *The Joy of Classical Music,* about her greatest passion in life, was scheduled to be published by Doubleday in October. Vicki thought it was a great accomplishment, but when she mentioned it to Ted he didn't seem impressed. She definitely began to better understand what she was going to be up against in marrying him, and now nothing would surprise her.

Like some of the other Kennedys, Ted's daughter, Kara, also had a critical opinion of Vicki, but at least hers had to do with wanting to protect her father. After all, she and her brothers had never known Ted to be so emotionally invested in any one woman, not even their own mother. They couldn't help but wonder if Vicki had some hidden agenda. That she seemed able to do what Joan had failed at, which was to not only captivate their father but help him to be a better person, didn't bode well for Vicki. The speed at which she'd gained influence over Ted was disconcerting. Was their father really just searching for a soulful connection with *anyone* because he felt so abandoned by his children after their failed intervention?

Over the next few months, the Kennedy progeny even began to suspect a financial component to Vicki's interest. They stood to inherit about $30 million, equally. A big question for them now had to do with how that amount might be impacted by their father's marriage. They couldn't very well sit down with him to discuss it, not after all that had recently happened. Therefore, in the true tradition of powerful family members who can't openly communicate with one another, such concerns had to be addressed via lawyers and other representatives. Through these channels, the Kennedy offspring came to understand and would have to accept that there would be no prenuptial agreement with Vicki. This shock would become the subject of a great deal of heated back-and-forth between lawyers. Finally, Kara drew a line and said she was sick of the fact that every time there was a disagreement about money, the family's pit bull attorneys had to be dispatched to settle it. That didn't get her far, though. She and her brothers were assured by their father's counsel that their inheritance was safe and they were told to just butt out. In their minds, it wasn't so simple, yet what could they do? They had to hope for the best. Making things worse for everyone, Vicki was hurt by the controversy and even angry about it. Wisely, though, she decided not to allow it to affect her. She knew how to pick and choose her battles, and she had enough on her plate trying to figure out her dynamic with Ted.

"From the time we were engaged, he used to push me onstage to speak at events," Vicki would recall. "That would just surprise me. So, my first trade union convention, it was the garment workers, we were in Florida. We weren't married yet . . . I remember walking in and they said, 'Ted! Ted! Ted! Ted! Ted!' It was exhilarating and he got up and then they introduced me and he said, 'Go on up, Vicki, say a few words.' I said, *'Ted —'* And I'm thinking he has totally lost his mind. What am *I* going to say? 'Oh, tell them the story of such and such. Go on, they want to hear from you, they'd love to hear from you.' And he used to do that to me all the time."

Vicki looked at Ted's coaxing her onto the stage with a little suspicion, especially given everything revealed to her by Joan. Was he just showing her off? Was she now just a little wind-up toy he could send out onto a stage to make himself look good? *I can still get the hot broads, can't I?* Though she decided to give Ted the benefit of the doubt, she would definitely keep her eye on him.

Ted and Vicki married in a civil ceremony on July 3, 1992, at Ted's home in McLean, Virginia.

THE BALANCE OF POWER

Summer 1992. Victoria Reggie Kennedy, wearing a colorful sarong, her brunette hair cascading to her shoulders, was talking to a longtime Kennedy employee as the two ambled slowly along the sand-and-pebble-covered beach of the compound. "I had worked for the family for many years as a property manager," recalled the caretaker, who's still employed there and asked for anonymity. "I understood the way the neighborhood functioned, which was as an open space for all of the Kennedys and their many friends."

In particular, everyone was free to visit, without advance warning, the so-called Big House, which is where the senator now lived with his elderly mother, Rose. Vicki had confided in one close friend that she felt just a little anxious whenever she walked by the wing where Rose — 101 by this time — was bedridden. Would that be her one day? Still living in this house in fifty years?

"They'd congregate in the enormous kitchen and anywhere else they liked, not only there but in all of the homes," said the caretaker of the Kennedys. "It had been that way from as far back as I could remember, when Rose lived there with Joe."

As he and Vicki walked the coastline, she asked for some information about how the estate was run, "what sort of security was in place," he recalled, "how paparazzi were kept off the property, that sort of thing." Vicki also wanted to know if there were specific rules in place for visiting one another. He told her that there were none; people just came and went from one another's homes as they pleased. Vicki stopped walking and turned to face the employee. "That really stinks," she said bluntly. He looked at her with surprise and asked, "Excuse me, ma'am?" Vicki sat down on an Adirondack chair and beckoned him to take the chair next to hers. Then, according to his memory, she said that she refused to allow her and Ted's home to be used as a "flophouse" for miscellaneous Kennedys and their friends. "That's *very* disrespectful to us," Vicki said. "Don't you agree?"

He didn't know how to respond.

After a thoughtful beat, Vicki said that she wanted the employee to change all the locks in the Big House and then make copies of the new keys not only for her and Ted but also for the many nurses and other caretakers charged with looking after Rose Kennedy. As he took notes, she continued by saying she would also need several DO NOT TRESPASS signs — maybe a dozen or so for around the property. Also, she said, there should probably be new signage around the pool that would keep everyone but her, Ted, and her children out of it except by invitation. She said she would need to think about the specific language, but that it would probably be along the lines of: FOR TED KENNEDY'S FAMILY ONLY.

"Will there be anything else, Miss Reggie?" asked the caretaker as he stood up.

Vicki rose, tilted her head back, and squinted up at the blazing sun through her large aviator sunglasses. "Yes," she said. "Maybe some earplugs," she added, "because once all those Kennedys figure out what I'm up to, I think I'm going to need them." She smiled at the employee and asked if she could count on him. "Of course, Miss Reggie," he said. He turned to leave. As he was walking away, she called out to him, "Oh, and one more thing."

He faced her again.

"It's *Mrs. Kennedy.*"

About a week later, Joan, who lived down the beach from the Big House, needed a half dozen eggs for breakfast. She asked her daughter, who was visiting with her two children, to run over to Ted's to raid his refrigerator. Kara sprinted over to her father's house, about a half mile or so. When she got there, she found all the doors locked. This was odd. Annoyed, she raced back to Joan's to get her keys. When she returned to Ted's, she tried to let herself in, but her key didn't work; it took her a few moments to figure out what was going on: the locks had been changed. Now she was angry. She stomped back to her mother's and called her father. The specific details of that call remain unknown, but what we do know is that Ted suggested that Kara give Vicki some time to adjust to her new role in the family. He was sure it would all work out for the best, he said — and, yes, by the way, he did have eggs in the refrigerator and he would happily bring them over to Joan himself. About an hour later, when Ted brought the eggs to Joan, he ran into Kara sitting on the porch, stewing. "Are you happy now?" he asked her. "Do I *look* happy?" she responded. He said he didn't want to talk about it, that if Kara had issues with Vicki she should take them up with her.

Later, according to this family account, Kara saw Vicki walking along the shore. She went up to her and asked for a word. She then told her that the compound had been run a certain way since her father was a child. She didn't think it was fair for Vicki to just waltz in and change things around. She said that she'd gone to the Big House that morning to get some eggs for her mother and the door was locked. Vicki asked what time it had been; Kara said it had been about seven. When Vicki then asked if Kara felt that was appropriate, Kara got a little heated. Yes, she said, going to her father's house to fetch eggs for her mother, was, in fact, quite appropriate.

Apparently, the two women then sized each other up: Kara, thirty-two, who had spent her entire life on these sacred grounds, and Vicki, a mere six years older, who was new to these shores. Vicki said she understood Kara's concern. However, her young children were both living in the Big House now, she explained, and she felt it wasn't safe for them to have people walking in unannounced at all hours of the day. She wasn't as concerned about Kennedys, she said, as she was about their friends, people Vicki didn't even know. As a mother, she said, Kara should understand. Plus, there was Rose Kennedy's privacy to also consider. If Kara wanted eggs, Vicki said, all she had to do was call first. She just didn't understand why this was such a big problem. In later telling this story to a friend of hers, Kara would recall, "What I wanted to say is, 'Well, Vicki, I think maybe a better question might be: Why are you such a bitch?' But I didn't."

Instead, Kara warned Vicki that she was going to make a lot of enemies in the family if she wasn't more careful. She cautioned her that no one wanted a new sheriff in town, not after all these years. Vicki was firm in her response. All she cared about, she said, was protecting her husband, her children, and Rose Kennedy. "But from who?" Kara asked. Maybe she expected Vicki's answer to be: "From the likes of you people." Instead, Vicki kept her cool, held her ground, and said from anything that invaded their privacy. All she was asking was that visitors called in advance before coming over to the Big House during early or late hours. In the afternoon, she said, she would allow more latitude.

"I actually think you may want to take the high road here," Kara suggested.

Vicki said that, unfortunately, her experience thus far with the Kennedys had shown her that "the high road doesn't always take you where you want to go."

According to this story, the two women stared each other down; finally Kara smiled and nodded. "Hmmm . . . you're very . . . interesting, aren't you?" Maybe it sounded condescending, but to hear Kara tell it later, she didn't mean it that way at all. She meant exactly what she said: Vicki *was* very . . . interesting. "I could say the same about you," she told Kara with a smile. The two then took a long walk together down the beach, just as

Kennedy women had been doing for decades, maybe commiserating about challenges they faced or maybe just getting to know each other. Who knows what they said during their stroll? Neither ever discussed it. But it had to have been . . . interesting.

About a week later, Vicki's NO TRESPASS-ING signs went up around the Big House. Now, instead of traipsing in front of the main house in order to get from one part of the compound to the other, Kennedys of all generations had to walk all the way down to the beach and then cross over to the other side. "This is absolute bullshit," said Joe Kennedy, speaking pretty much for everyone. "Who does she think she is?"

From this point on, Joe would have serious reservations about Vicki. "She's too big for her britches," he said, sounding like a man of the fifties, certainly not the nineties. "I have to talk to Uncle Teddy about her. He needs to straighten her out." If anyone in the family led a revolt against Vicki, it was Joe. Because he was the oldest son of the new generation, there was still a sense among some of the Kennedys that he was, at the least, the symbolic head of the family. No one wanted to cross him. No one, that is, except Vicki, who wasn't the least bit cowed by him. When the two were in the same room, she would always be cordial, but the tension between them was palpable. Once, in front of John,

Bobby Jr., and some other family members, she said to him, "You have a problem with me, don't you, Joe?" He said, "Should I?" She looked at him with indifference and said, "Probably," before walking away. John did a double-take. Smiling broadly, he then mouthed to Bobby, *"I love her."*

"I was contacted, I won't say by whom," said Dun Gifford, "to see if anything could be done about Vicki. I thought it was disrespectful. I was just a family friend, having not worked with Ted for years. I called him and told him, look, you have relatives opposed to your wife. He was not surprised; he already knew. He was calm. 'It's going to take time,' he said. 'Soon everyone will agree that she's a wonderful woman.' I told him I'd heard she was putting up signage. He said, 'Good for her, then. I say put 'em up if that's what it'll take for people to understand who's in charge now.' I thought, That's intriguing. *She's* in charge now? I liked Ted's attitude. I respected him for it."

Shortly after Vicki's signs went up around the house, similar ones started showing up around the Big House's swimming pool: RESERVED FOR THE SENATOR'S IMMEDIATE FAMILY. The problem was that most of the next generation — Kennedys, Shrivers, Lawfords, and Smiths — had been enjoying this enormous pool since they were children. Now they weren't allowed in it?

As if they were still children — and by this time they were all grown men and women, most of whom had kids of their own — they started to complain bitterly to their elderly parents, asking them to intervene with Vicki. Vicki couldn't believe it when Ethel, Eunice, and Jean pled the case for their offspring. "My God. How spoiled *are* these people," she wondered to one friend, "asking those poor women to talk some sense into the wicked stepmother? It's absolutely ridiculous."

The older Kennedy women asked Vicki to reconsider, but they certainly weren't going to beg. They then reminded everyone that Grandma Rose had always believed that swimming in the freezing ocean was much more invigorating, anyway. She used to swim in the sea every single day, no matter how frigid the water. "You can't use the Big House pool? Fine," Ethel told everyone. "Swim in the darn ocean and stop your bellyaching, you big babies. There are real problems in the world, or haven't you heard?"

One day, Ethel walked past Ted and Vicki's, and who should she see in the pool? Joan. She was splashing around the pool with Kara, playing with her two children. Did Joan count as immediate family? Maybe. But who knew for sure these days? "My God. Joansie, what are you doing in the pool?" Ethel asked, alarmed. "Didn't you see the sign?"

Joan had a feeling Vicki probably had a good reasons for the signs. Maybe what she had told Vicki about the family during their plane ride together had something to do with it. In any case, she knew she had a rapport with Vicki; she certainly wasn't afraid of her. "Yes, I saw the sign," Joan hollered back. "I'm babysitting Ted's grandchildren."

"Good answer," Ethel said.

Vicki's actions served a bigger purpose than just keeping people in line: it was her way of addressing the fact that many of the family members had so little respect for her. She knew she would have to make a big statement to them that she was there, she was Ted's wife, and that they would have to learn to live with her and understand her. It could be said that she pushed it to the extreme at first, but, as she put it to one relative of hers, "These are extreme people. You can't be subtle with the Kennedys. They don't understand subtle." So, yes, they got the message.

With the passing of the years, life with all its unpredictable twists and turns continued to unfold for the children of Ted Kennedy. Unfortunately, they abandoned their effort to get their father to stop drinking. He, in turn, eventually overlooked the insolence he felt they'd displayed during the failed intervention. As often happens in troubled families, it was all just swept under the rug and never again mentioned.

Happily, Vicki proved to be a good influence on Ted. She somehow even got him to at least cut back a little on his cocktails. He seemed in better shape for it, too; she also kept a close eye on his diet and had ordered the chefs to prepare healthier foods for him. He also worked her into his professional life.

"I guess he really was serious about [having a real] partner," Vicki would recall of Ted. "Over time, I started to be a part of meetings about strategy. Then I started to be a part of prepping for Sunday shows and a part of editing his speeches. We would be talking at breakfast about something and he'd say, 'That's really great, could you just do a one-pager on that while I take my shower?' Then they'd call from the office and say, 'Do you have time for a conference call with the Senator and his staff on such and such,' and I'd be a part of conference calls on strategy on a judicial nominee or on some other issue. It was just this seamless, total involvement in every issue he was working on."

"It would be untrue to say that she didn't like being at the center of so much power," said a friend of Vicki's. "Her parents were powerful, as was she; she definitely gravitated toward power. Being around Ted and the Kennedys? It was intoxicating, and she would've been the first to admit it. The fact that they slowly began to accept her into the fold meant a lot."

As much as some of the Kennedys hated to admit it, Vicki was actually good for Ted. Still, his sons couldn't bring themselves to reach out to her for a better relationship. They also rebuffed her advances in that regard. Ever loyal to their mother, as far as they were concerned, Vicki would always be an interloper. Many of their cousins sided with them. They were rarely openly hostile toward her, but an undercurrent of distrust about her would remain.

Kara didn't agree. First of all, she was proud to see Ted take another chance on love at his age. "Dad, anytime you open your heart," she told him in front of some of the family, "it's the right choice. So, good for you, Dad. Good for you." Also, as a woman and mother, she admired Vicki's strength and tenacity in carving out her own place in Kennedy culture. Kara now saw her as an ally in keeping her father healthy, and she didn't feel that being friendly with her compromised her relationship with Joan, either. Therefore, the two women became good friends, especially during the time Kara's marriage to Michael Allen ended. After having two children — Grace Elizabeth in 1994 and Max Greathouse in 1996 — the Allens divorced in 2001.

Meanwhile, about a year after his father married Vicki, Teddy Jr. married Katherine Anne "Kiki" Gershman, a clinical professor of psychiatry at Yale. The couple would go on to have two children, Kiley Elizabeth Kennedy in 1994 and Edward "Teddy" Moore Kennedy III in 1998.

■ ■ ■ ■

PART III
BEING KENNEDY

■ ■ ■ ■

THE CIRCUS

By the summer of 1995, John Kennedy and Carolyn Bessette had been together for about a year. They were now living in John's loft at 20 North Moore Street in Tribeca. John was generally happy with the way things were going with the woman he'd called "the one," even if the romance continued to generate headlines. For him, being a Kennedy had always meant forgoing privacy and dealing with daily intrusions — fans approaching for autographs, paparazzi taking pictures when least expected, all the sort of thing celebrities are used to, but, in John's case, magnified tenfold because of his storied lineage. The building in which they lived didn't even have a doorman; it was easy access for anyone.

That John was so good-looking didn't help, either. "Damn. If only I was slightly less photogenic," he used to joke when complaining about the photographers who would trail him for miles. He had good humor about it. Therefore, it was difficult for him to be sympathetic to Carolyn's angst about what he viewed as the relatively harmless act of people approaching for autographs and photographers taking pictures of her.

Carolyn felt as if she were being hunted and, in a sense, she was right. As the woman who had captured the heart of a man viewed as America's most eligible bachelor, she quickly became the source of great interest. Photos of her were sold to tabloids for thousands of dollars and, as she soon learned, even more if she was caught looking miserable. A sour face suggested she was unhappy, and what better story is there than the one about the woman who has it all but doesn't appreciate it? What right does she have to be so unhappy? After all, she's with John Kennedy Jr. "She would call me from an alley, her voice shaking," recalled Ariel Paredes, Gustavo's daughter. "She would say, 'These animals have been following me all day. I'm at the end of my rope.' I would tell her, 'Don't take it so seriously. They only want your picture. Just pose and forget it.' It's easy to give advice when you're not the one being followed by a pack of wild dogs."

In response to her complaints, John was impatient with Carolyn and simply wanted her to adjust. "Welcome to the circus," he would tell her, minimizing her feelings. "Just ignore the clowns, is all." The closest he ever came to being proactive about ditching the press was to call the Kennedys' wedding hairstylist, Lenny Holtzman, and ask for a disguise. "He would call me from the Barnstable Municipal Airport when he got to the Cape from Manhattan and say, 'Lenny, I need my bike and my disguise.' So I'd have to go and meet him with his bike, his wig, and a dress. He'd go into the ladies' room and change and get on his bike and ride right past the paparazzi. They wouldn't recognize him; he was *not* an attractive woman. I used to laugh so hard, I would pee in my pants."

"Don't talk those guys, whatever you do," RoseMarie Terenzio, John's assistant, would advise Carolyn of the paparazzi. "If they hear your voice, it's personal. Just be enigmatic and don't give them anything." Carolyn protested that advice, fearing it would just make her appear bitchy. "It doesn't matter," RoseMarie said. "You'll never win. Don't react because they want a rise out of you. That makes for an even better shot." When she could tell that she wasn't really being helpful, she suggested that Carolyn talk to John about it. "He's good at this sort of thing," she said. Carolyn said she had tried to talk to him, but, she added sadly, "He doesn't care about it at all."

"But John, that's not how you were raised," John Perry Barlow reminded him during the summer of 1995, while taking him to task about his reaction to Carolyn's discontentment. Barlow was right; John had been brought up to respect women, not disregard their feelings. He had once admitted to Barlow that he never wanted to become "that creepy Kennedy who doesn't care what his girl thinks about anything. I hate those guys." Barlow now warned him that he risked becoming "that creepy Kennedy" unless he paid attention to Carolyn's concerns. It wasn't easy. While John was certainly brought up a certain way by Jackie, he was also a Kennedy male raised in a Kennedy culture, where the men were generally selfish and entitled. It took some real introspection on his part to fully comprehend and then empathize with the depth of Carolyn's despair. He was eventually willing to put in the work, though, and dedicate himself to finding ways to help her cope.

In the end, John found there wasn't much he could do about "the circus" other than to make it clear that the clown act was no longer acceptable. Whereas the paparazzi army could once assume that John was fine with them and their intrusive ways, by the summer of 1995, those days were over. Now John wanted to at least try to protect his significant other. Therefore, when photographers approached, he would shout at them to back off, which was maybe an overreaction, but at least it was supportive of Carolyn. He'd also chastise people who jumped out at them from the shadows. Still, it took a lot out of him, just as it did Carolyn.

At the end of a particularly bad week of being hounded by the press, Carolyn and John were at their home with Anthony Radziwill when a friend came by unexpectedly. He walked into the apartment just in time to see Carolyn doing a line of coke from the coffee table. Both she and John were feeling no pain, he recalled; Anthony didn't seem to be indulging. " 'It's been a bad week,' John told me as he sat down and did a line," recalled the intimate. "I said, 'John, what the hell is this? This is new. Is this your thing, or is it Carolyn's?' He laughed and said not to worry about it. 'Look, I'm a Kennedy. Do you think this is the first time I've ever done drugs? Please.' Then he lay down in Carolyn's lap. As she stroked his hair and kissed his forehead, they actually looked peaceful together, I had to admit.

"An hour later John said he had the munchies. 'You sure you want to go out there and have to deal with who knows what?' I asked him. He smiled at me and said, 'Sure. Bring 'em on.' He then took Carolyn by the hand, and off we went with Anthony to get some pizza.

"As we walked down the street a couple guys approached. I thought, Oh boy, here we go again. But John said to them, 'You want a picture? Sure. Go for it.' He and Carolyn then smiled and smiled and *smiled* and posed and posed and *posed* to the point where Anthony and I were like, okay, Jesus. Enough, you guys. Then they waved goodbye to the paps and we all went on our way. John turned to me and said, 'This is not the real world we're in right now. It's only going to last about another hour.' "

Cocaine actually *was* new for John, but not because he lived a drug-free lifestyle. In fact, he and his friend John Perry Barlow had been doing acid and Ecstasy together for almost twenty years. Though his mother would, no doubt, have been quite upset about it, the first time they dropped acid was when John was just seventeen, right after Jackie sent him to work on Barlow's ranch in Wyoming for the summer. "John and I enjoyed LSD and MDMA for many years," Barlow recalled. "He was cautious, though, because of what he had seen in his family. But yeah, I mean, this was something we did from time to time to blow off steam and maybe look at life in a different way. It wasn't something he wanted a lot of people to know about, though, especially, his cousins. He didn't want them to think he approved of their own drug use, which he viewed as excessive, so he kept his own under the radar. Coke really wasn't his thing, though," Barlow continued. "John told me he viewed coke as merely a mechanism for getting stoned, whereas he thought of acid and Ecstasy as a way to experience life differently, especially when things started to get out of control because of his relationship to Carolyn. At that point, anything he could do to create the space to put things in perspective was what he would want to do."

BROTHERLY LOVE

As much as was known about John Kennedy Jr., one aspect of his life that he somehow managed to keep private was his relationship with his cousin Anthony Radziwill. Of course, there had always been pictures of the two published in newspapers and magazines as they grew up together, the sons of two famous sisters, Jacqueline Onassis and Lee Radziwill. However, few knew just how close they were and even fewer were aware of the private battle they waged for Anthony's survival. "It just goes to show that even a Kennedy could have a private life if he really wanted it," said Gustavo Paredes, "and John protected his relationship with Anthony. Though I was a third wheel at times, I was still there and can tell you they had a real, brotherly love. It was complex, though. They were competitive, whether it was sports or girls or just life. They also had a language all their own; they not only had pet phrases they used with one another, they could look at each other and say all that needed to be said. We knew that Anthony was John's soul mate and that none of us would ever have that kind of friendship with him."

Anthony had suffered from testicular cancer back in the 1980s. Though it was a scary bout with a deadly disease, the family got through it and Anthony remained cancer-free for some time. Unfortunately, in January 1994, the cancer came back at the same time Jackie first started battling hers. A month later, Anthony found himself at Memorial Sloan Kettering Cancer Center. "We got it all," said the surgeon after cutting a tumor from his abdomen. "Negative margins," Anthony was told, meaning no cancer.

John was relieved, as was everyone else. They all then went on with their lives, with Anthony asking his girlfriend, Carole Di-Falco, to marry him. However, after he proposed, Anthony started getting cold feet. He said he felt it was too soon after Jackie's death to have any kind of celebration. John, though, didn't believe his mother's passing was the true reason for the hesitation. In the company of two close friends at a bar, John broached the subject over beers. "John finally got the truth out of him," recalled one witness to the conversation. "Anthony wanted to wait for another doctor's report to make sure he was in good health. 'I can't do it to her,' he said, his voice shaking. 'I can't die on her.

It would be so fucked up to do that to Carole. She's such a good person.' "

Everyone at the table fell silent. John put both of his hands on his cousin's shoulders and looked at him deeply. "Listen to me. You are just fine, Tonypro," he told him, using a pet nickname. "I want you to live your life. Look at what we've been through as a family. That'll tell you that there's no time to waste."

By this time, all the fellows at the table had become emotional. "Fuck," exclaimed one of them. "If we get any softer, we're gonna start lactating, here."

When Anthony confessed that he was frightened about the future, John admitted that he, too, had his own fears and apprehensions, especially since the death of his mother. "But I think we have to catch this wave and ride it for all it's worth," he told his cousin. He reminded Anthony that this kind of optimistic outlook had been their philosophy going all the way back to when they were about ten years old and afraid to surf. He reminded Anthony that Ari took them both out into the choppy sea, surfboards in hand, and demanded, "Now surf, goddamn it. And don't come back until you do." Both boys were scared out of their wits. Somehow, though, they figured out how to do it, and surf they did, "and it was the best day, ever," recalled John. So, with that childhood victory in mind, John told Anthony he should face any challenges ahead and marry his intended. "Don't be a pussy, Anthony," he added with a smirk. His cousin was lucky, John concluded, that he'd found someone dumb enough to have sex with him, because, as he put it, "that has to be *real* unpleasant."

Anthony then said he wanted to confirm that John was going to be his best man; apparently, he'd already asked him. "Oh hell yeah," John answered. "After all, love is the thing that has licked him," he added with a grin.

". . . and it looks like Nathan's just another victim," Anthony responded, right on cue.

It was a line from *Guys and Dolls,* one of John's favorite musicals back when he was acting in college. Anthony knew it well, but no one else in their party had the vaguest idea as to what the cousins were talking about.

Shortly thereafter, Anthony did marry Carole in East Hampton with John as his best man. But then things took another bad turn. In the summer of 1995, Anthony's cancer returned. He was admitted into the hospital again, and another tumor was removed from his stomach. There would then be more chemo and more upset, but again it seemed that Anthony had escaped another close call.

Later that summer, many members of the Kennedy family came together at the compound, as usual. One night, John, Anthony,

175

Joe, Bobby, their cousins Christopher Lawford and Bobby Shriver, along with some other Kennedy men, congregated in front of a firepit to toss back beers and enjoy one another's company. Anthony seemed weak and looked thin. An hour was passed going down Kennedy memory lane as the fellows drank one beer after another, getting a little drunk. Later, as sometimes happened when the men of the third generation got a little loose, someone said something that set off a fight. Years later, in telling the story, Christopher Lawford couldn't even remember the specifics of the argument; it had been inconsequential. He also asked that the relatives involved not be identified.

"You should watch what you say to people," one of the men warned the other before bolting up and lunging at him. The two then toppled over each other, fists flying. "Hey, hey, hey! Break it up," Anthony said as he positioned himself to separate them.

"Somehow Anthony caught a fist in the face," recalled Christopher. "His nose started to bleed. John ran to him. 'Jesus Christ,' he said, 'you guys. *He's on blood thinners.*' We all sat there horrified as Anthony wouldn't stop bleeding. His shirt was covered with blood; it was everywhere. It looked like a crime scene. John kept saying, 'Fuck, fuck, *fuck,*' as he pressed a napkin on Anthony's nose. Anthony looked embarrassed as his hat fell from his head and we saw his balding head. He just kept moaning, a deep, guttural sound. 'What are you two, *still kids*?' John asked the guys who had been fighting. 'Grow up,' he said angrily. 'Come on, Anthony, let me take care of you.' Then he rushed Anthony away and back up to the main house, his arm protectively around his shoulders.

"While it was all upsetting, the way John had been with Anthony made a huge impression," said Christopher. "After they left, we just sat staring at one another. A couple of us were even close to tears. Joe was the one who finally broke the ice. 'Wow. That was real love right there, wasn't it?' he said."

Anthony's health challenge affected both John and Carolyn in many ways, not the least of which was that it forced them to take stock. For his part, John became more determined than ever to not only find purpose in his life but to be happy while looking for it. He'd already started on a road to self-discovery after Jackie's death, and now given what Anthony was going through, he definitely didn't want to waste any more time. He also sensed more strongly than ever that Carolyn should be at his side. Therefore, during the July Fourth weekend of 1995, he proposed marriage to her.

Carolyn, who was now twenty-nine, didn't accept right away, which surprised John. However, she was on her own journey. She needed time to be sure she could survive being a Kennedy, especially given the way she felt about the invasion of privacy inherent to the task. In the end, while she didn't really know if she could cope, she knew she had to at least try. "She held off the proposal for about three weeks," recalled RoseMarie Terenzio. "I actually think that made John even more eager to marry her. Eventually, she accepted his proposal. It was a lovely ring, diamond-and-sapphire and modeled after one his mother had that he knew she [Jackie] had loved."

A Sense of Purpose

Who am I? It was the existential question John Kennedy had been asking ever since the death of his mother. Never before had he found himself in such a serious search for identity, but now it was his most driving purpose. He sensed that marrying Carolyn would be a major puzzle piece in completing the picture of his life, but he knew there had to be more. John Perry Barlow recalled, "He once told me, 'You know, this is going to sound incredibly arrogant, but it would be a cakewalk for me to be a great man. I'm completely set up. Everyone expects me to be a great man. I even have a lot of the skills and tools. The thing is, I've been reading the biographies of great men, and it seems like all of them, my father included, were shit-heads when they got home. Even Gandhi beat his wife. What I think would be a much more interesting and challenging ambition for me would be to set out to become a good man — to define what that is, and become that. Not many people would know, but I would have the satisfaction of knowing.' "

As a Kennedy, of course, an integral part of being "a good man" had to do with giving back and being of service. The question by the summer of 1995 was: Just how would he achieve that goal?

While it's difficult to imagine that a weekend seminar about magazine publishing that his sister, Caroline, had suggested he take at the New School would have such an impact on him, it really did change John's life. He had always been fascinated with media and the way it had covered his family. Whether intrusive or from a distance, he realized that the press had been shaping public opinion about the Kennedys for decades. A student of political literature, he was well-read, even if he'd had so much trouble in school. He kept his library stocked with political biographies and other books of history, including many about his father, the President.

When John told Carolyn he was interested in starting a political magazine, she encouraged him in the idea. She even wanted to be a part of it with him, and he appreciated her support. John told her that a friend he'd known for more than ten years, Michael Berman, whose background was in marketing and public relations, had an idea for a magazine that would merge politics with personality. It would not be ideological but would

180

instead find an intersection between government and pop culture. He felt that one reason people were so misinformed about politics was because they were bored by it. Carolyn was intrigued, as were many others in John's life when he explained the idea.

Some were surprised, though, given the Kennedys' sometimes acrimonious relationship with the press. In 1998, at a publication party for Max Kennedy's *Make Gentle the Life of This World: The Vision of Robert F. Kennedy*, a book of quotes his father had loved and an examination of the way RFK had been influenced by the powerful thinkers he so admired, the author said, "I think there's a perception that we Kennedys are opposed to the public having a fuller understanding of who we are, of what makes us tick," Max, who was three and a half when his father was killed, added, "But it's not true. Yes, we have been opposed to much of what's been written about us, mostly because of the inaccuracies or because it digs too deep into private thoughts. But we Kennedys understand history and the importance of history. In fact, my mother has been my greatest encourager. She's the one who urged me to read my father's journals, to go through his notes and all of the index cards he had assembled during his life with quotes and other thoughts that had meant so much to him. My uncle Teddy had written a book about his brother called *Words Jack Loved*, and it was always my idea to do sort of the same thing for my father. But it was my mother who pushed the idea along, who felt it important."

John, as a magazine publisher, would certainly not shy away from being provocative. His mother, Jackie, had taken the same approach when she worked as a book editor at Doubleday. Although she was determined to keep her own life private, she understood the value of dissecting the private lives of public people to learn more about them and, maybe, in the process, more about ourselves. She once said, "I love people in the public eye who I sense have an inner life that is somewhat . . ." She paused. Then, with a conspiratorial look, said, "*Secretive.* I guess you could say I love people who have secrets," she added, laughing. "Isn't that just awful? But, really, what would be the point of writing about a celebrity if you weren't going to reveal his or her secrets?"

Such analysis of public figures had its place, though, where Jackie was concerned. If it was done with care and objectivity and the result of in-depth research, she respected it. However, if it was just done for purposes of titillation, she had no time for it and, in a sense, this was something she and Carolyn Bessette had in common. "At first I liked it," Jackie once told John Perry Barlow of being famous, "but then it made me feel like prey. Gradually, I realized that all this stuff in the press really wasn't about me. It was actually a comic strip that had a character in it that looked like me and did some of the things I did but wasn't me. It was something they were making up. And I read it quite avidly for a while, and then I realized it was making me sick, so I stopped."

In 1994, John said, "As I see it, even the trashiest tabloid writer has a responsibility that he clearly does not take seriously — shaping the way people think of others, and by extension, the way they perceive themselves. It's all tied together. When it's about politics, the way the media reports and distorts or otherwise makes decisions about the way to ultimately present information to the masses can, obviously, have huge ramifications. This is a subject that has long interested me."

For the next few months, Kennedy and Berman went about the complex business of trying to raise funds for their enterprise, which they'd come to believe would cost in excess of $30 million. John wanted to call the magazine *George* (an homage to George Washington). In a short time, enough advertising space was purchased to fill eight issues, and that was long before the first one was even published. Kennedy and Berman spent the next few months staffing the magazine's Broadway office space, starting with its creative director, Matt Berman (no relation to Michael), and its senior editor, Richard Blow (now Bradley; he uses his mother's maiden name).

In September 1995, John officially announced the publication of *George* at a much-touted press conference in Manhattan's Federal Hall National Memorial on Wall Street, which stands on the site where America's first President, George Washington, was inaugurated. He then displayed the cover of the first issue of *George,* featuring Cindy Crawford dressed as George Washington (it would be the October/November issue).

Later, John stood beaming with Carolyn as the couple posed for pictures. He was wearing a sharp, well-tailored blue suit, which she had picked out especially for the occasion, and a white pocket square, which he always wore for luck. "It felt like a victory not just for John, but for Carolyn," said Richard Bradley. "She was excited about John, about his drive and determination and the fact that he'd found something that gave him purpose. She wanted to be with him the whole way. She told me she had a sense that this was the first of a series of magazines John might publish, and she had an idea about a style magazine for men, something like *Esquire* but more mainstream.

"When you were with them, you felt John had really put forth a new power couple in the family, and there had been a lot of them, like Jack and Jackie, Bobby and Ethel, Sarge and Eunice. John had always had a thing about the Kennedy power couples of the past, and this was how he wanted to view himself and Carolyn. So, I guess one could say that Carolyn was becoming the woman behind the man, and John was happy and proud about it. I think his mom would have been as well."

THAT ONE FIGHT

Fall 1995. "Why in the world would you wear such a thing?" Ariel Paredes, Gustavo's daughter, was asking John Kennedy. The two were at the kitchen table of Ethel's home on the Cape gazing at a newspaper photo of John rising from the ocean while wearing an awful black swim cap. As he ate breakfast, John was surrounded by a stack of publications, research material for stories he was about to assign to reporters at *George*. He explained his reasoning behind wearing the cap. He hoped paparazzi would think it was so ugly, they wouldn't take his picture. "Kinda dumb, huh?" he asked.

"Yeah, real dumb," said Ariel.

"So now here I am, looking like a complete idiot in *The Boston Globe,*" John said.

"Wouldn't be the first time," Ariel added, laughing. As she spoke, John poured himself another bowl of his favorite cereal, Total Raisin Bran. Ariel rolled her eyes. "Worst cereal ever," she said as John poured milk on it. "You're such a . . . *dude.*"

John chuckled. He said that lately he was all business all the time with *George,* "so shut up and let me just have my dude cereal in peace, will you, please?"

Though off to a good start, within a short period of time *George* began to show signs of sales fatigue. It's a given in the magazine business that new publications have a difficult time in the marketplace and often don't make it. John had a lot at stake. "It felt personal to him, maybe too personal," said Michael Berman, who would eventually end up having a falling-out with John over the running of the publication. "This was his baby. He was living and breathing this magazine. It *had* to succeed."

Adding to John's complicated life these days was that Carolyn continued to show signs of insecurity. The longer she was with him, the more uncertain she seemed to be about their relationship. Some of her lack of confidence had to do with the response of others to John, which she witnessed on a daily basis. After all, it was difficult for people to avoid being swept away by him. His presence could suck all the oxygen from a room. No matter who was in his company, that person would become invisible. Carolyn had always been used to her own acclaim, though on a much smaller scale.

"Carolyn was accustomed to being the

most interesting person at a party," said a friend of hers from their Connecticut days, "and when it came to men, she was used to being the one being pursued. Once, we were together at a bar and a guy came up to her and hit on her hard. She flipped her long, luxurious hair, gave him a long look, and said, 'Go away, little man. I am *so* out of your league.' Maybe it was an act, but she at least appeared to be self-confident, before John. After John, things changed. When she realized she was so much in his shadow, it became a real issue. She started to feel that she was just an adjunct to him. It didn't feel good."

Making things even more complex for Carolyn was that she saw firsthand that John could have any woman he wanted. They seemed to fall all over themselves just to be near him, to breathe the same air. Carolyn couldn't help but be a little jealous of all the admiring glances thrown in his direction. Like everyone else, she knew of the reputations of Kennedy men and, as she got closer to the family, saw in the next generation some of the bad behavior of the earlier one. "I see what goes on in this family, and it scares me," she told her friend Stewart Price.

"But John is different," Price offered.

"It's a good thing, too," she said. "I know myself, and I'm definitely not that pathetic Kennedy wife who'll stay home with the kids while her husband is out screwing around," she said. "No," she added. "I'm that pissed-off Kennedy wife who'll be in prison because she took matters into her own hands."

Adding to the dilemma of her life was that every time John wanted to go to the Cape to be with his relatives, Carolyn didn't want to go. Not only did she still feel she didn't fit in, but by this time she also realized she was always being photographed while at the Cape. She'd previously thought photographers couldn't get close to her when she was at the Kennedys' sanctuary, but she was disabused of that notion one day when she saw a pack of paparazzi on a pier just shooting away at her. Now she felt she had to put on an act for public consumption, which added a new level of angst to going to the compound. She was still taking pills just to get through it, she confided in certain people, and an occasional line of coke, too.

It's sometimes said that every couple has that one fight that they can't get past, a disagreement that remains an issue between them no matter how many times they try to sort it out. If that's true, the question of whether Carolyn would accompany John to the compound to be with his relatives was their recurring argument, the one they just couldn't seem to settle no matter how many times they tried.

"Fine," John said one night in front of friends at a restaurant. "Don't come with me, hell if I care. I'm sick of having this same fight." Apparently, they were supposed to spend another weekend with the Kennedys, and Carolyn had made her objections clear. When her eyes filled up and she started to cry at the table, John became frustrated. "You're crying because you don't want to have fun on the beach with my family?" he said, being a little loud. "I don't get you, Carolyn. What's wrong with having fun?" He also noted that it was often the case that when she got to the compound she seemed to enjoy herself, especially with water sports. There were plenty of published pictures of her at least *appearing* to have a good time. So why fight it? In response to all that, Carolyn just rose and rushed off. John groaned. "Should I go after her?" he asked his friends. They all said, "Yes. Of course. What's wrong with you?" Sighing heavily, John got up and left the table. Fifteen minutes later, he returned. "She's gone," he said, looking disgruntled. "Took a cab back to the apartment, I guess. I'm so over her now. What a big baby."

John Perry Barlow, who was at the table, recalled, "He was really worked up. I said, 'John, so what if she doesn't want to go? Leave the poor girl alone. Stop badgering her.' He said, 'But it's my *family.* We're getting married, and she won't even give them a chance.' I said that she'd given them plenty

190

of chances. It wasn't easy blending in with that bunch, I reminded him, and he should know that by now. If they somehow make her feel badly about herself, I told him, he should be more understanding. 'Don't you ever again make her feel so small, do you hear me?' I chastised him. He felt badly by this time and said he was going to go home and apologize."

By the beginning of the new year, Carolyn was still deeply troubled and feeling maybe not up to the "job" of being with John. Unfortunately, a terrible argument in Central Park would come to define this time in her relationship to John for much of the public. It happened one Sunday morning in February 1996.

The couple was first photographed by paparazzi while they were arguing in front of the Tribeca Grill, where they'd had brunch. Then they were filmed screaming at each other and gesturing wildly. His face twisted with rage, John laid into Carolyn, and she returned his fury — as the media documented the entire combative scene. At one point, John snatched the engagement ring right off her finger. It was ugly, the two pushing and pulling at each other while screaming and sobbing. The whole world bore witness to it, too; it was big news everywhere, and to this day people still remember it and wonder about it.

"From a public relations standpoint where *George* was concerned, the fight was very bad," recalled Richard Bradley. "We were afraid of how it would affect advertisers, especially women's fashions and cosmetics. I know John regretted it but, unfortunately, it was Carolyn who suffered the most in the court of public opinion. On the video, she definitely looked like the aggressor. It helped to set in stone an unflattering image of her as being dramatic and unhappy. We all knew John had a temper, but the public didn't. It looked like Carolyn had brought out the worst in America's Prince, that she was changing him, and a lot of people held that against her. In the end, I think Carolyn was more angry at herself that she'd let John get to her in public than she'd been at whatever they were arguing about."

The dynamic between John and his sister, Caroline, had always been such that he was reluctant to disagree with her. Going all the way back to when they were children, he never wanted to fight with his only sibling. Jackie had raised them to work out any differences. Usually, though, John just let Caroline have her way. It was easier. He wanted to keep the peace with the one person in the world who meant the most to him, and anytime something came up that had the potential to be a problem between them, he would decide it wasn't worth it and shy away from taking a stance.

When it came to his love life, though, things became a little more complex for John. Caroline never approved of any of the women in his life, with the possible exception of the actress Christina Haag, who John had dated for a few years before Daryl Hannah and who'd also had the approval of Jackie. Because Caroline's knee-jerk reaction was to just be contrary about John's women, he had come to the conclusion — as did others — that she'd simply never be happy with anyone he chose. In her eyes no one would ever be good enough for him. Unlike other disagreements, where John would acquiesce, when it came to this subject he would listen and then just do what he wanted to do. Caroline would be vexed and her disapproval would fester between them for the duration of the relationship, but she was never able to actually make him end it with any woman.

True to form, Caroline Kennedy didn't approve of Carolyn Bessette. The first time anyone knew for sure there was a problem was back in 1994 at a holiday meal at Caroline and Ed's home. It was a festive occasion hosted by the Schlossbergs with John and Carolyn and Anthony and Carole in attendance. After dinner, they all clinked glasses and talked about their New Year's resolutions. Anthony vowed to stay out of the hospital. "Good luck with that," John said, ribbing him, as always. "And I think Carolyn's resolution should be to just marry John once and for all," Carole piped in, smiling at her friend.

"I don't *think* so . . ." said Ed Schlossberg.

"Oh? And why is that, Ed?" Carole asked, biting back a smile. She thought he was joking. He wasn't. "Because Caroline doesn't even *know* her," Ed said with a stern face.

Carolyn and Caroline just looked at each other in chilly silence. At that point, to hear Carole tell it years later, one could hear a pin drop. After a few awkward moments, everyone tried to recover and go on with dinner. However, it was clear that trouble was on the horizon.

When Carolyn later questioned John about the awkward moment, she felt let down by his response. He actually seemed fine with his sister not getting to know her. "She's not going to like you, so why bother?" he asked. This made no sense to Carolyn. One relative in whom she confided recalled, "She said, 'That's not how people in the real world are with each other,' to which John responded, 'Welcome to the Kennedys' world, where it's either sink or swim. My sister is the last one who's going to throw you a life raft.' Carolyn persisted. 'But I need to get to know her,' she told John. 'Maybe lunch or something?' No, John said. 'Just leave it alone, Carolyn.' The more she pushed, the more John resisted. 'Jesus, I *said* leave it alone, will you please?' he finally exploded. Then he left the room, annoyed. She told me she was upset about it and wondered what it all meant."

In the months to come, it became obvious that Caroline would never be close to Carolyn. They were just different kinds of women. Style and fashion meant a lot to Carolyn, for instance, and not much to Caroline. Caroline interpreted Carolyn's interest in clothing as a sign of her superficiality. Also, Carolyn was forthcoming and open as a person, whereas Caroline was much more subdued and harder to know. There were many other differences, but they were mere personality quirks. In short, Carolyn simply rubbed Caroline the wrong way. The truth was that John's fiancée wasn't her cup of tea. Though it bothered John, he knew better than to make an issue of it.

The highly public fight in the park, though, really illustrated why Caroline was so critical of Carolyn. She actually blamed her for it. She felt she'd been with John long enough to know what sorts of things pushed his buttons, and that she should've known to avoid those triggers while in public. "Get to know my brother," is how she put it. She was used to her cousins dragging the family name through the mud, but not John. She then had words with him about the melee along the lines of: "How do you think Mummy would like it?" He felt bad enough already; Caroline just made him feel a lot worse.

Caroline was now clear that John shouldn't marry Carolyn — at least not anytime in the near future. She felt that the fact that they'd been screaming in each other's faces was evidence enough that they weren't a good match. Certainly, she and Ed would never have had a fight like that. They were different people, though. They were so mild-mannered with each other, at least from all outward appearances, some people in their lives couldn't help but feel that maybe an explosive airing of feelings once in a while might actually do them a world of good.

The siblings debated John's engagement to Carolyn until there was nothing left to say about it. Finally, John felt the only way to smooth things over was to ask Carolyn if she would have Caroline be her matron of honor. However, Carolyn had two sisters with whom she got along well, so why would she want John's disapproving sibling to fill that role? The only reason, maybe, was because John had asked her. After some deliberation, she agreed.

What could Caroline say? Declining Carolyn's request would just cause more problems. Therefore, she agreed to accept the honor. The two then made a real effort to at least act as if they got along for John's sake. However, to say they were close during this time would definitely be overstating things.

ETHEL REACHES OUT
TO CAROLYN

Not only was John's sister upset about the display of temper in the park, his uncle Ted was also perplexed; he felt it out of character for John to be so out of control in public. Maybe Ted didn't know his nephew as well as he thought he did, though; John definitely could, when worked up, lose his temper in front of strangers. "He spoke to John about it to sort of parent him through it," Ted's good friend Senator John Tunney once said, "but he told me he didn't get far because the kid was so shaken and embarrassed. This kind of thing reflected poorly not just on John, but on the entire Kennedy family. Also, Ted knew John wanted to be taken seriously as a businessman with *George*. What had happened had been at odds with the image he was hoping to project in that regard."

Maybe it wasn't John who should be spoken to, Ethel decided. Perhaps it was Carolyn. She knew from the first time she met her that she wasn't what she appeared to be on the outside — "all smoke and mirrors" was how Ethel had put it. She noticed that things hadn't gotten better with the passing of time. Ethel knew that a large part of Carolyn's reluctance to be with the family just had to do with insecurity, and she felt she could help her in that regard. She'd actually wanted to sit down and have a frank conversation with Carolyn for some time and had just been waiting for the right moment. After the Central Park incident, she felt the time was right. Therefore, she asked her to Hickory Hill for a chat.

Carolyn was reluctant. She couldn't imagine what Ethel Kennedy would have to say to her privately, and she feared it had to do with the recent fracas in the park. If so, she wasn't sure how she'd handle being chastised by the matriarch. John left it up to her to decide whether to go, but he suggested that if she passed on the invitation it might be insulting. Finally, she consented to meet with Ethel, feeling she really had no choice. She wanted John to go with her, but he said he couldn't because he had magazine business in New York. She then asked her best friend, Jessica Weinstein, to accompany her, but she couldn't make it. Carole Radziwill was also unavailable. Her third choice was a good friend who asked to remain anonymous in this telling of the story. "She just needed a friend with her," said the source. "She was scared. I didn't know what to expect either, but I said yes, I would go."

Early the next morning, Carolyn and her friend found themselves on a private plane Ethel had sent to take them to Washington. They landed at Ronald Reagan Airport and were then picked up by a chauffeur in a white limousine, who drove them to McLean. Eventually, they pulled up to an enormous, white-brick Georgian manor, the sprawling main residence of the Hickory Hill estate. They were met at the door by an officious African American female in a black-and-white ensemble, not really a maid's uniform but more like a businesswoman's. "Welcome to Hickory Hill," she said before asking them to follow her.

"When we walked into the house, we were faced with this huge display of American history, all sorts of documents and artifacts," recalled the source. "In the entryway, there were dozens of framed presidential correspondence along with photographs of John, Bobby, and Ted. I noticed one letter of scribbled handwriting and asked what it was and was told that they were notes from JFK's last cabinet meeting. There was also a copy of JFK's inaugural address. There was even an original copy of the Emancipation Proclamation, which, we were told, was one of only forty in the world. I also saw letters from George Washington, Andrew Jackson, and

John Hancock. It was amazing."

The visitors were then taken through a maze of rooms and into a large, formal space that was described to them as "the drawing room." It was lovely, with hardwood floors, expensive rugs, and enormous picture windows that faced a stunning view of trees, flowery bushes, and marble statues of angels and saints. Antiques were placed about the room in just the right places. On either side of one of the main picture windows were two tall flags from JFK's Oval Office and RFK's Department of Justice office. There was more historic memorabilia everywhere, including photos of various Kennedys giving speeches and accepting awards. In the corner was an antique desk with a bust of Bobby Kennedy on it, which was surrounded by more family photos, all in silver frames.

It was early, and the housemaids were in the middle of their morning chores, preparing the room for the day. There must have been six women in crisp uniforms scampering all about, fluffing pillows, turning on certain lights, turning off others. Someone was vacuuming. Another woman was fumbling while trying to spark a blaze in one of the fireplaces. Someone else was arranging a huge assortment of exotic flowers in a large crystal vase. Another woman was perched precariously high atop a ladder and dusting books on a shelf she was barely able to reach.

"We heard someone say to be sure to keep the top of those books clean because Mrs. Kennedy might just get up there herself and run her fingers over them," recalled the source. "At just that moment, our greeter clapped her hands twice and announced, *'That will be all, ladies.'* They all then quickly started gathering their things. In maybe thirty seconds, they were gone."

After the two visitors sank into a comfortable, pale yellow couch, they were told to wait. Five minutes later, a maid presented them with a tray of hot tea and butter cookies. After the passing of about a half hour of eerie silence, Carolyn and her friend were beginning to wonder what was going on. Then Joe Kennedy, looking handsome in a blue suit with a red tie, appeared and introduced himself. He shook their hands. "My mother is dealing with a little issue in the kitchen," he said. "It's not a big deal," he added with a chuckle, "but if you see a tidal wave headed in this direction, get ready to start swimming." With that, he left.

"Finally, Mrs. Kennedy walked into the room," continued the source. "Carolyn jumped to her feet, which surprised me. It wasn't so much that she stood up as much as she did it as if she were a soldier coming to attention. I was about three seconds late. I remember thinking Mrs. Kennedy was more petite than I expected, but well put-together in a light pink linen pantsuit with pearls. She apologized, saying there was a plumbing problem. 'This place looks great from the outside,' she said, 'but if you scratch a little beneath the surface? Forget it. It's falling apart.'

"She asked who I was and why I was there," recalled Carolyn's friend. "When Carolyn explained that she just wanted company on the trip, Mrs. Kennedy looked skeptical and said, 'Yes. That and you were afraid to come here alone, weren't you, dear?' Carolyn's face got beet red. Mrs. Kennedy laughed it off and said, 'I get it. Don't worry. People think I'm scary.' Then, lowering her voice, she said, 'They think it because it's true.' We laughed nervously and sat down."

The three women talked for about an hour about a wide range of subjects, the gist of the conversation being the complications of dating and then marrying into the Kennedy family. Ethel acted surprised when Carolyn admitted to insecurity about John. "But you're so beautiful," she said, "and so smart. Why?" Carolyn said she felt not only in John's shadow but in that of every person who ever came into his orbit. "He's just such a big . . . *presence,*" she said. Ethel understood. "I went through that with Bobby at first," she said candidly. "Then I finally got it that the only way to survive in this family is to look in the mirror in the morning every single day and say, 'You know what? I am enough.' Plain and simple. That's it. 'I am enough.' Eventually it sinks in that, yes, you *are* enough, and that no one can ever take that away from you. Not even the Kennedys."

"We were so surprised," said Carolyn's friend. "She was so forward-thinking, so empowering. I guess I expected someone more traditional, strict, and old-fashioned. Then, becoming more firm, she said, 'Carolyn, I will tell you what I've told my daughters and my daughters-in-law. Be there for your husbands, but do not let them influence you into bad behavior. They will bait you. They always do. I've seen it for years. But you can't take the bait. You must be stronger than that.' Carolyn said something like, 'But John's temper is a lot to deal with sometimes.' Mrs. Kennedy became annoyed. She said, 'So? What else is new? You should see Joe's temper. You should see Bobby's. And you should see *mine.*' At that moment, the maid happened to be pouring more tea. 'Just ask her,' Mrs. Kennedy said. The maid looked at me, opened her eyes real wide, and sort of cringed. 'But not in public,' Mrs. Kennedy added. 'Never in public,' she said in a chastising tone. 'These men are hotheads. Don't let them goad you into acting improperly in front of the whole world. Do you know what I'm talking about?' Carolyn nodded."

"Let me tell you something, Carolyn,"

Ethel said as she rose when it was time for the conversation to end. "I think you're more powerful than any of the other women John has dated. You know why? Because you're smart," she said, "and because you have heart. So don't let John or those reporters or photographers or anyone else change who you are in here," she said, and then she tapped on Carolyn's chest. "Do you understand?"

Carolyn said she understood.

"Mrs. Kennedy walked us both outside," said Carolyn's friend. "We then hugged her goodbye and got into the car. As we were being driven down the long driveway and then out onto the street, I rolled down the window to wave goodbye, but she was gone. 'She's not really the goodbye-waving type,' Carolyn said. As we headed to the airport, we didn't say a word to each other. We were completely taken aback. I thought to myself, Well, okay, it makes sense. Look at all of the powerful women she's raised. Her daughter is the lieutenant governor of Maryland! That didn't just happen by accident. *Of course* this is how she thinks.

"Finally, Carolyn turned to me and said, 'I *am* enough, aren't I?' I smiled at her and said, 'Damn right you are.' And we just sat in silence for a little while and let that sink in."

Over the next six months, things definitely

seemed better for Carolyn. She still didn't love going to the Cape with the Kennedy herd, but Ethel's philosophy made a difference in her life. It was good advice. Maria Shriver would add, "We are *all* worthy — not because we've accomplished something or because we're part of a famous family. You're worthy if you don't make the team. You're worthy if you get Ds and Fs. You're worthy if you don't get into the best college. That belief is the greatest gift any parent can give his or her child."

Carolyn also seemed to be adapting to her high-profile relationship with John outside of the Kennedy enclave. "She would be at the compound wearing nice bright clothes, her hair falling free, very casual, no makeup," recalled Gustavo's daughter, Ariel. "Then, when she was getting ready to leave, she would change into all black clothing. She would then tie her hair up in a knot, a severe look, put on her makeup, and sometimes add a big hat and maybe sunglasses. This was her putting on her uniform, as if she was getting ready to go into combat. She would study herself in the mirror just before she and John would leave. She would then steel herself and declare, 'Okay, I'm ready. Let's do this.' That was her public persona. She had found a way to make it work for her. We felt, okay, it's time. Just be with John and get it over with."

Even though she was finding ways to cope,

John knew how much Carolyn would hate a big wedding, one swarming with photographers and reporters. How wonderful would it be, he mused, if they could just have a small, intimate affair, unlike the big, splashy occasions that had been previously orchestrated for many of his cousins. He knew it would be so appreciated by Carolyn. Could he pull it off, given that he was probably the most famous Kennedy of them all? Of course, as is well known by now, he did make it happen, and in the process of surprising Carolyn, he also surprised much of the world.

John chose Cumberland Island off the coast of Georgia as the wedding location, "as far off the beaten path as you can get," he told John Perry Barlow, who attended the ceremony. In the end, John would get his wish: not one photographer would be in sight to capture Carolyn's shining and eager face during the private and romantic ceremony. It took place in small wood-framed First African Baptist Church on Cumberland on September 21, 1996. The only lens man present was Denis Reggie (no relation to Vicki Reggie), who had been photographing Kennedy weddings since 1980.

Carolyn looked stunning in a forty-thousand-dollar pearl-colored silk crepe gown with a tulle silk veil, along with beaded satin Manolo Blahniks. She also wore long silk gloves. Her hair was pulled into an elegant chignon, the bun pinned with a clip that had belonged to Jackie. John looked perfectly attired in a single-breasted dark blue wool suit with a pale blue silk tie, white piqué vest, and his father's wristwatch. The photo of him kissing his wife's hand as the two left the church, taken by Reggie, is a classic. Anyone who has ever laid eyes on it remembers it fondly.

Of course, John's best man was Anthony, who was doing a lot better these days. For John, seeing him looking vital and handsome in a natty suit and tie on this special day was a real treat. "When you spot a John waiting out in the rain," Anthony said to John as he straightened his tie. John finished, "Chances are he's insane as only a John can be for a Jane." As usual, no one around them knew what in the world they were talking about. Never would they have guessed that these were lyrics from *Guys and Dolls* — so typical of John and Anthony.

■ ■ ■ ■

PART IV
FAMILY SECRETS

■ ■ ■ ■

THE PROBLEM WITH MICHAEL

To state that the cultivation of the family's public image was everything to the Kennedys seems somehow absurd. *Of course* they cared about how things looked. One would think, then, that they would have been able to find some way to stay clear of controversy. However, that's easier said than done for powerful, high-profile people like the Kennedys simply because the premise ignores the obvious: families are made up of individuals, and each person's life story is a unique combination of influences and circumstances. Put it this way: when someone from an influential family closes his eyes to go to sleep at night, his thoughts in those solitary moments usually don't have to do with the greater good as much as they do with whatever is ailing him personally — his vices, his challenges . . . his pain, his sorrows . . . his hopes, his dreams for his own life. If those concerns somehow dovetail with what's best for his family, all the better. Often, though, they don't. Certainly Michael Kennedy's experience was that he didn't much care about what was best for the family. He barely cared about what was best for *him* — and that was the problem.

To the outside world, it seemed as if everything came easy for Michael. By 1994, at the age of thirty-six, he seemed to be well-adjusted, successful, and even happy. Of course, that was also the case with most Kennedys of his generation. Privately, though, just as was true for many of his siblings and relatives, it was a different story. Behind closed doors, Michael had been struggling for most of his life.

Michael LeMoyne Kennedy, the fourth of Bobby and Ethel Kennedy's sons, was born on February 27, 1958. As a youngster, he was good-looking, with a thick head of dark hair, hazel eyes — almost green — and a gleaming but bucktoothed smile. One couldn't help but also notice that Michael had a weak chin, unlike his more square-jawed siblings. The way his face sloped to a point made him appear less powerful, maybe less formidable, than most of his relatives, but definitely more endearing. Even in photographs taken of him as an adult, he still looked like a little kid.

From the time he was about ten, Michael was a relentless loner, no easy feat given the number of boisterous family members in the household and how little opportunity there was for anyone to have a moment of solitude. Michael used to find ways to be by himself, though. There were times his mother couldn't even find him. When he was eleven and seemed to vanish, Ethel discovered him under a bed in one of the thirteen bedrooms of Hickory Hill. "What are you doing under there?" she asked. "Hiding," he answered. "From who?" The answer back was, "Everyone." He shared with Fina Harvin that his favorite hiding spot was in the hayloft of Hickory Hill's barn in a fort he'd make from hay bales.

Michael didn't always need to find a hiding place, though; he could somehow blend in, disappear into the crowd as if he wasn't even there. "Michael could hide in plain sight" is how Fina put it. "Mrs. Kennedy was concerned about him at an early age. The thing about Michael is that he was born with webbed feet. Maybe he felt insecure about it, I don't know. I only know that Mrs. Kennedy forbade everyone from ever mentioning it. She began to pay special attention to him. They got very close. The other kids started saying he was her favorite, and maybe he was." Michael always regretted that Ethel had had his toes surgically corrected. Joking, he used to say he felt the webbing might actually have helped to make him an Olympic swimmer.

Bobby Kennedy Jr. put it this way in his

book, *American Values:* "Michael was Mummy's favorite. But no one was jealous of her love for him because he was everybody else's favorite, too." He also wrote, "My mother's perpetual annoyance at me seemed less a rational response to my mischief than the outcome of some volatile chemical reaction; my mere presence seemed to agitate her. Michael provoked the opposite reflex: his proximity triggered in her a calming, soporific effect. When my appearance pitched my mom into a fit, my siblings knew to summon Michael to pacify her."

Prior to the age of ten, Michael had been an engaging child; he was funny, he loved to play, he was full of good humor. He would go into the servants' dining room and beg Ena Bernard and the other live-ins for cookies, and they couldn't resist giving them to him because he was just so cute. He'd always be sure to put extra ones in his pockets for all his siblings, counting them carefully to make certain he had enough. Ethel would chastise him, saying, "Leave those poor people alone," speaking of the help. "They have enough problems." Everyone loved him, though, and would smile whenever he came tearing into the servants' quarters. However, all that seemed to change in June 1968.

Like the rest of his siblings, Michael's eyes had always lit up whenever "Daddy" walked into the room. Bobby had been the kind of father who took the time to bond with each of his kids, and there were many of them by 1968, ten in all. Little Michael loved, in particular, those bedtime moments when Bobby would read stories from the Bible that somehow — at least the way Bobby read them — always seemed so exciting. While his son was just one of many, Bobby had a way of making him feel special, just as he did his other children. Nothing was more fun for Michael than when his father would take the boys into the bathroom and teach them how to shave — and this was years before puberty had set in for most of them — with just a bladeless razor running across cream-lathered, smooth faces. While Ethel was usually withholding when it came to doling out affection, Bobby was more forthcoming.

Michael was particularly affected by the war that was presently raging in Vietnam; February 1968 marked its deadliest period, with more than 500 Americans killed in action and more than 2,500 wounded. It was customary for all the kids to gather in front of the television and watch the news in order to stay informed. There was a point when Bobby thought maybe the smaller ones shouldn't watch the news, but Ethel disagreed, saying she felt they all needed to be aware of what was going on. While the others seemed able to take the bad news and not internalize it, Michael was somehow more affected by it, maybe even more scared of it.

When Bobby was taken from them, each child responded in his or her own way. Michael, for his part, just shut down — and he never opened up again. The change in his personality was instant, and permanent. It was as if life at Hickory Hill was just too much for him, what with all the kids, not to mention the animals — the snakes, hamsters, hawks, sheep, dogs, rabbits, pigs, iguanas, "and we even had goats, burros, and a bear," exclaimed governess Ena Bernard's daughter, Fina. "There was constant madness," she said. "When he was ten, Michael used to answer the phone, 'Confusion, here.' My mother became closest to Michael in a lot of ways. Mrs. Kennedy trusted him to her to make sure he got the attention he needed, to make sure he didn't get lost in the family. There were a lot of times you'd hear my mom and Mrs. Kennedy whispering about Michael, trying to figure out what else could be done for him. He was always a big concern."

As a teenager, because of his retiring personality, everyone began to think of Michael as being the most sensitive of the bunch. "Michael was a peacemaker," recalled his brother Bobby. "A family friend once made the observation that if Michael entered a room where a fight was about to break out, he would have a calming effect that would avert the conflict. As for himself, he never lost his temper and he never got flustered. Everyone who knew Michael eventually remarked on his extraordinary capacity to function in perfect calm amid chaos, whether it was dinner with ten screaming siblings, paddling a kayak through the most ferocious white water, or bringing a sailboat home through a gale. Most remarkably, he had the ability to inspire a similar composure in others." While it was true that some in the family viewed Michael as a calm center in the middle of a storm, others had a different view. "What we began to see is that there's a big difference between easygoing and sensitive and sad and isolated," said Noelle Bombardier, the property manager at Hickory Hill. "If anything, not only was Michael different, seeming disconnected and not really a part of things, as he got older something else seemed amiss: I think he actually began to lack simple empathy."

"If one of Michael's siblings was hurt playing or injured in sports, Michael shrugged it off, while the others glommed onto the wounded Kennedy," Joseph Gargan once recalled. "When one of the many animals that lived at Hickory Hill was ill, all of his siblings would be sick with worry — but not Michael. He didn't really seem to even care about his mom, or at least he didn't know how to show it; on Mother's Day, all of the children would make cards for Ethel, spending hours on their projects and then presenting them proudly on the special day. Not Michael."

It was true. Fina Harvin would sit Michael down and ask, "Don't you love your mummy? How come she didn't get a present?" He would look at her and just shrug. "Okay, but *next year,*" she'd say, "your mummy gets a card."

"Once, his uncle Ted was playing football with the kids and Michael took a tumble," recalled Leah Mason. "The Senator and Mrs. Kennedy and everyone else ran over to him to make sure he was okay, and Michael just sat there staring into space. 'Jesus Christ. This kid wouldn't know a real emotion if it hit him over the head,' the Senator said. Mrs. Kennedy smacked Ted hard across the chest. 'Don't say that, Teddy,' she exclaimed. 'That's not true.' "

Michael was self-aware enough to realize that something was different about him, as evidenced by a statement he once made to one of his closest friends when he was in his late twenties: "I *act* like I care. People *think* I care. But if I really analyze it, I mean if I *really* think about it, I realize that I actually don't care about much."

As he grew up, one thing was certain about Michael Kennedy: when it came to athletics, no one could hold a candle to him. "He was the greatest athlete of our generation," said Bobby Kennedy. "Timmy Shriver, a spectacular athlete, told me that Michael was so gifted that at one point he stopped being jealous and reconciled himself to admiring him. His speed was legendary. He could run circles around any of us in football, and I never saw him beaten in a sprint even when he raced two NFL fullbacks on Grandma's lawn. He could master any sport — squash, windsurfing, snowboarding, paddle tennis, golf — in days. More than once, his athletic ability saved his life. A skidding car threatened to crush him against another vehicle on an icy Boston street. Michael vaulted vertically, landing with a foot on each car before the crash, then surfed down Boylston Street."

"Even though athletic risk-taking was certainly par for the course for Kennedys, Michael was really over the top with it," added one friend of his who knew him as a young man. "This he cared about. *This*. Escaping death while kayaking or sailing or skiing was, from my perspective anyway, the one thing that truly animated him. Being a junkie for danger was okay, I thought. But it bothered me a lot when he would say, 'I'm just trying to figure out some way to feel alive.' "

When he was a teenager at St. Paul's boarding school in Concord, New Hampshire, Michael met the blond and lovely Victoria Denise Gifford — Vicki. Her father was the famous football player and television announcer Frank Gifford, and her stepmother the talk-show host and singer Kathie Lee Gifford. In the 1970s, Ethel had dated Frank, though not seriously.

Michael and Vicki had a whirlwind relationship before marrying in a Catholic ceremony at St. Ignatius Loyola in Manhattan on March 14, 1981. They would go on to have three children, Michael LeMoyne Jr. in January 1983, Kyle Francis in January 1984, and Rory Gifford in November 1987.

In academics was where Michael also shone, first at Harvard and then at the University of Virginia Law School, from which he graduated in 1984. He, along with his brother Max, also became one of the family's keepers of the flame; both would carefully study the smallest details of their father's life and times. When a writer wanted access to the Kennedy Library, it was usually Michael who would have to be convinced. "I'm going to sit behind you and watch you and make sure you get the right files and do the proper research," he told this biographer when I was working on a previous book about his family. He wasn't kidding. He did what he threatened to do, sat and watched and took his own notes on the research at hand, and he did so for more than six hours.

After he graduated from law school, Michael was recruited by his older brother Joe to join the company he had started called

Citizens Energy. Joe, when he was fresh out of the University of Massachusetts back in 1979, had started the venture to alleviate the burden of heating bills for the poor during the oil crisis of that year. Because he was so smart and industrious, Joe's company absolutely soared, even though it was rooted in philanthropy. Eight years later, when Joe entered the family business of politics and was elected to Congress, he put Michael in charge of Citizens. Michael and his partner, Wilber James, a former Peace Corps volunteer who had been with the company from its outset, then split up the Citizens empire: Michael became president and CEO of Citizens Energy, the nonprofit end of the company, and James president and CEO of Citizens Corporation, the profit-making arm.

During the course of about fifteen years, Citizens had all but moved away from its original strictly nonprofit mandate of delivering fuel and had become involved in global enterprises, with Michael strongly at its helm. Angola quickly became the most important foreign country of all Citizens' connections abroad. Stakes in an oil concession there eventually became hugely profitable. Citizens would even build a college in Angola, further cementing its connections there. In 1994, Michael earned almost seven hundred thousand dollars, but that was just the tip of the iceberg where his personal profit margin was concerned. In terms of stock options, he held at least ten million, and probably more. Such success didn't come without mounting pressures, though.

It was around 1994 that Michael began to drink heavily and also do cocaine. Some felt it had to do with his workload, others with trouble in his marriage. It could just as easily have been another way to isolate. Whatever the case, Michael's personality had now taken on a new and darker dimension. Whereas he used to be passive, when he started doing alcohol and drugs he became combative and angry, almost as if some sort of inner demon had finally been released. "I'm *Michael fucking Kennedy* and you don't get to tell me what to do," he shouted at one Citizens Energy officer during a contentious meeting. "I don't respond to threats," he said, his eyes flashing. "*I make them.* Now get out of my sight." The company executive on the other end of that rebuke later recalled, "That was so not like him to lose his shit like that. We were all just so stunned to hear him talk like that."

"The memory of him that stands out was at a fund-raiser for Patrick [Kennedy] in August of '94 at Hammersmith, our former family home," recalled Jackie's half brother, Jamie Auchincloss. "After Michael made his remarks and introduced Patrick, he didn't engage or schmooze. His vibe wasn't good, as if he had a chip on his shoulder. In speaking to him, he was so angry. It struck me that maybe he had some kind of chemical imbalance."

A week later, back at the Kennedy compound for the 1994 Labor Day celebration, Michael was still tense and unhappy, snapping at people. The poet Rose Burgunder Styron, wife of the famous novelist William Styron, was present with her husband and recalled Michael being "not very engaged. We always loved Michael, so we were worried. He had been a sweet boy who seemed to have changed. My husband suffered from severe depression," she said, "and Michael's behavior reminded me of it." When Fina Harvin saw him smoking a cigar, she went up to him and good-naturedly said, "Michael! That's not good for you." He became belligerent. "I'm a grown man, Fina," he said angrily. "I can smoke a cigar if I want to. So butt out."

"This ice cream smells funny," John said to Michael at one point as he held a bowl in front of him. "Smell it." It was an old joke, one John had played dozens of times. As his cousin slowly lowered his head to smell the dessert, John pushed his nose right into it. Michael was immediately enraged. In response, John said he thought *Carolyn* was the newbie on Kennedy turf, not Michael. Michael said all he expected of John was for him to act like a grown-up for once in his life. Then he took off.

"About an hour later, Michael had a loud argument with Vicki," recalled Theresa Lichtman, who worked at that time in the kitchen. "It got pretty volatile."

"What is it you want from me?" Michael shouted at Vicki, according to Lichtman.

"I want you to stop drinking," she said, upset.

"I think what you *meant* to say is: Michael, *maybe* we should have a little *talk* about your drinking," he said.

"That comment really set Mrs. Kennedy [Vicki] off," recalled Theresa, "and the next thing everyone knew, the two of them were off and running. 'I don't want to hear another word about it,' Michael said angrily. He held up his hand to silence her. 'End of subject,' he said. 'Now, just shut up about it.' It was so surprising."

Again according to Theresa Lichtman, at that point, Ted Kennedy went over to Michael and said, "Come on, kid, let me sober you up." He patted him on the shoulder and kissed him on the top of his head. Michael pulled away. "This isn't the eighties, Uncle Teddy," he said, "and I'm not a kid anymore. Leave me alone." Now the Senator was the one upset. "Whatever your problem is," he told Michael, angrily, "you'd better suck it up. *You're a Kennedy.*" He then walked over to Ethel and remarked, "I think that boy drinks too much." She looked at him with annoyance and said, *"Ya think?"* Then — all of this according to the witness — Ted said, "I don't know . . . maybe the kid is still dealing with Bobby's death." At that, Ethel got angry. "It's been almost twenty-five years," she exclaimed. "Don't you dare blame it on Bobby."

Also, at this time, Michael had been tasked with helping to orchestrate his uncle Teddy's latest run for the Senate, this year against an unknown named Mitt Romney. He had a hard time with it, his organizational skills lacking. Ted wasn't happy with his work, but Michael complained that it was impossible to keep his uncle on message. It was true that Ted's charm with the ladies was still an issue at the age of sixty-two, even if he was now married. "Senator Ted Kennedy at your service," he would say with a wink as he extended his hand to a lovely admirer. Michael would just shake his head in frustration.

"You have no idea what my life is like or what it feels like to be me," Michael told Vicki the day after Labor Day during dinner. He then got up and stormed off. Ethel hollered after him. "Michael! You get back here right now." He returned, his head hanging low. His mother then rose, looked up at him — he was at least a foot taller than she was — and smacked him hard on the side of his head with her open palm. "Grow up," she commanded. "Now, you apologize to Vicki," she added, all this according to Leah Mason, who witnessed it. Michael faced his wife and muttered, "Sorry, Vicki," as if he were twelve, not thirty-six. "Fine. Now go," Ethel told him. After he skulked away, Vicki started to rise, saying, "I should probably go after him." However, her mother-in-law placed a stern hand on her shoulder and pushed her back down. "No," she said. "I'll do it."

MICHAEL'S TEMPTATION

Though she was just a teenager, she somehow seemed older. Not only was it her appearance — her full and shapely figure, the heavy makeup, clothing that seemed more suited for a woman in her twenties — it was also the way she comported herself. Sixteen-year-old Marisa Verrochi — born on January 29, 1978 — wasn't one of those kids uncomfortable or awkward in social situations with adults, not wanting to make eye contact. When she spoke to grown-ups, she was smart and funny. When she listened, she was invested. However, no matter how mature she may have seemed, she was still just a young girl with the vulnerability normal to kids her age.

In recent years, Marisa had been troubled by family dysfunction, specifically her mother's alcoholism. Former schoolteacher June Marie Verrochi, a shapely, attractive blonde who usually wore her hair in a smart pageboy cut, was a popular, social woman with sparkling blue eyes and a gregarious personality. She and her husband, Paul Verrochi, and their children — Marisa and her brothers, Matt and Marc — lived in an massive nineteenth-century seaside mansion with a wraparound driveway behind elegant white wooden gates in Cohasset, Massachusetts, right down the street from Michael and Vicki Kennedy. Not only were the Verrochis one of the wealthiest families in Cohasset, they were extremely social and could always be counted upon to show up for philanthropic events. Paul was well-connected politically, too, having raised a fortune for Democratic politics. He was even thinking of running for office. Privately, though, the fights he and June had over her drinking were constant. Sadly, their three children would be raised in a household where there always seemed to be some sort of high-stakes drama.

Back in 1991, the ambitious and enterprising Paul founded American Medical Response — AMR; it quickly became the largest medical transportation company in the United States. "Paul was a great-looking guy," said Ren Ayers, who was Paul and June's personal masseuse, "a lot of dark hair, thick eyebrows. Square jawed. Muscular, built like a linebacker. Very personable. Good laugh. Though he could be quite stern, he sure did love his family." Thomas Davis, a friend of Paul's from Cohasset, confirmed,

"June and the kids were Paul's whole world. He was able to compartmentalize the arguments he had with June from the rest of their life together. 'I let her drink,' he told me, 'and I keep an eye on it. It's not the best situation, but she'll go to AA soon.' 'Soon' never seemed to happen, though."

Paul and June Verrochi were about eight years older than Michael and Vicki. The two couples had become close, their relationship solidified when Paul donated fifty thousand dollars to one of Michael's most passionate causes — handgun control. Soon after, at Michael's behest, Paul joined the board of Citizens Energy. By the middle of 1994, the two men were the best of friends; Paul was forty-four, Michael thirty-six.

Paul was always able to make Michael laugh, cutting through his apathy and giving some relief from his depression, whether by just hanging out watching sports on television, or going to a bar to toss back a few. "Why is he such a miserable fuck?" Paul used to ask Thomas Davis. "He's got the world by the balls. He's a Kennedy." Thomas would answer, "Maybe that's why he's such a miserable fuck."

When they were together, Paul and Michael sometimes commiserated about their troubled marriages. Of course, Paul was always worried about June's alcoholism. Michael's story was along the cliché-ridden lines of "Vicki doesn't understand me." Meanwhile, Vicki's friendship with June was more guarded, the reason being that Marisa had taken to complaining to Vicki about her. Certainly, with the exception of June's drinking, there wouldn't have been anything particularly unusual about the troubled dynamic she had with her daughter. It was mostly the result of teenage rebellion: schoolwork, boys, chores, and other typical adolescent discord. It was June's alcoholism that exacerbated the situation, making it so much more toxic. After a big argument with her mother, Marisa would inevitably run to Vicki, crying. Vicki would then end up being her counselor; she felt the need to be there for her.

At one point in mid-1994, Paul confided in Michael that June had either slapped or threatened to slap Marisa — Paul wasn't clear about it, maybe trying to protect his wife from judgment. Whichever the case, Paul was concerned. He also mentioned that Marisa had begun showing signs of the eating disorder bulimia. He didn't know how to deal with it. Michael's personal experience, he explained, was that when distance was put between his sisters and their mother, it often proved productive. Usually, the girls would go off camping for the summer months and that would be enough of a break for them to then return to a more peaceful relationship with Ethel at Hickory Hill.

By this time, Marisa, who was five years older than Michael's eldest, his namesake, had been babysitting for the Kennedys since about the age of fourteen. Michael suggested that, while they waited for this bad phase to be over between Marisa and June, maybe Marisa should move in with him and Vicki. He said he thought it might be a good idea for everyone.

Michael's suggestion struck Paul as a little strange. However, when he later mentioned it to June, she didn't think it was such a bad idea. Because June liked the Kennedys so much, she felt Marisa would be safe with them. She also pointed out that since they lived so close, it would be more like a sleep-over for Marisa than anything else.

Now Paul was conflicted. Of course he and June could probably use a break from their daughter's moodiness and sullen behavior, but wouldn't that have been true of any parents trying to raise a recalcitrant teenage daughter? If he couldn't handle his own kid, he had to wonder, what kind of father was he? Michael wouldn't let it go, though. He kept pushing the idea to the point where Paul actually began to question his determination to see it through. Over the course of a couple of weeks, Michael seemed downright fixated on the idea. Meanwhile, Paul continued to vacillate about it.

One night, Paul went over to Michael's home and found him and his brother Joe reviewing a mountain of paperwork with lawyers and business associates, all of it having to do with providing heat to the poor. Paul couldn't help but be impressed that the Kennedy brothers cared so much about those less fortunate; Michael was impassioned about it, in fact. When he talked to Paul about the mission of Citizens Energy, he also explained the Kennedys' long-held credo of being of service. Of course, this wasn't the first time Paul had heard such words coming from Michael, but on this particular evening he was even more moved by them. They actually influenced him to acquiesce and agree to Michael's plan for Marisa. Certainly, if the family's philosophy of selflessness could influence his daughter even just a bit, she'd be all the better for it. Therefore, in the spring of 1994, Marisa Verrochi moved into the Kennedys' home as their live-in babysitter.

Without the benefit of an eyewitness, it's difficult to ascertain exactly what occurred. Some have suggested that sixteen-year-old Marisa began to have a crush on the thirty-six-year-old Michael, which maybe wasn't so unusual for a teenage girl living in the home of a powerful and handsome Kennedy. Some say she even started acting on it by being flirtatious and forward. If so, obviously it would have been Michael's responsibility as a grown man, a husband, and a father, to put an immediate stop to it.

Apparently, he didn't.

On June 24, 1994, many members of the Kennedy family went rafting on the Kennebec River near The Forks in Maine on a trip organized by Michael's good friend John Rosenthal. In order to raft on the Kennebec, participants were required to fill out a Noncommercial Whitewater Rafting registration form for the Maine Warden Service. On this trip was a party of seventeen, including Michael and his brother Max and sister Rory, along with Marisa. Michael's three children were present, as well as other kids as young as eleven. However, Vicki wasn't a part of this trip. Instead, she attended a friend's baby shower.

During this particular getaway, people couldn't help but notice that Michael and Marisa would often slip off to be alone. Some began to wonder about it; it did seem peculiar. However, certainly no one would accuse Michael of doing anything improper to exploit the power dynamic of his relationship with Marisa. While something didn't seem quite right, no one could be sure that anything untoward was going on . . . or at least they *hoped* it wasn't. Michael was drinking a lot, though, at this time, and he always seemed to be high on something. It was becoming difficult to know exactly what to

KENNEDY STRATEGY SESSION

On January 3, 1995, an emergency Kennedy family trust meeting was called at Hickory Hill. Present were many of Ethel's children — Kathleen, Bobby, Joe, Kerry, Rory, Max, and Christopher, as well as Jean Kennedy Smith's son Willie. John flew in from New York, though Caroline did not attend. Ted Kennedy was present, as well. These kinds of family strategy meetings were common, or as the reporter Ben Bradlee, a close friend of JFK's who had been the executive editor of *The Washington Post,* said in 1995, "The Kennedys would call a major family meeting to talk about what to have for dinner that evening. So you can be sure that when something major was happening, they would get everyone available in a room to make decisions as to how to go forward. It would be all hands on deck, so to speak, or at least as many hands as Ted and Ethel could pull together. Brain trust? To them, that was just another name for family."

During this top secret strategy session, the Kennedys all sat in Ethel's living room and faced Michael, who was present with Vicki. One family strategist present, who insisted on anonymity to discuss internal deliberation, was a person who'd long handled the family's public relations. He brought with him an assistant and a secretary to take notes.

The family had come together to address Michael's obvious drinking and drug use. Not only was it upsetting his wife and family members, it had recently become the subject of an off-putting press report. The writer cited credible sources who suggested that Michael's behavior might affect Joe's career as a congressman and Kathleen's as a lieutenant governor.

Joe Kennedy had been a congressman in the Eighth District of Massachusetts since 1987. He was extremely popular, a politician known for getting things done. Privately, he was also known in the family as the brother with the shortest fuse. For instance, back in 1985 when he heard that his cousin Teddy — Ted's son — was considering running for the Senate seat once held by JFK, Joe was angry and everyone knew it. He was the oldest of the cousins and that was *his* seat, at least as far as he was concerned. It turned into a family dispute; in the end, neither man went for it.

Christopher Lawford explained: "By the

time Joe hit the testosterone-producing years of puberty, he had developed a fairly regular addiction to punching someone over something." He also noted that Bobby Jr. was often a target, and that he had suffered a "lifetime of beatings" from his brother. "He could be a lot nicer" is how his cousin John, who always had issues with Joe, once put it. It was always interesting that, as a grown man and politician, Joe obviously cared deeply about others, yet somehow he also gave the appearance of not caring as much for those actually in his life. Criticism of him in this regard was nothing new to Joe, though. He was self-aware enough to know that people thought he could be, as John put it, "a lot nicer." Or, as he once said, "I'm a dick and I know it. But at least I know it."

Kathleen was, by this time, lieutenant governor of Maryland under Parris Glendening. Of course, Ethel had encouraged her to run, as had Ted and everyone else, including his sisters Eunice, Pat, and Jean. Jean was another real role model for Kathleen; she'd recently been appointed U.S. ambassador to Ireland

In her platform, Kathleen was more conservative than many of her relatives. For instance, unlike her uncle Ted, she supported the death penalty and believed that criminals sentenced to life shouldn't be paroled, not as a deterrent, she explained to *Time,* "but because there are awful people who don't have a right to live. The Democratic Party got away from believing personal responsibility was part of our agenda. But I've always believed it was part of mine." She would remain a busy and accomplished woman, constantly giving speeches across the state, furthering her party's platform, and conferring with her brother Joe on policy. "Maryland became the first state in the country to require all kids to do community service as a condition to high school graduation, and that was what I worked on for a number of years," she recalled, "because I thought it was critical that not just Kennedys are told that they can get involved in changing their community, but that everybody should be able to do it."

There were other family members in influential positions who had a lot to lose if Michael's behavior became publicly known. This was serious business and the stakes were high, just as was always the case whenever someone of Michael's generation displayed behavior that threatened the family's image. Ted would always tell them, "You need to think like Kennedys and make better choices." However, they often didn't take his advice, and some even felt maybe he didn't have a lot of room to give it, considering some of his own choices.

"This was an intervention," said the source,

"where each person got up and faced Michael to let him know how his addiction had affected them. The point is that the addict has to then come to a full understanding of how his actions have impacted others and then make a decision to go into rehab, right then and there. Best-case scenario would have been to have a professional interventionist supervising things. That wasn't the Kennedys' way, though. They preferred to handle these sorts of things 'in-house,' so to speak.

"Michael didn't fight it; he said he'd go to rehab, but not immediately. He wanted a month to get his affairs in order. Everyone protested; no, no, no, they said, he should go right away. 'I'm the one who has a lot to lose, Michael,' Joe said, 'and I've been good to you,' he added, I guess referencing his handing of Citizens over to him. Michael muttered, 'Sorry, Joe.' "

Though he may not have shown it at the intervention, Joe's criticism was hard on Michael. The two had always been inseparable; it was one of the reasons Joe had entrusted Citizens to him. More than anything, Michael believed in Joe and felt, like everyone else, he could one day become President, maybe even using a possible governorship of Massachusetts as a stepping-stone. "This situation is fucked up," Joe concluded."

Ethel bolted out of her chair. "Language, Joe," she exclaimed. "*Language.* Everyone simmer down. We're *Kennedys.* Not hood-lums."

"No, Mummy," Joe said with impatience. "If we can't tell each other the truth, then why are we even here?"

According to witnesses, Ethel didn't respond; she just glared at her eldest until he averted his eyes and mumbled an apology. Michael then promised his mother he would go into treatment in a month and asked her to please just believe him. She agreed, but not before reminding him and everyone else present of what they had to lose. "People look up to this family," she said with icy tenacity, "and we must still make a difference, each one of us. But we can't if we're unable to control our weaknesses," she added, and then, staring at Michael, she concluded, "of which there are, apparently, many." She then asked someone to get her a notebook, after which she went into her purse and pulled out a red pen; Ethel always had a red pen on hand, never any other color ink. With pen and paper in hand, she asked the Senator, "So, what is it we're going to say, Teddy?"

As Ethel took it all down, Ted dictated a brief statement that basically explained that Michael had volunteered to enroll in a rehabilitation program in Maryland, the Father Martin's Ashley center in Havre de Grace, northeast of Baltimore. He would enter on February 1.

The press release would be issued to the media in the morning.

The press release would be issued to the media in the morning.

A DEAL WITH THE DEVIL?

Victoria Denise Gifford — Vicki — hadn't been raised to be a quitter. After all, her father, Frank, had been a Hall of Fame football player for the New York Giants back in the fifties, playing both offense and defense. He was as ambitious as he was talented, determined to not only make his mark on the sport but to also have his children use the example of his success as a guide for their own lives. Frank had married Vicki's mother, Maxine Avis Ewart, in 1952. They had three children, Jeff, Kyle, and then Victoria, on February 20, 1957.

After Frank Gifford retired from the Giants in 1964, he became a popular sportscaster on ABC's *Monday Night Football.* In the seventies and eighties, he was instantly recognizable as an affable, handsome personality with the square-jawed and chiseled-face looks of a movie star. In his private life, though, he had his challenges: Maxine suffered from multiple sclerosis, and even though their marriage had failed, he was determined to support her, making sure she had what she needed financially to do battle with her insidious disease. He was a good man who lived by the strength of his convictions.

Frank's daughter, the blond and blue-eyed Vicki, was also made of tough stuff. By the time she married Michael Kennedy in 1981, she was twenty-four, college educated, and raised to not only excel in life but to be smart about her choices. Still, some thought that she was too young to know what she was getting herself into by marrying into a complicated family like the Kennedys. She'd only had one boyfriend prior to Michael, and it was not serious. Michael was her first love, and he wasn't exactly easy to understand.

By 1994, after thirteen years of marriage, Vicki had long ago been disabused of any illusions she'd ever had of Michael being any different from many of his male relatives. He'd been cheating on her for years, and she knew it. That summer, while at the Cape, Vicki told one of her sisters-in-law that there were days when it was all she could do to force herself to get dressed, put on some makeup, and get on with things. Sometimes what she most wanted to do, she said, was to curl up into a little ball and never leave the house. If not for her kids, that's probably what she would do, she admitted.

At the time, Vicki and this sister-in-law were

walking along the beach in front of Rose and Joe's home, commiserating about their bad marriages. To stay or to leave, that was the dilemma. For now, these Kennedy wives decided to stay. However, they agreed that it was as if they'd made a deal with the devil. They couldn't help but reflect upon other women like them from the previous generation who, though deeply wounded by Kennedy patriarchy and infidelity, had made the same bargain. How often had they consoled each other while walking this very same stretch of shoreline? This wasn't the 1960s, though. It was 1994. However, apparently, some things never changed.

According to this account, the sisters-in-law also talked about something they'd both heard through the family's grapevine: Joan Kennedy had, in recent weeks, decided she wanted to see the bridge at Chappaquiddick her ex-husband, Ted, had driven off and killed Mary Jo Kopechne, back in 1969. Joan had waited twenty-five long, painful years before she could muster the courage to go to that fateful site and see it for herself. When she finally did, she thought she'd be awash in emotion considering the destruction that accident had caused to the Kopechnes and the Kennedys, not to mention her marriage. She had even had a miscarriage because of it. Instead, as she later told it, she felt . . . nothing.

"Poor Joan," Vicki said. "She's dead inside, isn't she?"

"Yes," her sister-in-law agreed. "Dead inside."

"Is the price of power just too high?" the sister-in-law asked.

According to this account, Vicki mulled over the question and, true to her pragmatic nature, answered, "Maybe. Or perhaps a better question is: Why can't these men just keep their dicks in their pants?"

About six months had passed since that moment on the beach shared by Vicki and her sister-in-law. Now it was January 22, 1995, three weeks since the family's intervention for Michael. Coincidentally, it was also the last day of Kennedy matriarch Rose Fitzgerald Kennedy's life. At 104, she'd been a widow for twenty-six years, since the death of her beloved husband, Joseph P. Kennedy, back in 1969.

Very early that morning before that sun had risen, Vicki awakened with a feeling of dread, a sense of alarm. Maybe it was an intuition that her grandmother-in-law was taking her last breath, or maybe it was something else. All she knew was that she was uneasy and couldn't get back to sleep.

Vicki rose from her bed, put on a robe, and looked around the room. It was dark; she turned on a light. That's when she realized Michel was not in bed. Confused, she left the room and slowly walked down the hall, searching one room after the other for him. Maybe he was in one of the children's bedrooms, she thought. A good and caring father, Michael would often lie in bed with one of the kids if the child awakened with a bad dream and called out for Mommy or Daddy. He wasn't in any of their rooms, though; in fact, he seemed nowhere to be found. *Something,* as she would later recall, then began to draw her like a magnet to the room Marisa Verrochi now slept in since having moved in with the family. Slowly, Vicki made her way to that spare room. She cracked open the door, peered inside . . . and that's when she got maybe the biggest shock of her life: Michael was in bed with Marisa.

She couldn't help herself; according to what she later told family members, Vicki screamed loudly, the piercing sound filling the enormous home and waking up her children, who began to cry. Michael then explained that he'd been drunk and had stumbled through the darkened house and somehow — he couldn't imagine how, he said — found his way into Marisa's bed. By this time, the teenage girl was also crying so hard, Vicki wasn't even able to get her side of the story.

With the scene so quickly out of control and emotions running hot, Michael started to babble on about his addiction. He said it was worse than Vicki knew and that he had hidden the severity of it from her for a long time. He must have been drunk, or high, or . . . who knows? He also pointed out that he and Marisa were both dressed in pajamas, so obviously nothing untoward was going on between them. Besides, she was only sixteen, he noted. (Marisa would turn seventeen in a week's time.) Why would Vicki think the worst of him?

Actually, to hear her later tell it to relatives, Vicki didn't know *what* to think. Her mind was a jumble; she needed time to figure it all out.

The next day, a distraught Vicki sent the kids to her father's home and Marisa back to that of her parents. She elected not to tell the Verrochis about what had happened, leaving it up to Marisa to tell them about it if she wanted to do so. But what to do about Michael? Vicki didn't know the answer to that question. All she knew was that she needed time.

A GRUESOME DISCOVERY

After the shocking discovery of her husband in bed with the family's teenaged babysitter, Vicki Kennedy knew she needed help. Could she go to one of Michael's siblings for it? She wasn't sure how they would react. Because they were so loyal to one another, she questioned how much support she could expect from them. Therefore, she went to someone else, a Kennedy cousin named Michael Skakel. This man was someone with his own checkered history; he'd actually been at the center of a murder mystery for the last twenty years.

It had all started back on October 31, 1975, six years before Vicki Gifford had even married Michael Kennedy. It was on that day that Michael's mother, Ethel, forty-seven at the time, first learned about a crime that would haunt her family for decades to come.

"What!" Ethel said, answering the phone in the pool house in her inimitable way that Halloween morning. She'd been getting calls

for hours and seemed particularly agitated, so much so that her property manager, Noelle Bombardier, knew to leave her to her privacy. When she finally emerged from the pool house, Ethel seemed weighted down with a problem. Once back in the main house, she received yet another phone call. *"What!"* Noelle stayed in the kitchen and heard Ethel's end of the conversation, which was mostly along the lines of her making exclamatory statements such as "There's no way," "It can't be true," and "I can't believe it."

"I remember thinking, My God, what is this?" recalled Noelle. "Was somebody sick? Did somebody die?"

Though a Halloween party had been planned for the Kennedys at Hickory Hill that night, Ethel had her own idea for mischief: She planned to go trick-or-treating with Elizabeth Stevens, wife of George Stevens Jr., the longtime producer and writer of the Kennedy Center honors; his father had directed Elizabeth Taylor in *A Place in the Sun.* It was typical of Ethel to want to have her own bit of fun on Halloween. Around five P.M., she pulled Noelle aside. "Help me get dressed," she told her. The two then walked up the long flight of stairs and down the hall to Ethel's bedroom. As Ethel started to don her costume, Noelle realized it was a black witch's ensemble, complete with pointy sorcerer's hat, clunky shoes, and a broom. After she put the outfit on, Ethel sat down at her vanity and began applying gobs of green makeup to her face. "So, how do I look?" she asked as she whirled around to face Noelle.

"Fantastic," Noelle said. "But I think you'll still be recognized. You *are* Ethel Kennedy, after all."

Ethel chuckled. "Don't worry," she said. "I'm going to wear sunglasses."

As the two women made their way downstairs, Noelle asked Ethel what was going on. Handing her the broom that was integral to her costume, Ethel said, "Come with me." She led her into the drawing room and quickly closed the sliding doors behind them. This was a spacious area designed in a Victorian style with royal colors of gold and burgundy. There were no couches; instead there were several round red oak tables with enormous matching chairs with red velvet coverings, all organized into separate conversation areas. It looked royal if not exactly comfortable. Right in the middle of the room on a silver pedestal and enclosed in a glass box was one of the strangest souvenirs one might ever encounter: a gleaming gold-and-white pope's miter. When she first started working at Hickory Hill, Noelle had asked to which pope it had belonged. With a mischievous glint in her eye, Ethel said, "Guess. And I'll tell you if you're right." Rather than reveal that she didn't know the names of very many popes, Noelle just passed on the offer. Therefore, in all her many years working there, she never did find out which pope had donated his miter to Hickory Hill.

"As you know," Ethel began, "I've had many calls today. They've been from the Senator. It looks like *maybe . . .*" She stopped and took a deep breath. *"Maybe, my nephew Michael Skakel . . . killed a girl."*

"Oh my God, Mrs. Kennedy. Who's the girl?"

"I think her name is Martha something or other," Ethel answered.

"How?"

Ethel said that the victim's body had been found in a yard, lying in a pool of blood with a broken golf club next to her. Shuddering, she said Ted told her it had been a particularly gruesome scene. She wasn't sure why he felt Michael Skakel might be the culprit, "but time will tell, I guess."

Years later, Noelle would recall, "Picture it: I'm standing with Ethel Kennedy in a Victorian setting in the middle of which is a pope's miter in a glass box. She's dressed in a witch's costume with green makeup on her face. And she's telling me that one of her nephews may have slaughtered a girl with a golf club. It was surreal, to say the least. I had to sit down. She sat next to me. 'I can't imagine that Michael would do something like this,' she said, trying to process things. 'Why, he's only fifteen.' 'Will he be arrested?' I asked. 'Who knows?' Ethel answered. 'Who the heck knows?' "

At that moment, the doorbell rang. Ethel took a deep breath. "Can you believe I have to go trick-or-treating now?" she asked. Noelle suggested that maybe she should cancel. "No. Liz is counting on it," Ethel said. Noelle then handed Ethel her witch's broom. Ethel looked at it and shook her head at the absurdity of it all. As she walked away, she turned back to Noelle and whispered, "Not a word about this to anyone."

Twenty years had passed since that fateful day in 1975 when Ethel Kennedy learned of her nephew Michael Skakel's possible involvement in the murder of Martha Moxley. However, by 1995, he still hadn't been charged; there simply wasn't enough evidence against him to support a conviction. However, the case would always linger in the background of his life and in those of the Kennedys. Some family members felt he was guilty of murder, while others weren't so sure. His aunt Ethel was one of those who believed in his innocence.

Michael Christopher Skakel was the middle son of seven children fathered by Ethel's brother Rushton Walter Skakel and his wife, Anne. The Republican Skakels and Democratic Kennedys had feuded over business for years before Ethel married Bobby, and even after the merging of the two families they didn't get along. Ethel says she was proud to now be a Democrat even if, by her own admission, she says her family "thought I was a little Communist" — and she wasn't smiling when she said it. "The Skakels supported Nixon, not Jack, in the 1960 election," recalled Ethel's brother Jim Skakel in a 1994 interview. "That was tough on Ethel. She managed to let it go without too much of a problem, though. I remember that when Jack was elected, Ethel got a nice block of tickets for the Inauguration. This was supposed to be a really big deal, of course. She gave them to our brother George to distribute to our family. Instead of doing that, George went into the streets and handed them out to bums and hobos. So, on the big day for the Kennedys, these smelly and messy guys ended up sitting right next to all the close friends and relatives of the Kennedys. Ethel was pissed. She gave George hell for that."

Michael Skakel didn't have much to do with his Kennedy relations until sometime in the mid-eighties, when he became sober after a long bout with addiction. He then began hanging out with the Kennedy brothers Bobby Jr. and David and, in the process, became an example of what life could be like sans drugs and alcohol. He'd had a tough childhood but was still a positive and happy person. Bobby would describe him as "a mix between John Candy, John Belushi, and Curly from the Three Stooges. People begin laughing as soon as he enters a room."

Largely because of his own recent dependency issues, Michael Skakel had recently become much closer to Michael Kennedy, especially after Kennedy invited him to join him on Ted Kennedy's senatorial campaign. (In order to distinguish the two, everyone soon began to call Michael Kennedy by his first name and Michael Skakel by his last.) The cousins' friendship deepened even further as they traveled to Cuba, Portugal, Angola, and Brazil together on business, this after Skakel took a job at Citizens Energy as its international director.

In the winter of 1994 — a couple of months before Vicki discovered him in bed with their babysitter — Michael Kennedy called Michael Skakel to ask if he could visit him and his wife, Margot, at their home in Windham Mountain for a week of skiing. Skakel agreed to the idea. A few days later, Michael showed up with his three kids, but not with Vicki. He explained that she wasn't well. In her place was Marisa. The Skakels couldn't help but sense that something wasn't right with the situation, especially when, on the second night, Michael asked the sixteen-year-old for a massage. "Sure," she said. After he then took off his shirt and lay on his stomach on the couch, Marisa straddled the thirty-six-year-old athlete and began to apply hot oils to his back, which she just happened to have handy in her purse. "You don't see something like *that* every day," Skakel would later recall. "It made me and Margot uncomfortable. So we went to bed and left the two of them in the living room." The next day, Skakel didn't ask Michael about it, and Michael didn't bring it up.

KENNEDY DETOX

On Sunday, January 22, 1995, the day after Vicki Kennedy's discovery of Michael and Marisa, she insisted that he needed to check into a rehab center immediately and *not* wait until February 1. If he was going to cite addiction as the reason he was in bed with Marisa, then fine, she said. He needed to address the problem right away. Without hesitation, he agreed; he must have known he didn't have much ground to stand on.

Like her husband, Vicki had also begun to enjoy the company of Michael Skakel, who was lately becoming fairly ubiquitous. She thought he could be trusted and seriously doubted stories that linked him to the brutal Martha Moxley murder. She admired this man who always seemed to have a rosary in his pocket and went to Mass almost every day, and actually felt a lot closer to him than she did to any of her other in-laws. Like her brother-in-law Bobby, she sensed that Skakel was a deeply empathetic person who had a real understanding of flawed humanity. She knew he wouldn't judge her husband, or even her, for what she'd recently discovered. Therefore, on Sunday, Vicki called Skakel to confide in him. He wasn't shocked by what she said she'd discovered in her home, especially considering what he and his wife had earlier witnessed of Michael and Marisa. Rather than ask a lot of questions, Michael decided to just do what Vicki asked of him, which was take her husband to the treatment center. Skakel speedily made all the arrangements and, shortly thereafter on that same Sunday, he and his cousin made the six-hour trip to Havre de Grace.

After a pleasant drive in the country, Skakel and Kennedy passed through the large wooden gates of Father Martin's Ashley center (which is today known as Ashley Addiction Treatment) and then down a long, winding driveway to an enormous brick-and-wood estate in the middle of about 150 acres of lush, green solitude. As the two men walked into the lobby, the polished marble floors, the winding staircase, the sparkle and gleam of it all made it appear more like a deluxe five-star hotel in the country than a rehabilitation center. On the other side of French windows in the distance was a spectacularly gleaming view of the Chesapeake Bay. Michael took a look around and exclaimed, "Okay, now *this* is how Kennedys detox. *This is how we fuckin' detox.*" Skakel was upset. He reminded Michael that this wasn't some sort of vacation, that it was serious. Michael laughed, told his cousin to lighten up, and suggested that they seek out the restaurant; he was "starving." At that moment, two women appeared in starched white uniforms with clipboards, followed by a couple of men who looked like nightclub bouncers. As he was being forcibly rushed off, a wide-eyed Michael Kennedy turned around, looked in dismay at a surprised Michael Skakel, and screamed out just one word: *"Fuck."*

After getting his cousin settled at Father Martin's Ashley, Michael Skakel spent the night in Maryland. Early the next morning, Monday, January 24, he attended the wake for Rose Kennedy, where he congregated with his many cousins. He couldn't help but notice that Ethel was preoccupied, no doubt fretting about her son. She'd heard that Skakel had secreted him into rehab early, and the fact that she couldn't get a straight answer about it from anyone had driven her to distraction. She didn't know anything about her daughter-in-law finding Michael in bed with Marisa — not yet, anyway — all she knew was that the plan they had all agreed to in their so-called "intervention" had not been followed.

"As soon as she saw Skakel, she rushed over

to him," Benedict F. Fitzgerald Jr., Rose's attorney, once recalled, "I remember it well. He was sitting down and he jumped to his feet. She was upset. She had real fire in her eyes."

"Where is my son?" Ethel demanded. What a sight these two presented. Picture it: Skakel was about six-two, Ethel *maybe* five-five. According to Fitzgerald, she drew herself up to her full height and lifted her head even higher. Standing an inch from Skakel, she looked up with a face of fury. "He's okay, Aunt Ethel," said her nephew as he tried to back away from her. However, every step he took backward resulted in a quick step forward from his menacing aunt. "I took care of it," he stammered. "Don't worry."

"Without consulting me?" Ethel asked. "What gives you the right? That is *my son. You do not have the right.*" She told him that the family had a good plan in mind for Michael; they had all agreed he was going into rehab on February 1. It was a strategy, she said, they'd come to after much deliberation and one that should never have been altered without first consulting her. They had a lot to lose, she said, by rushing things and making mistakes. "But you don't have the whole story, Aunt Ethel," Skakel protested. "Let me explain." Ethel shook her head. She was angry now and didn't want to hear another word from him. Maybe they could talk later, she said; if so, she'd let him know. He started babbling something anyway. In response, Ethel took both her hands and put them right in front of Michael's face as if she might slap him. Instead, as was her custom, she clapped loudly three times just inches from his nose — *clap! clap! clap!* "Michael! *Stop talking,*" she shouted at him. "That's enough. I will not listen to this." She then stared at him with hard eyes for a moment before she turned and walked away.

"This House Can Have No Secrets"

It didn't take long for the story to start spreading throughout the Kennedy family that the reason Michael's rehabilitation had started earlier than planned was because Vicki had found him with the teenaged babysitter. It was a close family; word traveled fast. As the story spread over the course of the next three weeks, most people automatically assumed Michael had been caught being intimate with the girl. If Vicki was being truthful about what she'd seen, why else would he have been in bed with Marisa? He was a Kennedy male who'd cheated on his wife in the past, and everyone knew it. Most had long ago accepted infidelity as just another facet of Kennedy culture. So maybe some were a little surprised because of Marisa's age, but they had little to no doubt about what had occurred.

On February 15, 1995, John Kennedy Jr. paid his cousin Michael a visit at Father Martin's Ashley. He took his friend Stephen

Styles-Cooper with him, trusted by John to maybe advise Michael since Styles-Cooper had once had a similar problem; his marriage had ended over an affair with a young woman of eighteen. Like John, he was now thirty-four. They drove out to the rehab center and met Michael on a patio with a view of the bay. He looked terrible, sleep-deprived and unshaven. If he thought rehab was going to be a piece of cake, he was mistaken. The counselors were brutal. "I'd say pleased to meet you," he told Stephen, "but I'm not pleased to meet anyone these days."

The three sat down at a small table overlooking the serene water, John right next to Michael. Someone brought over a silver carafe of iced water and poured it into three glasses. "Let me see a picture of this girl," John said. Michael told him he didn't have one. John didn't believe him. After some prodding, Michael reached into his pants pocket and extracted a dog-eared photograph of a young woman. He nervously placed it on the table. John took a look at it and shook his head. He expressed amazement that the facility's staff would actually allow Michael to keep a picture of Marisa. However, Michael sheepishly explained that the counselors had checked his wallet for such mementos, but that he'd hidden it in his sock. John then picked up the picture and studied it.

"*This* is the girl you're going to hell for?"

he asked. Michael explained that he liked Marisa, that he got a lot out of being with her. She wasn't judgmental of him, he said. She was kind. She was also innocent. John looked at his cousin as if he were out of his mind. "But she's just a kid," he exclaimed. "You don't want people to think you're a pedophile, do you?"

"She's seventeen, John," Michael protested. He explained that the picture was an old one and that Marisa was now a lot more adult-looking, all this according to Stephen Styles-Cooper. "I know people think I'm a sick fuck," Michael allowed. "But I'm not." He lowered his head. "No one gives a shit about me now, anyway," he concluded pitifully.

"That's not true, Michael," John said, putting his arm around his cousin. "*I* give a shit." He reminded him of what RFK used to always say: "Nothing is as good or as bad as it seems in the moment." He also talked about the fact that when they were kids, it was always Michael who would break up the cousins' little fights. "That's why we always called you the Peacemaker," he reminded his cousin with a smile.

John then asked Michael if he'd thought about what might happen to him if Marisa's parents decided to press charges for statutory rape. Again, Michael protested, saying that the two hadn't become intimate until Marisa was sixteen, legal age in Massachusetts. John said he felt that was still too young, no matter the law. "Michael then explained that he felt his entire life had always been out of his control, that, as a Kennedy, he'd always had to please people and toe the family line and live up to unreasonable expectations," recalled Stephen Styles-Cooper. "Finally, this was one circumstance, he said, where *he* got to choose, where *he* was in control — and it had to do with his decision to be with Marisa. John listened intently. Later, he would tell me that while he completely disagreed, in a weird way he sort of understood."

"But how could you do this to someone you love?" John asked, speaking of Vicki. Finally — a question to which Michael didn't have a ready answer. "Gimme that," an exasperated John finally said as he took the picture of Marisa and thrust it into his pocket. "This is mine now."

John then noted that Michael should have more consideration for his mother. After all, Ethel had been through enough in her lifetime, he said, and the last thing she needed was more heartache. Michael didn't seem too concerned, though. He reminded John that it had been Ethel who was the strongest advocate for Bobby to run for the presidency, that she had constantly warned him that if he didn't capture this moment in time for himself, he would live to regret it. It was true; as Michael's brother Bobby Jr. would later recall of his mother, "She knew he [RFK] would never be happy on the sidelines. Knowing his thoughts better than anyone, my mom goaded him with a piece written by his friend Jack Newfield in the *Village Voice,* which she carried in her purse for that purpose: 'If Kennedy does not run in 1968, the best side of his character will die. . . .' "

"Maybe Daddy would still be alive if she hadn't pushed so hard," Michael said. How, John must have wondered, did his cousin develop such a cynical view of what most people in the family viewed as Ethel's un-equivocal support for Bobby? Surely he must have recalled the times he and his siblings went from town to town alongside their tire-less mother campaigning as hard as they could for their father. John was unable to disguise his surprise. "My God, Michael," he exclaimed. "How long have you felt this way?"

"Since the day he was shot," Michael admitted. Moreover, he said he'd always been filled with such shame that he felt this way about his mother. It had been one of his dark-est secrets ever since he was a child. Even now, he couldn't believe he'd revealed it. He said he felt he was losing control of every-thing. "Then, Jesus Christ, Michael," John exclaimed. *"Take it back."*

John said he never wanted to hear Michael speak about his mother in that way again. Then he got up, stood behind his cousin, wrapped his arms around his chest, and kissed him on the cheek.

"We didn't say a word to each other on the almost four-hour drive back to New York," recalled Stephen Styles-Cooper. "John was preoccupied and didn't want to talk. I couldn't tell if he was angry, hurt, sad, confused . . . or what. He just shut down. When he finally dropped me off, we shook hands and he looked at me and said three words I never thought I'd hear coming from him: *'Fuckin' Kennedy curse.'* "

By the end of April, Michael Kennedy was out of rehab and back to work at Citizens Energy. Despite the fact that he'd recommitted himself to his job and was supposedly sober and also regularly attending AA meetings, he still wasn't willing to stop seeing Marisa. It was maddening to his friends. Because he was so proficient at what he did at Citizens, the passion he felt for helping the poor so evident to everyone, they just wanted him to focus on his work and stop obsessing over this teenager. It was as if he were under some sort of spell, though.

During more camping trips between May and July, Michael and Marisa openly conducted their relationship in front of friends and family. To say, though, that his siblings were upset about it would be untrue. It actually didn't seem to bother them much. Most figured that Michael and Vicki had some sort of unconventional understanding that was none of their business.

Meanwhile, Marisa had moved out of her parents' home and into that of one of her friends. Paul and June still had no real influence over her. She didn't want to talk to them about Michael, and there wasn't much they could do to force her. She was seventeen and felt she knew what she was doing, and that was the end of it for her. Meanwhile, because June was still battling alcoholism, it was all Paul could do to cope with her. Therefore, it was easy for both to be avoidant.

While Paul and June chose avoidance as their way forward, Ethel Kennedy wasn't inclined to handle much, if anything, in her life quite that way. Though the family, especially her sons, had tried to protect her, by the summer of 1995, she knew everything. A political strategist going way back, she was conscious of all the ramifications, not just the personal. Of course, she was worried about Joe's and Kathleen's careers, but she was also concerned about the future of those in the *next* generation who might want to serve. She feared Michael's actions were going to make it difficult if not impossible for them.

"Who knows, Mrs. Kennedy?" Leah Mason mused as she and Ena Bernard tried to calm Ethel down one morning. Ethel had earlier explained the problem to Ena, and then Ena told Leah. However, Ethel wasn't aware that Leah knew; the two employees decided it best that she be kept unaware. "Whatever it is, Mrs. Kennedy, maybe no one will ever find out about it," offered Leah. Ethel looked with suspicion at Leah, at Ena, and then back at Leah. Then, with annoyance, she said, "Not likely. Obviously this house can have no secrets."

From a more personal standpoint, Ethel was not only troubled about Michael but also quite angry at him. However, the obvious problem she faced was that Michael was a grown man in his midthirties with a son and two daughters of his own; there was only so much his mother could do to control him. Though she tried to reason with him, she got nowhere. "I swear to God, nothing wrong is going on," Michael promised her, according to one account. "Well, you must not think much of God," she shot back, "because that's a lie."

Ethel considered calling the parents of the girl — she always called Marisa "the girl" — and arranging a meeting with them to come to some resolution. She attempted to recruit Joe to help her in that regard, too. However, Joe said no; Michael and Marisa weren't disobedient high school teenagers whose folks could sit down together and hash things out. In the end, it would have to be just a matter of handling each difficult moment as it came their way.

One such moment occurred when Michael announced that he was bringing Marisa to the compound for Labor Day. As it did for most Americans, that holiday held special significance for the Kennedys as the symbolic end of the summer season; as usual, there were sporting events planned, dinners, parties . . . or, as John Kennedy Jr. used to put it, "the whole nine Kennedy yards." One of Michael's siblings recalled of Labor Day 1995, "Ultimately, Mummy made the decision that if Michael was going to bring the girl, they couldn't stay in our home. 'Fine,' he said. 'I've no problem with that.' So they stayed elsewhere; I don't remember where. As I recall it, Vicki and the kids didn't come to the Cape for the holiday."

That Labor Day, September 4, Marisa was photographed at the compound by the Associated Press wearing blue jeans, a black jacket, and a white blouse, her dirty-blond hair falling to her shoulders. "Wow. This is really something else," John Kennedy reportedly said when he saw the picture. "Aunt Ethel must really be on the warpath."

■ ■ ■ ■

Part V
The Caretakers

■ ■ ■ ■

THE COMFORTER

As a young widow, Ethel Kennedy was matriarch of a big family full of rowdy children. Luckily, she had help in raising them. There were two memorable people who were most influential in the lives of the third generation of Kennedys, and the first was a woman whose time with them as their full-time governess, their occasional cook, and sometimes even as their makeshift therapist would span an incredible forty-four years. Even after her employment was over she would remain close to all of them, especially to Ethel. Her name was Ena Bernard, sometimes lovingly known in the family as "Mimi."

Ena Bernard, a black woman who was descended from African slaves, was born in Costa Rica on June 18, 1908. After the death of her four-month-old second baby, Petronila, she fled an abusive husband, leaving her other child, a seven-year-old daughter named Josefina Harvin (known as "Fina," and born in January 1938) with a friend in Costa Rica while she pursued employment first in the capital, San Jose, and then in the United States. She then paid for Fina's care with wages she earned in America, but wouldn't see her again for nine years, just before her sixteenth birthday.

Ena's first job was as a domestic at the United States Embassy for Joseph Flack, the ambassador to Costa Rica. The salary was too meager, though, so she left after less than a year. An employment agency in Dupont Circle in Washington, D.C., then gave her two job opportunities. She settled on the Robert Kennedy household.

"It was freezing cold when my mother, who was forty-three, arrived at the Kennedys' home in October of 1951 to be interviewed for a job as their governess," recalled Fina Harvin. "Mrs. Kennedy — Ethel, who was just twenty-three — was immediately impressed with the way my mom took off her coat, folded it very neatly, and put it with great care on the banister. She thought that little gesture said a lot about her. 'I have to say, I love that dress,' Mrs. Kennedy said of my mom's red-and-white skirt. 'You know, I saw the exact same one at Peck and Peck,' which was an exclusive, very expensive store in Manhattan. 'Oh, please! This is a copy, Mrs. Kennedy,' my mother said. 'Do you really think I shop at Peck and Peck? I bought this thing on Fourteenth Street in

Washington,' which was a predominately black shopping district. Mrs. Kennedy liked that a lot. 'Well, good for you, then,' she said. 'I like a woman who's frugal. Just because you have money doesn't mean you have to spend it.' My mom laughed and said, 'Well, since I don't have it, I guess I don't have to worry about spending it.'

" 'I have the one girl, Kathleen,' Mrs. Kennedy said as they got to know each other. She and Bobby had just married a little more than a year earlier; he'd just graduated from law school. 'She's three months and a real handful,' she said. 'But I have a feeling there'll be more on the way. Would you be open to taking care of more than one child?' 'Of course,' said my mom. 'I love children.' "

Ethel thought for a moment. "You know what? I like you," she said confidently. "You're hired."

"Um . . . no, I don't think so," was Ena's response. "Why don't we sleep on it and talk tomorrow. By then, we should both know if I'm hired or not."

Ethel laughed. "That's a good idea," she said. The two women parted. The next morning, Ethel called Ena. "Well?" she asked. "I thought about it," Ena said. "And yes, I would be honored to work for you."

Despite Ethel's chipper attitude, Kathleen's delivery had been hard on her. She'd had a myriad of physical problems during the birth process, including a torn perineum; she was in pain for months afterward. Not many people knew about it; the Kennedys' family nurse since the 1950s, Luella Hennessey, is the one who told Ena. Though from all accounts, Ena and Ethel never discussed it — Ethel was extremely private when it came to these things. Ena took special care of the young mother during this difficult time, and Ethel would never forget her kindness.

It was Bobby Kennedy who felt that Ena should finally be reunited with Fina, whom she hadn't seen since she left Costa Rica. He then arranged for the teenager to come to America in 1954 when she was sixteen, just ten years younger than Ethel. Fina then moved into the Kennedys' home in Georgetown (this was before Ethel bought Hickory Hill from Jack and Jackie), where she would live with her mother in the servants' quarters. She and her mom were immediately at odds. "I was holding on to a lot of anger against her over the fact that she'd left me to raise some other woman's children," she remembers. "I hadn't seen her since I was seven. I'd never even heard of the Kennedys. So, when I moved into Georgetown, they were just this family that had stolen my mother. By this time, Mrs. Kennedy had not only Kathleen, but Joe and Bobby, Jr., too. It bothered me so much that when I would go to hug my mother, she would push me away and say,

'No, no, I don't like that, Josephina.' But if a Kennedy wanted to hug her, oh my God. She just loved it."

Ethel couldn't help but notice that Ena was more affectionate to her children than she was to Fina. "It's not your mother's fault," she told the teenager. "It's yours." She speculated that Ena felt guilty about having left her daughter in Costa Rica and told Fina, "You make her feel that way every single day of the week." Consequently, at least the way Ethel saw it, Ena didn't feel she deserved affection from Fina. It actually made her feel badly about herself every time her daughter asked for a hug, and so she pushed her away. "Stop blaming your mother for wanting to give you a better life," she told Fina. Fina said it made no sense to her that her mother was the one upset — *she* should be the one holding a grudge. "The way people feel usually doesn't make sense," Ethel told her. "Do you think it was easy for her, leaving you behind while she came to work in America?"

"But she missed all of my birthdays," Fina said, tears coming to her eyes.

Of course she did, and that was a shame, Ethel said. However, she also told her that she and Bobby gave Ena extra money so that the people caring for Fina in Costa Rica could give her a birthday party every year. Ethel even took Ena to the post office to make sure the funds were properly sent. She did this at every birthday for nine years. Upon hearing this, Fina burst into tears. "They must have pocketed the money, Mrs. Kennedy," Fina said sadly. "I never had one birthday party."

Ethel's heart went out to Fina. However, she held fast that none of this was Ena's fault. "I want you to work things out with her," she told her. "It's very important to me." Fina promised that she would try.

"Still, I went through this stage of really hating her," Fina now says of her mother. "Therefore, I wasn't an easy teenager. I had a chip on my shoulder."

"One memory that sticks out for me," Fina recalls, "is of the day Mrs. Kennedy asked me, 'Fina, have you eaten yet? Because dinner is being served in the servants' dining room.' I said, 'Yes, I *et* already.' I couldn't say 'eat,' my English was so bad. Mrs. Kennedy corrected me, 'No, no. You don't say *et*, Fina. It's *eat*.' I was so fresh, I said, 'Well, at least *I* speak two languages, Mrs. Kennedy. You only speak one.' My mother was mortified. 'Fina, don't you dare talk to Mrs. Kennedy like that,' she said. 'Now you apologize to her.' So I did. 'I'm very sorry,' I said, looking down at the floor. Mrs. Kennedy said, 'No, Fina. You look at *me* when you're talking to me, not at the floor.' 'But Mrs. Kennedy,' I told her, 'in Costa Rica when a white lady speaks to a colored girl, you look down when you speak back out of respect.' Mrs. Kennedy shook her head, no, no, *no*. 'You are in *America* now,' she said. 'And in America, you look that person in the eyes, no matter her color. You look that person straight in the eyes, Fina. Do you understand me? *Straight in the eyes.*' I never forgot that, and neither did my mom."

Fina also fondly remembers being chastised by Bobby Kennedy for coming home late one night after a Cotillion dance in the Grand Ballroom at the Presidential Arms in Washington. "You don't have a father," he told her when he caught her sneaking up the stairs to her room, "so that means you're my responsibility now, and this is much too late for you to be out. Now, go to your room, *Joe*-sephina, and not another word out of you!" Bobby always called her *Joe*-sephina, mispronouncing her name, which was actually enunciated with a silent "j."

Fina eventually enrolled in a Catholic boarding school in Georgetown. While she would spend the week at school, her weekends were with the Kennedys. Bobby used to drive her back to the school on Monday mornings, Ena in the front seat next to him and Fina in the back.

At this point, Democrats controlled the Senate and Bobby Kennedy was chief counsel. Because of his work on the McCarthy committee, he'd also been named one of

"Ten Outstanding Young Men" of 1954, a list created by the U.S. Junior Chamber of Commerce. "Even though he was very distinguished, the nuns were upset about him driving me to school," Fina recalled. "Oh, it was *such* a scandal. Here was this white man driving this colored girl and her colored mom to school, and he was a Kennedy! The nuns felt it was morally wrong. I was just one of a handful of colored girls in that school, if there were even that many. I ended up in a fistfight with one of the white students about it. The principal then called me into her office and phoned my mother. 'Your daughter doesn't belong here,' she told her. 'In fact, we're taking her to the train station and sending her back to you this very second. So you'd better have someone there to pick her up.' I was crying when I got off the train in Washington. Mr. and Mrs. Kennedy were there to meet me, along with my mom who was so embarrassed she could barely look at me. 'I'm very sorry that this is the way things are today,' Mr. Kennedy told me. 'We have to find a way to change this country, and we will one day. I promise you, all of this will change.' Mrs. Kennedy took my hand and said, 'Bobby will help make that change. It won't always be this way. He'll see to it.' Later my mother told me that when the nun called her to tell her I was being expelled, she accused her of sleeping with Mr. Kennedy. It was so embarrassing to her she made me promise never to tell either Mr. or Mrs. Kennedy about it."

Ethel had been around servants since she was a child and her affluent parents employed a large staff to care for the family in their own stately mansion. The Skakels embraced what would be considered an old-world, even Victorian view of the help in the sense that they believed that those working for them should observe and respect strict British customs and traditions. This sensibility had evolved because Ann Skakel had a friend, Alice Clark, who hailed from England and who employed a staff of dutiful English servants. After she and her husband raised their large family, they decided to return to their home country. However, they didn't wish to take their staff with them. Some would go back on their own, but most wanted to remain in the States. Ann had been impressed with Alice's obedient, respectful employees and felt her own paled in comparison. One day, she decided to dismiss everyone working for her and bring in Alice's entire staff. From that time on, the Skakels would be served by mostly English natives and with the formality particular to the way household workers comported themselves in that country, especially before the war. Though there was obviously a hierarchy at work in the Skakel home, one thing was also certain: the staff was not to be disrespected. Ann never browbeat her employees and definitely didn't let her children lord over them; Ethel would later also never allow her own offspring to mistreat the help.

Over the years, at Hickory Hill, Ethel's staff would never be strictly English; it would always be comprised of all nationalities. However, the way they behaved was still old world in nature simply because this was what Ethel had seen growing up. Some would wonder about it, especially as Ethel would speak of "tradition" when talking about what was expected of her staff. "What tradition?" her friend Frank Gifford once wondered. "Weren't you raised in Connecticut, Ethel?" he asked, kidding her. "Is this how they do things in Connecticut?" Ethel took the ribbing with good humor; she knew the way her help acted was probably more formal than the American norm for the times, but so be it. It was her estate and she would run it as she saw fit. "I'll have you know my family came from *Ireland* and *Holland,* Frank," she responded, "so put that in your pipe and smoke it."

Ethel had a little trick for determining a servant's character, especially if that person was to be in charge of others. It was something she had picked up from her mother. After hiring someone, Ethel would wait a few days and then, at about seven o'clock in the morning, present that person with an enormous slice of chocolate cake she proudly claimed to have baked herself — which, of course, was unlikely. "Please try this," Ethel would say. "Tell me how it tastes." If the employee would eat the cake at such an early hour, Ethel would glean from it that this was someone who could maybe be pushed around, not the best person for a management role. She would keep a close eye on that employee. However, if the hire refused the cake, Ethel would conclude that this was someone who could not be intimidated and was probably suitable for a supervisory role. Since Ena was eventually to be responsible for others working with the children at Hickory Hill, she became a prime candidate for testing, the old-fashioned way. One morning, bright and early, Ethel presented her with an enormous slice of chocolate cake. Ena said, "No, Mrs. Kennedy, not now. I'll save it for later." Ethel said, "But I insist!" to which Ena responded, "Well, I'm sorry, no." Ethel wouldn't let it go. "I really want you to eat this cake, Ena! Now!" Ena threw her shoulders back and declared, "I'm sorry, but I'm not gonna eat no chocolate cake at seven o'clock in the morning! I *said* I'll save it for later. *Mrs. Kennedy.*" *Good to know,* Ethel thought. Clearly, Ena wasn't someone who could be bullied, which would serve her well in dealing with insubordinate staff members but, as Ethel would soon learn, maybe not so well in dealing with her.

Ethel was also raised to understand that household staff members took pride in their work and that they should be allowed to do it in an environment that wasn't hostile toward them. Still, they knew their place. "Though in a sense we were thought of as part of the family, we still knew what Mrs. Kennedy referred to as our 'roles,' " said Leah Mason. "For instance, all of us, such as Ena and her daughter, Fina — who was not a staff member but as Ena's daughter always helped out where she could — Noelle Bombardier, Jinx Hack, Carol Gainer [both of whom were Ethel's secretaries], Sandy Eiler and Bob Galland [both of whom were "athletic directors," responsible for the children's sports activities], maybe ten of us in all, ate in a separate dining room," said Leah. "If Mrs. Kennedy walked into the room when we were eating, we would all jump from our chairs to attention. She would say a few words. After finishing, she would thank us, apologize for interrupting our dinner, and then take her leave. We would all then sit back down and return to our meals, though we'd all be a little rattled. It was unsettling when she surprised us in our private space."

By the time Bobby Kennedy was assassinated in 1968, Ena and Fina had lived at Hickory Hill for many years. Of course, both were devastated; Fina actually fainted while paying her respects at the Capitol and had to be taken by ambulance to a hospital. Despite what was, by far, the darkest time in her life up until this point, Ethel somehow marshaled the resolve to make sure that Ena's sixtieth birthday was acknowledged on June 18. She felt she owed it to her. After all, by this time Ena had been the family's governess for almost twenty years and had helped raise all of Ethel's children.

On the morning of her birthday, Ethel sent Ena off to do errands with Fina. While she was gone, Ethel instructed the other servants to decorate their dining room with festive red, white, and blue ribbons and balloons. She also had Leah Mason bake a double-chocolate cake, Ena's favorite. She then gathered all the younger children who happened to be in the house — Courtney, Michael, Kerry, Christopher, Max, Douglas, and Rory — and told them there was going to be a party for their beloved Ena. They were delighted, so much so that Ethel was pleased she'd had the idea if only to lift their spirits. Later that day, they all gathered in the dining room, along with the rest of the household staff. When Ena walked into the room with Fina, they shouted out "Surprise!" and began to applaud. Ena burst into tears. Ethel embraced her. It's interesting, though, that she and the kids only stayed for a short time.

"The last thing they need is *'Mrs. Kennedy'* putting a damper on their good time," Ethel later explained to her friend Elizabeth Stevens, who took her shopping for the day.

Still, despite their closeness, after Bobby was gone Ethel and Ena often found themselves at odds. "That's when a difficult phase began for Mrs. Kennedy and my mother," Fina Harvin recalled. "They really started going at one another."

While the servants at Hickory Hill would not be disrespected, they should also not act disrespectful. Insubordination had not been tolerated by Ann Skakel, and it would also not be condoned by Ethel. However, Ena was an outspoken woman who sometimes felt compelled to make her feelings known. She crossed a line one day in 1970.

Joe, Bobby, and David told Ena that they were angry at their mother for locking them out of the house because she caught them playing Tag on the Roof. This was a game they invented where they'd leap from the top of the barn, to the top of the toolshed to the top of the horse trailer and onto the roofs of any other buildings in sight. Ethel said she was tired of taking the boys to the emergency room with broken limbs. Ena had to agree. However, though she was often mad at the children, too — "She would praise us in English and get mad at us in Spanish," recalled Ethel's son Christopher — never would she want them kicked out. She couldn't imagine where they went when they were told to leave, and she didn't want to know.

According to Leah Mason, Ena decided to confront her boss about it on a day Ethel was scheduled to have lunch with Jackie. "If I say something while the other Mrs. Kennedy is there, maybe she'll side with me and things will go better," Ena told Leah. The two of them were standing in the pantry, speaking urgently to each other in hushed tones. Leah didn't think it was a good idea. However, because she was just twenty-one and Ena was sixty-two, Leah felt she should defer to her. When a suspicious Bob Galland peeked into the pantry and asked, "What are you two whispering about back here?" Ena waved a hand at him and said, "Shoo! Mind your own business." After he backed off, Leah said, "Please be careful, Mimi," using Ena's nickname. "Mrs. Kennedy isn't going to like this one bit. I'm afraid of what she'll do." Ena nodded. "Don't worry about me," she said confidently. "I know how to handle Mrs. Kennedy."

That afternoon, Ena was frying plantains as she did most every day, when she turned around and said to Ethel, "I've been holding this in, Mrs. Kennedy, and I'm sorry, but I just can't anymore. It's not good to lock the boys out of the house. I'm afraid that one day they will hate you for it. Especially David. He's only fifteen." She looked to Jackie for support, but apparently, Jackie knew her place — and it wasn't to align herself with a household employee's negative opinion of Ethel's parenting skills. Instead, the former First Lady just sat quietly with an amused look on her face, as if waiting for the show to begin — which took only about ten seconds.

Ethel, who was drinking coffee, almost did a spit-take. She jumped out of her chair and demanded to know how Ena could be so insubordinate, especially given everything she'd done for her and Fina. Ena turned down the heat on the frying pan and then whirled around to face Ethel. "I'm sorry, Mrs. Kennedy," she said, "but I have to speak my mind."

"Oh really? Since when?" Ethel demanded to know. "*Since when* do you have to speak your mind?" The argument escalated from there, with Ethel being particularly confrontational, almost as if trying to save face in front of Jackie. "You've got it all figured out, don't you?" she asked the governess. Finally, it ended with Ena exclaiming, "I quit." To which Ethel responded, "Good. Then pack your things and get the heck out of here. I don't need you, and neither do my kids." Ena stomped out of the kitchen and went to her room on the third floor, next to the former nursery, where she slept in a narrow twin bed surrounded by framed photos of saints of all races and colors and an enormous painting hanging over her headboard of Jesus on the cross.

The next day, when Ethel woke up, Ena was gone. " 'Fine and good riddance' was Ethel's response," recalled Leah Mason. " 'Can you imagine what would happen if I let her get away with that kind of impertinence? Why, it would be complete anarchy around here.' We all knew she was disappointed with Ena. After twenty years, she was used to Ena speaking out of turn, but doing so in front of Jackie was really unacceptable. Mrs. Kennedy told me to call the Kelly Girl temporary agency and have them send someone over. 'Just make sure she's a nice, quiet woman who doesn't have a burr under her saddle,' she told me. I decided to hold off on that task, though. It actually wasn't even my job to do such a thing, it was someone else's. So I just waited. I had a feeling."

Sure enough, two days later when Ethel woke up and came down to the kitchen she found Ena preparing Cream of Wheat for breakfast for the children. Ethel sat down. "I guess this means you're back?" she asked. Ena answered that she supposed so and then asked Ethel if she wanted some coffee. Staring hard at her, Ethel said yes. Ena walked over, poured hot coffee into Ethel's cup, and then turned around and went back to her work. Ethel said she was surprised by Ena's actions and that, considering how long she'd been at Hickory Hill, she couldn't understand why she'd ever be so outspoken in front of company — and especially in front of Jackie. "Here's an idea, Ena," she told her. "Why not have a *private* thought for once in your life?" She finished her reprimand by acknowledging something everyone working there knew about life at Hickory Hill, whether they wished to recognize it or not: a hierarchy of privilege existed and each of them had a role in it. Or as Ethel put it, "Everyone who works here has a part to play, Ena. *Know your part.*"

Ena Bernard would remain with the Kennedys, obviously knowing her "part," for at least another twenty years. The family also remained close to her after she retired; she and Ethel remained friends. Their relationship, and that of Ethel's with much of her help, might also act as proof that she is not a racist, as some have tried to claim over the years. As recently as July 8, 2018, a columnist for the *Boston Herald* wrote of her: "Her disdain for the black and brown women who have worked for her is well-documented."

Of course, just because a person is friendly with someone of a different race doesn't necessarily mean that person isn't a racist. But according to those who have known Ethel for many decades, the accusation is simply not true. The origin of this pernicious lie goes back more than twenty years to when an unkind book was published about her that stated that Ethel had, in her days as the out-of-control matriarch (the late sixties through the eighties), been especially unkind to her black employees, sometimes using a racist word to describe them. When the book came out, Fina brought it to her mother's attention. Ena was angry about it. "Never would Mrs. Kennedy call me such a name," she insisted. "That never happened."

While she would never use racist language, Ethel could still sometimes lose her head. "Yes, she could be mean to some of the black help," recalled Noelle Bombardier, but when she was under pressure, she could also be short to the whites, the Hispanics . . . Few escaped her temper during those difficult years after Bobby died.

"I remember witnessing a volatile disagreement she had with one of our housemaids, a Spanish woman named Connie," recalled Noelle. "Mrs. Kennedy and I were racing around her bedroom looking for a pair of designer shoes she wanted to pack for a trip to New York. She was agitated, upset that we couldn't find them. As we were ransacking the room, she hollered out for Connie to fetch a jar of her special face cream, which she also wished to pack. Connie didn't seem to understand. She disappeared for a moment and came back with, of all things, a box of

291

tampons. Mrs. Kennedy became angry and said a few things. Connie stood up to her and told her to never speak to her that way; she was definitely going too far. Before I could calm the situation, Mrs. Kennedy just took a big swing and slapped her hard across the face. Connie raced from the room, sobbing. Overcome, Mrs. Kennedy then collapsed into a chair, also crying."

Ethel immediately felt bad about the incident. "I'm sorry I did that," she told Noelle, still trembling. "That's not how we do things around here."

"Well," Noelle said, treading carefully, "we generally don't answer rudeness with rudeness, that's true, Mrs. Kennedy."

"But she pushed me into it," Ethel said in her own defense. "How dare she talk to me like that? Fire her, Noelle. There are rules to this way of life, and our maids have got to follow those rules. I want her out of here. Tomorrow."

Noelle recalled, "I managed to talk her out of it, saying we were already having a hard time finding good maids and Connie really was a good worker. I convinced her that it had all been a misunderstanding. Then I had Connie apologize to Mrs. Kennedy and told her to just stay clear of her for a while."

About a week later, Ethel hosted a party for Anatoly Fyodorovich Dobrynin, the Soviet Ambassador to the United States whose meetings with Bobby had been critical in solving the Cuban Missile Crisis back in 1962. It wasn't unusual for Ethel to host such receptions for important dignitaries such as Dobrynin. This one was attended by a wide array of political movers and shakers, as well as a host of family members, including Jackie, who moved with grace about the drawing room, engaging each guest as only she could. Her children, John and Caroline, were also present, as were Senator Ted Kennedy and his wife at that time, Joan, and the Shrivers, Eunice and Sargent. The servants had been preparing for this occasion for at least a week; Ethel had a long list of concerns having to do with everything from the preparation of the gourmet food to the placement of massive floral displays. Once a carefully planned party such as this one was finally under way, the staff always felt a great sense of accomplishment even though they wouldn't actually get to experience the festivities. "We would gather in the kitchen and peek out at the well-dressed, glamorous guests," recalled Noelle Bombardier. "In those moments, the stark difference in social standing was always so, I guess, *understood,* is the word, we in our starched uniforms gazing out at all of the beautiful people in their tuxes and gowns. We felt such satisfaction knowing we'd done our part to contribute to another special evening at Hickory Hill."

After the assassinations of President John F. Kennedy and Senator Robert F. Kennedy, the next generation of Kennedys—the children of JFK, RFK, their brother, Senator Edward Kennedy, and his three siblings Eunice, Jean, and Pat—would bear the weight of triumph and tragedy as they sought new ways to serve their country. Here is the widowed Jackie and her children, John and Caroline, at the President's gravesite in Arlington on May 27, 1964, the day he would have turned forty-seven. (*United States Army Corp of Engineers, Public Domain*)

The President and First Lady spent Christmas 1962 with Gustavo Paredes (left), who would go on to become a lifelong friend of John Jr.'s (here in his mother's lap). In front of John is his cousin and best friend, Anthony Radziwill. (*Cecil W. Stoughton/ John F. Kennedy Presidential Library and Museum*)

John Kennedy Jr. at about the age of three. Was there ever a cuter kid in the White House? (*Cecil W. Stoughton/John F. Kennedy Presidential Library and Museum*)

The Shriver family, in 1968, never thought of themselves as Kennedys; they were always proud of their own family identity forged by Eunice Kennedy Shriver (far left) and Sargent Shriver (far right). In the middle are Anthony, Maria, Bobby, Tim, and Mark. (*Paul Slade/Globe Photos*)

Of all the Kennedys of his generation, it was thought that Joseph Patrick Kennedy II (Joe) had the greatest chance of one day becoming President. Here he is at twenty-six, in 1978. (*Frank Teti Collection/John Fitzgerald Kennedy Library and Museum*)

Live-in housekeeper Ena Bernard loved the eleven children of Ethel and Robert Kennedy as if they were her own. Here she is with the two youngest, Rory, ten, and Douglas, eleven, in 1978. (*Frank Teti Collection/John Fitzgerald Kennedy Library and Museum*)

There seemed nothing his mother, Ethel, or his ten siblings could do to help David Kennedy battle his drug addiction. Here he is at a Kennedy family wedding in 1983. (*Russell Turiak/Getty Images*)

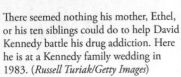

"I haven't seen anything like *that* come down the pike since Jackie Bouvier," exclaimed one Kennedy family lawyer about Victoria Reggie, who would become Ted's second wife. Vicki eventually ushered in a new era of respect for feminism among the next generation of Kennedy men. Here she is with Ted in May of 1992, shortly after they became engaged. (*Lisa Bull/AP/Rex/Shutterstock*)

Kara Kennedy (right) faithfully protected her mom from a relative she believed was robbing her of her fortune. "*I* advocate for Joan Kennedy," she told him. "Not you. And not anyone else!" Here are mother and daughter with Kara's child Grace on Labor Day 1996. (*Laura Cavanaugh/Globe Photos*)

It was John Kennedy Jr. who counseled his cousin Michael during a sex scandal in 1997 that would jeopardize Joe's chances of becoming Governor of Massachusetts. Left to right: Michael, John, and Joe. (*Rex Features*)

"So, this is the girl you're going to hell for?" John asked Michael when shown a photograph of the teenager at the center of the controversy—the young and pretty Marisa Verrochi. (*Kevin Wisnewski/Rex/Shutterstock*)

Though Victoria Gifford Kennedy tried to understand her husband, Michael, she had to make some very tough decisions about her marriage. Here she is supported by her mother-in-law, Ethel, on one of the worst days of her life, outside Our Lady of Victory church in Centerville, Massachusetts. Behind her is Michael's brother-in-law Andrew Cuomo and Victoria's father, Frank Gifford. (*Mark Lennihan/AP/Rex/Shutterstock*)

The burgeoning political career of Congressman Joseph Patrick Kennedy II was cut short after Sheila Rauch (left) wrote a controversial book about their marriage. Here are the two with twin sons Joseph III and Matthew. Joseph would grow up to become a successful congressman in his own right. (*Ira Wyman/Sygma via Getty Images*)

Though John Kennedy and his sister, Caroline, had to agree to disagree about his wife, Carolyn Bessette, they remained true to the family ideals passed on to them by their mother, Jackie. Here they are in Boston at the annual Profile in Courage Awards on May 29, 1998. (*Elise Amendola/AP/Rex/Shutterstock*)

"Do not let Kennedy men influence you into bad behavior. You can't take the bait!" Those were Ethel Kennedy's words to Carolyn Bessette after her very public spat with John Kennedy in Central Park. Here a glowing Carolyn poses at the gala event of the Municipal Art Society of New York in September of 1998. (*Sonia Moskowitz/Globe Photos*)

Kerry Kennedy Cuomo and her husband, Andrew Cuomo, arrive at the Spotlight Awards Benefit in New York on November 12, 2001. As often happens to political powerhouse couples, a total focus on public service eventually undermined their marriage. (*Kelly Jordan/Globe Photos*)

Robert F. Kennedy Jr. and his wife Mary Richardson Kennedy at a gala celebrating the Sundance Institute's twentieth anniversary in New York on April 23, 2002. Soon Mary would fall victim to the serious mental disorders that had plagued her for most of her life. (*Acepixs/Image Collect*)

In June of 2008, Ena Bernard, who worked for Ethel Kennedy for forty-four years, celebrated her one hundredth birthday. Here she is at the celebration with her daughter, Josefina, seventy-three, who grew up as part of the Kennedy family, having moved in with them when she was seventeen. (*Willie L. Hill Jr.*)

Kathleen Kennedy Townsend was just three months old when Ena went to work for the Kennedys in October of 1951. Here Kathleen, almost sixty, poses with Ena at her birthday party. (*Willie L. Hill Jr.*)

Ethel, just twenty-three when she hired Ena, had her share of big battles with her. Here she is at eighty talking over old times with her trusted friend. (*Willie L. Hill Jr.*)

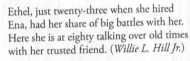

Ena was present for the birth of each of these Kennedy siblings. Top row, left to right: Bobby Jr., fifty-four; Max, forty-three; Fina, seventy-three; Kerry, forty-eight; Joe, fifty-eight, with his wife Beth, and sister Courtney, fifty-one. Bottom row: Kathleen, fifty-nine; Ena; Ethel, eighty; and Chris, forty-five. (*Willie L. Hill Jr.*)

Ted's two wives, Joan Kennedy and Victoria Reggie Kennedy, at Eunice Kennedy Shriver's funeral on August 14, 2009. Before Vicki married into the Kennedy family, Joan gave her fair warning: "Those men do not respect women. Period!" (*Darren McCollester/ Getty Images*)

Noelle Bombardier worked at Hickory Hill for many years as its estate manager. She quit after a botched kidnapping attempt of her daughter, Danielle. Here she's reunited with Courtney Kennedy Hill at a concert in Washington in 2006. (*Noelle Bombardier*)

Arnold Schwarzenegger deeply regretted ruining his marriage to Maria Shriver. "A lot of people, no matter how successful or unsuccessful, make stupid choices involving sex," he would observe. Maria filed for divorce in June of 2011. (*Reed Saxon/AP/REX/ Shutterstock*)

On June 22, 2013, Tatiana, Jack, Rose, and their parents, Ed Schlossberg and Caroline Kennedy, attended a ceremony to commemorate the fiftieth anniversary of the 1963 visit by President John F. Kennedy to New Ross, Ireland (where his great-grandfather had lived before he immigrated to Boston in 1847). (*Clodagh Kilcoyne/ Getty Images*)

After Rose Kennedy died, it fell upon Ethel Kennedy to take over as matriarch of a new generation of Kennedys. To this day, she continues to rule not only with love but an iron fist. Here she is awarded the Presidential Medal of Freedom by President Barack Obama on November 24, 2014. (*Michael Reynolds/Epa/Rex/Shutterstock*)

Congressman Joseph P. Kennedy III delivered the Democratic rebuttal to President Donald Trump's State of the Union address on January 30, 2018. After hearing his eloquent speech, many political pundits began to view him as the next great political hope for the Kennedys. (*Aflo/Rex/Shutterstock*)

Ed Schlossberg and Caroline Kennedy, together for thirty-eight years, have a bond that has never been broken. "Marriage is about forgiveness," she once mysteriously observed. Here they are arriving at the John F. Kennedy Presidential Library and Museum in Boston for 2018's Profile in Courage Awards on May 20, 2018. (*Steven Senne/AP/Rex/Shutterstock*)

THE MENTOR

Another person who had great influence over the new generation of Kennedys was a man who had been close to the family since the 1930s, someone they all loved and respected despite his eccentricities — and maybe even because of them. His name was Kirk Le-Moyne Billings, known to all as "Lem." No examination of the third generation of Kennedys could ever be complete without an understanding of Lem.

Lem was born in 1916 in Pittsburgh. In 1933, at the age of sixteen, he became best friends with the then-fifteen-year-old John F. Kennedy while the two were students at the Choate preparatory school and then later, for a year, at Princeton. "He was well-liked and someone to whom all of the other students seemed to gravitate, including Jack, who had really taken a liking to him," Senator George Smathers once said. "From the time Jack brought Lem home to spend Christmas with the Kennedys at Palm Beach [in 1933], Lem was a part of that family. Jack told me there was this instant camaraderie between not only him and JFK but with the whole bunch of 'em. There was always a lot of strange excitement around Lem. For instance, Jack told me that during the summer break of '34, Lem was burned by a defective hot water valve in the shower at the Kennedys' home and had to be hospitalized for three weeks. Whoever heard of such a thing happening? Only to Lem."

Lem was a tall, gangly fellow at six foot four with curly dirty-blond hair and large, thick glasses. One could tell that, in his youth, he'd been a college wrestler and crew captain. As an older man, there was imperiousness in the way he held his head; he walked with pride as if he knew his worth. Maybe he wasn't handsome in the accepted sense of the word, but his vitality made him seem somehow better-looking. He was well-mannered, extremely meticulous about all things, especially his appearance — only the best, most expensive wardrobe, for instance. While some might say he leaned toward being effeminate, no one in the family ever made fun of him; he was much too beloved. Sure, when he first entered the White House after Jack was elected, he stood between Pat Lawford and Eunice Shriver and, motioning all around him, struck a flamboyant pose and stole a line from Butterfly McQueen in *Gone With* the Wind: "Lordy! We sure is rich now!" But that was just Lem. He had his little quirks; for instance, though he was a year older than JFK, he fibbed during the first of his eleven oral history interviews for the JFK Library (in 1964) and said they were the same age rather than admit to his true age.

Lem would always have unfettered access to JFK and the White House throughout Jack's term as President. When Bobby and Ethel had their sixth child in 1958, they named him after Lem — Michael LeMoyne Kennedy. After Jack died in 1963, it was as if Lem, who was then forty-seven, had nothing to live for, his grief was so debilitating. Though he did go on, he was never quite the same.

Lem was delighted when Bobby decided to run for President in 1968, feeling as did everyone else in the family that this was their moment to reclaim what they'd lost with the murder of Jack. Of course, it wasn't meant to be. While losing Jack had been devastating, Bobby's death was more than Lem could handle. He completely spiraled out of control, turning to drugs and alcohol in his grief.

"The adults in the lives of the younger generation didn't spend a whole lot of time talking about Jack or Bobby because it always took them down a road that was off-limits," observed Ben Bradlee. "When they did speak of them, it was serious and solemn. But good ol' Lem had no fear of the subject. In the years after Bobby's death, he became even more open and excited about sharing his stories of the fallen Kennedy men. He was the one with the incredible scrapbooks full of correspondence, photos, and all sorts of other mementos. He was a font of information for pretty much every member of the younger generation. I think he made Jack and Bobby come alive for them with his great stories of courage and wisdom, and his hilarious tales, too. He made them human. He was, in many ways, a surrogate father, though he would always bristle at that notion. He never wanted to be thought of as a father figure, but rather a friend or perhaps a mentor. Thank goodness he was in the lives of Jack's and Bobby's kids, as well as Ted's, Eunice's, and all of them."

"You must stop turning away from your rightful place in history," Lem would tell the young Kennedys, especially brothers Bobby and David Kennedy and their cousin Christopher Lawford, the three to whom he had become closest. While he understood their need to search for their own identities outside the Kennedy legacy, he never wanted them to risk losing their true selves and abandoning their real responsibilities in the process. "Embrace your destiny, don't turn away from it," he would tell them. "And remember what Grandma Rose used to say: 'Never forget that you are a Kennedy. A lot of work went into building that name. Don't disparage it.' "

Though they didn't really have much to do with each other in that they were at different stations in the family pecking order — one a close family friend, the other an important household staff member — their loyalty and devotion to the Kennedys, as well as their pride of association, is what Lem Billings and Ena Bernard had in common as family caretakers. They played their rightful "parts," as Ethel Kennedy might have put it, in regard to the upbringing of her many children. In the process, both would find themselves depended upon during the most challenging of times, especially in regard to the difficulties brought on by her most troubled sons — Bobby Jr. and David.

····

PART VI
A TALE OF TWO
BROTHERS

····

MISFITS

It always comes as a surprise to those who have studied the Kennedy family that some of the younger generation were so eager to shed their identities as scions of one of the most powerful American families and seek out a darker underside of life. Maybe it shouldn't be so unexpected, though. Many of them, especially the young men, were raised by parents who had such great hopes for them that there was no way they would ever meet them, or so they felt. Before they knew who they were, they were required to know what they wanted to do with their lives, to be of service to others and — who knows? — to one day even become President of the United States. Given the tragedy of the murders of their beloved relatives and, in the case of Ethel's kids, the fact that they were being raised in an unstable atmosphere, it wasn't surprising that some of them turned to drugs and alcohol, and also not surprising that some of them wanted *anything* other than to be Kennedys.

In the summer of 1970, there was one Kennedy son — a fifteen-year-old with big, defiant eyes that were so blue they were almost turquoise, a tangled mop of blond hair, and an emaciated, malnourished physique — who found himself in dire straits. His clothing was damp and dirty — worn-out black jeans, a red T-shirt with holes in it, and a ratty blue denim jacket. The bottoms of his sneakers were falling apart. He wore no socks; didn't believe in them, or so he said. He was a runaway to big-city Manhattan, an escapee from the Kennedy compound in Hyannis. He and his cousin were standing at the foot of an escalator on the ground level of Grand Central Terminal. As a train stopped and passengers began to disembark and make their way to the escalator, the cousins would approach. "Got any spare change?" one would ask. Usually, he'd be ignored. Sometimes, though, he would get lucky and end up with a buck or two. Then, the two would take the money and hightail it to Central Park. Once there, they would score a small bit of heroin.

At this same time, three thousand miles away in Los Angeles, there was another Kennedy kid, this one sixteen. He looked like a true bum with disheveled, smelly clothing, his long hair past his shoulders and so skinny his cheekbones looked like small rocks on otherwise smooth adolescent skin. Sitting in the corner of a train's boxcar, he shared a joint with two other refugees from the Cape. While the train chugged along at a nice clip, this Kennedy kid turned to one of the other boys and asked, "So, where we headed?"

"Beats me," said the kid as he passed a joint. "Doesn't matter, does it?" he asked.

"Not really."

The first kid, the one in New York? That was David Kennedy.

The other one, in California? His brother Bobby.

THE TOUGH ONE

One day, when Robert Kennedy Jr. was about six months old, he was being cared for at his parents' home at the Cape by Fina Harvin. There was a knock on the door; it was the milkman making his regular delivery. Fina ran to let the serviceman in and, while in the kitchen, she heard a thud and a loud squeal. She then ran back to the bedroom and realized that little Bobby had rolled right off the bed and onto the floor. She scooped the crying infant up into her arms, sure she'd done the baby harm. At that moment, the phone rang. It was Bobby Sr., the baby's father. "I think I broke little Bobby," Fina said, crying. She explained what happened. "How high is the bed?" Bobby asked. She said it was about four feet. "Oh, that's okay," Bobby said, laughing. "Another foot, though, and the poor kid would probably be a goner." Thirty years later, when Bobby Jr. was giving a speech in Boston, he quipped, "People always ask me all the time how I turned out the way I did. Well," he said, pointing at Fina, "it's because that woman right over there once dropped me on my head."

Born on January 17, 1954, Robert Francis Kennedy Jr. was the third of Bobby's and Ethel's eleven children. He was nine when his uncle Jack was assassinated and fourteen when his father met the same terrible fate. As it happened, Bobby was one of the Kennedy children who was not in Los Angeles when his father was killed. At the time, he was in a Jesuit boarding school in North Bethesda, Maryland. A priest jostled him awake to tell him that there was a car outside, waiting to take him back to Hickory Hill. He didn't say why. It was one of his mother's secretaries, Jinx Hack, who told him that his father had been shot.

Hours after the shooting, Bobby found himself on Vice President Hubert H. Humphrey's plane, Air Force Two, with his older siblings, Kathleen and Joe, to meet the rest of his family already on the coast. He was at his father's bedside at Good Samaritan Hospital in Los Angeles when Bobby passed away. He then served as one of the pallbearers at his funeral. In the years that followed, he would speak of these memories with a certain detachment, as if it all had happened to someone else. Though he seemed to not connect to it, his entire life would be shaped and defined by this tragedy. It wouldn't be until he was perhaps in his forties that he really understood it.

"I have to say that I think it was simply because he was named after his pop that the adults in the family always thought Bobby was the leading contender in the race of who could one day be President," Christopher Lawford once observed. "He really didn't show any interest in social studies or politics, and I think he went out of his way to avoid such subjects in school. As much as the adults — especially his mother — wanted Bobby to be that person, that's how much he *didn't* want to be that person. He went the other way, as if to say, 'You know what? I am going to *so* not be that person, you won't *believe* how *not that person* I am going to be.' "

Being alone in the house with his mother was the last thing Bobby ever wanted, even when his father was alive. When RFK decided to campaign for the presidency in 1968, his namesake begged to be sent to a boarding school just so that he wouldn't have to deal with Ethel. "Are you scared of your mother?" Ena had asked him. "Of course, I am," he admitted. "Isn't everyone?" Ethel gladly sent him away. "I seldom lasted longer than a few days at home when I returned from distant schools for vacation," Bobby later recalled. "My homecomings were like the arrival of a squall. With me around to provoke her, my mother didn't stay angry very long — she went straight to rage. Her moods were like milk on a hot stove: one moment everything seemed fine and a second later the stove had disappeared."

In July 1970, a skirmish with the law would be the catalyst for Bobby's railroad odyssey. He and his cousin Bobby Shriver were busted for selling pot to an undercover police officer. Ethel didn't handle it well. It was just a year after Ted's misadventure at Chappaquiddick and was the last thing she and the rest of the family needed at that time. "She went on a tirade after the arrest and really laid into Bobby, tossing his skinny ass into the bushes outside their home and then evicting him from the house," said Joseph Gargan.

Eunice was just as angry, but she knew where to draw the line — she definitely wouldn't call her Bobby names or throw him out of the house; that wasn't her style. Instead, she sent him to his room for a couple of days and waited for Sarge — who had been in California — to return. After the Shriver parents reasoned things out with each other and decided on a course of action, Sarge sat down with Bobby and talked to him. Looking downcast, Sarge said he was gravely disappointed in his son and hoped to God he'd never repeat this mistake. Importantly, he also reassured him he wasn't a bad kid. He said he was a good son who'd just made a bad choice. Bobby Shriver recalls the way his father dealt with this episode as being a seminal moment in his life. "I knew from that moment on that my dad would have my back," he said, "and then I spent the rest of my life trying to make sure it wasn't necessary. When you know your father is there for you, it makes a big difference in the life of a teenager. I just wished Bobby had had this same kind of support. He'd really suffer because of a lack of it."

Bobby Shriver said he never did drugs again after that troubling incident. The same couldn't be said for Ethel's boy. Not only did he continue smoking marijuana, he moved on to heroin and other narcotics — and he even liked to brag about it. "Don't even *pretend* to understand me if you haven't done acid," Bobby would tell people.

One family friend recalls, "I remember Bobby and I got our signals crossed about something having to do with his drugs. He completely overreacted. He threw me up against a wall. 'I am the last person you want to fuck with,' he screamed at me, *'because I will fuck you right back.'* I thought, Okay, this guy's a loose cannon you don't want to ever cross."

Ena Bernard would take Joe and Bobby, sit down with them in the kitchen, and try to reason with them. "You have to be better boys," she would tell them while serving them heaping bowls of chocolate ice cream. "Why do you have to be so bad? Do you know how much you're hurting your mother?" She warned them that if they didn't behave, "I'll give you a pow-pow." That was her way of saying she was going to give them a spanking, though never once did she ever lay a hand on them. At the time, the kids were getting ready for a photo shoot for *Look* magazine, for an article about how well the family was faring after Bobby's death. Most of the Kennedy children disliked such photo sessions, where, as Bobby put it, "we have to be this nauseatingly smiling family when *none* of it is true." Ena promised the boys that if they would just tolerate the photo session they could then go horseback riding. All of the kids had horses in the Hickory Hill stalls and had been riding through the Virginia woods from a very early age, taught by Ethel to jump fences, high hedges and, on occasion, even automobiles. Ena could get the boys to do pretty much anything if she just promised an afternoon gallop as a reward.

By this time, Ena was deeply entrenched in the Kennedys' world. "My mother's nickname in our family became Banco de Costa Rica [Bank of Costa Rica]," Fina recalled with a chuckle, "because we would always go to her for money since we knew she could get it from Mrs. Kennedy. For instance, I once ran my American Express card up to six thousand dollars and couldn't pay it. I was so

311

THE SENSITIVE ONE

David Anthony Kennedy, born on June 15, 1955, was the fourth of Bobby and Ethel's eleven children. He'd always been a wiry little blond kid, somehow more handsome than his brothers with his cobalt-blue eyes being his most spectacular feature. They were alive with what seemed like immense intelligence, even when he was a little boy.

"Of all of us children, David was the closest to my father, and the most vulnerable and dependent upon him," Bobby Kennedy Jr. recalled. "My dad had a special bond with David. They were very much alike: shy, vulnerable, tough, fearless, kind, loyal, and principled. Of all his children, my dad reserved a special love for David, and David thrived on his affection."

Of course, like the rest of his family, David carried a heavy burden of trauma due to his father's death, but maybe even in a more direct way: he'd actually watched his father's murder on television. While his brother

313

Bobby was thousands of miles away at boarding school, David was right there in Los Angeles when the tragedy happened. "David was with his mother and some of his siblings," recalled Noelle Bombardier, who became close to the boy she called "my sweet David." She continued, "Tragically, he saw the whole thing on TV at the Beverly Hills Hotel, in which the family was staying."

It's been reported over the years that David was alone when he saw the news reports about his father. That's not true. He was actually with Bob Galland, the Hickory Hill staff member whose job it was to teach the boys sports, camping, and other outdoor activities. "We were watching TV and it just came on," said Galland. "I mean, there it was, Bobby shot and on the ground, and I jumped up to turn the channel, but I think I left it on for maybe five or six seconds longer than I should have, and David sat there just sort of transfixed. I think he was in shock. He was thirteen. What do you say? I told him, 'Let's go for a walk, let's get out of here and talk.' He looked at me with a sort of resigned expression, and I'll never forget what he said. He said, 'Man, they got him, too, didn't they? It's over. They got him, too.'"

Losing his father the way he did was something David, like all his siblings, could never reconcile. He wrote to his mother in a Christmas letter in 1968: "There will be no more football with Daddy, no more riding and no more camping with him. But he was the best father their [sic] ever was and I would rather have him for a father for the length of time I did than any other father for a million years."

Though David had always been close to his brother Bobby, they seemed to go their separate ways after their father died. Some felt it was Bobby who pulled away, and that the reason was because he was the one who'd encouraged David in drug abuse. "He was the older brother, and yes, David looked up to him," said one person on Ethel Kennedy's household staff. "When Bobby started with the drugs, David followed him down that road. The two boys enabled each other for a while until Bobby began to feel guilty about it. I think it caused a rift between them. A little while later, there was a strange moment when David started talking about being a railroad hobo, and Bobby got upset. 'He stole that story from *me* and made it part of *his* legend,' Bobby complained. Legend? I thought, My gosh, these kids are thinking about their legends, not their lives."

"Mrs. Kennedy had kicked David out of the house, as was unfortunately her way at the time," said Sister Pauline Joseph. "She thought he'd be in the backyard somewhere. He wasn't. She called me, frantic. I went to see her. She was in the kitchen, washing dishes with an apron on and looking like a typical mother. She had a lot of help for that, so I knew if she was doing chores herself she was upset."

"That boy has just vanished," Ethel told the nun while she scraped a plate hard, as if taking out her anger on it.

"Permission to speak freely?" the nun asked. She always asked the question when she was about to broach a sensitive topic. She never wanted Ethel to think she was being presumptuous.

"Yes," Ethel answered.

"It's not good to send your children away, Ethel," the nun said. "God's design for you as a mother is to always be there for them, no matter what. I know it's hard with teenagers, but why would you banish him?"

"Drugs," Ethel said, without turning around.

"Staying focused on her work, she told me she'd warned him that if she caught him smoking reefer in the house, he'd be gone," recalled the nun many years later. "She said she needed to set boundaries and stick to them. I think what really struck me, though, was that she said she felt so completely unappreciated. She believed her boys didn't value all she continued to do to make sure they had a good and safe life at Hickory Hill. 'Anyway,' she told me, 'I caught the boy smoking reefer and now . . . he's gone.' "

"Then we should pray for him, Ethel," said

316

the nun.

Still not turning around, Ethel shook her head vehemently in the negative. Finally, she faced Sister Pauline Joseph. "Here's an idea," she said, "*you* pray for him." She then took off her apron and handed it to the nun as if she were a servant. "I'm fresh out of prayers today," she added as she walked out of the kitchen. A second later, she came back into the room and said, "Oh, and by the way. You know what? I would appreciate it if you called me *Mrs. Kennedy,*" and then left again.

David had hightailed it to New York with Christopher Lawford. "A hitchhiked ride here, a bus ride there, a train ride onward, and the next thing we knew we were in Manhattan," Christopher recalled. "My mom lived in New York. We thought we'd bunk with her, but she said no way. She didn't have a lot of patience for runaway Kennedys," he said with a chuckle. "My father [Peter Lawford] was no help, either; he had his own addictions, his own issues, in California. So, for me, a child of two addicts, turning to drugs was a no-brainer.

"Once we got to New York, my mom made it clear that David was Aunt Ethel's problem, not hers. *I* was barely her problem. She wasn't about to babysit the two of us. She did call Aunt Ethel, though, to tell her that we were in Manhattan alone. 'Great,' Aunt Ethel said. 'The two of them together couldn't operate a transistor radio, and now they're on their own in New York? Lotsa luck.' "

Thus it happened that while Bobby was in California riding the railways, David was in New York sleeping in cardboard boxes in subway stations with his cousin. "We were fearless and up for adventure," Christopher Lawford recalled. "Looking back on it now, I guess we decided, you know what? We'll never be what our parents want us to be; we sure as shit aren't going to be anyone's President. So we may as well just take off and have a good time and see how the other half lives. It was rebellion, as plain and simple and as cliché as that sounds. It's what happens, though, when you're a kid and you have no hope that you will ever amount to anything. That's what you do. You lash out."

Throughout this turbulent time, Christopher Lawford says he had a small thought in the back of his head that maybe things might one day be different if he applied himself to figuring out a better way. It was just a tiny seed of hope, but one he sensed might grow if he took the time to nurture it. When he wasn't high, in those rare moments of lucidity when he could really take stock, there remained that persistent, almost nagging thought that maybe, one day, things could be different for him.

Sadly, David didn't share in his cousin's

small measure of optimism. "Taking morphine was when I felt for the first time that things were okay in my life," he would say. "The morphine was the thing that made me forget how miserable I had been since Daddy died. It was the thing that made me forget my pain."

FOOTPRINTS DEEPER THAN HIS OWN

Spring 1971. "You're the chosen one," Lem Billings was telling Bobby Jr. in the living room of his Eighty-sixth Street apartment in Manhattan, this according to Christopher Lawford. "You're the one. You're named after your dad. You have the looks. You have the charisma. You're smart. You're the one, Bobby. *You're the one.*"

In Bobby, Lem saw not so much his father, but rather a reflection of his uncle Jack. Like Jack, Bobby was imaginative, he was interesting, he knew how to relate to people and, maybe more important, he was humble. Bobby's father had been more of a warrior, and his son was the same. However, Bobby Jr. also had a certain vulnerability and empathy that, at least in Lem's mind, was reminiscent of Jack. In the eyes of many observers, though, Lem had transferred the deep emotion he'd had for his best friend to Bobby Jr. His biggest concern now had to do with the boy's education. After getting kicked out of

320

Millbrook, young Kennedy would also be ordered to leave Pomfret in Connecticut in the spring of 1971 for using drugs. Lem wanted him to buckle down and be a good student. He knew what Bobby Jr. would be up against when measured by his family's ancestral heroes. "Jack was lucky," Lem once said. "He didn't have a lot of Kennedys getting there before him. Everywhere a boy like Bobby looks, there are footprints, all of them deeper than his own." Lem just knew Bobby was special and could become President one day.

So adamant was Lem about Bobby's chances, the young man actually began to take his direction to heart. "I began to feel this strange pull that maybe it really *was* my destiny to be President," Bobby recalled, "though I was at odds with it. I knew it was what Lem wanted. But was it what *I* wanted? I wasn't so sure I was cut out for it. First of all, I wanted to be a veterinarian, and I knew that for sure. Also, I had a secret life that kept me . . . preoccupied."

Bobby was talking about his drug habit. Several nights a week, he would sneak out of Lem's apartment and meet his friend Allan Burke. The two would take off to Harlem, where they'd camp out with homeless drug addicts and act as if they were a part of the gang; still, Bobby wanted to be someone else. "We'd go to 116th Street and pay thirty dollars at one end of the block and then pick up the drugs at the other end of the block," Allan Burke recalled. "Or we'd go to what was called 'the shooting gallery,' an alley of addicts all shooting up. We'd do heroin with them and then fall asleep in a corner of the alley covered in vomit. The next morning, there would be poor Lem, pissed off at us, shaking us awake. I imagined the poor guy searching the ghetto, scared out of his mind, waking up homeless people, asking if they'd seen this kid as he frantically flashed a picture of Bobby. Eventually, he'd find us and drag us back to his apartment."

Bobby would finally earn his high school diploma in June 1972 from Palfrey Street School in Watertown, in which he had been enrolled by Lem. It wasn't a boarding school, so Lem arranged for Bobby to live with a family in Cambridge and then with him in New York on weekends.

In the spring of 1972, Bobby somehow managed to get into Harvard, mostly on the Kennedy name and influence, certainly not because of his grades. His drug abuse continued unabated. Making things worse for Lem was the way Bobby lied about it. Once, when Lem chastised him about it, Bobby shouted at him, "What? All of a sudden we have a big problem with lying?"

What did *that* mean? Was he referencing Lem's possible closeted homosexuality?

Maybe so, since that was the one thing Lem seemed to be concealing. Whatever the case, this amorphous notion that Lem was hiding something from Bobby, someone to whom he was so close, suddenly became a running theme in their friendship. "When Bobby started accusing Lem of not being honest with him, it hit Lem hard and made him feel as if a gulf was developing between them," recalled Allan Burke. "Before I knew it, the old guy was doing drugs with Bobby just to ensure commonality with him. It was such a violation of his role in Bobby's life, though, and Lem knew it. But Lem kept saying it was a way to be with Bobby on a deeper level. Bobby, though . . . well, Bobby just wanted to do drugs. He had no agenda other than to get high. I once asked him if doing drugs with Lem was maybe a way of bonding with him. He lashed out at me and said, 'When are you going to get this through your fat head? *I don't bond.*'"

THE WORST THAT
COULD HAPPEN

Bobby Kennedy Jr. was about twenty-five in 1978 when he met Emily Ruth Black, a fellow student at the University of Virginia Law School in Charlottesville. A graduate of Indiana University who had majored in political science, she was petite, bookish, five foot four with auburn hair and a bright, engaging smile. One of three children, she'd had a modest upbringing; her mother was a schoolteacher, her father owned a family business in wood lumbering. He'd died of a heart attack at a young age, just thirty-four, when Emily was two.

"I went with Emily and Bobby to a picnic one afternoon at a park in Liberty Hill in West Virginia," recalled Marjorie Dougherty, who had known her since childhood. "I remember he had this huge black-and-white falcon perched on his right hand. This enormous bird jumped from his right hand to his left when Bobby went to shake my hand, as if on cue. Bobby kept bragging to Emily that one day he was going to be President, and she believed him. It *was* intoxicating. She later told me that when Bobby took her to the compound to meet the family, her head was swimming. 'I felt like I was dreaming,' she told me. 'There I was on the beach, having a daiquiri with Jackie O. How can you not love that?' "

In 1980, Bobby went to work on his uncle Ted's failed campaign to challenge President Jimmy Carter for the Democratic presidential nomination; he was responsible for galvanizing voter support in the South. That same year, in August, Bobby asked Emily to marry him.

"Bobby's engagement to Emily was the worst thing that could ever have happened to Lem," observed Allan Burke many decades after the fact. "For sure, Lem felt he was losing Bobby. I remember being at his new Upper East Side home near the Guggenheim Museum one night with Bobby, David, and Christopher. Lem looked terrible, his enormous frame slumped into an easy chair, his face bloated, his eyeglasses all askew. I asked what was wrong and he said, 'I'm upset about this Bobby and Emily business. It's not right.'

"I also have this distinct memory of Lem sitting next to Bobby on a long couch going through an old family scrapbook, telling one great Kennedy story after another," said Allan Burke. "And as they were turning the pages, he moved just about a half inch closer to Bobby. Bobby moved a half inch away from Lem. Then Lem moved a half inch closer. Again, Bobby inched away. They kept doing this dance, all the way down to the other end of the couch. Finally, Lem got upset and said to Bobby, 'You won't even let our legs touch. Why is that, Bobby? *Why is that?*' Bobby shot back, 'Because it makes me feel weird, Lem.' Lem was mortified. The lines had definitely become blurred between being paternal and being, I don't know . . . maybe something else. And this longing or just this sense of things being not in alignment ate away at Lem."

By 1981, everything in Lem Billings's life had become exaggerated, all the good taking on a weird, eccentric, and fanatical turn. Now his home appeared like some sort of disorganized Kennedy Library, with family mementos strewn all about: framed photographs of Lem and Jack, letters they'd exchanged in glass cases, not only Jack's to him but, somehow, even his original letters to Jack. Everything Lem could put his finger on had some kind of compelling Kennedy backstory, some hidden Kennedy meaning, some anecdote that only Lem could tell. It was a real mess, though, not organized or well-kept.

A one-two punch of tragic episodes of gun violence really threw Lem at this time. The first was the murder of John Lennon in

December 1980 by Mark David Chapman in New York. It was followed just months later, in March 1981, by the assassination attempt on President Ronald Reagan by John Hinckley Jr. Both events stunned a nation fearful of gun violence yet also unwilling to do much about it in terms of legislation. For Lem, these two incidents brought back the horrors of Jack's and Bobby's murders. He became consumed with wanting to know more about both Chapman and Hinckley, digging into their backgrounds and trying to discern why these men had been compelled to such violence. He couldn't stop talking about them as he attempted to frame them into some sort of historical context and grasp at straws of any psychological parallels they might have had to Lee Harvey Oswald and Sirhan Sirhan.

When he was in his right mind, one still couldn't ask for a better instructor of Kennedy history than Lem Billings. However, when he was high, he would become incredibly sad and morose. In those moments, he would fall into great despair. He would complain that he'd never really lived his own life. Instead, he'd devoted all his passion and energy to the Kennedys, and he had to wonder whether it had ever been truly appreciated by them. After all, they'd gone on to marriages and children and even grandchildren, but he hadn't enjoyed any of those experiences. He'd hidden from everyone all aspects of his personal, private life . . . his longings . . . his dreams. He knew that most of them figured he was probably gay, but they didn't know for sure because he never confirmed it.

Allan Burke says he dropped in on Lem once and, since the front door was cracked open, he went into his home. He looked around but couldn't find his friend. He called his name; there was no response. He walked down the hallway and peeked into the bedroom, and there he found Lem tangled up in the arms of a man, someone they all knew from the Village. "Lem shrieked, jumped from the bed naked, and slammed the door shut," recalled Burke. "Five minutes later, the guy bolted from the room and out the door.

"I waited in the living room feeling so sorry I had ever seen anything at all until, finally, after about an hour, Lem came out of the room. He was emotional. 'Please don't tell the Kennedys,' he said. I said, 'But Lem, I think they would understand.' Deep down, though, I knew they wouldn't. This was the 1980s; they were devoutly Catholic . . . the boys all macho. No, they wouldn't have understood, and neither would Ethel or Jackie or any of the older ones, either. They would've thought he'd been keeping this secret for years and probably would've re-evaluated every single waking moment they'd ever spent with the poor guy. That was just the way it was back then. 'Not a day has gone by I don't wish Bobby was here,' Lem said, crying, 'until today. Today I'm glad he's not here. To see this.' That made me think, did Jack know? I asked, and he nodded. It made sense that it wouldn't have impacted their friendship. JFK was so inclusive in his thinking and had many gay friends. I wondered why Lem felt this kind of understanding wouldn't have also been Bobby's way. 'Only Jack ever understood me,' he said. I promised him I would never tell anyone. He thanked me and calmed down. I felt terrible because I figured everyone, on some level, already knew. I was only twenty-five at the time. It seemed to me that poor man had spent his entire life hiding, but the only thing he'd been truly successful at hiding was just how lonely he was."

Maybe the Kennedys didn't really know, after all. All they knew was that when Lem was a young man, he'd asked Kathleen ("Kick") Kennedy to marry him. "I never saw any evidence that Lem was gay," Bobby Kennedy now says. "To the contrary, he almost always had a steady girl. Nor did I hear even the hint of a rumor to that effect. If Lem had a secret gay life, it occupied very little of his time and energies and, in any case, that fact would in no way have diminished our friendship or the intensity of the love that

I and my entire extended family felt for him."

The fact that, in light of Bobby's engagement, Lem feared that their bond would somehow weaken just seemed to make things worse for him. "You can do what you want with Emily, fuck if I care," he told Bobby one drug-infused night, this, again, according to Allan Burke. "You never wanted me to be happy," Bobby responded, crying. "I don't know what you've wanted for me since Daddy died, but it's not to be happy."

"But why ruin your life, Bobby?" Lem asked. "We could have it all."

"Let me set this in a more understandable context for you," Bobby said angrily. "*We* can't have anything. There is no *we*, Lem. I'm not my uncle Jack. And I'm not my father, either. How many times have I told you that?" He then rushed away. Bobby, possibly because of his immaturity, could be incredibly unkind to his old friend. Somehow along the way, it seemed as if he'd begun to resent Lem, much as a son resents a father who can never be truly pleased. Allan Burke felt bad for Lem. "I'm sorry, Lem. He didn't mean that," he told him. "It's all right," Lem said sadly. "That's probably the most honest thing he's ever said to me."

CRUSHED

On May 27, 1981, Lem hosted Bobby's brother Michael Kennedy and his wife, Vicki, at his home for dinner. Lem had just bought a new fondue pot at Macy's and couldn't wait to use it. He and Vicki spent an hour in the kitchen chopping vegetables. Later, Lem, Michael, Vicki, and a few other friends sat around a coffee table in front of the television and dipped the veggies into hot cheese while watching the sitcom *The Facts of Life.* "It's so interesting, this older woman in charge of all of these young girls," Lem said of the show's premise, "and she's so devoted to them. They appreciate her so much," he concluded as Michael and Vicki looked at each other knowingly. After the show was over, they switched to melted chocolate, dipping cubes of fruit into the gooey confection. As they spoke, it became clear that Lem was more conflicted than ever about Bobby.

Harvey Blake Fleetwood, a good friend of Lem's, was present that night and recalled that Lem was eagerly expecting Bobby to arrive from Charlottesville the next morning. However, Bobby called to cancel, explaining that he decided he wanted to be with Emily. Lem was crushed. " 'I think I made a terrible, terrible mistake,' he said, crying," according to Fleetwood. " 'I took drugs with Bobby. It was wrong. I let him down. How could I have done that to him?' "

Stunned, Michael and Vicki didn't know what to make of Lem's confession. All Michael knew was that he didn't want to have a discussion about it in front of his wife. So he suggested they all get out of the house and go see a Sean Connery film called *Outland.* When they got home, Lem was still in a deep depression. "Michael, be a dear and get me a G and T with three ice cubes," he told young Kennedy — meaning a gin and tonic. Michael fetched him the drink — then three more like it in rapid succession.

Lem began talking about how much he missed Jack, what a good man he'd been, and how unfair it had been that he was taken from them. "Oh, dear Lem, you've got to stop living in the past," Vicki said to him, putting her hand on his. "Let us help you. Let's get rid of some of the stuff around here that keeps you in the past," she said, looking around at all the Kennedy memorabilia.

Lem nodded, saying she was absolutely right. "I think we should just get rid of *all* of it," he said. Michael suggested they donate it to the JFK Library and Museum in Boston. "What an exquisite idea," Lem exclaimed, suddenly brightening. "Why, we'll have to take a complete inventory of everything," he decided, "and we'll have to make sure we know when each and every photo was taken . . . and exactly who is in it . . . and we should write all of that down in a ledger . . . and then maybe we should talk to the people in the photos . . . and even record their memories . . . and . . . and . . ."

Michael and Vicki couldn't help but smile. They'd given Lem a new project, and it had to do with the Kennedys. He felt a lot better.

The next day, May 28, the lifeless body of Kirk LeMoyne Billings was found in his bed. He'd had a heart attack just one day before what would have been JFK's sixty-fourth birthday. Lem was sixty-five. All the Kennedys were filled with grief, of course. Andy Williams, who had been a best friend of RFK's, came by Lem's house that day and saw Bobby sitting in a corner, weeping. "He was just crushed," Andy recalled. " 'Lem was my true, true friend,' he kept saying. 'He'll always be with you,' I told him. 'Just as your daddy is still with me.' "

Lem's death would mark an inflection point in the life of Bobby Kennedy Jr. In the years to come, he would sometimes be filled with overwhelming regret about Lem, wishing he had been more considerate of him, lamenting his treatment of him, and just hoping that Lem knew how much he'd meant to him. He came to understand that, toward the end of Lem's life, their drug taking had twisted everything and had made them say things to each other they really didn't mean. Now Bobby just wanted to live a better life. He wanted to change. He wanted to be a better man . . . and he wanted to do it for Lem.

Bobby's Victory

At the beginning of March 1982, Ethel Kennedy walked into the servants' dining room at Hickory Hill during the evening meal. The staff all jumped obediently to their feet. Ethel motioned for them to be seated. "I just wanted you all to know that my Bobby is getting married next month to Emily Black, who I'm sure you've seen around here," she said. "So the month ahead will be busy." She explained that there would be parties being planned at Hickory Hill as well as other festivities designed specifically to celebrate the couple and to hopefully lift the general mood after Lem's sudden death. "It's been difficult for all of us," Ethel said, according to Leah Mason, who was one of those present. "Lem was a good friend of ours, as you know. But he would want us to soldier on." She then said that Noelle Bombardier had a list of duties for each staff member and that they should take direction from her. "Now, go back to your meal," she said. "I'm sorry to have disturbed you, but I thought you'd like some good news."

"She seemed exhilarated and revitalized, as if things were looking up," recalled Leah Mason. "But we all knew that Bobby Jr. still had serious drug problems. I would say we knew a lot more about his personal problems than probably we should have. Everyone on staff was always talking about it and worrying about it."

On April 3, 1982, Bobby, now twenty-eight, finally married Emily Black, twenty-four. After the wedding in Emily's hometown of Bloomington, Indiana, and the many celebrations later at Hickory Hill, the newlyweds moved to New York and into the home of Lem Billings, which he had bequeathed to Bobby. Bobby then got a job as an assistant district attorney (he'd failed the bar the first time he took it but passed on the second try), earning about twenty thousand dollars a year, while Emily, also now an attorney, began work as a public defender, earning an equal amount. However, it would appear that the marriage was troubled from the start.

Emily was a pleasant enough, well-meaning young woman, but extremely naive and ill-equipped to deal with the complexities of marriage to a troubled Kennedy. She couldn't deal with his wild mood swings, which tended toward deep depression, and most certainly his drug abuse was something with which she couldn't contend. Bobby's grief over Lem seemed even worse than the sadness of losing his own father. At the end of the day, he would come home from the office for dinner and then, two hours later, disappear with friends intent on scoring drugs in Harlem, three miles north of where they lived. Meanwhile, Emily would sit at home, scared for his safety. Then she would call her mother-in-law back at Hickory Hill, frightening Ethel and causing her more than a few sleepless nights.

Eventually, Ethel decided to send a trusted family attorney — a gentleman who asked not to be identified because still, all these years later, he said he didn't want to betray Ethel's confidence — to see if he could influence Bobby. During his visit, he found that Emily was in distress because Bobby wasn't home most of the time. One night, after she went to bed, the attorney sat and waited for Bobby to get home. He showed up after four in the morning, looking terrible, with dirty clothing, his hair unwashed. "Why are you doing this to yourself, Bobby?" he asked him. Apparently, Bobby didn't have an answer. He slumped into a chair, seeming ruined. "If I go into rehab and it gets out that they're treating *Bobby Kennedy Jr.,* how will *that* look?" he asked. "My mother will kill me." The attorney said, "That's as good an excuse as any, I guess."

Because he'd known him almost since birth, the lawyer felt he could be honest with Bobby. He observed that the deaths of Bobby's uncle, father, and now Lem had troubled him to the point where he'd lost all hope. Bobby agreed. He added that he was tortured by the way he had treated Lem. The attorney pleaded with him to get help, adding that this is what Lem would want for him. He then reached into his vest pocket and pulled a rosary from it. "This is your mother's," he told Bobby. "Take it. Pray."

Bobby took the rosary and, his head bowed, began to weep.

A week later, on September 9, 1983, Bobby decided to get treatment at a facility in Rapid City, South Dakota, "as far off the beaten path as possible," he said, "so as to not be recognized." On the way, in a jet twenty thousand feet in the sky, he secreted himself into a restroom for one last fix of heroin — and it was there that he overdosed. An ambulance and two police cars met the plane when it landed; the ashen and sick Kennedy was then taken to a nearby hospital.

Shortly thereafter, Bobby checked into Fair Oaks Hospital in Summit, New Jersey, for rehabilitation. He would eventually plead guilty to drug possession and be sentenced to 1,500 hours of community service and two years of court-enforced probation. Throughout the ordeal, Emily would stick by her husband's side. In September 1984, the couple welcomed a son, Robert Francis Kennedy III. Four years later, in April 1988, they had a daughter, Kathleen "Kick" Alexandra Kennedy.

As part of his community service, Bobby would volunteer at an environmental organization dedicated to eradicating the pollution of the Hudson River. It was here that he would find his calling as an environmentalist and, eventually, an environmental attorney. Bobby had read the activist Robert Boyle's *The Hudson River* and became enchanted by the locale, dedicated to preserving it. "You know, you can put your past behind you and find a new life," Boyle told him. "A lot of people go through addiction. But the Hudson River is your salvation, if you will, from the horrible life you have led. You can seek a new life through the river, and through ecology."

Bobby began work with the Hudson River Fishermen's Association — soon to be known as Riverkeeper — and while fishing and camping on the river banks, he says, he began to appreciate the beauty of nature "and the responsibility we all have to keeping it alive for generations to come." He and Emily bought a home in Mount Kisco, outside New York and not far from the Hudson.

"Once I realized and accepted that higher office — meaning the presidency, I guess —

was not for me, once I truly reconciled that I was not cut out for it, that's when my *real* life began," he observed. "When that pressure was off, I began to see more clearly that I could contribute in other ways, in cleaning up the planet, in being of service that way. I don't blame the stress of hopelessly trying to be what people wanted me to be for my addiction. That would be a cop-out, and besides, there were other issues. But once I was drug-free, I never looked back."

The happy arc of this story is that, finally free of the hold of addiction, Bobby would go on to his true calling as an environmentalist and, in the process, become a great influencer in the field, someone who could put the power of the Kennedy name to good use. With the passing of time, everyone in his life began to understand that Bobby really didn't belong in politics, that he could do the world a lot of good in his own way and in a way that would have made his father and Lem proud. He had done it, all right; he'd turned his life around after a fourteen-year drug addiction. It was a true victory. Never again would Robert Kennedy Jr. ever do drugs — and he remains clean to this day.

WILLFUL DAUGHTER

While Bobby seemed to be out of the woods, his brother David was still in the thick of it. Rather than be inspired by Bobby's victory, he resented it because it just made him look bad to his family, all of whom now wanted him to be more like his older brother. "I don't know what we can do, short of locking the guy in his room," Joe Kennedy told Fina Harvin. "It's like a slow death, isn't it? I can see that he's not going to make it."

Of all his siblings, David seemed to be the most open to his sister Kathleen's reaching out. She seemed able to connect with him in a different and maybe more meaningful way than other family members.

Born on July 4, 1951, Kathleen Kennedy, as earlier stated, was the oldest of Bobby and Ethel's children. An accomplished, award-winning equestrian at a young age, when she was fourteen she was thrown from a horse during a competition. "Bobby once told me that she was unconscious and bleeding internally," recalled Frank Mankiewicz, RFK's former press secretary, in a 2000 interview. "She was apparently rushed to a hospital in Cape Cod. It took hours for Bobby and Ethel, who happened to be en route to Hyannis Port, to be reached. I'm sure they were frantic. She eventually did recover, though I understood it was a long, tough road."

Kathleen recalls it a little differently. She says it took her parents four days to accept that her leg was broken because "you know, Kennedys don't cry and all . . . so I had to keep a stiff upper lip for a while. I learned then that, as the saying goes, 'you have to get back on that horse.' I think the accident taught me to be tenacious about life, to not let events that can occur by happenstance define you in a negative way."

For a little while, when she was a teenager, Kathleen dated Jackie's half brother, Jamie Auchincloss. "It was puppy love," he recalled. "We sent love letters to one another, that sort of thing. I found her interesting. She was a tomboy; I liked that. We were in sync because we were related to this royal family, yet we didn't really identify ourselves in that way. Though I was an Auchincloss, she was a *real* Kennedy — she didn't trumpet it like the rest of them. You had the distinct sense that she was her own person. One funny story comes to mind: she told me that when she was young and would write letters to her grandma Rose, the old woman would send them back to her with corrections in red pencil. I later learned that this was the case with all of Rose's grandchildren."

At the age of about fifteen, Kathleen transferred out of the parochial Stone Ridge Country Day School, a Catholic school, to Putney, a progressive secular school in Vermont. Many people thought her decision was a rebellion against Catholicism. She laughs at the notion and says, "No. I was rebelling against the idea of there being no boys. Stone Ridge was a single-sex school, and that made no sense to me. How were we as young women supposed to be in the world if we had no association with men? I just didn't understand it, so I campaigned hard to change schools and, somehow, I got my way."

Those who worked for Ethel recall Kathleen's Putney years as her most rebellious. In some ways, she began to mirror her mother's sometimes volatile nature. Noelle Bombardier, Hickory Hill's estate manager, recalled Kathleen, at about eighteen, coming back to Hyannis from Vermont for the summer break and deciding to celebrate the vacation months with a picnic she wanted to have with four girlfriends from school. She asked Noelle to go to the specialty cheese store where the Kennedys had an account and purchase a quarter pound each of Gouda and Gruyère cheese. Going the extra mile, Noelle also purchased a quarter pound of feta. When she returned to Ethel's, Noelle called out to Kathleen to tell her that she had returned and placed the three cheeses on a counter. Kathleen walked into the kitchen and became upset. "That's too much cheese," she said. "Why did you buy so much cheese?" She then picked up the block of feta and threw it at Noelle, hitting her on the shoulder.

"What is wrong with you, Kathleen?" Noelle demanded to know.

"That's just too much cheese," Kathleen repeated. "Go back and return it. You're wasting money. My mother hates it when you waste money, and you *know* that's true."

Years later, Noelle would remember, "It's funny, the silly little stories that come to mind when trying to recall a young girl you were around for so many years, but that incident occurs to me today whenever I think of Kathleen. Later, when I told Mrs. Kennedy about it, she wasn't surprised. 'She's just going through this teenage phase where she's nasty, angry, and never more self-righteous than when she's wrong,' she said. She then wanted to know every detail of Kathleen's picnic plans: How many girls? Where were they going? Would there be any boys? 'I know you want to protect her,' I told Mrs. Kennedy. 'But how? She's so headstrong.' Mrs. Kennedy looked at me and said one word: *'Shackles.'* We both then just died laughing.

'Look, she knows her own mind,' she finally said. 'It'll serve her well. All my girls need to be tough. When they grow up, they cannot be weak, and if people think they're bitchy, too bad. It's a small price to pay.'

"Of the four daughters, I would have to say that Kathleen was probably the most willful in high school and all the way through college," recalled Noelle. "Lots of teenage rebellion stuff, more than Mrs. Kennedy had with Courtney, Kerry, or Rory. She would holler at Kathleen, 'Good luck with that mouth when you grow up, because you're sure gonna need it.' Sometimes she could be sort of funny about it. For instance, she would tell me, 'Please, Noelle. I can't handle any more bad news about Kathleen right now. My diet pills are starting to wear off.'

"Looking back, I have to say that Mrs. Kennedy and Kathleen were exactly alike: strong-minded, opinionated, and determined. And also, as much as Mrs. Kennedy was infuriated by it, that's how much she cultivated it because she wanted those girls to be powerful in their lives. 'If we can just get through this bitchy phase,' she used to tell me, 'we'll be good to go.' "

After Putney, when Kathleen was at Radcliffe studying history and literature, she met David Townsend, a college tutor four years her senior. From the start, Kathleen and David's relationship seemed like a good one.

Townsend would go on to become a professor at St. John's, happy in his work, not at all eager to be in the public eye. "He's an intellectual," Kathleen would observe. "I mean, he teaches Greek and Einstein and Shakespeare and chaos theory. In other words, he's very strong."

The couple, who married in 1973, soon moved to Santa Fe, New Mexico, which is where two of their children, Meaghan and Maeve, were born.

DOCTORS' ORDERS

By 1983, Kathleen was thirty-two. Because her brother David had been to several treatment facilities that were ineffective, he had become a primary concern of hers. "She and her mother disagreed about his treatment, though," said Noelle Bombardier. "They disagreed about it *a lot.*"

One psychiatrist in Cambridge, Massachusetts, to whom Ethel had sent David had provided him with fifty prescriptions over an eighteen-month period, including Percodan and Dilaudid. As far as Ethel was concerned, this doctor knew exactly what he was doing — "Otherwise, how did he get his license?"

Kathleen didn't see it that way. "Doctors overprescribe all the time," she told her mother.

"Yes," agreed Fina Harvin. "I've read that doctors prescribe and prescribe and *prescribe* and they don't even check with each other to see what the patient is getting."

"Oh please," Ethel shot back. "Says who?"

"*Life* magazine," Fina exclaimed.

Ethel shook her head in dismay. "No. It's alcohol," she said. "*Alcohol* is what's ruining our youth today, not drugs."

Ethel added that many of her Skakel relatives were alcoholics and that if it was true that the disease was genetic then they probably got it from her side of the family. Even in the older Kennedy generation there were problems of this nature that had gone unaddressed. For instance, there was no doubt that matriarch Rose had long been dependent on sleeping pills and tranquilizers, especially as she got older, as was Ethel herself. "My sister was taking all kinds of pills in a way that was not safe," said Ethel's brother Jim back in 1994. "The drug Restoril was the one most prescribed to her and to the other Kennedys, probably Rose, too," he recalled. "That was the big sleeping pill back then, especially in our family. We all thought that if it came from a doctor, it had to be harmless."

Ten years earlier, in November 1973, the year of the tenth anniversary of JFK's death, Ethel spent most of her days walking around in a fog thanks to prescription medications. The milestone anniversaries of Jack's and Bobby's deaths — with so many television specials and news reports recounting the tragedies, as well as the inevitable books and magazines — would always send her into a downward spiral. On this anniversary, she hosted a memorial Mass at Hickory Hill, attended by most of the Kennedys, including Jackie.

"Just look at us," Ethel told Jackie, crying in front of Noelle Bombardier. "We're wrecks and we'll never get over it, will we?" A tearful Jackie had to agree. "The two women embraced and held it for a long time," recalled Noelle Bombardier.*

The next day, as Ethel and Noelle sat in the kitchen at Hickory Hill, they began to talk a little about Bobby. "Can I tell you a secret?" Ethel whispered. "For a moment after he was shot when he was laying there

* Ethel's relationship to Jackie has often been misunderstood. They're usually portrayed as rivals in accounts of their lives. Though they certainly had their contentious moments, it wasn't so black-and-white between them. Perhaps some proof of their rapport can be found in a letter Jackie wrote to Ethel on June 6, 1968, after Bobby's murder, which she addressed to "My Ethel." She wrote: "No one in the world could have ever been like you were yesterday — except maybe Bobby. I stayed up till 6:30 last night just thinking — and praying for you. I love you so much. You know that . . . Stas [her brother-in-law] will take little Bobby to Africa. I'll take them around the world + to the moon + back — anything to help you + them now and always." She signed it, "With my deepest love, Jackie."

on the floor bleeding, I thought he was going to live. Why, he opened his eyes, Noelle, and he looked right up at me. And I thought, Oh my God. He's going to live. *He's going to live.* Then, later, at the hospital, they put a stethoscope to my ear, and I could hear his heart beating. It was beating . . . beating . . . beating . . . but then . . ." Her voice trailed off. "Our life together had been so great and so exciting up until then, Noelle," Ethel said sadly. "And then, just like that, it was over." (This was a rare moment of candor; Ethel almost never talks about Bobby's assassination, even to this day.)

As if things weren't troubling enough, at this same time there was a break-in at Hickory Hill. Ethel had always refused to have a security system installed, which was surprising considering the tragedies of her life. "She said there were too many people in the household and that the alarm would forever be going off," said Noelle Bombardier. "Not only that, she used to always repeat her husband's mantra, 'Kennedys can take care of themselves,' which, of course, was tragically ironic. I spoke to Senator Kennedy about this matter many times. I didn't feel that any of us were safe, the staff included, at Hickory Hill and also at the Kennedy compound. He said he had talked to Mrs. Kennedy about it on numerous occasions, especially after Bobby was killed, but that she was adamant about it. 'She doesn't want to live in fear,' he told me, 'and I'm not going to fight her on it.'"

Maybe one of the reasons Ethel wasn't particularly conscious of danger was because the Kennedys had always lived with it, even before the assassinations. For instance, back in 1957, when Bobby was chief counsel of the Senate's racket committee hearings, he was charged with investigating criminal activity surrounding the labor-management relations. The most famous of his cases related to Jimmy Hoffa, a labor union leader with ties to organized crime. Bobby's family was constantly threatened during this time. "They had thrown acid into the eyes of a journalist from the *New York Post*," Ethel told her daughter Rory for her HBO documentary *Ethel*, "and they would say they were going to do the same to your children." Kathleen Kennedy Townsend added, "There was a period of time when we were going to Our Lady of Victory School, we couldn't leave with all the other kids. We had to go up into the principal's office and wait for Mummy to pick us up because it was too dangerous for us to just walk out of school." After the assassinations, death threats were an even more common occurrence. It could be said that the family was somewhat inured to the idea of violence even before Bobby was killed, and for Ethel, that didn't really change after his death — thusly, no security measures were in place at Hickory Hill or at her home at the compound.

One night, a vagrant broke into the house by scaling a fire escape and somehow ended up in five-year-old Rory's room on the third floor. (The Hickory Hill manse had five floors.) At the sight of the man coming in through the open window, Rory's cocker spaniel began to bark. Rory had to have been scared out of her mind. The man asked, "Where's Mommy's room?" The little girl pointed that it was down the hall.

When Ethel heard something in the hallway, she cracked opened her door to find the stranger on the other side. She screamed out in fright. The next thing she knew, all her sons had exited their bedrooms, run to the intruder, and tackled him to the ground. Then Ena came bounding out of her room with an African Masai hunting spear in one hand and an enormous wooden mallet in the other. She started madly pounding away at the intruder. Once he was subdued, they all waited for the police to arrive as Ena held him at bay with her spear. Though the telling of the story seems somewhat amusing, it was actually quite upsetting. Bobby later referred to the intruder as "a would-be rapist."

Shortly after the incident, Jackie was scheduled to once again visit Hickory Hill. Whenever she came to visit Ethel, it was usually with one or two security guards in tow. Ethel thought that was completely unnecessary but, as she put it to Noelle Bombardier, "to each her own, I guess. Jackie and I just handle things differently."

The morning of Jackie's arrival, Ethel walked into the servants' dining room as they were having breakfast. Everyone bolted to their feet. "My sister-in-law Jackie is coming to spend the day. I want you to take all the kids to the park," Ethel said, directing Ena, "and keep them there for the afternoon. And tell Jackie's security detail that I'm worried about the kids and that I want them with you for protection." Alarmed, Ena said, "Oh no, Mrs. Kennedy. What's going on?" to which Ethel said, "Nothing. Everything is fine. I just want those men out of the house." She also said that she would like the rest of the staff to stay away from the drawing room for a few hours. She asked them to find something to keep them busy. She thanked everyone and then walked out of the room. Everyone sat back down. "What in the world is going on?" Ena Bernard asked Leah Mason. "Search me," Leah answered.

After Jackie showed up that afternoon, she and Ethel made themselves comfortable in the drawing room. Jackie reached into her purse. She took a vial of pills from it, poured a few of them into the palm of her hand, and downed them with a glass of Chardonnay.

She handed it to Ethel, who did the same. Then, for the rest of the day, the two widowed sisters-in-law sat in the living room with their heads back and their feet up, listening to classical music and relaxing as they talked about good times and bad, cried a little about the way things had worked out for them, and promised each other that everything would get better with time. Everything just *had* to get better with time.

Now, with the passing of a decade, Ethel had become completely organized around the premise that the only way forward was for her to be in control of everything — every*one* — around her. However, in trying to control David, she began to lose sight of what might have been in his best interest. "But she just didn't know how to handle a drug addict," explained Leah Mason. "How was she to know? I mean, who was to teach her? No one knew what they were doing. The reaching out to professionals was always dicey; there was always concern that someone they couldn't trust would tell the world their secrets. Once, Mrs. Kennedy confided in me, 'I've buried him a hundred times, already.' I asked what she meant, and with a trembling voice, she said, 'In my head. Every time David is late coming home. Every time I don't hear from him. Every time I don't know what he's doing. I bury him in my head. It's a mother's worst agony, burying her child, constantly repeating itself.' David didn't realize what he was doing to her; how could he?"

"Once, David was sitting in the kitchen rocking back and forth in a chair, seeming in a trance, muttering something," recalled Noelle Bombardier. "Maybe he was high, I don't know, but as I got closer I realized he was saying, 'I hate her. I hate her.' I asked him, 'Who do you hate?' He said, 'My mother.' I asked him, 'But why?' He said, 'Because she can't love me, and I don't know why. Do you know why?' I said, 'No, David, that's not true. She may not be able to express this to you, but I know she loves you very much. I wish you could see that.' "

Sometimes, outreach from household help to David would put them at odds with Ethel, who thought everyone was coddling him. One day in the kitchen in front of staff members, Ethel really let Ena have it when she saw her hovering over David, who was nursing a hangover. "Mrs. Kennedy ordered David out of the kitchen and then tore into Ena, demanding that she stop trying to make David so comfortable as long as he was doing drugs in her home," said Leah Mason. " 'I am *not interested* in his comfort,' Mrs. Kennedy said. Ena challenged her about it. Finally, Mrs. Kennedy got within inches of Ena's face and, with a great deal of heated emotion, declared,

'You don't know what it's like for me as a mother. You have no idea. *No idea at all.*' Ena got indignant and responded, 'I have a child of my own, Mrs. Kennedy, or have you forgotten that?' Mrs. Kennedy shot back, 'Well, until *your* child is a drug addict, I don't want to hear another word out of your mouth. That is *my* son, Ena. *Stop enabling him.*' "

At this time, Kathleen surprised everyone by applying to the court to be David's trustee. People outside the family assumed that she wasn't happy with the decisions her mother was making and decided to step in herself. Maybe there's some truth to that, but she really couldn't have gotten far without the approval of the family's iron-willed matriarch. Kathleen felt her mother had had enough of David and could use some distance from the decision-making process. Even though her intention was not to usurp her mother, her actions did often spark tension. "*I* know what's right for my son," Ethel told her in front of witnesses during one angry altercation. "He's *my* child, not yours." Generally, though, Ethel was happy her daughter had taken control of the situation and understood that she did it out of concern for her.

Outlining her own plan for him, Kathleen sent David to a rehab center that had previously treated Christopher Lawford. It didn't work. Then she sent him to England to be treated by a surgeon pioneering neuroelectric therapy. That, too, was not successful. Months later, she checked him into Massachusetts General Hospital. The treatment didn't take. After that, she chose another rehab center in Spofford, New Hampshire. No go. Then, in March 1984, she checked him into St. Mary's Rehabilitation Center in Minneapolis. Nothing seemed to work.

Throughout this time, Kathleen was consumed by her brother's illness, agonizing about whether she was making the right decisions and blaming herself that nothing she did made a bit of difference. The toll David's addiction took on her was incalculable, the stress wearing her down. She now appeared to be much older than her thirty-three years. Extremely thin, she sported a short-cropped, easy-to-manage haircut and wore large, thick, and not very becoming glasses. She almost never wore makeup. Not only was she David's advocate, she had a busy career working as a property program analyst at the Massachusetts State House in Governor Michael Dukakis's Office of Human Resources. Of course, she also had her family, three children by the onset of 1984. She was definitely stretched to the limit.

A Gathering of the Original Eleven

In April 1984, Ethel wanted to host a gathering at Hickory Hill of what she called "the Original Eleven." This was a congregation of all her children but no spouses — at this point just Kathleen and Bobby Jr. were married — or significant others, boyfriends, girlfriends, or other people who always seemed to be hanging around the estate. Sometimes getting "the Original Eleven" together was a lot of trouble; everyone always had commitments, some lived a great distance from Hickory Hill, some just didn't want to show up because they didn't know what to expect, especially lately. The problem with the Kennedys was that things could change dramatically in just a day or two; there was no telling what the temperature might be by the time the gathering was to take place. Often, these meals ended with a family dustup or, as Bobby would call it, "typical Kennedy family drama." However, Ethel maintained that it was important for the family to get together, check in with one another, and update one another on whatever was going on in their lives. Therefore, she would plan these dinners far enough in advance so that no one could beg off.

On this night, it was extremely tense as everyone gathered around Ethel's dining room table, obviously because of David's problems. "They tried to ignore what was happening to him so that they could just have a nice meal together," Leah Mason, Ethel's employee who was helping out with kitchen duties that day, recalled, "but it was impossible. Talk about the elephant in the room. Ena and the waitstaff kept bringing out one dish after another while Mrs. Kennedy and Kathleen kept *ooh*ing and *aah*ing over the food, trying to keep everyone upbeat. Bobby and Joe were talking in an animated way, joking with each other. I kept peeking out from the kitchen, trying to see if everything was okay. At one point, I saw David slipping down in his chair. His brother Max kept nudging him, but it wasn't working. I didn't want Mrs. Kennedy to notice, so I came out of the kitchen with some Irish-style mashed potatoes, put the serving dish down on the table, and then whispered urgently in his ear, *'Sit up. David. Right now.'* And he did. I knew that Mrs. Kennedy saw me out of the corner of her eye; I caught her scowling at me as I slipped out of the room."

After the first couple of courses, David began nodding off. Though his mother and siblings talked rapid-fire around him about current events and kept trying to bring him into the conversation, he was disinterested. It became clear that he wasn't going to last through the entire meal.

"David, sit up," Ethel finally exclaimed, unable to continue to act as if he were okay.

"Oh my God. Just get off my case, will you please?" he grumbled. According to the witness, Leah Mason, there was silence, or as she put it, "you could hear a pin drop." Ethel stared intensely at David for a moment before saying in a loud voice, *"If you want to go, David, just go.* But don't expect any of us to care about you if you don't want to be a part of this family. I have had it with you. *I swear to God."*

David looked at his mother with disdain. "Figures you would say that," he remarked. At that point, a couple of his siblings tried to talk to him, murmuring in low voices for him to be calm, to not cause a scene, to "please, just for once" let mealtime unfold without drama. It was too late, though. Ethel slammed both hands on the table, causing the plates and silverware before her to rattle. "I don't know what you want from me," she shouted at her son angrily. *"What do you want me to say?"*

David jumped out of his chair, stood up, and faced his mother, his face beet red with fury. *"How about that you love me?"'"* he screamed at her. "How about that there's nothing wrong with me? How about that you're proud of me? How about any of *that*?" He then ran out of the room.

Ethel stared straight ahead, not making direct eye contact with anyone at the table. There was a moment of silence — maybe a minute, maybe less — before Kathleen began to apologize profusely for her brother. "He didn't mean it, Mummy," she said. "He's just. . . . he's just . . . he's just . . ." Ethel didn't want to hear it. The Kennedy matriarch slid her chair out from under the table, stood up, said "Excuse me," and left the room.

Ethel Kennedy, a woman still so traumatized by having witnessed the murder of her beloved husband, now found herself woefully lacking in her ability to deal with or even understand her son's drug addiction. "One night soon after, Mrs. Kennedy hosted a party for the RFK Human Rights organization at Hickory Hill," recalled Noelle Bombardier. "She tried to be upbeat, typical Ethel Kennedy, gay and happy and flitting about, the perfect hostess. At one point, though, she disappeared into the bathroom. She was gone a long time. I went to find her to make sure she was okay. When I put my ear to the door, I heard that she was crying. I was about to knock and ask if she needed something. However, I didn't. I knew she would have been embarrassed. So I decided to let her have her privacy."

On April 19, David Kennedy flew down to Palm Beach, Florida, to be with some of his cousins as they visited their grandma Rose for the Easter holiday. About a week later, Ethel got the call: David had been found in his hotel room, dead of a drug overdose. He was only twenty-eight.

BLACK MIST

Not surprisingly, David Kennedy's death cast a pall over Hickory Hill, with all its residents, Kennedys and staff members alike, trying their best to process many different layers of grief and trauma. "Usually, the estate was filled with noisy activity, but after David's death there was such immense sadness, I didn't think any of us would get through it," said Noelle Bombardier, speaking for the household staff. "We went about our duties as if in a daze. I would find myself struggling to hold back tears. As much trouble as David had been, he'd also been such a gentle soul. He would come into the servants' dining room and sit with me sometimes. We would talk about marriage and children, and he would say, 'I don't think that will ever happen for me, Noelle.' I would ask, 'But why, David?' And he would answer, 'Because I'll never be special to anyone.' "

After David's death, her coworkers felt that Ena Bernard, who was sixty-six, should take some time off. After all, she had known David since the day he was born and had helped care for him as an infant. "She almost had what they used to call a nervous breakdown," said Noelle Bombardier. "She seemed to not be present. You'd talk to her and she wouldn't hear you.

"I remember the family had David laid out in the drawing room in his casket. It was open and people kept going in, falling to their knees, crying and praying. Ena refused to look at David that way. She simply couldn't do it. I asked, 'Why are we doing this? Why such torture?' and one of the boys said, 'I don't know why, Noelle. It's killing us, but it's tradition and it's what Mummy wants.' "

Immediately after the funeral, Ena had to go to the graduation of her grandaughter — Fina's daughter — from Florida State University. "Somehow we got her on the plane," said Leah Mason, "and she went to the ceremony. But by the time she got back after a few days, she was really undone. We were all concerned about her."

Many of Ethel's grown children who lived elsewhere came back to Hickory Hill with their own spouses and children for a while just to be together under one roof. As is the case with many families who suffer such trauma, though, David's death was rarely openly discussed. There were isolated camps of siblings where the subject was raised —

one brother might feel free to discuss it with another over a beer while two sisters might find emotional refuge in each other at lunch — but there was no true family reconciliation of the tragedy. Once David was gone, his passing was just viewed as too painful to process. Exactly as they'd handled JFK's and RFK's deaths, the Kennedys — and not just Ethel's family, but all of them — tried to avoid the subject. Something was missing, though, a piece of them, and they all knew it. Bobby, in particular, took it badly. He realized it could have been him. Had he not found a way to deal with his own problems, there was no way he would have survived it. He wondered why he was so fortunate and David not as blessed.

"Mrs. Kennedy went into a deep depression that I would say lasted at least a year," said Leah Mason. Ethel still had many social and philanthropic obligations. She was determined to keep her schedule and maintain that stoic "Kennedys don't cry" image the world had come to expect of her. However, it was now more work for Ethel than ever before, than even after Bobby was assassinated. Maybe it was because she was older and not as resilient as she'd been back in 1968. Plus, the deep wound from Bobby's death was still present. While she could appear remarkably unruffled in public, she was actually deeply sedated. She was also going to Confession twice a week, as if grappling with some sin she felt was beyond atonement.

"I would catch her just staring into space, seeming lost," said Leah. "It was as if she was in a black mist. I remember there was a lot of discussion about a photograph of David that was in a silver frame on the mantel over the fireplace. Should it stay? Or was it a bad reminder? How would it affect Mrs. Kennedy? The kids? Some days it was there. Other days Ena took it and hid it.

"Mrs. Kennedy's friend Liz Stevens would come by often and sit with her in the kitchen, trying to console her. I overheard Mrs. Kennedy tell her, 'I have a hole in my heart that will never heal. I just have to live with it because when David died, my chance to be a better mother died with him.' I remember feeling upset hearing those words; my knees felt as if they would buckle. I had to stand with my back against the refrigerator. Mrs. Stevens just held Mrs. Kennedy's hand. There were no words."

In Her DNA

Though Kathleen Kennedy Townsend had done all she could think of for her brother, she had to accept once he was gone that her efforts had been in vain. There was nothing she could have done, and for a woman who describes herself as "a results-oriented person," this was not easy to accept. Her way of coping was by becoming incredibly busy. Maybe as a distraction from her sorrow, she began to balance motherhood with public service pursuits. Inspired by her work a couple of years earlier in 1982 as her uncle Ted's campaign director for his Senate seat that year, she had already started to lean in the direction of politics as her way to fulfill the family's mandate to serve. At first, Ethel wasn't sure how she felt about it.

In some respects, Ethel Kennedy still thought politics was a tough business better suited for men. She was a woman of her time in that she held fast to some old-fashioned ideas, some of which flew in the face of the reality of her life. "She was in transition by the 1980s," said her daughter Kerry. "She would say, for instance, that women shouldn't work, but then all of us knew that she worked harder than anyone. She was always packing her bags, going off on one important activist trip or another to distant corners of the globe. That was hard work, whether she viewed it that way or not." Kathleen added, "Our mother was a feminist long before the phrase was coined and long before she even knew she was. She'd raised us girls to have minds of our own. She never wanted us to be limited by societal restrictions. Never. It was a slow process, I think, throughout maybe the seventies and eighties as our mother, like many women, came to terms with what their roles could and should be in society."

Like her mother, Kathleen, too, was in transition. Her journey to eventually becoming lieutenant governor of Maryland in 1995 really started with David's death.

In a lot of ways, Kathleen had wanted to be a stay-at-home mother. She had the perfect husband for it, too; David Townsend was nothing if not a family man. Still, Kathleen felt the pull of familial duty and honor to be a part of "the family business." After all, it was in her DNA, wasn't it? Kathleen says, "I think the women's movement influenced me to recognize that maybe I had strengths in me I hadn't known. Or at least it made me wonder if there was more for me."

Kathleen had inherited the burden of expectation, and she knew she had to carry it. On November 24, 1963, two days after her uncle Jack died, her father had written her a note that said, in part: "As the oldest of the Kennedy grandchildren you have a particular responsibility now . . . Be kind to others and work for your country. Love Daddy."

Four years later, in April 1967, Bobby Sr. toured the Mississippi Delta at the behest of civil rights lawyer Marian Wright Edelman to see firsthand the poverty there. Because of media coverage of the visit, many Americans would be stunned by the impoverished conditions and quite shocked to learn that this kind of terrible hardship was going on in their country. It would end up bringing to the national consciousness the seriousness of the hunger problem in America and start a real movement to reform food assistance programs. "He arrived home clearly moved and emotionally exhausted from seeing such dire poverty," Ethel recalled of her husband. "I remember it was a lovely evening and the table in our dining room was set," added Kathleen, who was sixteen at the time. "We had a really nice dining room with the chandelier and crystal glasses, a cook to cook dinner and somebody to serve it and Daddy was there and he said, 'I've just been to Mississippi and I saw a whole family living in a room the size of this dining room. Do you know how lucky you are?' He was shaking. '*Do you know how lucky you are?* You have to do something for our country. You have to give back.' " There was great injustice in the world on many fronts — poverty, illiteracy, racism — as Bobby kept reminding his children, and they should all try to do something constructive about it.

In 1986, when she was thirty-five, Kathleen officially decided to take the leap and enter the political arena by running for a seat in the House of Representatives in Maryland's Second Congressional District, which, by the way, was strongly Republican. From the start, it was clear she would have some work to do to be a good fit for politics. "Her voice is high-pitched and not authoritative sounding," noted one of her cattier critics in *The Boston Globe*. "She has thick glasses. She's not really attractive, is she?" *Time* couldn't help but notice "her slip showing and her hair a mess."

"Sexism is something Kathleen had to deal with from an early age," recalled Noelle Bombardier. "Maybe she wasn't as pretty as her sisters, but Kathleen was never one to obsess about fashion and makeup. She was anything but superficial. Still, she was stung by criticism of her appearance, as was Mrs. Kennedy. 'So this is what it comes to now in being of service?' Mrs. Kennedy raged. 'It comes down to how *pretty* we are?' We all felt it was ridiculous, but despite the great advances made in the seventies, these were still the times in which we lived."

Besides any apparent image problems, a big mistake for Kathleen in 1986 was her decision not to use her Kennedy family name, eliminating it from most campaign posters and bumper stickers. "She wasn't 'Kathleen Kennedy,' she said. She was 'Kathleen Townsend,' " recalled David Burke, who had once been her uncle Ted's chief of staff, in a 2000 interview, "and she was proud of her husband and her children and the nuclear family she created for herself. 'I'm running as my own person,' she said. But I remember thinking it was a risk. Ted felt the same way. The Kennedy name obviously had a lot of cachet. Kathleen was a risk-taker, though. I think that said something about her."

"My mother wasn't so sure that dropping the Kennedy name was a good idea for me," Kathleen said. " 'It carries a lot of weight,' she said, so why would I not take advantage of it? I think my mom realized she couldn't have it both ways," Kathleen concluded with a smile. "Either she had raised a daughter to believe she was capable of making her own important decisions, or she hadn't. Of course, she had."

"As women, it is time to stand up for ourselves and for our ideas," Kathleen said at one campaign rally. She wore a sensible navy-blue skirt and white long-sleeved blouse with a high-buttoned collar. She had a simple gold necklace around her neck, a pin at her shoulder, and a large diamond ring on her finger, the only thing that suggested Kennedy status. Her earnestness was her best quality. While she spoke to a small crowd in the parking lot of a schoolyard, her sisters Rory, Kerry, and Courtney stood at her side, beaming. Kathleen was strong and persuasive.

The next day, an editorial in the press noted that Kathleen was "big on rhetoric, short on specificity. People do seem to gravitate to her, though," the writer pointed out, "but likely not because of what is being said but because of who is saying it. One can't help but be transfixed by the lineage of Camelot. Now, if only Ethel and Ted would show up at one of these rallies."

When strangers asked her about her father, Kathleen was able to talk in detail about his achievements and the effect he still had on those who remembered him well; the same held true for her uncle Jack. However, she would visibly bristle when asked about Kennedys not in public service. "Tell me, were you upset when your aunt Jackie married that awful Greek?" an older woman asked Kathleen as she stood before her, paper in hand for an autograph. Kathleen caught her breath in surprise. A flicker of annoyance crossed her face. Then, looking directly into the stranger's eyes, she asked, "Would you not agree that a woman has the right to choose who she wants to be with, and that the rest of us should hold no judgment about it?" The stranger looked at Kathleen with a blank expression, muttered, "Um . . . sure, why not?" and then thrust the paper at her for her signature.

"That's the downside of being a Kennedy," Kathleen later told one reporter. "There's a lot of nonsense out there about us, and because I am out here in front of people the assumption is that I have to address it. I don't. My platform is not the Kennedys. It's education. It's taking care of our kids."

Unfortunately, her campaign never gained traction. "By Election Day, the party had pretty much written her off," Karen Tumulty reported for CNN, "removing her name from its list of priority candidates. She lost by eighteen percentage points — the only Kennedy ever to lose a general election. What she needed to learn was how to break the Kennedy mold without destroying its value."

In the end, Kathleen was defeated by the incumbent Republican, Helen Delich Bentley, 59 percent to 41 percent. "It was pretty devastating," recalled Ethel. "After all, Grandpa [Joe] had always said, 'We don't want any losers around here. In this family we only want winners.' So Kathleen felt she'd let us down, especially me. Of course, that wasn't true, at all. We were proud of her for going for it. I always told her, 'Whatever it is. You have to go for it.' "

Of course, years later, in 1994, Kathleen became Parris Glendening's running mate and then, in November of that year, he became governor of Maryland and she his lieutenant governor. "It was a slow but I think sensible evolution," she would conclude. "I took my licks," she said, "or as my mom would say, 'Kennedys die with their boots on.' In other words, we just keep on going; we don't stop."

FRESH START

After his brother's death, Bobby Kennedy Jr. wanted to do everything he could to live a good, sober, and happy life. Considering everything he had been through — life on the run as a Kennedy refugee, the loss of his mentor, Lem, the drug overdose — he felt lucky to just be alive and was grateful that God had spared him, even if He hadn't done the same for David. He continued to devote himself to environmental concerns as well as to his marriage; and he and Emily had another child to join Bobby III, a girl born in 1988 whom they named Kathleen ("Kick" for short, after Bobby's deceased aunt by the same name). By the early 1990s, though, the relationship had run its course. Some people in their lives insist he cheated on Emily and, truth be told, it certainly wouldn't be out of the realm of possibility. One thing was certain: As a response to what happened to David, Bobby felt that life was too short to be unhappy. He deserved happiness, he told

Emily, and so did she. He wanted them both to have fresh starts. Therefore, in 1993, the couple separated and she filed for divorce. It wasn't ugly, though. It was a relief, some in the family felt, to see two people make a decision that they weren't right for each other and then end things without a lot of acrimony.

That same year, Bobby — still technically married — began dating a best friend of his sister Kerry's, an uncommonly attractive and vivacious brunette named Mary Kathleen Richardson. Mary and Kerry had known each other since they were fifteen; they met on their first day at Putney boarding school in Vermont. "The next weekend we hitchhiked to Boston to see my siblings Michael, Bobby, David, Courtney, and Kathleen, and for the rest of her life, she spent nearly every weekend and vacation with our family," Kerry would recall. "We were roommates from the time we were fifteen until thirty, when I got married [in 1990]."

Mary had been a straight-A student at Brown, where she and Kerry were also roommates. "We were inseparable," Kerry recalled, "we shared friendships, a closet, a cash card. People couldn't tell our voices apart. Mary was brilliant, strikingly beautiful, radiant, luminous, spiritual, funny, fun. At any time there would be a handful of students waiting for when Mary might be free for a talk, but what they really wanted was a listen. Even as a teenager, Mary listened with compassion to all our adolescent pain and confusion, affirmed our feelings, and made us whole."

Whereas Emily was homespun, Mary — seven years Bobby's junior — was sophisticated, with long, dark hair past her shoulders and brown eyes that were her most spectacular feature; they were large, soulful, and endlessly intelligent. Raised Catholic, she was one of six siblings born to a father who was a professor at Hoboken's Stevens Institute of Technology and a mother who was an English teacher in public schools. A big presence on the New York social scene for a while, hanging out with notables like Halston, Calvin Klein, and Andy Warhol (who mentions her several times in his published diary), she was popular, someone to whom others seemed to gravitate. "Mary combined that RFK/roll-up-your-sleeves/get-the-job-done ethos with Jackie's otherworldly elegance, including the breathy voice," recalled Michael Mailer, a close friend of hers during this time.

A graduate of Brown, Mary was smart, creative, and an architectural designer at the prestigious design firm Parish-Hadley. There was also something sort of edgy about her. She had been a family friend for years, her status in that regard making her a little off-limits and taboo, which, admittedly, also made her all the more appealing to Bobby.

Her attributes aside, Mary did have some particularly troubling emotional issues. She suffered from depression. All her friends and family members knew it because, throughout her life, it had been so absolutely debilitating. At twelve, she stopped talking for almost two weeks, either unable to express her emotions or unwilling. She was diagnosed with anorexia as a teenager and at twenty-two ended up being treated for it in Boston's McLean Hospital for more than three months. Whenever things took a bad turn for her, she would talk about suicide. At twenty-five, she tied a plastic bag over her head, but then panicked when she began to run out of air and ripped it away. At twenty-six, she took two hundred barbiturates, regurgitating them before they could take effect. Her eating disorder continued unabated, with bingeing and purging. She became addicted to alcohol and prescription medication. However, in 1989, she finally took hold of her life, went to AA, and became sober. Clean living, though, did not mean an end to her emotional problems. She could still fall into the darkest of moods, becoming agitated over seemingly nothing, and then lash out. John Hoving, a social worker and friend of hers, recalled, "What Mary projected to the world was not someone with an illness. She kept most people at arm's length, giving the impression that she had it all together. But I lived it. There was no way that this woman was not very, very sick. In two seconds flat, she could flip from anger and rage into white-picket-fence mode, put on her Martha Stewart face, and convince anybody, including her own family, that she was in control of her faculties, environment, and personal matters. It was always jarring."

Obviously, all the Kennedys knew of Mary's problems, though with the exception of Kerry, they were unaware of her suicide attempts. Because he, too, had struggled so much in his own life, Bobby's heart went out to Mary. He was still sober after his overdose back in 1983, but it had been difficult for him. He felt he understood Mary's demons and wanted to help her, especially because he still felt guilty about what had happened to David — or as his brother Douglas put it: "He had this Saint Francis complex where he felt he could save people, and Mary fell into that realm."

Before he knew it, Bobby had fallen for Mary.

In March he flew to the Dominican Republic for a quick divorce. Mary was six months pregnant by this time and he wanted to get on with his life with her. Emily didn't fight it.

Though Mary was in love with Bobby, she wasn't so naive as to think he was someone in whom she could fully place her trust. After all, from the time she was a teenager, she'd known what Kennedy men were generally

379

like; it's not as if she was blind to their failings. Not only was Mary Kerry's best friend, long before her first date with Bobby she had worked for him at the RFK Center for Justice and Human Rights (before it became known as Robert F. Kennedy Human Rights). She'd also designed the logo for Joe when he started Citizens Energy — she'd compiled its first annual report as well — and then volunteered for Joe's campaign when he ran for Congress. So, suffice it to say, she'd been around Kennedy men for some time and knew how they generally treated women. "She knew the score" is how one of her friends put it. Even given what she knew, though, officially marrying into the family after being around them most of her life was a heady thought for Mary.

"Does it make me sound shallow that I really want to be a Kennedy?" she asked her friend Alyssa Chapman. The two were in Macy's in New York trying on expensive dresses. It was October 1993 and Bobby had said Mary should "go wild" with her spending as his present to her for her thirty-fourth birthday. "Does it sound like I have stars in my eyes?" Mary asked. "Because you know that's not me."

"No," Alyssa assured her, according to her memory of the conversation. "Every girl wants to become a princess. The Kennedys are about as close to royalty as you can get." However, she added, given what Mary had seen in the family, was she really sure that this was what she wanted for herself? "It's not all golden," she reminded Mary. Mary said she understood the two sides to being a Kennedy and that she was willing to take a chance that there would be more sweet than bitter. "Do you love Bobby?" Alyssa asked. "Or just the idea of being a Kennedy?"

"Both," Mary said, trying to be honest. "I don't know how you can parse it out," she reasoned. "It's what he brings to the table, isn't it? Being a Kennedy."

In Mary's view, Bobby's whole world glimmered with promise. She had long admired his determination to be of service, and his work as lead attorney for Riverkeeper had made her understand the importance of caring for the environment; she hoped to contribute to that effort. He believed he could make a difference, and she loved that about him. Moreover, she had great respect for his devotion to his children. She believed that when they had kids of their own he would be a strong and dependable father. She recalled that she'd lost her own father when she was twelve to colon cancer; he'd gone into the hospital and passed away quickly before she even had a chance to say goodbye. Therefore, she said, she felt that the sudden loss of a beloved father was something else she had in common with Bobby. "So, yes," she decided, thinking out loud, "it's more than just being

Maybe it wasn't so surprising that Mary Richardson was concerned about Bobby's ex-wife, Emily, with whom Bobby maintained a good relationship. The former spouses spent a lot of time together, too much as far as Mary was concerned. Mary's antenna was up about Bobby. While he insisted that he and Emily were simply co-parenting their children — she would remarry shortly after the divorce — Mary didn't know if she should believe him. The fact that trust had become an issue for her so early in their relationship probably should have raised red flags for both of them. However, Bobby felt Mary would learn to have faith in him with time, and that he should just continue to be as honest as possible when it came to Emily. As long as he didn't have any secrets, he felt, things would work out.

One day after Bobby took the kids on a picnic with Emily, he returned home to his pregnant fiancée and found her in a rage. She was convinced that something was going on with Emily. She was so hysterical, she had completely unraveled. It was as if she had dreamed up a scenario of infidelity while Bobby was gone and then spiraled out of control within a few hours' time. Though Bobby insisted nothing was going on with Emily, Mary wouldn't accept it. One thing led to another and, before he knew it, she hauled off and punched him right in the face. Because she'd had some boxing training, she knew how to land a right cross, and in doing so, her diamond engagement ring cut deep into Bobby's cheek. When Mary saw the blood, she burst into tears and crumpled into a heap on the floor. All this melodrama over nothing was more than Bobby could handle; he screamed at Mary and took off to get medical treatment.

The next morning found the couple full of apologies: she for not believing and then hitting him and he for not being more sensitive to her concerns. Mary begged Bobby to forgive her and pleaded with him not to tell Kerry or any of the other Kennedys what had happened. He agreed to come up with a lie to explain the stitches under his eye. When Bobby said he'd had a gardening accident as a way of explaining his injury, Kerry didn't believe him. After all, she and Mary had been best friends for years. "Mary's was a classic mental illness," she recalled, "which made her so unlike herself — kind, generous . . . perfect friend, force for good on our earth — that it was as if she'd been invaded by a foreign body. Every time I saw it happening, it scared me. I never held her accountable because that was her disease, not who she was as a person, and we all knew it."

As much as she loved Mary, Kerry began to question the wisdom of her brother's decision to marry her. Kerry didn't know what to expect of the union and was actually fearful about it. "It's true what they say," she told one relative. "Our greatest fears lie in anticipation," she said, quoting Balzac.

Even Ethel could see trouble ahead and tried to reason with Mary. After all, she knew her son well and recognized that even sober he wasn't easy. "None of the men in this family are a walk in the park," is how she so aptly put it. She'd known Mary since she was young and wasn't sure she was cut out for life as a Kennedy wife. Mary told Ethel she was eager to marry her son. Finally, according to one verifiable account, Ethel just warned her flat-out: "I know him better than anyone, and he's not for you. Not right now, anyway. Because I love you, Mary, I must insist that you wait." Mary disagreed. She said she knew what she was doing. Therefore, on April 15, 1994, she and Bobby Kennedy were married.

"Bobby was determined to make it work,"

said one of his relatives. "At the wedding, I pulled him aside and said, 'Man, I'm a little worried. Will you be okay? I mean, she hit you, Bobby. She actually hit you.' He looked at me, smiled that great smile of his, and said, 'Look, God has given me opportunities my brother David will never have to once and for all be happy, to have a good marriage, to have more kids. I don't want to waste time analyzing it and trying to figure it all out. I just need go with my gut that Mary is the one. So, yes,' he concluded, 'I'll be okay. I'm sure of it.' "

■ ■ ■ ■

PART VII
THE RECKONING

■ ■ ■ ■

HEAVY IS THE HEAD

By September 1996, it had been more than a year and a half since Michael Kennedy and Marisa Verrochi were found in bed by his wife. It speaks to the distant and strained relationship she had with her parents that Marisa still had not fully disclosed to them what was going on. June and Paul Verrochi would later be clear that they still didn't know about Michael. This strains credulity. After all, many people in their hometown of Cohasset were whispering about the relationship and wondering about it. Marisa had even been photographed at the Kennedy compound, with the pictures being published in the local newspapers. How could they not have known? "They continued to look the other way" is how one friend of the family's explained it. "They knew, but they didn't want to know."

In September, things took a dramatic turn when Marisa — who would turn eighteen in four months — enrolled in college. She now said she wanted to look to the future and close the book on Michael. She felt she deserved a new life and didn't want him to be a part of it. However, Michael refused to let her go. Instead, he continued to call upon her and surprise her with unwelcome visits. He even began to stalk her, or at least he kept showing up at places uninvited.

It was starting to get ugly, so much so that Michael Skakel took it upon himself to take Marisa to a mental health professional to help her sort through her emotions. However, when word got back to Michael that Skakel had done so, he was upset. It was just a matter of time, he feared, before word would leak out about him and Marisa via someone they couldn't control — the therapist. The cousins had an argument about it, with Michael accusing Skakel of not being on his side but being, instead, on Marisa's. Then, at this same time, Marisa became angry with Skakel for even confirming to Michael that he'd taken her for help. Everyone seemed to be turning on one another, as often happens when people find themselves complicit in the keeping of secrets.

When Marisa enrolled in college, she and her father began to have a bit more communication, related to her tuition. However, he still didn't push her about Michael and she still wasn't forthcoming about it.

Meanwhile, Ethel had still not gotten

anywhere with Michael. Compounding her confusion, she'd recently begun to interpret his bad decision-making as a personal affront. "I feel like he's punishing me for something," she confided to one good friend of hers, "but for the life of me, I don't know what for." Her friend was an Englishwoman about ten years Ethel's senior who'd once worked for her mother back when Ann Skakel had a house full of British servants. She and Ethel had forged a friendship when Ethel was a teenager, and all these years later they remained friends. She was divorced with no children. "One does wonder," she responded. She was taken aback by Ethel's observation in that it suggested a surprising level of introspection. Perhaps Ethel was growing? If so, this confidante couldn't resist taking her lead and building a bit on her theory. "Maybe Michael is in pain," she offered, "and maybe he wants *you* to feel what *he* feels."

Ethel let the hypothesis sink in, but not for long. "Are you suggesting that all of this is *my* fault?" she asked. No, of course not, her friend answered. She then tried to explain that her conjecture had nothing to do with Ethel's possible culpability. Rather, it was a mere speculation as to why Michael might be lashing out. "So, it's always the mother's fault, isn't it?" Ethel asked, still missing the point. "No, that's not it at all," her friend said, and by this time she was sorry she'd ever gone down this road with Ethel. "What I meant was —" Ethel cut her off. "Stop talking," she said angrily. Then, walking away, she muttered, "I have better things to do with my time than to explain to you how *families* work."

"I thought to myself, Oh well, same old Ethie," recalled her friend, using her nickname for her. "I wasn't offended. After all, I'd known her for more than forty years."

Years earlier, Ethel would probably have left things as they were; certainly she was used to putting a person in her place without much regret. Maybe she really *was* growing, though, because the next day she called to apologize. "I have a lot on my mind," Ethel said, "and I took it out on you. I'm sorry."

Ethel also revealed another reason she'd been so upset. She said that the night before she'd decided to attend an Al-Anon meeting in order to become better educated about substance abuse. To that end, she and her friend Elizabeth Stevens — who'd suggested the idea — drove to the church in which the meeting was being held. They then sat in the car outside for an hour until finally Ethel decided she couldn't go inside. She feared being recognized and didn't have it in her to deal with it. She felt terrible about it, she now said. Why, she wondered, couldn't she put her pride aside long enough to help her son?

Trying to reassure Ethel, her friend said it was admirable that she'd at least tried to attend the meeting and that maybe next time she'd be able to do so. "Meanwhile, don't worry, Ethie," she advised. "Michael is smart. He'll figure this thing out," to which she responded, "I'm afraid there's a big difference between intelligence and wisdom."

"Relax and try not to let it all get to you," concluded Ethel's friend.

"I will," Ethel said.

"Heavy is the head, Ethie," said her friend.

"Excuse me?"

". . . that wears the crown."

Ethel chuckled and said, *"I wish."*

"I DON'T FEEL THINGS"

Likely one of the reasons June and Paul Verrochi were able to avoid the subject of their daughter, Marisa, and Michael was because none of their friends who'd heard whispers about the relationship had the nerve to bring it up to them. That changed, though, when a good friend of June's named Linda Del Vecchio decided to broach the subject.

Linda had been hearing stories about Michael and Marisa for at least a year. During a luncheon at Ye Olde Union Oyster House in Boston on November 3, 1996, she tried to bring things out into the open by asking June about Marisa and Michael. June, immediately defensive, said that Marisa was almost eighteen, old enough to make her own decisions. It was then that Linda posed the question: "But how long has this been going on? I've heard it's been for some time." That's when June lost it. She started to sob so hard, three waiters rushed over to help. "On some level," she managed to say, "I think I always knew."

However, she said she was afraid to have it confirmed because she was worried about what it might do to her daughter if she was forced to admit it.

"You must talk to Marisa immediately," Linda told June. "Promise me you will," she insisted. Through her tears, June agreed. Then, she had a thought. "Vicki once told me that Michael had a repressed Catholic upbringing," she said. "Do you think that has something to do with it?" she asked. "Who cares?" Linda responded. Then, as if still trying to put the pieces together, June further observed, "He's lived such a spoiled, entitled existence. Maybe that's what this is about. Maybe he believes he can get away with anything." Linda became exasperated. "*Who cares* what his issues are, June?" she exclaimed. "He's too old for Marisa. Get your daughter away from him. *Now.*"

That night, June called Paul, who had gone to Washington on business. She anxiously told him about her luncheon and asked him to return. He canceled his meetings and came back to Cohasset the next morning.

Marisa had classes that day, November 4, but later in the afternoon she was confronted by her parents. Feeling cornered, she denied she and Michael were anything other than just friends. June and Paul said they didn't know whether to believe her. Upset, Marisa left their home in tears, went back to campus, and . . . called Michael. Details of the conversation between the two are unknown, but based on Michael's subsequent call to Michael Skakel, it's clear that he understood the gravity of the situation.

Michael Skakel happened to be sailing with Michael Kennedy's brother Max when he got the call on his cell phone. Though there was poor reception, Kennedy's message was clear: "Get your fat ass back here immediately," he demanded, "because all hell is breaking loose." He told Skakel that Marisa's parents had confronted her, but that she had denied everything. "It looks like the shit is really going to hit the fan," Kennedy said. Skakel agreed that he would return.

After discussing it more fully, June and Paul began to believe that Marisa was covering for Michael. Late that evening, an incensed Paul confronted Michael after pounding on his front door and demanding to be let into the house. The two men then had a heated conversation, during which Michael insisted that he and Marisa had never been anything more than just friends. Michael said he was insulted that Paul would ever think otherwise.

As soon as Paul left, Michael got on the telephone with Marisa to tell her about the visit. Because he was so upset and talking so quickly, Marisa couldn't quite figure out what he had told her father. However, based on his emotional state, she surmised — incorrectly

— that he had pretty much come clean about everything. Now Marisa was the frantic one. In her mind, the secret was out. She felt she had no choice but to tell her parents what had been going on, starting with her mother.

Early the next morning, November 5, Marisa met with June and this time confessed everything, all of it tearfully coming forth with an abundance of emotion — even the surprising and upsetting revelation that the relationship with Michael had actually begun back when she was just fourteen! This would have been two years before Vicki found Michael and Marisa in bed together. In fact, it would have been two years before Marisa had even moved into the Kennedy household! Was this possible? Though Michael, in months to come, would steadfastly deny it, it was Marisa's testimony to her parents just the same.

"No, no," June protested. "I don't believe you, Marisa," she exclaimed.

According to one confirmed account, Marisa looked her mother squarely in the eyes and said, "Yes. You do, Mother. *You know you do.*"

Now there was no stopping the chain reaction.

June called Paul. He raced over. Marisa then told him the same story.

Livid, Paul stormed out of the house and went straight to Citizens headquarters. In front of stunned witnesses, he burst into Michael's office, his anger flaring. Michael immediately stood up from his desk chair, drawing himself to his full height and lifting his head as if hoping to intimidate Paul. According to witnesses, Paul drew back as if he were about to punch Michael right in the face. He didn't, though. Instead, he broke down into tears. "How could you do this?" was the only question he could ask Michael. "This is my *daughter,* Michael. How could you do this?" He must have asked the question ten times. Michael didn't have an answer, though. Finally, a distraught Paul screamed at Michael that he was a pathetic excuse for a man and left the premises without incident.

Michael was haunted by Paul's question. *"How could you do this? How could you do this?"* If anything, the altercation with his former friend brought to the fore something Michael Kennedy had suspected all along, which was that he didn't feel much genuine emotion with regard to Marisa. "Paul asked me how I could do it," he recalled to one relative. "And he kept asking me and asking me *and asking me.* And the only thing I could think of was that I was sure someone with a heart could've answered the question. But that wasn't me. I'm not normal," he sadly concluded. "I don't feel things."

Two days later, on November 7, at about three in the morning, June Verrochi climbed up onto the roof of the family's six-story Commonwealth Avenue town house. It was pouring rain; she was barefoot and in a white silk nightgown. As a small crowd gathered on the sidewalk below, June didn't make a move. She was dangerously close to the edge. Someone called Marisa, who then called Michael Skakel, who summoned the police. Both rushed to the scene. An hour later, they watched as firefighters used a one-hundred-foot ladder to bring June down from the roof. Once she was safe on the ground, June collapsed — not into her daughter's arms, but rather into Michael Skakel's. He then accompanied her to Massachusetts General Hospital.

The next day, a spokeswoman for June said that she had not intended to try to commit suicide. She explained that June had "received some very disturbing news and was taking doctor-prescribed medication." She added, "We're not going to discuss it any further."

After news of June's breakdown made the papers, Vicki once again confronted Michael about Marisa. According to a friend of hers, she was as clear with him as she could be: "I want the truth, goddamn it, Michael. You've lied so much, you've forgotten what truth is even like." Maybe he knew she was right, because this time Michael was candid: Yes, he and Marisa had been involved, he confessed, but he thought maybe it was over. He wasn't sure.

In his defense, Michael noted that his psychiatrist had recently diagnosed him a sex addict and figured that this condition was at least partially responsible for his behavior. Michael said he was surprised; he'd thought of himself as either a psychopath or sociopath and believed that this was why he'd always been unable to connect with his feelings or would mimic emotions he couldn't really experience. He was heartened, he said, to be told that true a psychopath or sociopath — they're actually two different conditions with similar characteristics but key differences — doesn't question his lack of emotion; it actually never occurs to him to do so. The doctor told him he probably had suppressed his feelings after his father was murdered rather than experience deep and prolonged grief, and that the family's historic pathology of avoidance just served to feed such behavior. All this made sense to Michael. It felt like an answer, anyway, to questions about himself he'd been asking for years. Now, he said, all he wanted was to learn to be a better man. He was going to check into a rehab facility in Arizona and get help, he told Vicki. Would she come back to him if he officially ended it with Marisa?

If?

Vicki said absolutely not. Was he out of his mind? He had put her through too much, and she was done with him. She was sick of his endless self-absorption; every concern of his was about himself and how he felt about things and what he was going through. What about her? "How little you must think of me," she said angrily. She then swept up their children and fled to her father's mansion in Connecticut, moving in with him and Kathie Lee Gifford.

Soon after, she filed for a legal separation.

RUN WITH THE FOX

It was December 18, 1996. Ethel Kennedy was sitting in a back booth of a restaurant at the Boston Harbor Hotel at Rowes Wharf with Michael Skakel. At sixty-eight, she seemed older than her years, maybe closer to eighty, her face deeply etched by years of worry, frustration, and anger. She was wearing a black leather raincoat, her hair beneath a small matching leather hat. She was deep in conversation with her nephew about the situation with her son Michael.

While Ethel always knew that Skakel cared deeply about her family, some of her sons had recently told her they believed he was a traitor and more loyal to Marisa than to the Kennedys. Complicating things, rumors continued to circulate that Michael was somehow responsible for the death of Martha Moxley. Skakel had lately come to believe that Michael and Joe were actually the ones encouraging a criminal investigation against him because they believed he was a turncoat.

The question of Skakel's loyalty to the Kennedys came to a head at the end of 1996 when Paul Verrochi gave him letters he said Michael Kennedy had written to his daughter. Paul said he did it to prove to Skakel that Michael was still in pursuit of Marisa, even though she'd made it clear that she wanted nothing more to do with him. It stands to reason that Skakel, if he was really trying to be helpful to the Kennedys, would have been judicious in the handling of this correspondence. Certainly, he would have realized how damaging it could be in the wrong hands. However, Skakel decided to give them to, of all people, Vicki. That bizarre decision, compounded with the fact that he had taken Marisa to a therapist, made him seem suspect. "Nobody can stab you in the back quite like the guy who says he loves you" is how Joe Kennedy put it.

Ethel wasn't sure what to think about any of it, which is why she arranged the meeting with Skakel. According to what Skakel would later recall, she put her hand on his, leaned in toward him, and simply said, "I know everything." She searched his face, waiting for a response. "Everything, Aunt Ethel?" he asked. *"Everything,"* she repeated in a low voice.

Ethel told Michael that the family now had to focus on giving Joe a fighting chance to be governor. He was a good man, she insisted, who'd worked hard to be of service, just like his father. He had great ideas for the state, she said, and he deserved the opportunity to act on them. It would be completely unfair if the unfortunate business presently unfolding between Michael and Marisa were to jeopardize Joe's future in politics. She had always been worried about the impact of the resulting scandal should Michael's indiscretion become widely known, and her fear had not eased with the passing of time. She was also concerned, she added, because lately she really had to question Michael Skakel's allegiances. Was he loyal to the Kennedys or to the Verrochis? "Pick a side," she demanded, reminding him that loyalty was everything to the Kennedys. "Whose side are you on?"

"Yours," Skakel exclaimed. "I've always been on your side, Aunt Ethel."

If that was true, Ethel said, then why would he have given Vicki those damning letters Michael had written to Marisa? That made no sense to her. Skakel explained that he did it so that Vicki would understand, once and for all, that she needed to end her marriage to Michael. He did it, he said, not only for Vicki's sake but also for Michael's. "But that is not your place," Ethel exclaimed. "And why," she further inquired, would he take Marisa to a therapist?

"Same reason."

"That is not your place, either," Ethel said,

her temper rising. *"Both* are her *parents'* place, *not yours."*

"I'm sorry, Aunt Ethel," Michael said.

Ethel studied her nephew's face carefully. "Let me tell you something my mother used to say," she said, staring hard at him. "You cannot run with the fox and hunt with the hounds."

"What does that mean?" he asked.

"Figure it out."

In His Father's Shadow

Joseph Patrick Kennedy II was born on September 24, 1952, the second of Ethel's brood after Kathleen. He was just eleven in 1963 when his uncle Jack was assassinated. On the day JFK was buried, Joe's father, Bobby, wrote to him: "You are the oldest of all the male grandchildren. You have a special and particular responsibility now which I know you will fulfill. Remember all the things that Jack started — be kind to others that are less fortunate than we — and love our country." Six years later, his father was also taken from Joe. He'd been in boarding school when it happened and was flown across the country to be at his father's deathbed.

"Unlike some of his brothers and sisters, who may have been a little too young to have many precious memories of their father, Joe really had a history with him," observed Ben Bradlee. "He thought of him as a real hero. Once he was gone, he missed him terribly. No one in the family would ever forget that he had walked up and down the length of the train that carried Bobby's body from the funeral Mass in Manhattan to Washington, introducing himself to more than a thousand mourners and thanking them for their sympathy. He was only fifteen and, by the way, was wearing one of his father's suits. I heard Ethel later said, 'He's really got it, that kid. He's got it.' "

With the passing of time, there's little doubt that it was the loss of his father that fueled a kind of burning anger in Joe, just as in others of his relatives, and that it was this rage that fueled his tempestuous youth. Expelled from or otherwise dropping out of a number of schools, including the University of California, Berkeley, in 1972, from which he departed of his own volition, Joe was pretty much always in trouble. He and Ethel were always at odds. Maybe making things more complex for him was a pervasive feeling among the adults in his life that Joe wasn't all that bright. "It's just a shame that Joe isn't smart," Rose Kennedy once told her secretary Barbara Gibson as the two strolled along the beach. "Him being the oldest," Rose said with her clipped Boston accent, "it would be so much better if he was the smartest." Barbara said she sensed that the boy was doing his best. "Oh, I'm sure he is," Rose said, "and that's what I'm afraid of." When Barbara suggested that they just had to hope for the best from Joe, Rose countered with, "Hope all you like, dear, but we Kennedys prefer reality." Joe — as an adult — would come to believe that the entire time he was in school he was an undiagnosed dyslexic, and that this was the reason he'd had so much trouble with his studies.

Complicating his life was a fear in Joe, deep and ingrained, that he couldn't measure up to his father. Though he sat in Bobby's chair at the dinner table now, he believed in his heart that he would never be able to replace him. Still, as the oldest male, Joe was a father figure to many of his siblings and cousins; he did his best to keep them all in line, though he was rarely successful. As a result, many people in the family felt he had a chip on his shoulder. "I think Joe would think he was a wimp if someone told him he was a good listener," observed his first wife, Sheila Rauch Kennedy. "This is a man who has described himself as the family pit bull." Though others have been more charitable, they made the same point. "He's the family cynic" is how Michael once put it. "He's not always kind." Joe was especially competitive where his cousin John was concerned. After all, in his mind he was the one actually doing what people expected of him, but John was still the family's Golden Child. The two were not that close. "I think he loved John, hated John, and wanted to *be* John all at the same time"

408

is how Christopher Lawford put it.

One of the great trials of Joe's life unfolded in 1973.

On Saturday, August 11 of that year, Ethel and Ted sat down with Joe to have a serious talk. He had to stop being so irresponsible, Ted told him. His many siblings were looking to him as an example. "You've got to start making good decisions," he told him. "Remember that character is easier kept than recovered," he added. The family was counting on him, Ted told his nephew. He could be valuable in government one day and it would be a shame for him to squander the opportunity to serve.

At this time, the country was in the midst of the Watergate scandal, which would culminate with President Richard Nixon's resignation within a year. Ted and Ethel both thought the administration was full of liars and that the country was in dire need of a reset. It motivated them both to want to make sure the new generation of Kennedys was at least *trying* to better themselves in hopes that maybe one day they might be of real service. Ted said he would do anything he could for his nephew Joe, as always, and that if he felt he was about to make a wrong choice to please just call him and ask for help. He would drop everything, he said, and race over to him so that they could talk it out. Ethel agreed. "Be responsible. You're about to turn twenty-one. It's time to grow up," she said. "You are Joseph P. Kennedy the Second. *Act like it.*"

In his defense, Joe said he was trying his best but never got credit for anything he ever did right, only grief for what he'd supposedly done wrong. He was sick of it, he said. When would the two of them ever give him a break? After all, his uncle Teddy had done any number of terrible things, and "he turned out okay, didn't he?" Bringing up Ted's indiscretions right in front of him was going too far. "Spoken like a true failure," Ethel exclaimed. "You never disappoint, do you?" Then, according to this account, she walked up to Joe and, in one swift motion, hauled off and slapped him hard right across the face. "You'd better stop talking right now," she said angrily, "or I swear to God, *I will beat the Kennedy right out of you.*"

A couple of days later, Joe and David, then eighteen years old, along with David's girl-friend, Pamela Kelley, attended a barbecue on Nantucket with some other friends. Kelley's family members were permanent residents of Hyannis Port; her sister Kim had dated Bobby. Somehow Joe ended up behind the wheel of a Jeep, with David, Pamela, and four other girls crammed into it. He was joyriding. "It was typical Kennedy horseplay," Pamela Kelley would recall. "We were all

410

laughing as Joe spun the Jeep 'round and 'round and 'round until it started flipping over. I remember David and I holding on to the roll bar to keep from flying out, and I can still in my mind's eye see David's face as we were forced to let go of the Jeep. That's the last thing I remember." As a result of the accident, Pamela would be permanently paralyzed and forced to spend the rest of her life in a wheelchair. David would suffer injuries to his back, the treatment of which would factor into his deadly drug addiction.

The next day, a solemn Ethel sat in her kitchen at her home on the Cape, nervously drumming on the table with her fingernails while perusing the damning police report. Ena and her daughter, Fina, were also present. Fina sat down next to Ethel and put a comforting hand on her shoulder. To make her smile, she remembered that when Joe was about five, Fina — who was nineteen at that time — would say, "I heard from a little birdie that you were a bad boy. Is that true?" The wide-eyed tot would look all around him and ask, "Really? A little birdie? Was it yellow?" Then, pointing to a bird on the fence, he would ask, "Was it that yellow birdie right over there? I'll bet it was. Was it?" The memory worked; Ethel's face lit up if only for a second. "He was such a sweet boy," she said.

Noelle Bombardier, also present, recalled,

"As Ethel tried to concentrate on the police report, Ena said, 'Don't worry, Mrs. Kennedy. Whatever Joe did, I know he's sorry. You're right. You've raised him to be a sweet boy.' Ethel shook her head. 'Maybe. But he could be such a powerful force for good.'"

After she left the room, Noelle urged Ena and Fina to sit down with her at the table. "But we're not *allowed* to sit in here," Ena said. "Oh, just for a second," Noelle told her. "I promise we won't get arrested." The three women sat down, Ena very reluctantly. They were then joined by Leah Mason.

"We have to try to help Mrs. Kennedy through this tough time," Noelle told her coworkers. "If you see one of the kids misbehaving, come to me with it, not her. She has enough on her mind." Ena, feisty as ever, snapped back, "Well, if you ask me, she needs to love 'em more and holler at 'em less." Then she got up. "I have work to do," she muttered as she walked away. "She sure speaks her mind, your mom," Noelle told Fina. Fina chuckled and said, "Yes. I'm just glad Mrs. Kennedy didn't hear it."

At just that moment, Ethel entered the kitchen. As she passed by, she took notice of the women sitting around the kitchen table. "My, my, my," she said as she breezed through. "Must be so nice having nothing to do. Maybe I should take a vacation, too." Once she was gone, Leah said under her breath, "Good idea, Mrs. Kennedy, and maybe we can help you pack." Her remark caused the ladies to break into gales of stifled laughter.

After the accident, Ethel, Ted, and a few of the Kennedy lawyers tried to figure out a fair way to compensate Pamela for her life-altering injury — not much, as it turned out: a total of about seven hundred thousand dollars, which would be doled out in increments over the years. It wouldn't even dent the Kennedys' family fortune. "But how long will she be getting that money?" Joe asked in the company of a family attorney. Ethel slammed his chest hard with the palm of her head. "For the rest of her life, Joe," she exclaimed. *For the rest of her life.*

In 1976, Joe graduated with a degree from the University of Massachusetts Boston. That same year, he founded Citizens Energy, the successful nonprofit designed to provide heating oil to low-income families, which he would later turn over to his brother Michael. He also managed his uncle Ted's reelection campaign. He was twenty-four at the time and much like his father; he had the same earnestness about being of service to the underprivileged. He was also interested in politics, unlike his father's namesake, his brother Bobby. "He had it in him at an early age," Bobby Jr. would say of Joe. "He was well-read, even if others didn't know it at

413

first. He had ideas. When we all gathered 'round the dinner table, some of what we said didn't make a lot of sense. We were allowed to have varied opinions, though. Joe always made sense. You'd hear him reason something out and think, yes, that's a leader in the making. He had a sense of things that eluded most of us."

In 1979, Joe married Sheila Brewster Rauch, a young woman three years his senior for whom he fell hard. Sheila hailed from a good, upwardly mobile background, daughter of Rudolph Stewart "Stew" Rauch Jr., chairman of the Philadelphia Savings Fund Society, the first savings bank to organize and do business with the United States (back in 1816). She was pretty and dark-haired, with an outgoing personality. She got along well with Ethel, too, which was important. "My Joe will give you a beautiful life," Ethel told Sheila on her wedding day, "and I promise you, kiddo, you will love every second of it." Though he'd had an irresponsible youth, Ethel hoped it was now over and that Joe was ready to be serious as a husband and father.

The Kennedys went on to have twins in 1980 — Matthew Rauch and Joseph Patrick III.

In 1986, when Phillip "Tip" O'Neill announced his retirement, Joe decided to run for his seat in Congress, which Tip had held since 1953. It seemed somehow to be his destiny in that his uncle JFK had held that same seat from 1947 to 1953. Of course, everyone in the family was excited by the idea, especially Ethel, even if she did have some reservations. Her husband's were big shoes to fill, and she had never been quite sure that Joe was the one to fill them. Still, now that he had stepped up to the plate, she wanted to give him a chance to hit a home run.

For his part, Bobby Jr. was relieved that the pressure finally was off him.

Joe won the election in 1986 and then again in 1988, 1990, 1992, 1994, and 1996. His victories weren't small ones, either. He was incredibly popular with voters in Massachusetts. He had good ideas, was devoted to serving and doing whatever he could, especially for the underprivileged. Whereas his cousin Patrick had mental health as primary concern as a legislator, Joe was invested in helping the lower and middle classes sustain themselves with affordable housing, whether it was by passing legislation to make credit available to working Americans having trouble purchasing homes or by creating hundreds of thousands of affordable housing units by virtue of tax credits that would stimulate growth.

Still, from the start, Joe Kennedy was controversial. He was often argumentative with colleagues, too often showing his temperamental side. He was sometimes absent from important committee hearings. A female lawmaker told *Time* that when Joe noticed her adjusting her bra strap during a caucus meeting, he leaned in and whispered to her, "Need any help with that?" Beneath the surface, people who got to know Joe well felt, was a vast insecurity, and maybe it had to do with Ethel. "There was this huge fear of failure," one staff member reported, again to *Time,* "which his mother continued to promote."

Ethel remained a discouraging factor in Joe's life even after he was in office. No one could really get a handle on why. Obviously, she should have been proud of him, and probably on some level she was. However, she constantly reinforced that he would never be in government what his father had been, as if she felt Joe was in some sort of competition with RFK. It seemed irrational — and it hurt. "When he would get off the phone with her," the former aide recalled, "he would literally look deflated, as if he could never hope to live up to who his father had been, not only in his life but in his mother's." As much as it hurt, maybe Ethel's critical nature also motivated him to be bigger and better, because Joe Kennedy was quite successful in Congress. Even his mother couldn't take that away from him.

In 1993, a *Boston Globe* poll showed that Joe was a likely successor to the popular incumbent governor, William Weld. However, Joe decided to stay in Congress, feeling that a governorship was slightly premature for him. "That was the biggest mistake he'd ever made in politics," Ethel would later say. She was probably right. With timing being almost everything in politics, that had been Joe's time and he missed it. If he had run, he almost certainly would have won, his future as a politician assured.

By 1996, Joe had been a Massachusetts congressman for almost nine years. He was still young — he'd just turned forty-four — was tall and good-looking, about as handsome as his cousin John. With tousled dirty-blond hair, penetrating blue eyes, tall and muscular and well-dressed, when Joe stood on a stage behind a lectern he was a commanding presence. "He was extremely well-spoken," Senator John Tunney observed in 1998. "He didn't need a script and was always better without one. I remember Ted once saying, 'There has to be a lot in a politician's head that isn't written down.' His own son Patrick paled by comparison to Joe. Pat was vulnerable; he appeared to want to please. That worked for him, though. People liked his sense of empathy. Joe was more commanding and powerful, anything but vulnerable. He was a type-A personality, a real fighter . . . and he'd been one ever since he was a kid. The challenge for him was to find a way to move out from behind his father's shadow. I felt he was doing so. I think a lot of people felt that way. He was a good politician in his own right, and he proved that."

By this time, Joseph P. Kennedy II had his eye on being governor. He felt he was ready, and everyone in the family, even his usually disapproving mother, had to agree. Part of his platform had to do with pushing for legislation requiring banks to let consumers pay off debt at the rate they incurred it at as long as they agreed to cut their credit cards in half and not use them. In one speech at this time, he said: "We are at a point where people have to make the difficult choice between paying off their debt and heating their homes. It's not right. It's not fair. It's a choice no one should have to make. This is a crisis we face in this country, in this state, and it's really not that complex. Part of it has to do with the way banks blanket consumers with credit card applications, people who are already in trouble. There has to be some regulation in place. It's one thing to induce people to save and quite another to induce them to go into debt."

"He understands that politics is about people," said his uncle Ted of Joe to *The Wall Street Journal,* "*all* the people, not just the so-called elite. He gets it. Of the next generation, he will go far, and we Kennedys will always stand behind him." Off the record, Ted was even more effusive. In the company of that same reporter for *The Wall Street Journal,* he turned to Vicki and observed, "You want to know who the next President is in this family? Well," he added while smiling broadly at his nephew, "you're lookin' at him."

WHAT WOMEN WANT

Everyone knew that if Michael Kennedy's relationship with Marisa Verrochi were to ever be made public, it would have a terrible impact on the political career of his eldest brother, Joseph P. Kennedy II. Therefore, when Joe's office began receiving phone calls from reporters at *The Boston Globe* inquiring about Michael and a "family employee," he and his family became alarmed. Joe's staff tried to discourage writers from digging too deeply. However, it was clear that *someone* was cooperating with the *Globe* — and the Kennedys feared it was either the Verrochis themselves or, worse yet, maybe even Michael Skakel. "There was a lot of paranoia going on" is how Bobby Kennedy put it. As Joe tried to get a handle on what was happening, another story was about to make headlines, this one directly involving his marriage to Sheila.

By the end of the 1980s, Joe's marriage was in trouble and he wanted a divorce. When that divorce was granted in 1991, he left behind a hurt and disillusioned Kennedy wife. Amy Thompson-Huttel, a friend of Sheila's who had worked at Citizens Energy, recalled, "Sheila told me, 'He could be so much nicer as a person. When I see him in public and he's in politician mode while smiling, shaking hands, kissing babies, and being *that* guy, all I can think to myself is, Oh my God, he's so fake. That is not who he is at all. He once accused me of only being concerned about our family, not our country. Who says things like that to his wife? I had to accept that family would always come second to his political career.' "

It was telling that Sheila had even become afraid to go into Joe's study at home for fear of disturbing him. She would stand outside the door as she tried to make up her mind whether to knock, or just walk away. Usually, she would choose the latter rather than dare to disturb him and risk taking his mind off politics.

One story that says a lot about Joe's opinion of Sheila was one she told Amy Thompson-Huttel. It was a Sunday morning, Sheila recalled, just a normal day at home. The couple was having breakfast, the kids playing in the background. Joe was reading a newspaper. Sheila asked, "Can I have some of that to read?" Without looking at her, Joe said, "Sure." He then peeled off the comics section and, without even looking at her, handed it over.

Around the time of his divorce from Sheila, Joe became serious about a former staff member, Anne Elizabeth Kelly — known as Beth — and wanted to marry her. She was sweet and supportive and not as formidable as Sheila, which was good news to Joe. Sheila suspected that Joe had been with Beth long before she'd known about her, and that he'd been dishonest about it. She felt she had to take it in stride, though. "I married a politician and then I'm surprised when he lies to me?" she asked someone in her circle.

Since divorce is not recognized in the Catholic Church, Joe would be unable to marry Beth in a religious ceremony. If he did so in a civil ceremony, he then wouldn't be able to partake in the Church's sacraments, such as Holy Communion and Penance (Confession) — and neither would Beth, who was also Catholic. This situation was untenable for Joe. Still, on October 23, 1993, Joe married Beth anyway in a non-Catholic ceremony. Afterward, he applied to the Roman Catholic Archdiocese of Boston for an annulment of his marriage to Sheila. He explained that he hoped to rectify his standing with the Church and then remarry Beth in a religious ceremony. However, Sheila wouldn't allow it. She and Joe had been married for twelve years, she said, and had two children; she felt that if she agreed to an annulment it would be "lying before God." She wanted to "defend my marriage." Joe was furious at her for taking such a position; more than anything, he hated being defied, especially by females. At one point, he even had the temerity to tell her, "I will not allow a woman to stand up to me like this." Her hurt response: "Why don't you try talking to me as though I was someone that you actually loved?"

The contention between Joe and Sheila over the annulment would rage on for three more years. In the end, Joe would win the battle; the annulment was granted in October 1996 *without* Sheila's consent. Everyone in the family was surprised that he'd been able to pull it off. "That was definitely Kennedy money at work" is how one intimate of the family's described it. Sheila was distraught. It had meant everything to her to not have her marriage annulled, yet Joe didn't seem to care. It was as if he wanted what he wanted, and that was the end of it for him. Even Ethel wasn't comfortable with the annulment. She said she wasn't sure how Joe had managed it and didn't want the details. In her gut, she felt there was something not right about it and that he would live to regret it. "Just remember this moment," she told him, according to one family source. "That's all I have to say, Joe. Remember this moment."

There had actually been some precedent,

with Ted having had his marriage to Joan annulled so he could do the same thing — marry Vicki in the Catholic Church. However, Joan had reluctantly given him her blessing; she didn't fight it like Sheila. Ethel couldn't help but fear that there would now be trouble. She always had an intuition about people, especially other women, and she knew that even though Sheila had been a retiring personality in her marriage, she was smart, well-read, and educated. "She's not going to let him get away with it," she said. "Do you think she's just going to go away? She's not." Ethel was right. Sheila did *not* accept the ruling. She appealed it.

In considering her journey, it's easy to recognize the slow burn of Sheila's life as she found her own power and went from being a wife her husband thought was only smart enough for the newspaper funnies to one who undertook the mammoth amount of research necessary to challenge him over a Catholic annulment. He really didn't think she had it in her, and his underestimation of her would be to his great detriment, especially when Sheila sought to take their battle before the court of public opinion. She decided to write a book about the entire story.

Sheila's proposed book was the subject of a conference at Ted Kennedy's home in March 1996 with the family patriarch, Ted, his nephew Joe, and two of their political operatives, both attorneys. According to one of them, Ted told Joe that he needed to stop the book from being published. When Joe asked how, Ted said Joe should just call Sheila and tell her the whole family is against it. Joe said he'd already tried Ted's suggestion, but that he'd gotten nowhere with it. "Jesus. What the hell did you *do* to that woman, anyway?" Ted asked, frustrated. "Nothing," Joe said. "I gave her everything," he added. "I gave her our *name,* for Christ's sake."

"That's when Ted became annoyed," recalled one of the observers to the conversation. " 'Back in my day,' he said, 'women knew how to act. Now, Joan? She knew how to toe the line. She was a Kennedy wife and knew how to act like one,' he said, riled up. 'She did what I told her to do, like a good girl.' Joe then made the observation that it was the 1990s, not the sixties, and that women were now different. At that, Ted threw up his hands. 'Your ex-wife needs to play by the rules,' he said angrily, 'and the first rule is: *we make the rules.* An attack against one of us is an attack against all of us,' he bellowed as only the Senator could bellow."

In March 1997, Sheila's memoir, *Shattered Faith: A Woman's Struggle to Stop the Catholic Church from Annulling Her Marriage,* was published. It turned out to be a well-measured, thoughtful account of her investigation into the process of annulment, the

425

hypocrisy she found within the Catholic Church, and stories of other women who'd been faced with similar circumstances. It was with her assessment of Joe's character, though, that she did the most damage. She portrayed him as being argumentative, temperamental, and emotionally abusive. She said he had no time for her or the kids once he got into office. He berated her, she alleged. He browbeat her and called her a "nobody." What's worth noting, though, is that not a lot of the book is devoted to her analysis of Joe, and what's there is in prose that appears to be carefully written with an eye toward avoiding offense.

In April 1997, Massachusetts governor Weld finally made it clear that he would not be running for reelection. This was good news for Joe, who was still considering the position. There was a big party at Hickory Hill after Weld's announcement, a celebration of just what might be in store for the family. "This was really the realization of a generation of dreams," said Christopher Lawford. "Look, we all had been groomed for the presidency since the time we were little kids. Now Joe was on his way there. The governorship was clearly just a stepping stone to the presidency, and we all knew it. Everyone was excited, Aunt Ethel and Uncle Teddy especially. The stakes had suddenly gotten a whole lot greater. Even Joe was sort of over the moon, and believe me, he wasn't a man necessarily given to false hope or to unrealistic expectations. 'I can do this,' he told me. 'You *will* do this,' I said to him. 'You've been *bred* to do this, cousin.' He looked at me, flashed that great Kennedy smile, and said, 'Yeah, Chris. You know it.' "

Prior to the publication of Sheila's book, most people — not just the family but much of Massachusetts — seemed to agree that Joe had a good chance at winning an election. *After* the book, and most especially after Sheila's television appearances promoting it, things took a sudden turn; Joe's popularity took a real hit. Sheila did a lot of damage quickly. One *Boston Globe* poll showed that only 17 percent of voters were now likely to vote for him after the book's publication. "It was a real boomerang effect," said Christopher Lawford. "*So* fast. Like within *weeks.* One minute we were all sitting on top of the world. The next, we were sliding off it, and it was slippery, all right."

During a subsequent meeting at Hickory Hill with staff members and family, the Kennedys tried to determine a plan going forward. Joe said that after everything he had done for his state, and considering all his great plans for the future, he refused to believe that an ex-wife's little book could ruin everything. It was incomprehensible to him. It was also wrong, he said, and he added while slamming his fist onto a desk, *"I'm just not going to accept it."*

"What a shame," Ted said. "Massachusetts is being been robbed of such a strong leader." There was so much work to do, and his nephew was the man to do it, Ted said; the people of the state deserved him, and he couldn't believe that it was all because of *a woman* that everything was blowing up around them. He asked if what Sheila had written was true. Could they challenge it? It was all true, Joe admitted. "The truth is whatever it looks like, though," he added, spoken like a true politician.

"Oh, who cares?" Ethel snapped, annoyed. "The truth is overrated, anyway." Ethel's was an interesting observation, especially given that the truth had often been a flexible proposition in Kennedy history. For instance, back in the 1950s, when JFK was seeking the nomination of his Democratic Party for President, his opponent, Lyndon Baines Johnson, played a dirty trick on him the day before the vote. He had his people slip under the hotel doors of every delegate a yellow sheet of paper informing them that Kennedy suffered from Addison's disease — which was true. Bobby Kennedy responded by getting doctors to lie and say his brother was completely healthy — which was untrue. However, Ethel definitely approved.

Bobby had been famously quoted as saying he believed people to be divided into two groups, white hats and black hats: the Kennedys being the white hats and everyone else the black. (Incidentally, from that time on, Johnson was viewed as a black hat; at Bobby's funeral when he tried to kiss Ethel on the cheek, she turned her head to make sure it didn't happen.) Ethel wholeheartedly agreed with Bobby's classification of friends and enemies. It was easier to make this distinction, though, when the traitor was outside the family. When the enemy was within, it was tougher for Ethel to be as definitive. That's why she was torn about Sheila. While she wanted the women in the family to be strong-minded and independent, she also wanted them to be loyal. "Not only should the wives know where the line is," she said in speaking about Sheila, "but also," she added, raising her voice, *the cost of crossing it.*" As far as she was concerned, Sheila had definitely crossed that line. If not for the fact that Ethel loved her grandsons by Sheila — Joe and Matt — she would never have had anything more to do with her. "I'm not one to say 'I told you so,'" she said at the meeting, "but doggone it, Joe. Didn't I?" What could he say? Mummy was right again; it was impossible to diminish her prescience. So now what?

"We should just say everything in the book

is a lie and leave it at that," Ethel concluded. "A nice blanket statement without being specific." No, Joe said. He felt that this position would open them up to scrutiny as Sheila and her defenders would then go through the book point by point to prove its accuracy. He was right. This wasn't the fifties. It was the nineties. Because of the family's checkered history, the public was a lot less inclined to just believe them these days without question.

"What do women want, anyway?" a frustrated Ted asked, according to this account. "That's what I don't get. *What the hell do women want?*"

"Everything, I guess," Joe answered, shaking his head in dismay.

According to the witness, five minutes later, the phone rang. Ethel picked it up. *"What?"* she demanded in her own inimitable way. There was a pause. Then, without saying another word, she slammed down the phone. "Who was that?" Ted asked.

"Speak of the devil," Ethel exclaimed. "It was Sheila."

Joe was surprised. "I should talk to her," he said.

"What for?" Ethel asked. "I think we've all seen how effective *that* can be." After a beat, she then asked, "Are we done here?" to which Joe responded, "Actually, Mummy, I was thinking —" Ethel cut him off. *"We're done here,"* she concluded in a voice that forbade argument. She then rose and left the room.

As he had demonstrated throughout his life, Joe Kennedy always leaned toward sexist behavior. It was decided, however, that in his response to *Shattered Faith,* he should do whatever necessary to hide that particular inclination. Wisely, he didn't try to argue with Sheila's depiction of him. He fell on his sword without obfuscation or even the kind of self-righteous detachment many politicians do so well. "There are certainly things I wish I never said and I presume Sheila feels the same way," he allowed. "I am terribly sorry for any of the mistakes I made in our relationship. I have deep regrets about my relationship with Sheila. [It had] in so many ways deteriorated . . . you say things you wish you never said."

Unfortunately, Joe's subsequent speaking appearances about Sheila and her book did little to assist him in the court of public opinion. Ethel became angrier every time she saw him on television. The official line was enough to satisfy the public, she felt, and every time her son tried to elaborate he got himself into trouble, especially when his words were taken out of context upon later publication in newspapers. "Oh my God, Joe. Stop talking," she told him. "Remember one thing: people can't quote silence."

Many people now took a dim view of Joseph P. Kennedy II, and there wasn't much he could do about it. Even to this day, what remains surprising is how one book by one author could do so much damage. Maybe it wasn't so surprising, though. Its narrative fed right into the popular notion that not only could a Kennedy male get away with pretty much anything, but also that his toxic masculinity knew no bounds. In Sheila's case, the takeaway was also that he would even try to find ways to twist to his advantage the tenets of Catholic law. Not since Mary Jo Kopechne had the story of one woman done so much harm to the family's public image. Maybe one of Joe's brothers put it best when he concluded: "Karma's a bitch, all right. And her name is Sheila."

Sheila Rauch Kennedy continued to appeal the church's decision to annul her marriage to Joe, fighting it long after most people forgot about her book and long after many other women might have abandoned the battle. In 2007, her efforts finally paid off when the annulment was overturned. As of this writing in 2018, Sheila has remained successful in seeing to it that her marriage to Joseph Kennedy remains intact in the eyes of the Catholic Church.

"SURRENDER THE *ME* TO THE *WE*"

On April 25, 1997, just days after Joe made his statement about Sheila's book, the proverbial "other shoe" dropped: *The Boston Globe* finally broke the story of Michael's relationship with Marisa Verrochi. The headline on the front page was a stunner: "Controversy Surrounds a Kennedy's Alleged Affair with Baby-Sitter." While the paper didn't identify Marisa, it did note the names of her parents. The report also clearly stated that the relationship with Michael started when Marisa was fourteen. (Maybe that was true, but Vicki discovered Michael and Marisa in bed on January 21, 1995, when Marisa was sixteen — the legal age of consent. She would turn seventeen a week later, on January 29.)

The news sent shock waves throughout the media, with the *New York Post* using the headline that Ethel Kennedy hated the most: "They're at It Again! RFK Son 'Slept with Schoolgirl, 14!' Could Even Face Statutory Rape Rap." One of Ethel's assistants recalled,

433

"That was the one, even more than *The Boston Globe,* which really upset her. I watched her tear that front page up into little pieces. Back in her day, she told me, she had an enemies list of reporters who spoke out of turn. Pretty much nothing was ever revealed about her kids in the 1960s unless she approved it. Reporters knew better than to cross her. Those days were long gone, though. 'The damn seventies changed everything,' she told me."

Almost everything that had occurred between Michael and Marisa was now out for the world to weigh in on, and it was unlikely that the verdict in the court of public opinion would be sympathetic to the Kennedys. Some people in the family — like John, a magazine editor in his own right — were surprised it took so long for the story to be revealed. He understood the way media worked and, like most of the Kennedys, he was almost certain that Michael Skakel was a source for the original story in the *Globe.* "*Finally,* I agree with Joe about something," he said. No one quite knew what to do about Skakel yet, but they were definitely suspicious of him.

The day the news broke, John telephoned some of his older relatives to see how they were handling it. When he called Eunice, he first spoke to her household chef, Randy Beatty. Beatty catered the food service for five sitting presidents, including inaugural dinners for Carter, Ford, Bush, and Clinton. He had been the executive sous chef at the Smithsonian Institute just prior to working for the Shrivers. Now he was working in the Shrivers' enormous (ten bedrooms, eleven bathrooms) stately Colonial Revival–style mansion on Harrington Drive in Potomac, Maryland. "Very nicely, John asked me how I enjoyed working for his aunt and uncle," Beatty recalled, "and he tolerated my answer good enough, though I could tell he was anxious to talk to Mrs. Shriver. They got on the phone, and she lowered her voice to an urgent whisper as she spoke to him."

That night, the Shrivers hosted a dinner for Ted Kennedy and his wife, Vicki, as well as Tim and Mark Shriver and their wives, Linda and Jeanne. They ate in the enormous, white-walled dining room with its cathedral ceiling and huge ornate hanging chandelier. This was truly a magnificent space, with its own fireplace, which was always in use, even in summer; its magnificent oil paintings from the Shrivers' time in France; and its expensive antique furniture with chairs that weren't exactly comfortable because of their straight wooden backs and firm custom-made cushions, but that Eunice liked because of the way they forced guests to sit up straight. Each of the four corners of the banquet-sized room featured built-in shelves in which family photos taken over the years were proudly displayed in silver and gold frames. At the far end of the room was an enormous floor-to-ceiling window that showcased the lush grounds of the estate, all beautifully illuminated as the sun went down.

The Shrivers and their six guests were gathered in one corner of an enormous antique dining room table that could easily seat thirty. "They were open, not hiding their conversation whenever I walked into the room to serve them," Beatty recalled.

"I feel just terrible," Ted said at the dinner table as Beatty served heaping helpings of his special, red flannel hash. The Senator wondered if he'd somehow failed Michael and what he might have done to prevent him from making such bad choices. He recalled once being in a car with him and noticing that the way the sun hit him and the shadows fell on him made Michael looked almost exactly like his father. "The resemblance was so striking, I had to just sit there and stare at him for a moment," Ted said wondrously. On the other hand, he was also angry at him. He felt that Michael had been selfish by indulging in an affair with someone so wildly inappropriate. "In this family, you have to surrender the *me* to the *we*," he observed.

Eunice noted that Michael had never really been the same after Bobby's death. Sarge agreed that he became a different kid. The problem, Sarge noted, was that he was a grown man with children of his own. If he didn't know better by this time than to make such bad decisions, what could any of them do about it? He wasn't a youngster anymore, Sarge said, and they couldn't coddle him or treat him like one. He also said it was time for Ethel to stop infantilizing her children, hollering at them and putting them in their places "like they're ten, when they're what? Forty?" Eunice had to agree with him. She said she believed that Ethel, in her heart, felt she'd done a poor job with her children when they were young and that she was now trying to make up for it. This was why, said Eunice, Ethel often treated them as if they were still just teenagers. She remained optimistic, though. "We will survive this," she said, "because that's what we do. We survive."

Later the atmosphere cheered up over crème brûlée desserts when Ted, always the raconteur, began telling jokes and stories. For instance, he told everyone a humorous anecdote about having recently sailed with First Lady Hillary Clinton. "So we're coming onto shore from a very pleasant outing when she looks around and suddenly seems insulted. 'Why isn't the presidential flag flying?' she asks me. 'After all, I *am* the First Lady, you know?' I stare right at her and say, 'I don't know why, Hillary. Maybe it's because I'm not the President?' " Eunice shrieked with delight, "No," she exclaimed, "that can't be true. That's hilarious, Teddy.' "

After dinner while in the parlor having coffee, Ted, Vicki, and the Shrivers tried to craft some sort of response to the *Globe*'s story. They realized that they couldn't completely deny the report; it was all true.

The next day, despite the Kennedys' attempt to explain things in a vague statement of support for Michael, the *Globe* feature would start an avalanche of bad publicity for them. By the middle of the summer there were probably few people in the United States unaware of the story of "Michael Kennedy and the babysitter." What was maybe most ironic about what was happening was that Michael was actually doing a lot better. He'd just gotten out of an Arizona rehab, where he'd been in treatment for substance abuse and sex addiction. He was also on new medication to treat depression, which doctors determined had probably been a problem for him since he was a child, and which had clearly not been addressed. The new treatment made a big difference, and people noticed it straightaway. He felt *good* for the first time in a long while, maybe the first time ever. Also, he was said to have passed a lie detector test relating to Marisa and her age when he first started having sex with her. What was not revealed, however, was that the test was administered by someone working for one of his own lawyers, arguably not the best-case scenario if on a search for the truth.

Obviously, the timing of the news about Michael couldn't have been worse for Joe. He'd already taken a big hit in the polls because of Sheila, and now this latest story threatened to complete his undoing. "Well, it's a big family," he said on Capitol Hill during the first week of May 1997. "There will always be a few little problems along the way," he added, sputtering. "And this one might not be such a little one for everybody, but, you know, I am proud of my family."

It was now felt by much of Joe Kennedy's base that he was being unfairly tarred by his brother's scandal, that a good man might be kept from being of future service through no fault of his own. "It's the spontaneous combustion problem," noted the political consultant Lou DiNatale. "You're standing next to someone who goes up in flames, and you're covered with gasoline. What happens? You go up in flames, too." With this one-two punch — Sheila's book along with Michael's misdeeds — Joe could see nothing but a raging fire engulfing him as his political career went up in smoke.

ETHEL SCHOOLS THE NEXT GENERATION

As her son Joe's political career was being decimated by the actions of his brother and his ex-wife, Ethel Kennedy continued to view what was going on as a problem bigger than just present concerns. She feared the way the *next* generation of Kennedys — the fourth — would interpret what was happening and how it might inform their view of politics. "They see what we've been through and they maybe start to think politics isn't worth it," she said in the spring of 1997 at the start of the new Cape Cod season. She and Joe and Beth were talking on the veranda of her home, along with Ted and his sons, Patrick and Teddy, and Ted's longtime friend Dun Gifford. Gifford, a lifelong resident of Nantucket, had, after his time working for the Kennedys, gone on to create Oldways, a company whose mission was to promote healthy eating. His company would actually become a major force behind the rise in popularity of the Mediterranean diet in the United States. He

440

was visiting the Kennedys with his wife, Gladys.

"Kids see all this mud being thrown at our elected officials and they figure, heck no, that's not for me," Ethel said. Ted had to agree.

"As the family matriarch, Ethel felt a responsibility to make sure the younger generation understood what was expected of them," said Dun Gifford. "There was this sense that because of the recent shenanigans, some of the kids might grow up thinking politics was not for them," he recalled. "I happened to be at her home with Ted on one of those days Ethel got the kids together to talk a little about the family business. 'Does she do this a lot?' I asked Ted. 'All the time,' he told me."

After Ethel went to fetch one of her many dusty scrapbooks, she sat down on one of the wicker chairs. She then gathered around her some of those youngsters of the next generation. Among them were Joe's twin sons, Joe III and Matthew, who were sixteen; Bobby's son Bobby III, who was thirteen; and his daughter Kathleen, who was nine. As they sat around their grandmother, Ted and Dun sat directly across from her, smoking cigars and sipping tumblers of scotch.

According to Dun Gifford, beneath each photograph in Ethel's scrapbook was a segment of an important speech correlating to the picture. "Ethel pointed to each photo and then read aloud the caption," he remembered. " 'This is your uncle Jack when he was elected President in 1960,' she said. Then she read aloud from his inaugural speech: 'Let the word go forth from this time and place, to friend and foe alike, that the torch has been passed to a new generation of Americans . . .'

"She showed a picture of Bobby after the assassination of Martin Luther King in 1968 and read his famous lines: 'What we need in the United States is not division; what we need in the United States is not hatred; what we need in the United States is not violence and lawlessness, but is love, and wisdom, and compassion toward one another.'

"Then from Ted's Democratic National Convention speech in 1980: 'For me, a few hours ago, this campaign came to an end. For all those whose cares have been our concern, the work goes on, the cause endures, the hope still lives, and the dream shall never die.'

"The kids listened, not saying a word, just immersed in their family history lesson," said Dun Gifford. " 'This is what we do in this family,' Ethel told them. 'We serve. We lead.' They nodded. 'You must never be afraid to serve,' she told them. 'It's a great privilege and honor to serve. If you listen to your heart, it'll tell you how you can best do it.

Do you understand?' They all said yes. 'Fine, now get outta here,' she told them as she slammed the scrapbook closed. 'Go play.' They all scattered. Ted and I then watched the kids run down to the beach, tripping over each other, roughhousing with one another, just as Kennedys had been doing for as long as I had known them."

Not Every Wrong . . .

Though it had been building for years, the scandal of Michael Kennedy and Marisa Verrochi was resolved so quickly that one of Michael's siblings described its resolution as "a house of cards that just sort of folded in on itself."

Any case against Michael fell apart in May 1997 when Marisa and her parents, Paul and June, each gave conflicting stories about Marisa's relationship with Michael and when it began, whether at fourteen or sixteen. Then they said they didn't want to proceed with any charges. June was too sick with her alcoholism to ever withstand a trial, and Marisa just wanted to get on with her life. Meanwhile, Vicki refused to testify against her husband, still loyal to the Kennedys despite everything she'd been through. As it turned out, the only one committed to justice seemed to be Michael Skakel.

Skakel stated to authorities that Marisa had told him the relationship started when she was fourteen. It didn't matter, though. His statement would be considered hearsay evidence in court and thus would be inadmissible. It would ruin his relationship with the Kennedys, however, many of whom now felt sure he was a turncoat, as they had expected. When they confronted Skakel, they almost ended up in a bar fight. Skakel asked for understanding and told Joe Kennedy he thought of him as a brother, to which Joe shot back, "Oh yeah? Think again." Even Ethel was done with Skakel now. The only Kennedy on his side was Bobby Jr., who still thought of him as a good man. "He's been trying to save everyone, left and right," he said at the time. "But you know what they do to saviors," he added. "They crucify them."

As hard as it was to believe considering all the damage it had caused, the entire Marisa Verrochi saga was wrapped up in a few days. Michael simply couldn't believe it. According to one of his attorneys, when he realized he was in the clear, he blinked several times as if he wanted to cry. But there were no tears.

Once it was all over, there were rumors that the Verrochis had been paid off by the Kennedys to make it all go away. While it certainly makes sense that a prominent, wealthy political family might attempt to settle an ugly situation with a cash payout, not a shred of evidence exists to support the allegation. Paul Verrochi, who was quite wealthy, has strongly denied it. However, if one were to ask him today when his daughter and Michael started having sex, he would probably say fourteen. Be that as it may, he decided to take the difficult position that not every wrong has its remedy.

Meanwhile, despite everything that had happened with his brother and ex-wife, it would seem that Joe Kennedy's political career wasn't over, at least not yet. He was still hoping to salvage it. On June 8, he spoke before nearly three thousand delegates at a state Democratic convention in Salem, trying to raise money for a bid for the party's nomination for governor in 1998. Mostly, he was trying to gauge the public's reaction to the idea. He told the crowd: "I had had a marriage that didn't work out. I can't tell you, and I can't put into words, how sorry I am about that. I said things that I wish I'd never said, and I did things I wish I had never done. I've told you [turning to his wife, Beth], I've told Sheila. I've told anyone who cared how sorry I am. On the matter of my brother. I am so terribly sorry, so very sorry for what has happened to the Verrochi family. I extend to them the deepest apology I can summon. I love my brother very much. I will always love my brother, and I will stand with my brother."

Unfortunately, polls conducted after Joe's speech made it clear that the tide had turned against him. Two months later, in August, another family meeting would be called to determine a course of action. The road ahead was obvious: Joe would have to drop out of the running for governor. "This was tough," recalled Christopher Lawford, who wasn't at that meeting but, of course, knew of its particulars. "Aunt Ethel, Uncle Teddy . . . Bobby Jr. . . . Kathleen . . . Michael . . . all of them . . . all of us . . . everyone was devastated. Talk about shock and awe."

POSTSCRIPT

In 2000, Michael Skakel was finally arrested and charged with the murder of Martha Moxley. Two years later, he stood trial. Most of the Kennedys — like Joe — were not surprised and leaned toward his guilt. Others — like Bobby — continued to believe in his innocence. Skakel was convicted of Martha's slaying and sentenced to twenty years to life in prison. However, in 2013, a judge granted him a new trial, citing evidence that his lawyer hadn't properly represented him in the original proceedings. Skakel was then released from prison.

With the passing of the years, Bobby Kennedy Jr. became even more convinced of his cousin's innocence and worked hard to exonerate him in Martha's murder. In 2016, he wrote *Framed: Why Michael Skakel Spent Over a Decade in Prison for a Murder He Didn't Commit.* Later that same year, the Connecticut Supreme Court reinstated Michael's conviction.

In 2018, Michael's conviction was overturned by the Connecticut Supreme Court, forty-three years after the crime, citing what was described as representation by his attorney so ineffective that his right to a fair trial had been violated. Unless prosecutors decide to retry him, which is unlikely, Michael Skakel, now fifty-eight, will remain a free man.

As for Marisa Verrochi, she went on with her life and today works in education and is happily married with children.

Marisa's parents, Paul and June, divorced in 1999. Two years later, June died of alcoholism. She was fifty-one. A year later, Paul married a socialite and businesswoman from the Boston area. He remains a health care professional as well as a philanthropist involved in a number of children's charities.

TRAGEDY ON THE SLOPES

"If there's one myth about the Kennedys that ain't no myth, it's their incredible athletic competitiveness," Frank Gifford once recalled. By 1997, Michael Kennedy's father-in-law had long ago retired from professional football and was now commentating for ABC Sports. However, he still enjoyed the sport and loved to play with his relatives by marriage. "Playing touch football with them at Hickory Hill or Hyannis Port was insanity," he remembered. "Even for a guy who played for twelve years with the Giants, it was dangerous. You had to stay constantly alert because they hurled their bodies around like kamikazes."

Probably no better example of the Kennedys' obsession with competition and with pushing the envelope was the longtime family tradition of combining skiing with football — which they called "ski football." Many outsiders considered it a reckless folly, which was maybe one of the reasons the Kennedys glommed on to it. For them, it was fun, it was thrilling, it was maybe even deadly — everything these lifelong daredevils felt they needed to make ski football worth their time.

The family — adults of the third generation, Jack's, Bobby's, and Ted's offspring, along with their young children, the fourth generation — would divide themselves into two teams and then take off down the slope at treacherously high speeds, often without helmets or poles. They would remain in close proximity to one another, weaving in and out as they hurled the ball at one another and achieved touchdowns at demarcations decided upon in advance, usually enormous aspen trees. Whenever the Kennedys played this makeshift sport, they were chastised by the ski patrol. However, since having the popular family on any icy slope was good for business, there was no way the Kennedys would ever be penalized or banned, regardless of how dangerously they played their hair-raising sport.

After the Christmas holiday of 1997, many members of the Kennedy family decided to spend the week on the snowy slopes of Aspen. Ethel, who was nursing an injured shoulder from a recent fall, was happy these days, especially since Michael was out of trouble. She was worried about him, though. It was as if a light had gone out in him; he wasn't quite the same, she said. Some wondered what she was talking about; when was he ever happy? "Man, you're a *Kennedy,*" his brothers and cousins kept telling Michael. "You have to pull it together." He was reminded that others in his family had also made terrible choices and that, somehow, they'd always managed to get past them, go on with their lives, and, most important, still find ways to be of service. "Come on. That's just Kennedy 101," said Ted's son Patrick. Michael knew, though, that he would never be able to run for office. Of course, there were some Kennedys who didn't hunger for politics, but at least *they* had a choice. Michael would never have it. "And for what?" asked one of his frustrated relatives. "For Marisa Verrochi? Really? *For Marisa Verrochi?*"

Even Ethel had a change of heart where Michael's marriage was concerned, which surprised some in the family. After Vicki cleared Michael in the Verrochi case, her mother-in-law told her she would understand if she went through with the divorce. She felt that Vicki had proven her loyalty to the Kennedys and that she had more than enough reason to no longer be married to her son. She told her it was her decision and that she would not interfere with it, and also she assured her that if the couple divorced she would always consider her a daughter and a Kennedy. "Because you have been loyal to us, we will always be loyal to you," she told her. "On one hand, Vicki appreciated it," said a friend of hers, "but on another, she was like, 'You know what? I don't need *your* permission to do anything.' She had some deep-seated resentment toward the Kennedys by this time; it was hard not to."

It was all Vicki could do lately just to be in Michael's company. Every time she looked at him she wondered how her life had gone so wrong. Family members were stunned in the days before the skiing trip when she and Michael had a loud argument. "I was wrong and I swear to you, I'm very, very sorry," Michael told her. Whatever was at issue in that particular moment, Vicki wasn't prepared to accept an apology for it. Instead, she said a few angry words to Michael and rushed off. Embarrassed, he turned to uncomfortable observers and said, "As you can see, my wife and I are working on open and honest communication. So far, so good." Deep down, he knew the truth: he'd ruined their life together and would likely never be able to make it up to her.

Vicki had to admit, though, that she was still vacillating about the divorce. Though she'd filed the papers and they would be finalized in about a month, to say she was absolutely certain that she wanted to break up the family would be untrue. There was still a small chance that she would take Michael back, if only for the sake of their kids.

Though he had lost so much, he still had his children. "I tell my kids every day that I love them," he once said, "because I want them to be very clear about that." One relative recalls Michael right after the holiday playing touch football with his son, his namesake, Michael, who would turn fifteen in about a month. "Little Michael was peppering him with observations about the Patriots, his favorite team," recalled the source. "He'd make a statement and then eagerly add, 'Right, Dad?' Then another and . . . 'Right, Dad?' Michael still walked on water where his kids were concerned, especially his son, and he felt the same about them. Nothing could ever change that."

On New Year's Eve — December 31 — the family congregated at the Sundeck restaurant atop Aspen Mountain, waiting for the other skiers on the slopes to clear out so that they could have enough freedom to play ski football without interference. The ski patrol was constantly warning them not to play the makeshift sport because of the obvious danger attached to it. Inevitably, one of the family members would always end up declaring, "Too bad. We're the fuckin' Kennedys," and that would be the end of the debate; the game would continue.

As melancholy as he was at this time in his life, Michael Kennedy was always enlivened by skiing. "In all my life I've never seen anyone ski as beautifully as Michael," said his brother Bobby. "He had the quick feet of a professional mogul skier and as fluid a movement as I've ever seen on any skier. Bob Beattie, who coached the U.S. Olympic team, once said that Michael was the best natural skier he had ever seen."

Though Michael loved it and was the best at it of all the family members, Vicki hated ski football. For years, she'd been telling anyone who would listen — not many — that she thought it was risky. She would just as soon not even watch, though she did trust Michael to make sure their kids were safe. Therefore, she stayed behind in Vail at Frank and Kathie Lee's home while the other Kennedys went to the Aspen slopes.

What happened that day occurred so swiftly and was so shocking, some of those who witnessed it can't really remember it clearly. The fact that it happened to Michael, of all the Kennedys, the one who was the most athletic, the most daring . . . the best at everything sports-related, made it all the more impossible to fathom. It happened at lightning speed, too, not allowing time to process it or to even later clearly recall it. When trying to catch a pass of a blue Nerf football, Michael somehow misjudged things and skied right into a tree, his head hitting first with a stomach-turning cracking sound. He wasn't wearing a safety helmet. Of course.

Everyone ran to him, stunned. As others gathered and became hysterical at the sight of Michael's crumpled body, Rory started to pound on her brother's sternum until she managed to elicit a weak pulse. She turned him onto his side so that he wouldn't choke. "Michael," she screamed at him, "you have to fight! Don't leave us, Michael. Please. Please."

"By this time, Michael's children — Michael Jr. [fifteen], Kyle [fourteen], and Rory [ten] — had also gotten to the scene," said R. Couri Hay, a reporter and family friend who was also present. "Crying, they fell to their knees and began to pray, their prayers interrupted with cries of 'Please, God, not my daddy. Not my daddy.'

"Finally the paramedics arrived and started working on Michael, but it was too late. He was gone. Rory tried to shield the children from what was happening as the paramedics put a cervical collar on Michael and then placed him on a toboggan. She continued to urge the kids to pray for their father.

"I started to back away from the scene because I realized that this had suddenly become an intensely personal and tragic family moment," R. Couri Hay continued. "As the toboggan took Michael down the slope, I took his poles and slowly skied behind it. At this point, it was just silent. Everyone was in shock. It was surreal. Eerie. Cold.

"I looked around. People were crying. The sun was setting. It was getting dark."

LOST SOUL

The days that followed Michael Kennedy's sudden death were a blur.

There was the wake in Hyannis Port at the compound, Michael lying in state in the drawing room of his mother's home, just as had been the case with his brother David. His family members and friends passed by his casket, each kneeling before it, crying and praying. All nine of Michael's siblings and their spouses as well as their children tried to console one another. Meanwhile, photographers in helicopters and airplanes flying above the compound tried to get blurry shots of the Kennedys on the beach walking together quietly.

Vicki was bereft. Who knows what the future would have held for her, Michael, and their three children? The book was now closed for good, though, and the ending more tragic than she could ever have imagined.

At the center of this circle of grief was the family's matriarch, Ethel, doing her mighty best to lift everyone's spirits while she herself was all but crushed by the weight of her own despair. It had been almost thirty years since her husband's murder, but somehow this latest family tragedy returned her to its pain and sorrow. She missed him more than ever and felt that if he were alive he would know better than she how to handle their son's death.

Seeing her children's longtime governess, Ena, now eighty-nine, walk through the door with her daughter, Fina, fifty-nine, was almost more than Ethel could bear.

By this time Ena was retired; she'd reluctantly left the household a few years earlier simply because she was just too old to continue working. Ethel had kept her on as long as she could because she understood that Hickory Hill had been Ena's home since the day it was purchased in 1956. By the beginning of the 1990s, when Ena was in her early eighties, Ethel suggested that Fina move back into the estate to care for her. Fina, now divorced, obtained a transfer to Virginia from her employer, American Express, so that she could, again, live with the Kennedys. Ena would then continue to work at Hickory Hill and at the Kennedy compound well into the decade doing easy jobs like arranging flowers or polishing the silverware, with Fina always keeping a close eye on her. Finally, when the winters became too hard on Ena, Ethel set her up in a house in Florida, which is where she now lived. It just so happened that mother and daughter were together for the birth of Fina's grandson in Washington, where Fina lived, when they saw the news about Michael's death on television in the hospital's waiting room. The two then flew up to Hyannis Port to be with the Kennedys.

People in the room immediately rose out of respect as soon as they saw Ena. Ethel collapsed in her arms, her ironclad façade crumbling before everyone's eyes. "Oh my God," she exclaimed. "I can't believe you are here, Ena. What in the world are you doing here?"

"Where else would I be, Mrs. Kennedy?" asked the elderly woman.

As she remained in her embrace, Ethel then noted that Ena had been at her side the day Michael was born. Ena comforted Ethel as best she could, but she, too, was upset. She seemed to be trembling. "You did very well with him, Mrs. Kennedy," she managed to say. "This is not your fault —"

"I know that," Ethel said, cutting her off.

"It's nobody's fault," Ena continued.

"Ena, *I know that,*" Ethel again said. While she was obviously devastated, she wasn't going to blame herself. All of it was God's plan, she concluded, and she'd accepted it. When Ena asked if there was anything Ethel needed, she said that all she needed were her prayers.

"May God bless Michael," Ena then said, "and welcome him home." Then Fina took Ethel into her arms. Like her mom, she, too, had helped care for the infant Michael. "He was a good boy, Mrs. Kennedy," Fina said, "and a good man. I have so many wonderful memories of him." She and Ethel then held a long embrace.

A funeral Mass at Our Lady of Victory Church was attended by all the family, their friends, as well as many politicians, with, of course, Vicki and her and Michael's three children in the front pew of the church.

Maybe it was understandable that Bobby Jr. would seek to frame his brother in a positive light in his moving eulogy of him. Of course, privately, the Kennedys knew the truth: Michael had gone down a bad road and had ruined any number of lives in the process, including his own. But the question remained: *Why?* What drove him? Was he traumatized because of his father's death? Was he crippled because of drugs? Was he suffering from a mental disorder? His family remained at a loss to explain it. All they knew with certainty was that they must honor him. No matter his faults, he was their beloved Michael, and they would preserve his memory. Some observers felt Bobby's words during the service didn't really reflect the reality of Michael's experience, though. Instead, they felt it to be a romanticized version of events. However, there are still kernels of truth in Bobby's words and, no doubt, the sentiment behind them was heartfelt.

Bobby said, in part: "I was so proud of him this past year. He handled the chaos with characteristic calm. The personal issues with which he struggled were not about malice or greed. They were about humanity and passion. His transgressions were the kind that Christ taught us are the first and easiest to forgive. He died, three years sober, on a forty-degree day under a blue sky in the company of his children, his family, and friends he loved. He caught the ball, turned to a friend, and said his final words: 'This is really great!' The last thing he saw was his children. The next thing he saw was God."

"By the time we got to the cemetery, everyone was feeling such tremendous grief, you couldn't even speak," said football star Brian Holloway, a close friend of the family's. "We just put our arms around each other because there weren't any words. I was standing right next to John at the family plot where David was also buried. John and I looked at each other and nodded sadly, and then I put my arm around his shoulder. He did the same, put his arm around mine."

A few months earlier, John had addressed Michael's and Joe's problems in *George,* penning an editorial that some viewed as a harsh indictment of them. Actually, it was a condemnation of the media's coverage of the dual scandals and of the public's opinion that high-profile people like the Kennedys aren't allowed human foibles. However, Joe didn't quite see it that way and told the press, "I guess my first reaction was, 'Ask not what you can do for your cousin, but what you can do for his magazine.'" John didn't much care about his opinion, though. He was more concerned with how Michael felt about it, and called him to make sure he understood. He said he was fine, but worried about John's relationship with Joe. Days later, he got the two of them box seats to a Boston Red Sox game and suggested they go together. Of course, John and Joe didn't want to do so, but Michael insisted. The cousins then had a great time at the game and, remembering their bond as kids, couldn't help but wonder how they'd ever become so estranged. Joe took the blame. "While I was trying to figure out how to be a good politician, you were trying to figure out how to be a good person," he told John, according to this account. John confessed that he always felt naive and soft next to Joe. He respected the fact that Joe took his work in Congress so seriously. He urged Joe to stay in the game and not allow Michael's scandal and Sheila's book to ruin things for him. He also promised to campaign hard for him if he decided to run for governor. The cousins had reached a détente, and it was all because of Michael — the one John had always referred to as "the peacemaker."

The tragic death of Michael LeMoyne Kennedy would have a reverberating effect throughout the whole family, especially on his brother Joe's political career. Joe spent a lot of time discussing his future with Ethel, Ted, and others in the family who'd always believed — hoped — he would one day be President. In a few months' time, though, he would leave politics altogether, citing "a new recognition of our own vulnerabilities and the vagaries of life."

"Not only did Joe fear he'd never gain political traction again due to recent family travails, he didn't want to try," recalled Richard Burke, who had been an aide to Ted Kennedy. "He was exhausted. Politics had taken a toll on him; he wanted a different life. He once said something about being a politician, and Ted corrected him: 'You're not just a politician. You're a Kennedy.' That had always been a lot to live up to. He might have survived Sheila's book if that had been the only thing working against him. But combined with what Michael had done? It was like a whole river of shit engulfing him."

Though Ethel was gravely disappointed, she wasn't particularly surprised. After all, she'd always known that Joe's career could be adversely impacted by Michael's actions if they ever became public, and she had a bad feeling about the way Joe had treated Sheila before she'd even written the book. That didn't mean she wasn't crushed, though, by the knowledge that Joe would now be the first Kennedy to ever drop out of politics. In all, he spent six terms in the U.S. House of Representatives, until January 1999. In his last speech on the floor, he delivered a passionate speech asking for unity and forgiveness in the midst of Congressional debate regarding the articles of impeachment of President Bill Clinton.

Gayle Fee, the reporter for the *Boston Herald* who covered the story of Michael and Marisa extensively, says that according to her sources, the Verrochi family was purely satisfied by the way things had worked out. "They didn't really even do anything to exact their revenge, did they?" she noted. "They didn't testify against Michael, seek to have him charged with statutory rape, or push to have him incarcerated. Yet they'd still managed to get justice just by letting things unfold naturally and, in a sense, altering American history forevermore. After all, Joe had been on the road to becoming governor, and probably later President. But now that was never going to happen, was it? In their eyes, it had been better for them to just sit back and watch the favorite son be completely destroyed by his brother's transgressions than it

■ ■ ■ ■

PART VIII
THE IN-LAWS

■ ■ ■ ■

THE OUTSIDER

Two days after Michael Kennedy's death, while the family was still in shock and sequestered in their homes at the Cape, there was a bit of controversy caused by Kerry Kennedy's husband, Andrew Cuomo.

Mary Kerry Kennedy — known to all as Kerry, born on September 8, 1959 — was the seventh child of Bobby and Ethel. She and Andrew Cuomo had been married since 1990. When she married him, Kerry was young, blond, and gorgeous at thirty, two years his junior. A graduate of the Putney School, where she and Mary Richardson had become best friends, and Brown University, she received her law degree from Boston College Law School. Like her sister Kathleen and many of her brothers, she had a real hunger for politics, but unlike Kathleen, felt it was not a good fit for her. She wanted to find other ways to be of service.

Kerry began working as a human rights activist in 1981 as an intern with Amnesty

International, traveling to El Salvador to investigate claims against the U.S. immigration system relating to refugees from that country. She would, in years to come, travel to Kenya, South Korea, Northern Ireland, China, Vietnam, and India among other countries, leading delegations devoted to children's and women's rights, domestic violence, workplace discrimination, and other violations. She became the president of the Robert F. Kennedy Center for Justice and Human Rights, founded by Ethel and designed to urge Congress to keep human rights violations front and center among its concerns, and also to supply activists around the world with funding to continue their good work. Over the years of being a public servant, Kerry's résumé has become long and impressive; she hasn't stopped fighting for people since the day she started doing so in 1981.

Of Italian American descent, Kerry's husband, Andrew Cuomo, was lethally attractive. Tall and dark, with black hair and deep-set eyes, Ethel once called him "a picture-postcard career politician," meaning that, in her view, he looked exactly as a politician should look and, sometimes to the dismay of certain of her family members, acted like one, too, which, it would seem, was the problem after Michael's death.

After Michael's passing, much of the grieving Kennedy family was gathered in Ethel's living room, watching television news reports. They were so numb, they could barely speak to one another. Suddenly, there before them on television appeared Andrew, explaining to a reporter that the Kennedys were all mourning, that it was a bad time for them, and that they hoped for the space to mourn in private. What he said was actually quite benign, and also true. The fact that he said it at all, though, was the problem. "Who made *him* a Kennedy spokesman?" one of the family members said, bolting up from his chair. According to this relative, "Everyone had been so solemn and then, suddenly, so agitated as we reacted to this breach. You just didn't do that. You didn't break ranks and go rogue like that. It felt like Andrew just wanted attention, that it was an opportunity for him to get in front of a camera. No one was happy about it."

Rory, still traumatized by the ordeal of having tried to save Michael's life with mouth-to-mouth resuscitation, confronted her brother-in-law as soon as he walked back into the house. "Andrew," she exclaimed, "why did you do that?" Confused by his sister-in-law's annoyance, he explained that he felt someone needed to address the media. He said he realized that the Kennedys were all too distressed to do so and he thought he would step in for them. He thought they'd be grateful, not upset. As he explained himself, he began to get a little defensive. "First of all, Andrew, I would correct your attitude," Rory told him, sounding much like her mother. "And second of all, you shouldn't have done it."

Even the visiting Ena Bernard knew better, Rory noted. When Ena picked up the phone and it was a reporter, she told him, "I take care of the Kennedys. I don't help you write stories about them." She then slammed the phone down, exclaiming, *"Ay caramba!"* How was it, Rory wondered, that Ena had more sense than Andrew? She then turned around and left the room; Andrew also stormed out. "You know what I like about that guy?" one of the Kennedy brothers asked no one in particular. "Nothing."

The next day, Andrew complained to Bobby's wife, Mary, that Rory had been dismissive of him and that the two had had a bit of a dustup. Mary wasn't the one for him to turn to, though; she'd never liked Andrew. She found him rude and abrasive and only tolerated him because she knew he made her best friend happy. If it had been up to her, though, she would never have selected him for Kerry. "I'm sorry, but I don't want to hear your outrage right now," she told him in front of some of the other Kennedys. "Poor Michael is dead. Show some respect." Andrew made a few excuses, and then, flustered, announced to everyone in the room, "Look, I'm out of here. You won't be seeing me for a while," to which one of the Kennedys responded, "Well, that's the dream, anyway."

Of course, Andrew Cuomo is today serving his third term as governor of New York. However, his early days with the Kennedys are considered by many political historians to be his origin story. By 1997 he was Secretary of the U.S. Department of Housing and Urban Development. A member of President Bill Clinton's administration, he was the former assistant secretary for Community Planning and Development. Philanthropically, he had also distinguished himself in myriad ways, not the least of which by establishing HELP, a successful foundation dedicated to the assistance of the homeless. Even though he and his family were obviously already quite influential in government, it was as Kerry's husband and because of his high-profile link to the Kennedys that Andrew became really well known to most of the country. To the Kennedys, though, he seemed as if he liked the spotlight just a little too much, and if a *Kennedy* thought a person was hungry for attention, that was really saying something. Moreover, they also felt he wasn't kind, that he was brash and inconsiderate. However, he was married to one of their own. So, of course, they had to accept him. For Kerry's brother Douglas, though, that one

THE CUOMOS

Kerry Kennedy had always been clear that she'd never endure the sorts of unhappy marriages she'd seen all around her from the time she was a child. A romantic at heart, she always felt she'd be one day swept away by someone like her father and have a storybook romance like her mother's. "I envy your beautiful memories of Daddy," she once told her. She'd been engaged to a young man in college, someone for whom she fell hard. Tragically, he had a heart attack and died while having a snowball fight. It was devastating. Therefore, at the time she met Andrew, in 1989, Kerry was fragile. He helped heal her heart. He was warm and open, from a family that reminded her of the closeness of her own. Friends would note that when he looked at Kerry it was as if he were gazing at an apparition; he seemed to not believe his good luck in finding and then falling for her. He proposed on Valentine's Day 1990.

"When the engagement was announced, the

media was giddy with anticipation about the melding of these two powerful political families," legendary White House reporter Helen Thomas recalled in a 1999 interview. "The usually staid *New York Times* wrote something like 'This story has just about everything: love, politics, history' . . . the whole she-bang. There actually were some similarities between the two families: both hailing from immigrants — Ireland and Italy — both beginning journeys as underdogs in America, gaining money, power, and influence along the way, and then using it to do battle on the political landscape. But the Kennedys had so much more clout than the Cuomos on a national stage. I think some of them wondered why the heck they were even being compared to the Cuomos. They considered themselves so much *more* of a dynasty with so many *more* political power brokers. Andrew's father, Mario, had long been in Democratic politics; he'd served as the fifty-second governor of New York for three terms, from 1983 to 1994. So the Cuomos basically just had him at the top of the family tree and Andrew on the next limb down. Still, when he and Kerry married, a lot of people looked at it as the merger of two political powerhouse families."

Some reports had it that the Cuomos hoped that being linked with the Kennedys would advance Andrew's political aspirations.

However, because of the scandals that had long been a hallmark of Kennedy history, Mario wasn't sure that aligning with the beleaguered family would do him or his son much good. "We don't engage in scandal" is how Andrew put it. "That's not who we are."

The Kennedys would soon learn that Andrew wasn't necessarily a lighthearted person; many people found him to be downright humorless. What had always been true about the Kennedys was that, despite any problems, they liked to have fun. In that respect, Andrew didn't fit in with them. When he was with his brothers-in-law either at Hickory Hill or at the compound, he wanted to discuss policy, while they wanted to play football. For them, policy was dinner-table conversation, not really for the outdoors. However, even in that dining arena, Andrew didn't seem to blend in. He was never able to squeeze in a word between the many viewpoints, opinions, and criticisms. He actually began to not enjoy being around the Kennedys. That was fine with Kerry, at least at first. She'd had enough of her family anyway and was eager to get to know his. Typical of their differences, when the families began to plan the wedding, Andrew said he didn't want any toasts to be offered at the reception. This took the Kennedys by surprise; the giving of a toast was a family tradition at any gathering, big or small. However, Andrew was

CUOMOLOT

Andrew Cuomo, tall and lanky in his checkered swimsuit, was lounging by the pool one day with one of Kerry's brothers when Ethel approached in her colorful muumuu. "About last night," she began, standing before Cuomo and looking down at him critically. Surprised by her presence, Andrew jumped to his feet in respect. She nodded and told him to sit back down. "You're from an Italian family, Andrew," she then said. "I thought for sure that Italians were fun. But you. You're such a wet blanket. Has anyone ever told you that?" she asked. He looked at her with a stunned expression. "Close your mouth, Andrew," she told him. "You'll catch flies." Was she being insulting? Her beguiling charm and easy naturalness often made it hard to figure her out. It was her laughter as she sat down next to him, though, that answered the question.

Though Hickory Hill was an expansive estate and Andrew and Kerry certainly had their privacy, he was not accustomed to the place's rabble-rousing culture. On this sunny afternoon, Ethel was referencing what had happened the previous night when a Kennedy tried to push Andrew into one of the estate's two swimming pools. The two men almost came to blows over it. "We *are* fun," Andrew protested. "But within reason. Why is it so wrong that I don't want to be shoved into a pool when I'm wearing a suit and tie?"

Ethel nodded. "Okay. Fair enough," she agreed, though secretly she no doubt disagreed.

The two then had an animated discussion about public housing and the devious methods of slumlords in this country, a topic that had obviously become a priority of Andrew's because of his work with HUD. He explained that Mario had started as a lawyer for the underdog, and that he had now proudly taken up the fight himself, a battle Ethel admired and one that sounded a lot to her like something her late husband might have waged. Andrew was also invested in the Office of Fair Housing and Equal Opportunity (FHEO), which had been started under the LBJ administration. Ethel had had mixed feelings about LBJ back in the day but believed deeply in FHEO and its work in fighting discrimination in public housing. Andrew had recently beefed up its staff, wanting to make sure that each and every complaint ever lodged would be dealt with quickly and handled fairly. It wasn't just lip service for him, either. He had deeply held convictions and was passionate, which was clear whenever he talked about his work as an advocate.

In the year that they lived together at Hickory Hill, Ethel began to understand what Kerry saw in Andrew; she became a staunch advocate not only for him and his undertakings but also for the marriage. She began to think that maybe one of the reasons her sons didn't like Andrew was because they were jealous of him. He was a good man, she said, who kept his head down and did his work without distraction. He had a strong work ethic, which she felt some of her more undisciplined sons might consider worth emulating rather than criticizing.

Andrew soon became a fan of Ethel's as well. "My mother-in-law was a firsthand witness to pretty much everything I ever learned about the Kennedys in school," he said at the end of his year at Hickory Hill. "I admire her, probably more than she knows. I now understand that she's been Kerry's greatest influencer."

After that first year at Hickory Hill, the Cuomos settled in a large six-bedroom home in an upscale neighborhood in Queens. They had three children, twins Cara and Mariah in 1995 and Michaela in 1997. Andrew and his mother-in-law continued their close relationship, speaking on the phone several times a week.

While he was well-meaning in his work, it was also true that Andrew Cuomo was a tough boss; most of his aides were intimidated by and even afraid of him. Even those who admired him had to admit that they thought he was a bit of a tyrant. "Every day was blood-sport battle for Andrew," said one assistant of his, "and he eagerly put on his armor to engage in it. It was difficult for him to turn it off when he got home, and from what I understood, he could be less than warm to Kerry, particularly on days when tensions ran high at the office."

Also, because of his heavy workload and his commitment to it, Andrew had become an absentee father. By the end of 1997, Kerry was frustrated. She told her sister-in-law Mary that Andrew was always gone, traveling for work. She'd actually fallen into a pretty good routine with the kids in his absence. When he was finally around, however, his presence threw things into chaos. "To be honest, I'm starting to think it's better when he's not here," she said. "First of all, my expectations are lowered, and secondly, things just run more smoothly." Even when he was home, Kerry complained, Andrew seemed checked out. He was preoccupied, and maybe with good reason. After all, he was contemplating a run for governor. She started to feel selfish wanting more from her husband, and then *that* didn't feel good, either.

Even given her present dissatisfaction with him, Kerry felt Andrew had good ideas for the state of New York and that he could make a real difference. "What if this is his moment?" she asked her brother Joe. His response was, "Pretty much always in politics, it comes down to one of two things: 'I hate that guy' or 'I don't hate that guy.' With your husband, I'm pretty sure it will be 'I hate that guy.' "

Kerry wasn't offended by her sibling's observation. She knew how her brothers felt about Andrew. By this time, he knew it as well. "They can't stand it," he said of them, according to one account. "They just want us to be as miserable as they are."

Andrew didn't see the problems he had with Kerry as being insurmountable. He was still completely devoted to her and the children and felt he was giving to them as much as he had to give. Meanwhile, Kerry didn't want to sabotage his chances of being governor with a high-profile separation and possibly even a messy divorce. She wanted to support him; she felt it was her duty, and she wasn't going to let him down. Still, she wanted to honor her own concerns, too. Rather than cause any sort public sensation at the wrong time in her husband's career, she instead asked him if he would attend

■ ■ ■ ■

PART IX
RUNNING OUT
OF TIME

■ ■ ■ ■

A Culture of Caring

By the beginning of 1998, John Kennedy Jr. and his new wife, Carolyn Bessette-Kennedy, found themselves locked in a routine so familiar to anyone who has ever found himself on constant alert due to the illness of a loved one. The phone would ring in the middle of the night, jarring them from a restless sleep. John would answer it, panic rising in him. He'd then sit up in bed and listen as Anthony's wife, Carole, told him that his cousin was again in the hospital. "I'll be right there," John would whisper into the phone, not wanting to disturb Carolyn. He'd then leap out of bed, tell Carolyn to stay put (she never would, of course), throw some clothes on, race down to the street, and then hop into a taxicab headed to the hospital. Once there, he and Carolyn would find a weeping Carole pacing back and forth while doctors worked on her husband. As they awaited word, Anthony would suddenly stabilize. The next morning would inevitably find the best

487

friends joking about it always having to be "about" Anthony, and why it was that he refused to ever let anyone in his life have a decent night's sleep. A couple of days later, Anthony would be released. John and Carolyn would be relieved. With the passing of a few days, they might actually fall into a habit of sleeping well . . . that is, until the cycle would repeat.

The rest of the year and into the first six months of 1999 would involve more emergency hospital visits and more close calls. Of course, there were always Kennedys, Shrivers, Lawfords, and Smiths coming and going from the hospital, all of whom cared deeply about Anthony. There were also many strangers who kept showing up — friends of friends who wanted the best for him, not to mention the families of other patients who became familiar faces simply because they were also in the hallways every day, pacing the floors, worried about their own loved ones.

"You meet so many people in these circumstances — so many strangers — and you bond with them in the hallways of hospitals and in coffee shops there, and you hear their stories," Gustavo Paredes recalled. "John called it 'a culture of caring' and said that somehow in the midst of all the pain and suffering he started to recognize something so wonderful, so heartwarming — an inherent goodness in people. 'It makes such an impression on you, how wonderful people are at their core,' he told me one day at the hospital. 'It's so powerful, you never want to forget it. You want to hold on to it forever.' "

THE WEALTH OF
THE NEW GENERATION

At the same time that John Kennedy was trying to cope with Anthony Radziwill's devastating illness, he was also taking meetings
with other members of his generation in the
offices of Park Agency, Inc., the family's team
of business managers in New York. The Kennedys were in the process of attempting to
restructure and redistribute their tremendous
wealth. Of course, because of their mother's
marriage to Aristotle Onassis, John and Carolyn were more than set financially for life,
with each being worth as much as maybe $50
million by 1998. "It was hard to imagine how
much money they had," said one of their
cousins, laughing. "We would think, wow . . .
John's that rich but yet doesn't spring for
dinner?" Still, despite his tremendous wealth,
John attended all the meetings at Park
Agency, Inc. — and there were many of them
— feeling that even though he didn't need
the additional money, he was entitled to it, as
was his sister; he wanted to be a part of the

proceedings. Caroline, though, didn't attend a single one. When it came to discussing money with her cousins, she drew a line in the sand. She sent her husband to one of the meetings, and he then reported back to her that John had it covered. The Schlossbergs could safely stay out of it.

Prior to these meetings in 1998, most of the Kennedys of the third generation had their inheritances completely tied up in trusts and other entities that had been created with tax strategies in mind; it all made it difficult for them to access any funds, even for emergencies. In a sense, it wasn't exactly what the patriarch had had in mind. Back in 1940s, Joseph P. Kennedy used to tell his wife, Rose, "I'm making all this money so that my children don't have to, so they can go into public service." In other words, he wanted at least his own children to be able to access their cash, and probably, if he had been asked, he would have liked his grandchildren to have the same access. However, after RFK died in 1968, Rose Kennedy began to clamp down on the way the family's fortune was being spent.

By 1970, each of the families — Kennedys (Jackie's, Ted's, and Ethel's), Shrivers, Smiths, and Lawfords — were allocated about $150,000 a year, a sizable amount for the times with the average per capita income being $9,350. However, Ethel's Hickory Hill

491

was an expensive enterprise. Unlike, for instance, Sargent and Eunice, who had their own thriving philanthropy to finance Timberlawn (their estate from which much of their youth charity was run), Ethel was entirely dependent on the Kennedys' largesse. She was also having trouble accessing her own family's wealth, which had been put into complex Skakel investments that would frustrate and exasperate her throughout the seventies and all the way into the nineties. The third generation — her children and their cousins — also had trouble accessing trust funds and annuities as they got older, which is why some of them ended up finding their own ways of making money. Joe Kennedy II started Citizens Energy, for instance, and when his brother Michael took over the company (when Joe became a congressman), it continued to turn a huge profit and provide many millions of dollars for both of them. Others weren't as lucky. For instance, *Newsweek* reported that Bobby Jr. and his wife, Mary, might be forced to sell their house in Bedford because it was no longer sustainable. "Compared with his wealthier relatives, Bobby and his siblings were paupers," *Newsweek* noted. "His father had spent much of his inheritance on his 1968 presidential run. What was left went largely to his widow, the remaining amount divided among the eleven children." It wasn't true that RFK had used his inheritance to finance his presidential run, but the essence of what *Newsweek* reported of Bobby's siblings having to figure out their finances was true. "Of course, it overstates it to say that any of the Kennedys were ever paupers as *Newsweek* suggested," said the family's attorney Benedict F. Fitzgerald Jr. in an interview in 2012. "But prior to 1998, many of them did have to find ways to make a living in order to augment trust funds that were not easily accessible to them."

Things changed dramatically for the next generation in 1998 when the Kennedys decided to sell off the Merchandise Mart in Chicago — a family enterprise bought by the senior Joe in 1945 for $12.5 million — as well as other massive holdings. This financial reworking was the purpose of all those meetings in 1998 of Kennedy heirs at Park Agency, Inc. The properties that were to be sold consisted of 5.3 million square feet of office, retail, and showroom space — including the Apparel Center in Chicago, the Washington Design Center, and the Washington Office Center, both in Washington, D.C. All of it was sold for $625 million, and the sale was made for one reason: to once and for all seed the lives of the next generation, or as the *Chicago Tribune* put it, "The transaction fulfills a plan by the Kennedy family to sell real estate to satisfy the goals and financial needs of a growing number of family members." A small percentage of the wealth — which would still be managed by Park Agency, Inc. — would be split among all the members of the next generation, the children of Jack, Bobby, Teddy, Eunice, Pat, and Jean. They, in turn, would be free to distribute it to their offspring as they saw fit. Suffice it to say, this 1998 business maneuver would serve to finance a whole generation of Kennedy heirs, and the one after that one, too . . . and likely many more to come.

Pretty much every member of the next generation of Kennedys — and that's twenty-seven cousins, Kennedys, Lawfords, Smiths, and Shrivers — immediately received about $10 million each from the Chicago sale to do with what they liked, and many more millions — don't forget, the sale was for $625 million — which would be invested for them. Today, some of the Kennedys, such as Ted's children, Teddy and Patrick, are said to be worth about $20 million each, most of it from the sale, but also from inheritances. Bobby and Joe Kennedy are today worth $50 million — about $10 million liquid of which came from the Chicago sale and the rest from their own lucrative work: Joe's with Citizens Energy and Bobby's as an environmental attorney. While the wealth of the new generation is complicated in that they all have their own accountants and have invested in their

494

own ways, one thing is certain: if not for the 1998 sale, the Lawfords and Smiths, for instance, and some of the Shrivers, too, would have been in trouble. (Maria Shriver would never have to worry, though; her marriage to Arnold Schwarzenegger set her up nicely.)

Ethel Kennedy's present wealth is estimated at "just" $50 million, but a lot of that is old Skakel money she was finally able to access in the 2000s and not from the Chicago sale. Both she and Ted, whose estate was also estimated at $50 million, decided *not* to profit from the sale of the Merchandise Mart, trickling any of their parts down to their children.

Ethel's son Christopher Kennedy is quite wealthy after having run the Merchandise Mart as its president and later a top executive, even after the sale; he gave up the job in 2011. He remains one of the overseers of the family's investments. Today, thanks in part to his twenty-five years with the Mart, he is worth at least $50 million. When Christopher ran unsuccessfully in the Illinois gubernatorial primary in 2018, he would not reveal his net worth.

As for the fourth generation — the *children* of the third — most are also quite wealthy, again from the Merchandise Mart sale. For instance, Congressman Joe Kennedy III — son of Joe II — has an estate valued at at least $40 million; he's by far one of the richest of all congressmen. Even Conor Kennedy — Bobby Kennedy Jr.'s son — is worth at least $10 million, and he hasn't done a thing to earn it other than to just hire the best accountants to invest what has trickled down to him from the Chicago sale.

Of course, John and Caroline did well when Jackie died and would never have to worry about money. Still, Caroline, like all her cousins, profited from the 1998 sale. Today her proceeds from the sale — including what was invested for her and not just what she received in liquidity — combined with what she already had and invested from her mom (and then, later, from her brother) makes her, by far, the wealthiest Kennedy of her third generation. In 2018, her wealth was estimated at about $250 million.

Once, John Perry Barlow asked John about the big 1998 money deal, which John had begun to refer to as "the Big Chicago Fire Sale." Barlow said, "That's gotta be a lot of money for you, John." John responded, "Well, you know, I don't necessarily worry about money," to which Barlow quipped, "Spoken like a man with a lot of money." John smiled and said, "Yeah, well, you got me there."

CAROLYN'S EMOTIONAL AFFAIR

"I love you," John told Carolyn one day in front of friends. The two had just had a quick argument while having cocktails with friends at MercBar in Soho. No one seems to remember what was at issue; it was just a flash of anger between them, regrettable in that it had occurred in front of people. Embarrassed, John was now trying to make amends. "I *said* I love you," he repeated to Carolyn. There was no response from her. Instead, she turned to someone else at the table and, picking up the menu, said, "Hmmm . . . I wonder what the specials are tonight." John shook his head angrily.

After Michael's recent death and in light of Anthony's ongoing battle for life, things had become a lot tenser between John and Carolyn. When the two showed up for the family's 1998 Fourth of July celebration at the compound, they seemed to be barely speaking.

Carolyn felt that John had changed. She said, "It's as if the light in his eyes has dimmed." Others in his life had to agree; he seemed edgy and irritable, and they attributed it to the ongoing anxiety over Anthony. "I felt John was becoming detached from his emotions," said John Perry Barlow. "It was as if he was afraid to feel, or maybe he had forgotten *how* to feel after spending so many years suppressing emotions while trying to be strong in the face of Anthony's cancer."

It could be said that Carolyn already had enough on her plate just getting through the day. When she thought about the future with John, she admitted to feeling trapped. Was divorce even an option? She'd never gotten over her parents' divorce and had always said she'd never end a marriage of her own. As well as that conviction, she also couldn't help but consider the public's opinion of her. "People already hate me," she lamented. "What will they think of me if I divorce John F. Kennedy Jr.? I won't even be able to leave the house. I just want a normal life," she complained. Some felt she should've thought about that *before* she married a Kennedy. "But I'm tired of being made to feel like I'm broken," she also concluded — and *that* made her friends feel sorry for ever having had any judgment about her at all.

A big mistake Carolyn made, her friends felt, was in quitting her job when she started dating John. She had loved her work at Calvin

Klein and had been there for a number of years. She abandoned it in order to see what else might be out there for her. However, once she became consumed by her relationship with John, she never pursued other opportunities. There's no doubt, looking back, that a woman as ambitious as Carolyn would have benefited from having something else in her life other than her husband. Though she tried to stay busy with charity work, it wasn't enough to give her a sense of fulfillment. "I know now that I need a purpose," she told one friend. "I don't know what that is, though. I feel lost."

Unfortunately, John's own work wasn't going well. Advertising was down at *George* because sales had plummeted. There seemed no way to save it. He was at the office late almost every night trying to come up with a plan. Carolyn had supported his venture, wanting this success for him. Lately, though, she seemed to have lost all interest. "I certainly didn't think it was going to become his whole world," she explained to Carole Radziwill. "It's like the clock is ticking and we're running out of time to be happy."

One *George* executive recalls Carolyn calling John at the office and trying to get into a fight with him about his long hours there. John had just about had it with her. "I don't want to hear anything else from you unless it's 'I love you and I understand,' " he said, shutting her down and then hanging up on her.

Considering that John seemed so emotionally unavailable to her at this time, maybe it wasn't that surprising that Carolyn felt the need to connect with someone else, a person who might hear her problems and offer empathy and advice. In a best-case scenario, she would have continued to turn to her husband and hope to find a better way for them to communicate. Or she could have gone into therapy and utilized a psychiatrist to try to work through her marital issues. Instead, she turned to a male friend, someone she'd known from her days at Calvin Klein. The two had reconnected in the spring of 1998 after running into each other at a benefit dinner. Since he had known her before John, she felt he could better understand the changes she'd undergone in her life since becoming a Kennedy.

The two began to meet regularly for coffee. Years later, he would remember, "We ended up on this complicated journey having to do with her confiding in me because she felt I was a safe place for her. I wanted to be there for her. She was a wonderful person. Something about it felt wrong, though. We both knew it."

One night, when John was out of town, Carolyn and her friend had dinner together, which he would later say "felt a little bit like a date." Afterward, she went up to his apartment and they continued a conversation having to do with John not wanting her to go on his trip with him. She was crying, he was consoling her, and somehow they ended up kissing. It was brief, he remembered, but consensual. Then she pulled away and said, "No. What am I doing? I can't be here right now," and quickly gathered her things and left.

The next day, Carolyn called and said the kiss could never happen again. She was extremely regretful. She wanted to continue the friendship but said that it could be nothing more. She also said she felt she had to tell John about the kiss. "I told her it was a big mistake," recalled her friend. "However, she said she couldn't lie to her husband. 'That's just not who I want to be in this marriage,' she said. But it was nothing, I told her. Why cause trouble? She was adamant about it, though. It started to feel to me like she really wanted to blow things up between them and that she was maybe using me to do that."

Two days later, Carolyn's friend was jolted out of a sound sleep at about two in the morning by the sound of his intercom buzzer. When he went to the speaker and asked who it was, the voice on the other end said it was a police officer who needed emergency access to the building. Against his better judgment, he let the person in. Minutes later there was a pounding on his door. He opened the door to find John Kennedy on the other side, his face twisted in anger. Before he had a chance to say a single word, John swung a haymaker at him, clocking him on the side of his head and causing him to crumple into a heap on the floor. According to him, John then looked down and hollered at him, "Stay away from my wife! Do you hear me? *Stay away from my goddamn wife.*" And then he left. The entire incident — from the time the door was opened to the time John ducked out — took maybe thirty seconds.

"The next day, Carolyn called, full of apologies," he recalled. "I told her we were finished, that I didn't want our friendship to continue. She agreed, said she was sorry, and hung up. I didn't feel like it was over, though. I was right. A couple weeks later, she called me and we started up again with the sharing of her life. We were close to having sex and we both knew it. There was something wrong about it, yet there was also something exciting about it. It was hard to know what to make of it, actually."

JOHN'S POLITICAL MUSINGS

Because she already wanted more of his time, no doubt Carolyn would have also been concerned about John's latest curiosity: he was contemplating running for the United States Senate in 2000, for Daniel Patrick Moynihan's seat.

"I think I'm ready to make the leap," John told his close friend Gary Ginsberg. To test the waters, Ginsberg met with Republican strategist Roger Ailes, who at the time was building Fox News, in order to evaluate John's viability as a candidate. Though decidedly on the other side of the aisle, Ailes was someone who always had his finger on the pulse of current-day politics and, Ginsberg felt, could be trusted to venture an informed opinion — and then to keep that opinion to himself and not go to the press with it. The two had lunch to discuss John's possible candidacy, which in the end Ailes felt was feasible. When Gary reported this good news back to John, he was heartened by Roger's enthusiasm. It was in line with what other political strategists and reporters on the beat had told him.

"Most people felt sure that John could win that Senate seat should he go for it, and that there was no reason he shouldn't at least try," said family attorney Benedict F. Fitzgerald Jr. "I think a concern of John's, though, was that Hillary Clinton was making overtures for that seat after she and her husband were out of office. John didn't want to run against her."

Besides the fact that the Clintons and the Kennedys were close, John was sure he wouldn't win against Hillary. Not only that, he felt bad for her considering what was going on at the time with the Monica Lewinsky scandal. However, John's cousin Kathleen urged him to not allow too many side issues to influence his decisions going forward in politics. "There will always be one thing or another," she told him, according to one account, "and you have to take some things into consideration, but not everything." In November 1998, Kathleen would win another term as lieutenant governor of Maryland, so John had a lot of respect and appreciation for her point of view. "I'm wishy-washy, I know," he told her. "I need to be more like you." She countered with "No. Be more like *you,* John."

Key in the equation as to whether John should run for office would be, of course, his wife's attitude about it. How would Carolyn ever be able to adjust to life as a politician's wife? She was still having trouble reconciling things as just the wife of someone famous. Add politics to John's celebrity and there was no telling how it might impact her life.

Still, there was a lot of optimism about John's future. "There was never any doubt in my mind that John planned to run for the U.S. Senate in the next decade," said his friend the noted historian Douglas Brinkley. Or . . . maybe something else? "John had talked a lot about possibly running for governor in 2002," confirmed RoseMarie Terenzio, "and I think he would have ended up doing that. It came up a lot between us and between him and others. Something was going to happen for John in government. We just didn't know yet what that would be."

COULD THERAPY
BE THE ANSWER?

By March 1999, Carolyn's emotional infidelity with her male friend had been going on for about ten months. While John thought it had ended with his visit to the man's apartment, it hadn't; Caroline had continued with it and kept it from John. He wasn't so checked out that he didn't have his suspicions, though. One night, Carolyn ducked out, saying she had something to do. When John followed her to her confidant's apartment, he was crushed and felt betrayed. He was also furious. He sat outside the building for two hours, fuming. He later told one friend that when Carolyn emerged, he grabbed her hard by the arm, threw her into a cab, and got her home, where they really had it out. He then spent the next couple of nights at the Stanhope Hotel.

On some level, John actually felt it would have been better if Carolyn had been physically intimate with the trespasser in their marriage. At least then maybe he wouldn't have felt the relationship was so important to her. Under those circumstances, he might have considered it an insignificant one- or two-night stand. It would have hurt, but perhaps it could have been worked out. This kind of infidelity, though — which he called "emotional foreplay" — was worse in John's mind in that he felt his wife was breaking a marital trust and sharing with someone else that which she should have been sharing with him. He was crushed by it, especially when Carolyn became defensive and said she felt she deserved the relationship. If she couldn't have candor with John about her feelings, she felt she had a right to seek it out elsewhere. Since she had continued the friendship after saying it had ended, now John wasn't so sure Carolyn hadn't also crossed the line sexually. If she had lied to him once, why not twice? "Of course, his pride kicked in, too," recalled one of John's former coworkers at *George.* "After all, he was freakin' *JFK Jr.* He could have the pick of the litter if he needed 'companionship,' and he'd managed to resist it. So who was *she* to cheat on *him*?

"He told me he was going to go to the guy's place and this time really pulverize him. I begged him not to, telling him that he was lucky the man hadn't gone to the press with that first punch. I told him I felt he and Carolyn needed to go into couple's counseling and work this thing out, that Carolyn's affair of the heart wasn't the real issue, that it was a symptom of a bigger problem. I know others had been telling John the same thing."

After he cooled off, John realized his friends were probably right; there was a reason Carolyn had turned to someone else, and he had to own it; it was as much his fault as it was hers. His mandate had always been that he wouldn't have the same kind of marriage as many of his cousins, and now it would appear that he was headed down that exact same road. He felt he needed to stop and reevaluate things before they got out of hand.

By the middle of April, John and Carolyn were in couple's counseling.

On May 1, the Kennedys attended the White House Correspondents' Dinner; certainly one photograph of the couple taken that night with Carolyn — sporting a long Gaultier clamshell necklace — happily nestled on John's lap is, today, an enduring image of this time in their lives. "They never looked more content and in love than they did that evening," recalled White House reporter Helen Thomas. "I thought, My God, this is Jack and Jackie all over again, isn't it? They were so compelling; you actually couldn't take your eyes off them. The way photographers swarmed them, it really reminded me of the old days, the so-called Camelot days."

It was definitely true that when the couple

was in public, they seemed to be incredibly content with each other. Looking back on photographs like the ones taken at the Correspondents' Dinner begs the question of how Carolyn was able to pull it off. Was it all an act? While it's easy to paint complex relationships with a wide brushstroke, it's usually not wise. The Kennedys certainly had their personal problems, but that didn't preclude them from also having moments of great happiness, especially after they started marriage counseling. Based on what we now know about her, Carolyn wasn't a good actress. She wore her heart on her sleeve. It's a safe bet that when we saw her looking pleased with John, in that moment she'd found a measure of contentment. Conversely, when we saw her looking sad or discontented, those emotions were authentic as well.

A WOMAN'S INTUITION

"You are enough." Those had been Ethel Kennedy's words to Carolyn Bessette-Kennedy more than three years earlier in March 1996 after the infamous argument in Central Park. Since that time, Carolyn and Ethel had gotten closer; Carolyn would often call the Kennedy matriarch for words of encouragement. However, an interesting twist had recently occurred in the way Carolyn interpreted Ethel's advice. Rather than imbue her with courage to socialize with the other Kennedys at the compound, it gave her the resolve she needed to decline invitations there. It emboldened her, in other words, to make her own decisions relating to whether she wanted to attend family gatherings. Sometimes, she would be up for them and she would go. John would be happy. Other times, she would decline. John would then be unhappy. That was fine with Carolyn as long as she wasn't being forced to do something she didn't want to do. Ethel actually approved. It wasn't exactly the takeaway she had expected from her advice, but it was still good, she said, that Carolyn wasn't being cowed by anyone and that she was living her life her own way.

In the summer of 1999, John and Carolyn were invited to the wedding of Ethel's daughter Rory. By this time, Rory — the daughter Ethel gave birth to in 1968 after Bobby was killed — was a Brown University graduate who was beginning a career as a documentarian; in a few years' time she would direct and coproduce the Emmy-nominated series *Pandemic: Facing AIDS.* She was marrying a guy named Mark Bailey. The wedding was to take place at the compound, of course.

Immediately, Carolyn didn't want to go. Besides the fact that if she never went to the compound again, she would have been fine, she had a real instinct about this particular occasion. She couldn't really explain it; she simply didn't want to go. It quickly became a real point of contention between her and John. Finally, John said that if Carolyn was insistent, she would have to call Aunt Ethel and tell her. He wasn't going to do it for her. John suspected — and probably hoped — that she wouldn't have the nerve to do it. Carolyn had a good relationship with Ethel, though, maybe better than John understood.

The next day, Carolyn made the call. She told Ethel that she realized some people might take issue with her for not being with John, but she simply didn't have it in her. She hoped Ethel would understand.

Much to Carolyn's relief, Ethel didn't put up a fight. She said it was fine with her, and would also be okay with Rory and Mark, if Carolyn begged off. Things were changing in the family, Ethel explained. She used to always say, "Hyannis Port is where the Kennedys belong." Lately, though, she knew that wasn't always true. Many members of the younger generation had begun prioritizing their own pursuits over occasions at the compound with relatives. She had no choice but to get used to the idea. For instance, she said that Patrick — Ted Kennedy's son — wasn't going to be attending the wedding; he planned to be in California for a Democratic fund-raiser. In addition, Caroline — John's own sister — would also be absent; she and her husband, Ed Schlossberg, and their children would be vacationing elsewhere. According to a source with knowledge of the conversation, Ethel told Carolyn, "Tell John his aunt Ethel wants him to stop being such a jerk about this thing." After promising to see each other soon, the two women hung up.

When Carolyn, her spirits now lifted, reported to John everything Ethel had said, he still wasn't happy. That's when his personal assistant, RoseMarie Terenzio, decided to take up the cause. She stepped in and telephoned Carolyn and managed to convince her to change her mind.

Of course, John was delighted by Carolyn's decision. In response, he made many promises about their future, among them that he would never force her to go to the compound with him again — this would be the last time. His joy was shadowed by concern, though. He knew she felt forced into doing something she'd been quite clear about not wanting to do. Now he just wanted to get the wedding behind them so that he could refocus his energy on saving his marriage. He still loved her very much.

Obviously, Carolyn wasn't happy, either. She put John on "probation" and said she would know how she felt about him and about their marriage in three months. Of course, she still loved him and there was no denying it. But was that enough?

THE MASTER OF DISASTER

"Where are you, man?" John wanted to know. "You're gonna make us late."

"I can't get there in time," Gustavo Paredes said on the other end of the phone line. "You guys go ahead without me. I'll meet you there."

"Typical, Gustavo," John said. "Now we're gonna be late."

"Yeah, I know."

It was July 16, 1999, and John Kennedy and Gustavo Paredes planned to fly, along with Carolyn, to the Cape for Rory's wedding. John would fly his new Piper Saratoga, purchased a couple of months earlier, which was more luxurious, comfortable, and better in performance than his Cessna 182. On the way, they would drop off Carolyn's thirty-four-year-old sister Lauren at Martha's Vineyard. Lauren, a human rights activist, was just as striking as Carolyn, with her long dark hair and impossibly thin figure. She looked like a catwalk model and had dated

514

Eunice's son Bobby. She didn't mind flying with John and had done so a number of times in the past. She and her sister would sit in the two seats behind John and try to catch up, straining to hear each other over the din.

Gustavo knew that his mother, Provi, was already at the compound, helping Ethel with wedding preparations. "Be careful up there, John," he told his longtime friend.

"Don't worry about me," John said. "I know what I'm doing."

"Yeah, that's what I'm worried about," Gustavo said, laughing.

John loved to fly, and everyone in the family knew it. Ever since he was a small child, he had loved planes. Back when his father was President, he actually thought Air Force One belonged to him. Were his friends and family members worried about his flying? Some were, but for the most part there was a pervasive sense that John was somehow invincible. After all, he'd always been in one scrape or another, so much so that they'd lost count of the number of times one limb or the other was in a plaster cast. No matter the circumstance, he always seemed to emerge with a loopy grin and a great story. "You never imagined that anything could ever happen to him," said John Perry Barlow, who first introduced John to flying in Wyoming in a Cessna. "He was the one who took care of everyone else. Plus, even if you were worried,

515

there was nothing you could do about it. Ever since his mother died, he was determined to make every second count. If you loved him, you wanted him to live the kind of life he wanted for himself. You felt like he *deserved* to fly.

"When he bought the new plane, we chuckled about it among ourselves because John was the kind of guy who would lose his car keys or his wallet every day," Barlow added. "He was that guy whose socks never matched, so it could be said that precision and accuracy wasn't his forte. A lot of his klutziness had to do with his ADD. So the idea of John flying? Each time he went up in a new plane, it was a little scary. I mean, if you knew the guy. We didn't call him the 'Master of Disaster' without good reason. Since I'd introduced him to flying, I always felt responsible for him and tried to keep an eye on him, but I admit there were times I was sorry I had endorsed the idea."

Carolyn had originally been dead-set against John's flying. However, during those times he convinced her to go up with him and it was just the two of them, she couldn't help but note the advantage of being, at long last, alone with the man she loved with no interruptions. It was almost cosmic, she would have to admit. Therefore she actually began to look forward to those solitary moments with him. Still, though, she was usually on edge. Though she would try to relax and would sometimes be able to do so, for the most part she was nervous. "If John had ever decided to abandon his beloved hobby," said Gustavo Paredes, "she definitely wouldn't have fought him on it, put it that way."

On the evening of Friday, July 16, 1999, at about eight-thirty, John took off in his Piper Saratoga from Essex County Airport in Caldwell, New Jersey, headed first to Martha's Vineyard and then to Hyannis Port, with Carolyn and Lauren. As we all know, they didn't make it. The plane ended up nose-diving into the Atlantic Ocean off the coast of Martha's Vineyard.

John Perry Barlow had a conversation with John just two weeks before the tragedy during which he warned him of the danger of depending on his own perception while flying in hazardous conditions rather than on a plane's instruments. "I told him I felt like he knew just enough about flying to be dangerous," John would recall. "My exact words to him had been, 'You're always late because you are constantly enchanted by whatever is going on in the immediate present. This means you're going to fly yourself into conditions that wouldn't have existed had you left on time. Which means that you will find that you are flying on instruments whether you have an instrument rating or not.' " In fact,

John didn't have an instrument rating, meaning he was only certified to fly under visual flight rules. "I have just one thing to ask of you," John Perry Barlow recalled telling John. "Which is if you lose sight of the horizon, don't look for it. Just put your eyes on the instruments and believe them. Pay no attention to what may seem to be going on outside the aircraft. But when John flew into the vicinity of Martha's Vineyard about an hour later than he'd planned, he lost sight of the horizon due to a well-known ocean effect that I had encountered many times while flying back east. And he did exactly the wrong thing."

Since that awful night, details of this great American tragedy of July 16, 1999, have been dissected and analyzed so repeatedly by reporters, newscasters, historians, biographers, and, of course, close friends and family members, there seems little reason to explore any of it again. Suffice it to say, it was later speculated that John may have suffered from spatial disorientation, meaning that, due to foggy bad weather, his balance and depth perception were compromised, making it impossible for him to distinguish the plane's position in the sky. "In other words," said one investigator, "up became down. Down became up."

The National Transportation Safety Board also hypothesized that tension could have played a part in John's inability to control the plane. According to the Aeronautical Information Manual, "stress from everyday living can impair pilot performance, often in subtle ways. Distractions can so interfere with judgment that unwarranted risks are taken, such as flying into deteriorating weather conditions to keep on schedule."

Whatever the case, much of America would wake up the next morning to ominous televised imagery of nothing but vast blue ocean and the sound of solemn newscasters fearing the worst about a man some lovingly called the "Prince of Camelot."

It was Anthony who was tasked with tracking down Caroline Kennedy at Mountain Village Lodge in Idaho, where she and her family were vacationing, to give her the news. This was where the Schlossbergs had planned to celebrate their thirteenth wedding anniversary and also Ed's fifty-fourth birthday (both on July 19). Anthony had trouble reaching her, but finally, with the help of the local police, managed to leave a message for her at about four-thirty in the morning on the seventeenth. She called him back immediately. "It's John," he said. "His plane was supposed to arrive here hours ago. He hasn't shown up."

From that moment on, it would be just one frantic call after another from Caroline to friends and family, including her uncle Ted, as she and Ed tried to figure out exactly what was happening. That evening, the Schlossbergs boarded a private plane, headed back home to New York. "I helped them with their luggage," recalled Ken Nedeau. "Few words were exchanged, but you could see the panic in Caroline's eyes."

Once they got back to New York, the Schlossbergs would retreat to their home in Sagaponack, Long Island. Though everyone in her midst tried to be optimistic about John's safety and that of his passengers, Carolyn and Lauren, Caroline seemed to know better. "I can't feel him," she told Ed. "Usually I can feel his presence. But I can't now. I think he's gone."

"The Worst Day of Our Lives"

At first, Ethel Kennedy wasn't going to accept any bad news about John, no matter what she was being told or how many times she was told it. When Ted called her at five in the morning that Saturday to inform her that John's plane had gone missing, she said she was sure it would be found. She refused to accept any alternative. She then commenced with preparations for Rory's wedding. She'd seen a lot of tragedy in her seventy-one years — she'd buried a son just a year and a half earlier. Not again, though, she decided, and not John. It was as if she felt that if she kept busy with wedding plans, maybe enough time would pass and John would just show up. "He always pops up at the last minute," she said, echoing the thoughts of many others.

With the passing of more anxious hours, Ethel began to fear the worst for John. Of course, she had also grown fond of Carolyn. She often spoke of that first dinner at her home, the one for which "the newbie" seemed so ill-prepared. "Why was she on that plane?" Ethel kept asking. "I told her not to come. We talked about it. She said she wasn't coming and I told her it was okay. I thought we agreed. So *why was she even on that plane?*" Very upset, she said she believed Carolyn must have had some sort of instinct about the trip, something that was warning her not to take it. "Oh, how I wish she had listened to it," Ethel said.

When Gustavo Paredes walked into Ethel's house without John, he was swarmed by Kennedys because they all knew he was supposed to have been on the flight with John. They figured that if he was safe, then maybe . . .

"Oh my God," a tearful Provi Paredes said, rushing to her son. "I thought . . ."

"I'm okay, Mom," he told her, holding her tight. He explained that he'd missed John's flight and had found another way to get to the compound.

"But what about John?" Provi asked, her tone urgent.

"I don't know," Gustavo said helplessly. "I just don't know."

Provi then went to sit in the kitchen with Ena Bernard and her daughter, Fina, both of whom were distraught; the two had known John since the day he was born and had flown in for the wedding. "My mother tried to remain stoic," said Fina, "as did Mrs. Kennedy. I was more emotional. It was a terrible time; we just didn't know how it was going to turn out, but we feared the worst. I remember that the phone never stopped ringing. At one point, my mother picked it up, listened, and then slammed it back down. 'It was a reporter who wanted to know what we ate at the rehearsal dinner,' she said. 'Can you believe it?' "

At midmorning, Holly Safford, the caterer hired for the wedding, called to ask Ethel if there had been any change in plans given the nature of what was being broadcast on the news. Holly had been catering Kennedy events for almost ten years, ever since Rose's hundredth birthday back in 1990. She understood Ethel's exacting nature. She liked to tell the story of the day she opened her mail to find a sheet of white paper upon which had been drawn a small pencil sketch of a three-dimensional square. She read the note. "Holly, this is *exactly* the size crouton I want in the Caesar salad. No bigger than this, please. [signed] Mrs. Kennedy." That was Ethel's way.

Ethel insisted to Holly that everything was still, as she put it, "a go." Holly Safford recalled, "She told me, 'We're going to have a wedding today. I promise you.' She would not give in to fear, she said, and no one else should, either. There were still calls to make, details to review. She had promised Rory it would be a special day, and she didn't want to let her down. Rory had been on a sort of uneven emotional keel ever since Michael's death. Eighteen months had passed, but of course she wasn't over it. She deserved to be happy, Ethel told me, and this day had been planned with every intention of seeing her smile again."

At about noon on Saturday, the catering trucks appeared at the compound and with them dozens of workers carrying trays of foods and placing them on long banquet tables that had been set up under large tents. "Keep that stuff covered," Ethel ordered. "We get an awful lot of bugs around here." She then watched as three florist trucks pulled onto the property. From them emerged six men, all in white and dressed for the occasion, each carrying large arrangements of mostly red roses. Ethel rushed over to them to tell them where to set up the flowers, "Definitely out of the sun at least until the ceremony," she instructed, "or they won't stand a chance."

Ted Kennedy had been on the telephone for hours, trying to get information about John and then calling all his relatives to pass on what he knew. At one point, he decided he wanted to get out of the compound for an hour. He knew, though, that the perimeter was crawling with reporters. At that moment, he saw Provi and Ena getting into a car with Fina. "Where are you ladies headed?" he asked. They said they were going into town to pick up some things the caterers had forgotten. "Mind if I hitch a ride?" he asked. He then got into the backseat with Fina, and as the car pulled out of the compound, Ted ducked low so as not to be seen by paparazzi. "My God," he said as the little coterie made its escape. "We Kennedys have had bad days, but I dare say this could be the worst day of our lives. I'm not sure how we'll be able to handle it if John is gone. I actually don't think we could do it." He asked Ena to please be available to Ethel if necessary. "I think she's going to need you," he told her. He suggested she stay in town a little longer than she'd originally intended. Of course, Ena said she would do just that; "anything for Mrs. Kennedy."

Meanwhile, out on the veranda of her home, Ethel sat in a rocking chair talking to Sister Pauline Joseph. "She seemed older to me than ever," said the nun. "I wondered if maybe this was one tragedy too many for her. We noticed Rory and Mark walking on the beach, arm in arm, seeming so sad. They were both thirty, their lives together just beginning, but on such a dreadful note. Above them was a helicopter, I assumed from the media, probably photographing them. 'Not one second of peace, I guess,' Mrs. Kennedy said, finally looking at me. 'Do you think I should go out there, or should I just leave them be?' she asked. 'Go,' I told her. 'They need you, Mrs. Kennedy.' She nodded, rose, and then began walking slowly down the pathway toward the beach. I noticed she was limping. I hadn't noticed it earlier and wondered about it."

Ted returned to the compound at about this same time. As he settled in at his home, he relayed to family members the story of his brief escape with the help of Provi, Ena, and Fina. "They know so much more about our pain than we do about theirs," he said of them. "I've always marveled at their allegiance to us." Moments later, the phone rang; it was the Coast Guard.

After talking to Rory and Mark, Ethel made her way back to the porch of her clapboard home. As she gazed out at the ice-blue cold sea, she noticed Ted walking across the expansive green lawn between their two homes. His head was bowed, his shoulders slumped forward. Ethel didn't make a move. Rather, she just stood as if frozen in place as she watched the senator with apprehension. As he got closer, she noticed Ted's face lined with worry, his expression grave. Once he reached her, she listened as he said a few words. Then, as others looked on with heavy hearts — some of her children and grandchildren, members of her staff, as well as strangers who'd come to prepare for the festivities — Ethel Kennedy buried her face in both her hands. She then collapsed into Ted's arms.

BOOK II

■ ■ ■ ■

PART I
DAUGHTER OF
CAMELOT

■ ■ ■ ■

PROLOGUE:
PINKIE SWEAR

Spring 1973

"I don't know about this," twelve-year-old John Kennedy was telling his sister, Caroline. "When Mummy finds out, we're gonna be in big trouble." The siblings were standing out on a runway at Hanscom Field in Middlesex County, Massachusetts. A flight instructor named Matthew Johnston was standing before them, along with Lem Billings, the family friend who'd taken many of the next generation under his wing, particularly Bobby Jr.

Lately, fifteen-year-old Caroline Kennedy had become fascinated by the idea of flying. She loved looking at pictures of airplanes in magazines and had become fixated by the idea of soaring into the sky. It was one of those crazy ideas that would never amount to anything in the lives of most children. When she would mention it to her mother, Jackie would always say, "Absolutely not." John had been talking about planes since he was three, and she wasn't discouraging of it. However, Caroline was old enough to know better.

Undaunted by her mother's disapproval, Caroline somehow coaxed Lem Billings into signing the permission forms that would allow her to just go up in an aircraft for a quick trial run experience. Why Lem would do this is anyone's guess. He had to know Jackie would not approve. Some in the family would later say Lem probably felt that his best friend — Caroline's late father, Jack — would have wanted his daughter to have the experience, even if just to get it out of her system. Instructor Johnston was ambivalent, though. Many years later, he recalled, "When I said I needed to get Jackie's permission before I could take the kid up, Billings got aggressive with me. He said he was sure it was fine and for me to just let the papers he'd signed be sufficient. Against my better judgment, I said okay. I would just take her up for a quick flight, I told him, not an introductory lesson. In a formal intro, I would let the student actually fly the plane."

"You guys wait here," the instructor told John and Lem as he handed the boy a pair of binoculars. Johnston then helped Caroline into the passenger seat of the cockpit of a blue-and-white Cessna 172. He got into the pilot's and, five minutes later, the plane was slowly pulling out onto the main runway. Caroline, beaming and waving at her brother through the window, was obviously excited. He waved back. Minutes later, the Cessna sped off and then was up . . . up . . . and away.

About a half hour later, Johnston finally brought the plane down. By this time, his young passenger's eyes were as wide as saucers. Yes, Caroline said, she definitely wanted to take further instruction. "Me too," John piped in. *"Me too."* The flight instructor explained that John was too young; fifteen was the cutoff age. "I told him to wait a couple years and come back," Johnston recalled. "He frowned at me. Then Caroline wondered how they would convince Jackie. Lem said, 'Oh, just leave that to me.' He was confident, but John wasn't having it. He said that their mother would never let Caroline fly. 'She's going to be very cross with us for even coming here,' he said. I remember thinking, That's an odd thing for a kid to say — 'very cross.' It sounded like something maybe he'd picked up from his mother."

According to what the instructor recalled, Caroline knelt down to John's level. Holding him by his slim shoulders and looking him straight in the eye, she said, "John, you can't let people tell you what you can and cannot do," she said.

"Even Mummy?" he asked, his eyes wide with surprise.

"Yes. Even Mummy."

535

Matthew Johnston recalled, "As I watched, Caroline made them do a pinkie swear. She told her brother, 'I promise to help you make all your dreams come true, and you have to promise to help me make all of mine come true — and that includes going up in this plane.' They then locked their little fingers. 'Okay, I promise,' John said seriously.

"Lem didn't like it at all," said Johnston, "the part about them not allowing people to tell them what to do. 'That is not right, you two,' he said, glaring down at them. 'It's precisely *because* you are Kennedys that you have an obligation to your family and even to your country. This isn't about your dreams, it's about your obligations. You are old enough to know better. I never should have brought you here,' he said angrily. He was all bent out of shape. 'Now, let's go,' he demanded. Chastised, the two kids didn't say a word. Lem then began walking quickly, and the siblings followed, holding hands, John tripping over his feet trying to keep up. Caroline turned and looked at me with a sad face and waved. I waved back."

The next day, Matthew Johnston got a call from Rose and Joe Kennedy's attorney Benedict F. Fitzgerald Jr. "From my understanding, Jackie called Rose, agitated about Caroline being taken up in a plane," remembered Fitzgerald. "She didn't know how to handle the situation because Mr. Billings, a trusted friend of the family's, had been involved. She asked Rose what could be done about it. Rose called me to ask what I thought. I happened to be a licensed pilot. I had bought my first plane when I was a teenager. I also served as a pilot and flight instructor in the Navy. I taught [baseball stars] Ted Williams and Jimmy Piersall how to fly. Therefore, I understood flight instruction and was astonished that any licensed instructor would have taken Caroline up without parental authorization. I told Rose I would handle it.

"I then called the gentleman and had a reasonable if also firm conversation with him, telling him that the Kennedys were agitated because of what he'd done with Caroline. He was extremely apologetic. He asked if he should call Jackie to express regret. I told him I felt that would just make things worse, to just bow out at this point and never do such a thing again, not only with Caroline but with any adolescent without parental approval. I then reported back to Rose that I had taken care of it.

"The next day, Jackie called me and thanked me. 'We cannot tempt fate in this family,' she told me. 'We've had enough tragedy. I will never let my children fly. Never.' "

"Just the Three"

Winter 2000

"How do you manage to go on after such a tragedy?" a reporter was asking Caroline Kennedy.

"Oh, you just do," she answered wearily. "You do it for the children. You have no choice, really. You have to soldier on." Her answer sounded much like one her mother might have given back in 1963 after her father was assassinated. Like Jackie, Caroline always made it sound so easy, as if it was all just the natural order of things: "One pulls it together because one must" is how Jackie put it. In truth, though, as most people might imagine, it wasn't quite that simple.

By the beginning of 2000 it had been more than six years since Jackie died and barely six months since John's passing. Caroline, now forty-two, was petite at five foot three, four inches shorter than her mother. Her brown hair was most often cut to her shoulders and simply parted in the middle. She usually wore little makeup. "Unlike Jackie, I guess you could say that from the time she was a young woman Caroline would never be thought of as necessarily glamorous," observed Letitia Baldrige, Jackie's former White House social secretary, in a 2005 interview. "She was utilitarian in appearance. In other words, she wasn't one to pore over fashion magazines in search of the latest styles. I think she preferred casual wear for an easy-to-manage appearance. As long as she looked put-together and represented herself and her family with good taste, and she always did, she was fine."

Maybe not in style, but certainly in character, Caroline was much like Jackie — powerful, determined, and with a will of iron. She and her husband of fourteen years, Ed Schlossberg, lived comfortably in an eleventh-floor co-op on Park Avenue. Their home, with its modernist decor, was magnificent with its picture gallery (a large ornate room in which the Schlossbergs displayed their expensive works of art), dining room, kitchen and pantry, library, study, four bedrooms, and four and a half baths, all with high ceilings and city views. The Schlossbergs also owned a country home in the Berkshires and a summer home in the Hamptons, the previously mentioned Sagaponack house. Their marriage was strong and steady, in no small part due to Caroline's insistence that she retain her own identity; if she had learned anything from her mother, it was to never lose herself in her marriage. She never officially changed her name to "Caroline Kennedy Schlossberg," for instance. It would always be "Caroline Kennedy."

For Caroline, the woman recently referred to in one newspaper editorial as "the only remaining child of Camelot," the grief she felt over John's sudden passing remained mind-numbing, despite what she suggested in press interviews at this time. "After John's death, she was in bad shape," said her housekeeper and longtime friend, Marta Sgubin. "She was shattered. She cried all the time, constantly. I saw her many times with her uncle [Ted], her head on his shoulder as she cried and he comforted her." Marta started working for Jackie as a nanny in 1969 when John was eight and Caroline eleven. After the children no longer needed a nanny, she stayed on as the family's chef. Now, all these years later, Marta still worked for Caroline; she still does.

People in her life say that Caroline has always felt misunderstood where John was concerned. Her detractors charge she was hell-bent on having her way with him, no matter the dispute. As his older sister, yes, she could be bossy and even she would have to admit to it. "But there was no one in her life Caroline cared about more than her brother," said one of her longtime friends.

"She loved him so much that I think she would agree that sometimes she became overbearing, almost as if she was his mother. But after their father died and their mother went into a tailspin, it was up to Caroline to look after John, and she did, and she always would. He knew it, too, and I think that's why he never came out too strongly against her. 'We always had this sort of unspoken communication,' she once told me, 'and even when he was mad as hell at me, I know he got it that what I really wanted was the best for him.'"

People also accused Caroline of being deliberately contentious where Carolyn Bessette was concerned simply because she didn't like her. She knew she'd been hard on Carolyn. However, people who know Caroline best say that besides the fact that she had little in common with Carolyn, she also had a gut instinct about her. Early on, she intuited that she wasn't strong enough to survive life as a Kennedy. She feared that she'd buckle under the pressure and that, in doing so, she would bring John down with her. After Carolyn was gone, though, Caroline would have some tough moments wondering if she should have done more to help her, especially given that the two did have similar views when it came to privacy and the stalking media. "In the end, if she was going to beat herself up over anything," said

Caroline's friend, "it wasn't about John. It was about Carolyn. I think she wished she'd been just a little bit more generous with her, that's all."

Making things all the more complicated for Caroline was the fact that her cousin Anthony was now also gone. "When John passed, Anthony was the first person I thought of," recalled Gustavo Paredes. "I wondered, 'How in the world is he ever going to deal with this?' The last time I saw him was at John's funeral; he was a pallbearer. I could see then that his life was already over." Less than three weeks later, Anthony would follow his best friend in death, passing from this world to the next in a New York hospital in his wife, Carole's, loving arms. "Loss upon loss," is how his grieving mother, Lee Radziwill, put it; she had used the same phrase after Bobby Kennedy followed his brother Jack in death. "This was hard on Caroline, too," said Gustavo. "She grew up with Anthony. She loved him, too."

For the rest of the summer of 1999 the Kennedy family tried to get Caroline and Ed to the compound to commune with the family there, but to no avail. When the season turned, Ethel invited them to Hickory Hill several times and, again, was turned down. Caroline and Ed chose to spend less time, not more, with the Kennedys. Caroline found it uncomfortable to be around so many of them, just as her mother had at times; extended family was best in small doses. One wonders if she knew that she and her late sister-in-law, Carolyn, shared this feeling.

"When Jackie was alive, it was just the three of them — Jackie, Caroline, and John," said Christopher Lawford. "So many times, I would hear the question posed to Aunt Jackie, 'So, who's coming?' whether it was an invitation for a dinner or a clambake or something else. Jackie would always answer the same way: 'Just the three.' John loved being with the cousins, always did. You had a sense, though, that Caroline was just getting through it. She and Maria were close and she had a rapport with Kara. But for the most part, Caroline didn't really fit in. When both Jackie and John were gone, a lot of people felt that maybe the connection to Caroline would be broken, too."

THE JACQUELINE KENNEDY YARDSTICK

Because of the way she captivated most of the country while being raised with her little brother, John, in the White House, Caroline Bouvier Kennedy would always be viewed by a generation of people as "America's daughter." Today she has a wealth of happy memories of those Camelot days — the trips overseas with her mother, the glamorous First Lady, Jacqueline; the fun moments of dancing in the Oval Office with her father, the handsome President Kennedy; the friends she made in the private school her mother organized in the White House, not to mention her pony Macaroni, whom she would ride on the grounds. Born on November 27, 1957, Caroline actually began learning vocabulary during the 1960 campaign, her first words being "plane," "goodbye," and "New Hampshire." Jackie once said, "I'm just sorry more states don't have primaries, because if they did we'd have a little daughter with the greatest vocabulary in history."

Everything changed when Caroline was five. That's when, on November 22, 1963, her father was assassinated. Unfortunately, she also has vivid memories of that dark time. Today, she can still recall details of the funeral, for instance, and even remember with clarity that historic moment when John, on his third birthday, saluted their father's coffin. John didn't really remember it. "If only I could remember," he would say with longing. However, Caroline could call up all the details, including the unspeakable grief, and it would take years of therapy for her to even begin to reconcile it.

"In 1969, Jackie told me that when Caroline was about eight, she started taking her to the noted therapist Erik Erikson," Joan Braden recalled in a 1998 interview. Joan, the former personal secretary and economic assistant to Nelson A. Rockefeller, was also a campaign worker for the Kennedys and a close friend of the family's. "He said that Caroline was suffering from an identity crisis. I laughed and told her that she should stop with the headshrinkers; they didn't know what they were talking about. 'But she's just *so* unhappy,' Jackie said. 'She walks around all the time with her little hands clenched in fists; she seems angry at the world.' "

Jackie explained to Joan that — at least according to Erikson — Caroline had lost her father at a time in her life when she was just beginning to understand her identity and her place in the world. The sudden loss of her father made her question everything, including her own mortality. In an effort to protect her innocence, it had been Jackie's well-intentioned decision to at least *try* not to allow Caroline to see her grief. Yet the youngster still understood that her mother was all but broken. "My mommy cries all the time," she told one of the nuns at school when she was little. The inadvertent message to Caroline, again according to Erikson, was that turning away from sadness and not addressing it was acceptable behavior. This belief, he told Jackie, could only lead to trouble for Caroline as an adult.

Caroline would see a number of psychologists until she was about twelve. At that time, Jackie feared that therapy was only keeping her daughter tethered to her grief and stopped sending her.

A year after Jack's death, an anguished Jackie moved herself and her two children to Manhattan to start life anew. As a child, Caroline attended the Brearley School and the Convent of the Sacred Heart, both in New York City and within walking distance of Jackie's apartment.

"I think by about the age of eighteen, Caroline came to the conclusion that she would probably never get over Jack's death, but that she needed to find a way to get past it long enough to get on with her life," said Joan Braden. "While she never wanted to disgrace him or her family name, Caroline also viewed the royal and heroic 'Camelot business,' as she called it, as not really being rooted in much reality. She became bored hearing from her mother and [maternal] grandmother, Janet [Auchincloss], how Kennedys were supposed to act. After all, it could be said that she saw a bit of bad behavior in a few of her relatives. 'Can we please stop acting like we're one big happy family?' I once heard her ask Jackie. 'Why are we always trying to make our story so perfect when it's not perfect at all, and shouldn't have to be perfect.' Jackie actually agreed with her. 'Of course, dear,' she told her. 'When we're at home, we can act any way we please within reason. But out in the world? Out there, we are Kennedys and we must *be* Kennedys. That's what's expected of us.' "

Caroline graduated from Concord Academy in Massachusetts in 1975. She then received her bachelor of arts degree from Radcliffe in 1980, and by 1985 was attending Columbia University Law School. She then toyed with becoming a photojournalist, just as her mother had once been, and even interned at the New York *Daily News* in 1977 for $156 a week.

A year later, in 1978, Caroline ended up in a brief romance with *Rolling Stone*'s cofounder and editor, Jann Wenner, ten years her senior and recently separated from his wife. Jackie wasn't happy about it. She liked Wenner well enough, but she didn't want him around her daughter. First of all, he was still married; she was adamantly against extra-marital affairs. Also, she sensed an ambiguity about his sexual orientation; he wouldn't officially come out until after her death. Her biggest concern, though, was about his drug use.

Jackie had just joined Doubleday as an editor that same year when Wenner took her to lunch at a New York restaurant to talk to her about a book relating to *Saturday Night Live.* Right in the middle of his pitch, he had a nosebleed that wouldn't stop — apparently the result of a previous night's cocaine binge. As Jackie looked on, horrified, concerned waiters descended upon them from all fronts with towels and ice packs; it was a bloody mess. Later, Wenner was quoted as saying, "My God. *I bled all over Jackie, just like Jack.*"

Despite the unfortunate misadventure in the restaurant, Jackie did arrange for Doubleday to buy Wenner's book idea: *Rolling Stone Visits Saturday Night Live.* However, dating Caroline, even briefly, put him on Jackie's bad side; she wanted nothing to do with him for about two years. Then, after the romance was over and she had cooled off a little, they resumed their friendship.

In 1980, Caroline began working as a research assistant at the Metropolitan Museum of Art. Lisa McClintock, who also worked there, remembers her as being "personable and smart." She also recalls a day she was lunching with Caroline when Jackie walked into the restaurant. Though Caroline looked uncomfortable, Jackie sat down and joined them. At one point, when Caroline went to the ladies' room, Jackie began to pepper Lisa with questions. Was Caroline having fun working there? Did she know a lot of people? Jackie said that she was worried about a daughter who, as she put it, "isn't at all like her brother, who you can't shut up." She said that Caroline was "more reserved, like me" and asked Lisa to keep an eye on her and maybe encourage her to be more outgoing. "I would love for her to be more social," Jackie said. Jackie said she also felt that some of the young men Caroline had dated when she was a teenager "only wanted her because of who her parents are, and that can't feel good to a young girl."

"I gathered that John got away with more," Lisa McClintock continued, "whereas Caroline had it tougher. Boys, dating . . . teenage rebellion . . . all of that was harder with Caroline than it was with John. Caroline told me that when she would go to Europe for the summers and end up on the front cover of those fan magazines with different young men in nightclubs, her mother would become unglued."

"My God, how do I navigate this treacherous mother-daughter business?" Jackie once asked Olga Price, who was one of her housekeepers in the 1970s. "I want this to be such a lovely time in Caroline's life, but she is *so* difficult."

Olga recalled, "I asked Mrs. Onassis, 'Weren't you difficult?' She laughed and said, 'Oh, I was much worse. Mummy used to say I went from adorable to intolerable overnight.' " She added that Janet Auchincloss told her the only way teenage girls ever break away from their moms is to first resent them. " 'Otherwise, they'd probably never leave home,' Janet said, 'but then when they come back, they do so with all their hearts, that is if you give them enough time.' "

Adora Rule, who was Janet Auchincloss's longtime assistant, recalled that when Jackie brought her children to Hammersmith Farm — the family estate in Newport — there were sometimes disciplinary problems. "They came several times a year," Adora recalled, "and I often noted that, as a mother, Jackie could be much harder on Caroline than she was on John. For instance, when Caroline was about fourteen she made a smart remark about something to Jackie. 'How dare you?' Jackie told her angrily. 'Why, so help me, God, Caroline, I will slap the taste right out of your mouth.' Instead of being quiet, the teenager said something else, and sure enough Jackie hauled off and slapped her hard right across the face in front of a room full of people. 'Mummy used to do that to me when I was your age,' she said, 'and now you are forcing me to do it to you, too.' Caroline screamed bloody murder and ran off, sobbing and humiliated. Maria [Shriver], who was sixteen, looked at me with wide eyes as if she was horrified and had never seen anything like it. 'My mummy would never do that to me,' she said. But Jackie had her ways, just like her own mother had her ways and, yes, both could be stern."

Maybe Caroline said it best when she was about eighteen. After apparently having an argument with Jackie, she stomped into her grandmother's drawing room and came across Adora, who was typing correspondence in the corner. "You know, not a single day goes by that I don't measure myself by the Jacqueline Kennedy yardstick," Caroline said, flustered. Adora threw her a curious glance and said, "But I think your mother expects much less of you than you do of yourself."

"Well, I think you don't know me or my mother very well at all, now, do you?" Caroline shot back.

"Oh my. I didn't mean —" Adora said, beginning to apologize.

"Indeed," Caroline said, cutting her off.

RENAISSANCE MAN

The early 1980s, which was when Caroline first began to date Ed, was a period in her life during which most people felt she was at her happiest. "I think falling for Ed was a magical time for her," said Gustavo Paredes. "They went to Aspen together quite a bit, they went to museums, concerts. They spent a little time with the Kennedys at Hyannis, and, of course, lots of quality time with her mother at Red Gate Farm. They never crossed swords, at least not that any of us knew. He was reserved, though, not easy to know. I remember him as this tall man, prematurely gray, sturdy-looking. He didn't waste time on unnecessary friendliness."

"Ed had a house in Chester, Massachusetts, which I believe his parents had given to him, in the Berkshires," added Adora Rule. "I remember it had a wraparound porch and a vegetable garden, which Ed was obsessed with tending. It was rustic and lovely, perfect for weekend getaways. They spent a lot of time there in their own little world. Caroline told me that the attraction where Ed was concerned was simple: she'd just never met anyone quite like him before. He was so smart and so unique as a person; she said she couldn't help but fall for him."

Eleanor Doyle, Chester's postmaster, recalled Ed and Caroline as being "like everyone else. They walked around in blue jeans and blended in," she said. "They were just normal people. They took part in local activities, frequented the village's eateries, and contributed financially to the Chester Historical Society, now located in what was formerly our minuscule town jail. You'd never have known they were rich and famous city people, or 'flatlanders,' as we call them today."

Edwin Arthur Schlossberg, born on July 19, 1945, was twelve years Caroline's senior — the same age difference that had existed between her parents (JFK was thirty-six and Jackie twenty-four when they married). He was definitely a jack-of-all-trades, which may be why some in Caroline's life were never able to get a handle on exactly what it was Ed did for a living: he was an author, a poet, a painter, a designer . . . and an architect. He'd also been a city planner and, at one point, even a screenplay writer, or as John once said, joking, "Pick a job, Ed. Any job."

Schlossberg hailed from an Orthodox Jewish family, his great-grandparents all Ellis

Island immigrants who'd been born near Poltava, Russia. He was raised by his parents, Alfred and Celia Mae Schlossberg — known as "Mae" — on New York's Upper East Side. Because Schlossberg's father was the founder of Alfred Schlossberg, Inc., a successful textile-manufacturing firm in New York, Ed enjoyed a comfortable youth, with summers spent in the family's vacation home in Palm Beach (not far from the Kennedys' residence there). He attended Manhattan's Birch Wathen Lenox School, following his older sister (by seven years), Maryann, who'd also been enrolled. He received his doctorate in science and literature from Columbia University in 1971. "I combined physics and literature. I was using two different ways of talking about the world," he recalled of his doctoral thesis. "It was an imaginary conversation I was having in my head between Einstein and Beckett, two of the most brilliant thinkers I had encountered."

As an artist, Ed had many showings in New York, during which he demonstrated an avant-garde style, painting in watercolors and oil and also employing abstract construction elements such as aluminum and Plexiglas. Eventually, he started his own firm, Edwin A. Schlossberg, Inc., which, according to an early business brochure, specialized "in the multimedia designing of museums and educational environments."

Ed would always be regarded for his taste in art and furnishings — even later giving speeches at the Merchandise Mart in Chicago (which was owned by the Kennedys) about design trends. However, he viewed himself as an academic and knew he had a way of looking at the world some found peculiar. Therefore, he was uncomfortable in the public eye. He especially shied away from giving press interviews. The *Chicago Tribune* managed to get one with him after a Merchandise Mart speech, as long as the reporter agreed to ask no questions about the Kennedys. "Publicity doesn't interest me," Ed said. "The thing that interests me is work. We're living in a culture that if you spend a lot of time thinking about what other people think about you, it distracts you from what you care about. I like what I do, and that's what interests me."

Chris Kennedy, Ethel's son who was executive vice president of Merchandise Mart properties, said of Ed, "To a lot of people, Ed comes across as quiet and shy, but he's actually much the opposite when you know him. With Ed, it's impossible to plumb the depths of his intellect. He is one of the smartest people I've ever known. But he never chats up, runs off at the mouth. People who know Ed talk about him as a true Renaissance man. His big theme is engaging his audience in his designs. I compare him to Ben Franklin. He's playful with inventions.

He loves to see people's reactions."

Looking back today, many in Caroline's life feel that the death of her cousin David was the impetus for the growth of her romance with Ed. Caroline had been in Florida with David when he died of an overdose in April 1984. Distraught, it was Ed to whom she turned. He was a soothing and stable presence in her life during this terrible time. He also did something for Caroline for which he would become known in years to come: He kept her isolated from anyone, including family members, he felt might interfere with her grieving or would have questions she didn't wish to answer. It was then that the template for her relationship with Ed was designed; he was her protector. Because of this purpose in her life, Ed would sometimes be thought of as the enemy by many of Caroline's relatives, especially her cousins. It didn't help that he was rarely diplomatic. Instead, he was often assertive and not always kind. "Who the hell does he think he is?" became a constant refrain when it came to Ed, and it would remain so for decades to come.

A Mother's Work

Ed Schlossberg was pretty much swept away by the Kennedys from the beginning. "Honor. Family. Loyalty," he ticked off when explaining his fascination about them. "These are values they preserve which I think are important." Also, he would say that he'd read up on the history of the patriarch, Joseph P. Kennedy, and that he appreciated the fact that he "had the guts to go after what he wanted for his family, and get it all. That's worth respecting."

One woman more concerned about Ed's decision to marry Caroline was his mother, Mae. She and Alfred had been married for many years, but it hadn't always been easy. Whereas Mae was an expressive woman, Alfred could often be distant and emotionally detached. Mae believed in communication, almost to the point where her need to discuss every little thing drove her husband mad. During a disagreement, he would seethe silently while she fought for an airing of their differences. "When you're married to the same man for decades," she once told Sarah Abelman, a close friend of hers — the two attended Park East Synagogue together — "you learn to adapt. But it takes work." Sarah's daughter, Rebecca, who as a young girl was a good friend of Maryann Schlossberg's (Mae's daughter), recalled, "Mae told my mom, 'I never know what Al's thinking. Most of the arguments we have had in our marriage, I've basically had with myself.' "

Sarah Abelman continued, "Mae was an open book. If she thought it, she said it. She tried to teach Ed and [his sister] Maryann to be the same way, to not bottle things up. In the end, Maryann turned out just like Mae, candid and in touch with her feelings, whereas Ed became exactly like Al — not forthcoming, withholding."

Mae was a petite woman — not even five feet tall — with penetrating dark eyes, a bright welcoming smile, and a shock of black hair that came to a sharp widow's peak. Though small of stature, she was a forceful personality, definitely nobody's pushover. She commanded respect and she got it, especially from her children. Though they often felt she was a meddling mother, in her mind intrusion was a mother's responsibility. As they were growing up, she wanted to be involved in every aspect of their lives and have a say in all of it, from their choice of studies to their choice of romantic partners, or, as she liked to put it, "being a Jewish mother requires commitment."

Early in her son's relationship with Caroline, Mae wanted to reach out to Caroline and Jackie to get to know them better. Ed was reluctant. He didn't want to expose his outspoken mother to Caroline and Jackie, at least not yet. Rather than wait for Ed to arrange things, after a few months Mae took matters into her own hands and simply called Jackie herself. "Our children are dating and I thought it would be fun for us girls to get together," she said, according to one account. Jackie obliged.

A few weeks later, Mae, Jackie, and Caroline went to lunch at Fraunces Tavern, one of the oldest restaurants in Manhattan. It had been Mae's suggestion. The women dined in the Bissell Room, elegantly furnished with eighteenth-century decor. However, because it's known for its whiskeys, beers, and cocktails, Mae — who enjoyed the occasional cocktail — wanted them to relax and get to know one another.

According to family history, as soon as they settled themselves in their chairs opposite each other, Mae reached over to Jackie, took both her hands into her own, and, looking deeply into her eyes, observed that what had happened to JFK in Dallas must have been horrible for her. Remarking that she still hadn't gotten over it herself, she then wondered how Jackie had ever been able to get through it. As the story goes, Jackie smiled enigmatically and slipped her hands out from under Mae's. Then she lifted her head slowly, gazed about the room with interest, and said in that breathy voice of hers, "My, my, *such* an interesting place. Don't you agree?"

Mae quickly came to understood that Jackie was guarded; of course, this couldn't have been much of a surprise to her since the former First Lady's public persona had certainly preceded her. What she didn't know was that Caroline was even *more* reserved. "Mae worked for more than an hour trying to engage Caroline," recalled one relative of hers. "Much to her dismay, neither she nor her mother would have even one cocktail. It wasn't the open airing of feelings Mae had hoped for, put it that way."

Though Mae would be gracious and tell family members she found Jackie and Caroline "perfectly lovely," in truth, she was concerned. She knew her son well and couldn't imagine him being married to a mirror image of himself, someone who was also closed off and reluctant to reveal anything. She had hoped Caroline might be the kind of woman who would draw Ed out, but she quickly came to the conclusion that someone needed to draw *Caroline* out.

Not surprisingly, Jackie and Caroline found

Mae too familiar, bordering on intrusive. In the end, Jackie and Mae would never really be close. In fairness to both, however, Jackie was about twenty years younger than Mae, so that age disparity likely had as much to do with their lack of camaraderie as any difference in their personalities. Mae would have a difficult time getting to know Caroline as well. It would not be for lack of trying, though. Because Mae was so persistent, there would be many more such get-togethers with Jackie and Caroline. She would not stop trying to get to know them.

MUMMY'S WHARF

There was an old beaten-down wharf on Martha's Vineyard in front of Red Gate Farm that was really not much more than a shoddy and wobbly assembly of wood planks, with no guard railing or sides, just a flat surface that was in such close proximity to the ice-cold water below it that high tide inevitably just completely engulfed it. Certainly no boat had pulled up to this wharf in years. It was a barely standing relic of another time, maybe once used by fishing boats. John and Carolyn liked to call this little, somewhat precarious spot "Mummy's Wharf."

Jacqueline Kennedy had bought Red Gate Farm back in 1978 as a summer retreat; she and her children, relatives, and friends spent many happy times there. Early in the morning, Jackie could usually be found standing on Mummy's Wharf, gazing out at the sea, meditating, praying, or just thinking about her life and times — who could know what went through her head in such private moments? "What's she *doing* out there?" John would ask Caroline as, from a distance, the two watched their mother in her solitude, draped in the morning mist. He found the place cold and unwelcoming. Even as the sun would begin to filter through the gray sky, John would worry. "It's still freezing out there, and that thing looks dangerous," he'd say of the wharf. "Let's go get her." No, Caroline would always say — "let's just let her be." It was as if Caroline knew, or in some way could relate to, her mother's need to process things, to not just live her life but to take ample time to analyze it, maybe understand it a little better.

Though many of her family members thought of her as a deep thinker, Caroline wasn't as religious as many of her cousins, most of whom were steeped in Catholicism. Sister Pauline Joseph recalled, "In my company, Mrs. Kennedy [Ethel] quoted a Bible passage to Caroline after John's death: 'Trust in the Lord with all your heart and lean not on your own understanding; in all your ways submit to him and he will make your paths straight.' Caroline smiled and nodded, but I could tell that it didn't resonate with her." Many of her cousins committed themselves to going to church weekly and, in some cases, even daily. They were tethered to prayer, to fellowship, to their faith, but not Caroline. She went to church on occasion, but she was spiritual, not religious. Ethel wished she had her faith on which to lean, or at least a complete trust in God when things happened that made no sense, such as John's death. "With her heart breaking, many of us wished Caroline would turn to the Lord," said Sister Pauline Joseph, "but she had her own way of handling things."

After her brother's death, Caroline Kennedy would bundle herself up in a warm fleece jacket, her head in a favorite colorful scarf that had once belonged to her mother, and retreat to Mummy's Wharf so that she could be alone with her grief, trying to reason it all out. Ed would join her sometimes and the two would talk, but then he would inevitably turn around after about fifteen minutes and make his way back up to the main house at Red Gate, leaving his wife alone with her thoughts.

THE RICHES OF MARRIAGE

Caroline had always known that Mae Schlossberg had concerns about her son, Ed, marrying her. Mae brought it up several times, saying she was worried about their communication skills. Caroline didn't take it too seriously; she felt Mae was entitled to her opinion and she would work it out herself with her husband when the time presented itself. When Jackie heard about it, she didn't necessarily agree with Mae. "Well, it's been said that silence is one of the great arts of conversation," she observed, quoting Cicero. Jackie did agree with Mae, though, that there could be problems ahead for Caroline, but for a different reason. Ed just wasn't stimulating enough, at least in Jackie's view. She found him pedantic, staid, and a little old for his age. Some people who knew about her critical opinion of him — like her sister, Lee — believed that what Jackie actually felt, at her core, was that Ed just wasn't "good enough" for her daughter.

Janet Auchincloss's longtime assistant, Adora Rule, says she was at Janet's home, Hammersmith Farm, tending to Janet's needs in the summer of 1985 when Jackie and Caroline came to visit. They became engaged in an emotional conversation about Ed over breakfast one morning. "Jackie and Caroline were in the kitchen with me, Janet, and Margaret Kearney, who had been Janet's late husband Hugh Auchincloss's personal secretary, when the subject turned to Ed. Jackie said she was happy to have Caroline date him, but to marry him? No."

"I want your life to be a great adventure, like mine has been," Jackie told Caroline, this according to what Adora recalled. "I have had *such* a great life, Caroline," Jackie said, "and you deserve one, too."

"But Ed can do that for me," Caroline protested.

"No," Jackie said, shaking her head. "He's just not that exciting, Caroline. He's a homebody. Why, you're going to live in *New York* for the rest of your life," she exclaimed with a shudder. Jackie said she wanted Caroline to travel more and meet all sorts of "new and exciting men," just as she had done when she was her age.

Certainly, Jackie did have a spectacular life, but if one analyzes it, she actually didn't have a lot of "new and exciting men." She'd had Caroline's father, of course, who went from senator to President, making Jackie a First Lady, obviously a once-in-a-lifetime experience. She'd also had the Greek tycoon Aristotle Onassis, a marriage that was a whirlwind for her. Then she went right to Maurice Tempelsman, a diamond merchant who was safe and easy, treated her well, and gave her a sense of security, though not much stimulation. However, she was in her forties by the time Maurice came along, and she was ready to settle into a more "sensible" lifestyle. Caroline was only twenty-seven. Jackie didn't want the history of her romantic trajectory to be a straight shot to Maurice without having the experience of at least a Jack and an Ari along the way. "Ed's just not . . . interesting," she repeated. "I mean, do you really find him so?" she asked her daughter.

"Well, *I've* never been interesting to anybody, either," Caroline said glumly. She dropped her eyes, not elucidating further. Though Jackie didn't seem surprised to hear such self-deprecation, the other women were taken aback. "But that's just not true, dear," Margaret Kearney said. "Why would you say such a thing?"

"Suddenly, I saw that there was another problem at the root of things, and that was Caroline's lack of self-esteem," recalled Adora Rule. "From the way Jackie then spoke to her, I realized that this was nothing new, that this had been an issue in the past. She told Caroline that she *was* interesting and that she had *so* much to offer. 'Someday, people will brag that they even *knew* you,' she said.

"I suddenly understood that it must have been hard for Caroline to live in her mother's shadow, to be the only daughter of Jacqueline Kennedy Onassis. What a heavy load that must have been for a young girl. Finally, Caroline just got up and rushed away, crying. The episode was brief, but I'd never previously witnessed anything like it between mother and daughter, and believe me, I had been around them a lot. After Caroline left, it was just me, Jackie, Janet, and Margaret."

"All I want is for her to have a thrilling life," Jackie said. "Is that so wrong?"

"That's the wish of most mothers, isn't it?" Margaret asked.

"I certainly hope not," Janet answered. "The riches of marriage are not in its thrills," she concluded. She delivered the pithy aphorism in the way Janet was known to deliver her best lines, with great authority. At this point, she was just at the onset of Alzheimer's disease, with her short-term memory diminished, though not her long-term. "I'm afraid you have romanticized Jack and Ari," Janet told her daughter. "Neither one was good to you, Jacqueline. Maybe they were exciting men, but good husbands they were not." Perhaps that wasn't really the point, though,

Janet offered. If Jackie's intuition was telling her that Ed wasn't right for Caroline, for whatever reason, then it was her responsibility as the mother to disallow the marriage. She also added that Caroline was "young and pretty. Someone better will come along," Janet said. "You can get her settled later. The bloom won't yet be off the rose. I hope."

Jackie stood up and walked over to her mother. Bending down, she took Janet's face in both her hands. She kissed her on the cheek. "You're right, Mummy," she told her. "When you're right, you're right." Then, with a distant kind of smile, she left the room.

■ ■ ■ ■

PART II
THE POLITICS OF
MARRIAGE

■ ■ ■ ■

"MARRIAGE IS ABOUT FORGIVENESS"

Caroline Kennedy and Ed Schlossberg would finally marry in Hyannis Port on July 19, 1986, Ed's forty-first birthday. "The weather was perfect," recalled the family's chef, Neil Connolly, "a gorgeous July day that every bride would wish for. There were breakfasts, boat lunches for the Senator and his guests, and a parade of elaborate dinners. That morning I accompanied Jackie on foot as she crisscrossed the grounds of the compound, making last-minute arrangements to ensure the day would go smoothly."

Jackie asked Ethel to be responsible for the hairstyling and makeup of the women in the party, and also some of their friends and relatives when necessary. "Nothing too fancy," Ethel cautioned as she walked into one of the rooms in her home in which the bridesmaids' hair was being styled. "And nothing too sexy. We're going to a wedding, not a nightclub. And don't forget," she hastened to add, "the shorter the skirt, the longer the confession."

Ethel also presented everyone with what would today be considered a "nondisclosure agreement," a contract stipulating that every person involved in the wedding was restricted from talking to the media about it. "She actually had a stack of such documents — 'one for you, one for you, and one for you,' she said as she went around to each person," said Lenny Holtzman, the Boston stylist chosen by Ethel.

It would be a lovely wedding at Our Lady of Victory in Centerville, a few miles from the family's compound. Caroline's stunning clover-appliquéd white silk organza wedding trousseau was designed by Carolina Herrera. Ted walked her down the aisle. John was best man. The next morning, there was a spectacular fireworks display over the bay at sunrise. Jackie, in a green crepe sheath by Carolina Herrera, graciously made it a point to dance with as many of the men in the Schlossberg family as possible; there obviously wasn't one present who didn't want a chance to have her in his arms.

After the wedding, a reporter asked Caroline what she would now be called, and, annoyed by the media intrusion, she responded with a curt *Caroline.*

Within a couple of years, Jackie began to appreciate Ed and what she called "that unique place in which he lives." She would tell relatives that in getting to know him she'd come to realize that not all artists are easily accessible, and it sometimes takes effort to understand them and the way they occupy the world. Also, she decided that he really did make her daughter happy and, she concluded, maybe that was better than a life of thrilling adventures.

After Caroline and Ed had children of their own, mother and daughter became even closer. Jackie wanted nothing more than to have a close relationship with Rose, Tatiana, and Jack; all three loved their "Grand Jackie" very much.

Meanwhile, Mae and Alfred had their own rapport with the children, but, as it would happen, over the years there wouldn't be much mixing with the Kennedys. If ever there was a case of people just not finding common ground because they were so different, it was so for the Kennedys and the Schlossbergs.

Caroline's father in-law, Alfred, died in 1995. He was eighty-seven when he succumbed after a two-week bout with pancreatitis, leaving Mae, eighty-five, sadly on her own.

In the ensuing years, Mae continued to reach out to Caroline, always taking her side whenever there was any sort of disagreement with Ed. As the two women got to know each other — especially after Jackie's death — they became even closer. After a long and happy life, Mae Schlossberg died peacefully in May 2005 at the age of ninety-four.

Everyone had to agree, though, that Caroline and Ed had what appeared to be a good relationship. One relative recalled asking Caroline about her philosophy relating to marriage and she said, "Marriage is about forgiveness." It was a provocative observation, but what did it mean? Before that relative had a chance to pursue it, Caroline changed the subject.

SHARE YOUR PAIN

Like Jackie and Mae before her, being a good mother mattered to Caroline Kennedy. For instance, if there was a school dance at Brearley for Rose or Tatiana, she always wanted to be one of the mothers on the committee. "Even though she was so famous and standing out always made her feel self-conscious, she did it anyway," said one of Caroline's closest friends. "She would also be one of the dance chaperones, if need be, or one of the moms filling plastic cups with soda — whatever it took. She would also be the mother waiting patiently in the car in front of the school for her girls at the end of the day, and no, she would not send Marta or some other person working for her to retrieve them. It was her job, and she not only wanted to do it, she absolutely loved doing it. She would send Jack off on a crosstown bus to Collegiate. She would then walk her girls ten blocks to their school, Brearley, and coordinate things so that she could pick them up at the end of the day on her way home, with Jack in the backseat after having met him at the bus stop."

Family members recall what happened when six-year-old Jack came home from school one day and complained that, in class that day, everyone was told to pick a partner for a project. No one picked him. He was embarrassed and sad and felt isolated. Of course, Caroline was alarmed. She pushed the matter with him until learning that it was often the case with the boy that he was left with no partner, that the teacher had to select someone to work with him. When Caroline then went to the school to have a conference with the instructor, she was told that Jack was shy and didn't open up to the other students enough for them to feel friendly toward him. It reminded her of herself when she was that age. She was often bashful, worried about what people thought of her as the daughter of a President, what they expected of her, and whether she could live up to those expectations. She and Ed then worked with Jack every day for months, trying to teach him social skills that they felt might help him with the other students in school. Their at-home suggestions worked; Jack became a popular kid in just a short time. Ed was proud. "You're a good man, Charlie Brown," he told his son one day in front of others when he saw how well his boy was working on a science project in tandem with a friend.

After John's death, Caroline's life became less structured, her time for her children compromised by her grief. She was more snappish. For instance, in front of one mother at Brearley, she told eleven-year-old Rose, who was apparently having a bad day, "Life is not hard, Rose. You just insist upon *making* it hard." The little girl just gazed up at her mother, not knowing how to respond.

Just as her mother had done before her where her father's death was concerned, Caroline wanted to protect her children from the sadness and pain of losing their uncle John, to whom they were close. It was pathology so clear to the older members of the family who had seen Jackie do it and who had also done it themselves to their own children. It was the reason Caroline spent so much time on an analyst's couch as a child, and she knew it. She recognized it as a problem, but she didn't know what to do about it.

It just so happened that at this same time, Caroline's cousin Maria Shriver was writing a children's book about death and dying and how to explain all of it to youngsters. The idea was borne of the questions her own children had asked her after the death of Rose Kennedy, as well as Maria's own experiences with the subject in a family that had seen its share of death but never wanted to discuss it. Maria talked to Caroline about being more open with her grief and resisting the temptation of trying to shelter her children from it. "They know what's happening," she told her cousin. "Let them in. Let them share your pain over John."

It wasn't easy, and probably if she were able to go back all these years later and do it again she would be even more open to the idea, but Caroline did at least make an effort to shed her tears openly.

In that first six months, the last thing Caroline wanted to do was make any personal appearances. However, she had made a commitment to appear at a dinner celebrating the twentieth anniversary of the John Fitzgerald Kennedy Library and Museum on October 4. Ed suggested she cancel, but she felt obligated. Looking wan and unwell, she stood before an audience and said, "There are a few people I would like to salute. The first is my brother, John," she said, choking back tears, "who brought his own sense of purpose, idealism, and fun to the public service which I hope that we can all continue." After she finished, she ran backstage and broke down. It was too soon.

Two weeks later, Caroline was back at the JFK Library with the Senator. The two were reviewing footage of John that was to be incorporated into a video tribute of him for the library's research department. "This is tough," Caroline was overheard telling her uncle Ted. According to witnesses, she seemed to be unraveling. "I know," Ted said as he reached out and pulled her into an embrace. After a few moments, Caroline tried to move away. "No, not yet," Ted told her in a tender voice. He then pulled her back into his arms and repeated, "Not yet."

THINK BEFORE YOU SPEAK

While Caroline was working on a marriage that was being conducted out of the public eye — or at least as much as possible considering who she was in our culture — her cousin Kerry Kennedy was having a different kind of marriage with her husband, the politician Andrew Cuomo. Despite the fact that she knew her union to him was flawed, it had been Kerry Kennedy's decision to be at Andrew's side throughout the time he campaigned to be his party's nominee for governor of New York prior to the 2002 state convention. It wasn't easy, but life with him had always had certain challenges. He was constantly on the road, for instance; never did he turn down an opportunity to speak, shake hands, and interact with his constituency, especially if it had to do with fundraising. His absence left Kerry feeling sad and alone. However, because she feared Andrew would have trouble getting the nomination if he was in the midst of a high-profile separation, she tucked away any personal grievances.

At one point during the two-and-a-half-year run-up to the convention, Andrew was living in New York while Kerry and the girls were in Washington. That situation proved to be untenable; his daughters missed him as much as their mother did. Soon they would all relocate to Bedford, close to where Bobby and Mary lived, which at least gave best friends Kerry and Mary more opportunity to be together in Andrew's absence. No matter what was going on privately, though, Kerry still believed in Andrew's vision for New York, especially when it came to programs for the poor and for women's rights. She'd forsake much of her own human rights work in order to stump for him, giving many compelling speeches in support of his agenda. She was able to raise millions for his campaign.

From the beginning of Andrew's interest in being governor, it had been the strong advice of Democratic policy makers that he hold off. They wanted him to defer to the first black nominee, Carl McCall, at the time New York state comptroller. Two decades older than Andrew, McCall also had multiple terms in the New York Senate under his belt. It was *his* time, they argued, not Andrew's, especially because, if he won, McCall could end up the first black governor in the state's history. Besides, they said, how could Andrew run against an African American in the New York primary without appearing to be race-baiting every time he criticized him? In appearing to do so, he would make an enemy of the entire black community of New York, even though most of this faction had been supportive of his father.

"The guy can't win for trying," admitted Ted Kennedy in one private meeting at his home about Andrew's chances. "Whatever he says or does is wrong, and that's just because of the way he *is*. That's politics," he said. "Politics is perception." He also noted that Mario Cuomo had had the same problem. "That bunch has never exactly been likable, have they?" he asked. The Senator reminded those in the room that many people didn't take to Mario, including Democrats, despite his three terms as governor.

Maybe part of the reason Andrew appeared unlikable on the public stage was because he actually wasn't the nicest guy in the world, and he couldn't hide it. Put another way, most of the Kennedys were better actors. Certainly Joe Kennedy was not known to be particularly pleasant to his team, either. To some staffers, he was known for the remark "I would like people who work for me to show initiative. *But only when I want them to.*" However, Joe always came across well before an audience. His uncle Ted, even when his behavior was at its worst, still translated to the public as a decent fellow. Andrew couldn't seem to disguise the fact that he was hard-nosed and difficult.

The real killer of Andrew's campaign, though, was his much-reported criticism of Governor George Pataki as having taken a backseat to Mayor Rudy Giuliani during the tragedy of September 11, 2001. The gaffe happened while Andrew and Kerry were traveling with reporters on a bus. Maybe he thought it was off the record, but it wasn't. "He stood behind the leader," Andrew said of Pataki. "He held the leader's coat. He was a great assistant to the leader. But he was not a leader."

All Kerry could do was shake her head and bite her lip. She'd been around politicians her entire life and knew the second she heard those words tumbling from her husband's lips that he'd made a huge blunder. "Kennedys always think before they speak," she said (though of course that was hyperbolic at best), "and my uncle Ted says you don't always have a chance to correct something when you misspeak. It just becomes the record, for better or worse, and usually for worse."

While Andrew's remark seems a little benign all these years later, it really did ruin everything for him. Using 9/11 as a political talking point? No. It was too early, and regardless of how Pataki had performed during the crisis, it was not deemed appropriate as far as most traumatized New Yorkers were concerned. When the comment made the front pages of Manhattan newspapers, it was all over for Andrew. Looking back years later, he would have to note, "One stupid remark on the most sensitive topic in a generation communicated one thing: arrogance."

On September 2, 2002, a week before the primary, Andrew withdrew from the race. He had no choice; he was never going to get the nomination, anyway. Former President Bill Clinton introduced him to the cheering crowd, telling him he was proud of him and that he should be proud of himself. He would be back to race again one day, or so Clinton assured him and the audience.

At this same time, Andrew's sister-in-law Kathleen Kennedy Townsend had just lost her bid for governor of Maryland. Because the state's incumbant, Parris Glendening, hadn't been eligible to run again due to state term limits, Kathleen was nominated by her party. In the end, Kathleen lost to the Republican U.S. Representative (Congressman) Robert Ehrlich of Arbutus, 48 percent to 52 percent. "I'm just happy to now focus on my family," she said, seeming relieved.

It was a triple defeat for the family in that Mark Shriver had hoped to move up from the Maryland House of Delegates, where he had served since 1995, representing Montgomery County, Maryland District 15, to a seat in Congress for the Eighth District of Maryland. He was defeated in the Democratic primary by Chris Van Hollen. He took it harder than Kathleen; he really wanted to serve. It was a bitter disappointment. (He would then join Save the Children and serve as senior vice president for U.S. Programs until 2013.) This was definitely not a good time for Kennedys in the political arena.

Meanwhile, Andrew Cuomo was crushed. He would look back on his run for governor many years later with great regret. "I'd disappointed my wife, my parents, my supporters, myself. I hated feeling like a public spectacle. As I stood onstage, I felt my last bit of dignity drain out."

It would get much worse. About a week after Andrew dropped out of the race, Kerry made clear her feelings about the future of their marriage. She'd been there for him throughout his campaign, but now she was done. In January 2003, she hired a divorce lawyer.

Six months later, while still technically married to Andrew, Kerry would have a brief affair with a restaurateur named Bruce Colley. It wouldn't mean much to her, though, and, in fact, became the catalyst for her to examine how she really felt about being involved with anyone while still married to Andrew, even if she was separated. It had always been a part of Kennedy culture that the *men* were the ones who had the affairs, not the women. Though this really wasn't an affair in the strictest sense, it was close enough — and the press about it was relentless and unforgiving. She had to ask her mother, her chief adviser, how she felt about it.

Ethel had changed a lot in recent years, especially after Michael's death. She was more subdued, not as volatile. Perhaps a lot of it had to do with growing older — she was seventy-four — and mellowing with age. A person would be hard-pressed to remember the last time she'd snapped someone to attention by clapping her hands in front of his face, or forced someone to eat a slice of chocolate cake in order to test that person's mettle. She'd also relaxed many of the rules when it came to the household staff, saying that she now felt maybe life was too short to worry about old-world servant protocol. "I guess you could say that my perspective has totally changed with the years," she told one intimate. Indeed, she'd been through a lot and had found a place within where she was just more peaceful.

Whereas Ethel once would have advised Kerry to work on her marriage for the sake of the family, now she was a little more lenient in that regard, too. She still wouldn't condone an extramarital affair, though. If anything, she urged Kerry to get her divorce and start a new life with her children. Therefore, within weeks of it having first been reported in the media, Kerry ended her brief relationship with Bruce. As for Andrew? She was finished with him, too. She would move forward with the divorce.

■ ■ ■ ■

PART III
"THE KENNEDY
CURSE ENDS HERE"

■ ■ ■ ■

TED ADVOCATES FOR KARA

It was January 2003. Senator Ted Kennedy, who would turn seventy-one in a month, was sitting in the office of the president of the Dana-Farber/Brigham Cancer Center in Boston, Massachusetts. Before him were six large computer monitors. As he watched and listened, a half dozen of the most prestigious, skilled medical professionals in the field of cancer research offered various opinions and conclusions. Occasionally, Ted would turn to Vicki and whisper something in her ear. She would nod and take a quick note on a large yellow pad in her lap. In front of her on a coffee table was a stack of medical books. Now and then, she would lean over to them and riffle the pages of one until she found a passage. She'd hand the book to Ted for his review, pointing at the paragraph as he read it. He'd nod his appreciation. Though the information being imparted was grim, the rapport shared by the Kennedys was apparent as they took it all in and assessed it.

By this time, Ted was older, but he actually looked better than ever. His work in the Senate continued to be important to him, as it was to the country. A year earlier, the No Child Left Behind Act, which he had cosponsored, was signed into law. In the end, it gave states more fiscal freedom but also required substantial education allocations. He had also won an increase in the federal minimum wage. On this day, though, Ted had concerns that were more personal; he was determined to not allow yet another tragedy to occur in his life or in that of his family. A month earlier, his forty-one-year-old daughter, Kara, called to tell him that she'd had an annual physical and that the results had come back problematic. Her doctor suggested she have someone with her for a conference, during which he would provide more information. Kara wanted Ted to be at her side. Of course he would be there for her.

As father and daughter sat before him, the doctor pulled an X-ray out of a manila envelope and held it up to the light. He then began a series of solemn sentences with phrases such as, "this spot here . . ." and "that spot there . . ." The summation finally ended with the jarring words: "Kara, I'm afraid it's lung cancer." As Ted took in Kara's dazed expression, he knew for sure she wasn't actually hearing anything the doctor was saying; she was practically in a state of shock. Holding her hand and trying to keep his own composure, Ted began to ask questions, the last of which was: "It's curable, right, doc?" The physician asked if he could be frank. Ted turned to Kara. She nodded. "Senator, I'm not one to play the numbers game," the doctor began, "and you never can tell with these things, of course. But, at least in my opinion," he continued, now looking at Kara sorrowfully, "I would say you have less than a year."

A silence fell between them as the news sank in; the three stared at one another.

"Doctor, I would say that you're wrong," Ted finally said, his voice steady. "I would also say that as much as we respect you, we're not going to accept your prediction." He then turned to Kara and said, "Don't listen to him, kiddo. Don't listen to him at all."

"I'm sorry," the doctor said apologetically, "but . . . I . . ."

As he and Kara rose, Ted said it was fine. He appreciated the opinion. He would require a lot more information, though. "We Kennedys don't give up, as you may know," he concluded.

The doctor nodded as he shook Ted's hand. He put his hand on Kara's shoulder. "I'm sorry to have been so blunt," he said. She smiled and looked right through him.

Now, a month later, six doctors who had earlier examined Kara were weighing in with opinions on video screens while Ted and Vicki watched and listened; Kara was not present. The image of William Travis, the chief of pathology from the Armed Forces Institute of Pathology, flashed on a TV monitor. Looking grim, he noted that small-cell lung cancer was a disease not known to be treatable. Another doctor, this one from Johns Hopkins, agreed with Travis that there was nothing that could be done. He said he was afraid that Kara had, as earlier projected, about one year to live. A third added, "This particular tumor is known as a 'really bad active.' There is not a favorable prognosis to be had here." Three more had similar opinions.

Another physician present for the tribunal, but in person, was Dr. David Sugarbaker, a young chief of thoracic surgery at Dana-Farber/Brigham specializing in the treatment of mesothelioma. He'd earned his degree from Cornell University Medical School. A day earlier, he'd received a call from Dr. Edward J. Benz Jr., president of Dana-Farber. Benz told him about a "VIP patient facing a critical situation." He asked Sugarbaker to sit in on a video conference of doctors scheduled to take place the next day in his office. "Who's the VIP?" Sugarbaker asked. "Kara Kennedy." The name "Kennedy" sent a shot of adrenaline through the young doctor. "Her father is Senator Ted Kennedy," he was told.

As David watched Ted ask questions to the assembled physicians, he would recall, "I was surprised by his depth of knowledge. Obviously, he'd done a great deal of research in a short period of time and had talked to a number of professionals about his daughter's problem. He took in all of the opinions, all of the information, none of which was sugar-coated. Most fathers would have been out of their minds hearing such dire predictions for the mortality of a daughter, but the Senator was methodical, dispassionate. Serious."

Dr. Sugarbaker wasn't nearly as pessimistic about Kara's chances as his colleagues. "I say we begin with a simple evaluation process," he offered. "Let's go step by step and find out if this tumor has metastasized. I would biopsy the lymph nodes to see if they're involved. Perhaps we can then remove the tumor." One of the other doctors said that it was a complete waste of time to do any surgery at all. He noted that small-cell lung cancer has usually gone through every lymph node by the time it's diagnosed, and that it's already "widely metastatic" by diagnosis. He felt that immediate chemotherapy was in order, followed by radiation, but surgery was useless.

"I disagreed," Dr. Sugarbaker would say many years later. "I wasn't going to say my proposal for surgery would definitely work, but I felt there was hope whereas the others didn't. So I presented my case — biopsy, surgery, chemo, radiation. The Senator took in all of the opinions. He and his wife sat silent for a moment. Then he turned to Bill Travis's monitor and asked, 'Bill, what do you think?' Travis mulled it over and said, 'You know what? I actually think I agree with David here. If it were up to me, I'd want it [the tumor] out, and then I'd want to see how it goes from there.' That was all the Senator needed to hear. 'I appreciate your input, everyone, as does my wife,' he said. 'I'm also sure I speak for Kara when I say thank you. My family has been through this kind of thing before,' he explained. 'When my son Teddy had cancer, they told me he wouldn't make it. They said his chances were bleak. But we Kennedys are made of tough stuff. That was almost thirty years ago, and thank the good Lord, my son is still with us today.' "

Ted paused. "In the end, I think you have to be pretty decisive about these things," he declared. "My father always told me, 'If you have a second choice, then you don't really have a first choice. So I've made my first choice," he said, ". . . and it's Dr. Sugarbaker," he said, turning to the physician. "I'm going to explore Kara's situation with him. So, once again, thank you, all," he concluded.

"And with that," recalled Dr. David Sugarbaker, "all of the monitors went to black."

A few weeks later, Kara had biopsy surgery at Brigham to determine if the cancer had spread to her lymph nodes. Ted and Vicki paced the waiting room anxiously during what was actually a minor procedure. Days later, the couple was seated in Dr. Sugarbaker's office — again, without Kara — when he gave them the good news: the biopsy results were negative; the cancer hadn't spread. "I actually think we have a good shot at this," Sugarbaker told the Kennedys. "I say we go in, we remove the tumor and part of the lung, and then we just see how it goes. I believe we have a good chance for longer-term survival."

Ted smiled broadly. "This *is* good news," he exclaimed. Tears filled Vicki's eyes.

On the day of the surgery, Ted called a summit in Dr. Sugarbaker's private office at Brigham and Women's Hospital, which is connected to Dana-Farber. It was a dark, wood-paneled sanctuary. There were shelves with hundreds of medical books on the walls, along with striking black-and-white photographs of historical figures such as Albert Einstein and Winston Churchill. Sugarbaker's father was also an oncology surgeon; his antique medical instruments were displayed in lit glass boxes. There were also antique clocks everywhere; Sugarbaker was an avid collector. Ted loved sitting in this room in its heavily stuffed burgundy leather chairs. He said it felt not only like a safe haven but, as clocks ticked all about him, also a reminder of the inevitability of time's passing. "How many people with personal stories of pain and anguish have sat in this room and tried to come to terms with the inevitable chaos life presents?" he once mused. "And how many of those people were reminded in looking around this office that we must make the best of every single second as it ticks by?"

Many doctors and nurses connected to Kara's case were present to say hello to the Kennedys before they got to work on Kara. Ted, Vicki, Teddy, Patrick, and even Kara's former husband, Michael Allen, chatted with the medical team, wanting to know them, eager to hear their personal stories. "The Senator thanked each and every person," said Dr. Sugarbaker, "shaking hands, getting to know them, connecting with them. Each of us has a life story that extends far beyond what we are capable of doing for our patients," the doctor observed, "and Ted wanted to know those stories, as did his family members. I found it remarkable. So many people are either put off by doctors and nurses, maybe intimidated by them or maybe viewing them as just servants. What I got from the Kennedys was a personal approach to respect. After we all extended our hopes for a successful surgery for Kara, we left the Kennedys to get down to business."

The family made itself comfortable in Sugarbaker's office rather than stand vigil in the public waiting room. Meanwhile, Ted left the room and sat down on one of the two chairs in front of the desk of Mary Gillan, Sugarbaker's secretary. During the last few weeks, the two had developed a cordial relationship; she was so protective of the Kennedys she put extra drapes in front of her office window so that no one could peer in and spy on them. "What would you like for lunch, Senator?" Mary asked. "I'll order ahead to Pat's Place [the hospital's family-owned deli]."

Ted brightened at the mention of deli food. "Whaddaya got?" he asked. "Just don't ask my wife or I'll be stuck with cottage cheese."

Mary went into her desk, pulled out a menu, and handed it to him.

"Do you have children?" Ted asked Mary as he perused the menu.

"No, Senator," she said. "I'm a widow, no kids."

Ted nodded. "Lots of freedom, then, huh?" he asked, smiling.

"Lots."

"Steak and cheese sandwiches for all," Ted finally said, handing back the menu. "Oh, some kind of rabbit food for Vicki," he added with a smile. "Say, let me ask you, Mary, is there a Catholic church nearby?"

"The hospital has a chapel," she answered.

Ted frowned. "No, I think I need a real, honest-to-God church."

Mary, who happened to be a former nun, offered, "There's the basilica in Mission

601

Hill." She said that it was one of the oldest churches in the country, built in the 1800s, and that legend had it that people from all over the world have prayed there for a cure to illnesses. Her brother and his wife had an autistic child, and they often went to that church to pray for his healing. Ted had never heard of it, unusual since he was from the Boston area. "How did that one that slip by the Kennedys?" he asked. "Because we know our churches, believe me."

How far? Three blocks. Fine, Ted said, he'd walk over while Kara was in surgery. No, said Mary. It was in a rough part of town. She'd call a car service.

An hour later, Ted and Vicki walked inside the ornate church, whose complete name was the Basilica and Shrine of Our Lady of Perpetual Help. For the next three hours, they knelt and prayed, occasionally lighting candles. Finally, one of Ted's aides came to the couple to tell them that Kara's surgery was finished. They then raced back to the hospital.

Ted, Vicki, Patrick, Teddy, and Michael Allen all got to Dr. Sugarbaker's at the same time. Mary took the anxious family members into her boss's inner sanctum. She left them there and closed the door.

Five minutes later, David Sugarbaker, still in scrubs, came bounding into the suite, rushing right past Mary's desk. He glanced over at his secretary and noted the concern on her face. Then, as he opened his office door to face the Kennedys, he flashed a smile and gave her a big thumbs-up.

STRATEGY FOR HEALING

"Wow. Kara's doing unbelievably well, isn't she?"

Ted Kennedy was talking to his sons as he sat in front of a heaping plate of pancakes, scrambled eggs, and bacon.

"This man knows exactly what he's doing," Ted continued, motioning to David Sugarbaker at his side. It was eight in the morning, two days after Kara's surgery. Ted was holding court in a far corner of Pat's Place delicatessan — the hospital's go-to for good food. He and his sons would have breakfast, lunch, and dinner here every day for as long as Kara was in the hospital. This morning, they were in the company of Dr. Sugarbaker. "I'm just the surgeon," the modest physician told them. "Kara did all the real work."

"Kara was in the hospital for ten days after her surgery," recalled Dr. Sugarbaker. "We kept her in ICU a couple extra days just to be safe. The Senator came every morning at seven. He'd received permission from the hospital to set up an office in a large room down the hall from Kara's — desks, computers, printers, file cabinets, everything he'd need, with a secretary's station . . . phone lines, the works. He couldn't take a day off, he explained, yet he needed to be at the hospital. So we had government officials coming through every day, senators, congressmen. President Bush was about to declare the war in Iraq, so there was a lot of discussion about whether it was justified. There were serious things going on in the world, so I admired the way the Kennedys were able to compartmentalize and keep their focus on Kara. Teddy and Patrick would come to the hospital in the morning and would join their father in Pat's Place. Then all three would go to Kara's room. Later, I would follow with my own examination of her."

"I'm ready for the next phase," Kara told Dr. Sugarbaker on that second day. Though still physically weak, she was anxious to get to her chemotherapy.

After the diagnosis, Kara said she was paralyzed with fear, as was everyone else in the family. Patrick couldn't even look at her without bursting into tears. They all felt helpless and didn't know how to address it. For her part, she receded into what she called "a really dark place." Because she'd been such a heavy smoker, she was swamped with guilt. After all, she had two small children at home

— Grace was only eight and Max was six. Therefore the idea of leaving them without a mother was devastating. How, she asked herself, could she have been so stupid as to not have quit smoking years earlier? "I was paralyzed," she said. "Fear will do that to you, I guess."

Kara said that loved ones kept telling her she had nothing to worry about because she was such a fighter. Her response to that observation was: *Thanks very much, but what are you talking about?* After all, she'd always had the luxury of a soft cushion provided by her family's wealth and status. It had made everything possible for her, from a happy social life to a great education. Money was always at her disposal; she lived an entitled, privileged life. When did she ever have to fight for anything? She once recalled hearing one of her cousins declare, "We don't have to worry about shit," followed by the favorite refrain, *"We're the fuckin' Kennedys."* She would remember being put off by the observation. Of course, the Kennedys had plenty to worry about, but Kara likely understood where her relative was coming from, even if he did have a pretty crude way of expressing it.

It was Patrick who reminded Kara that her childhood had been no bed of roses. Raised by unpredictable, alcoholic parents, she spent most of her youth trying to figure out how to

606

survive in a family in which behavior was always at odds with personal responsibility. Usually feeling abandoned by either Ted or Joan, she and her brothers had to turn to one another for strength. They certainly weren't getting it from their mother, and the only time they got it from their father was when they were sick. Unlike her brothers, though, Kara had rarely been ill, at least not physically. However, she did feel desperate and anxious for most of her youth. How many times had she run away? When Patrick posed the question, Kara realized she couldn't even count the times, there had been that many. "Every day, you had to fight," Patrick told her. "All three of us had to fight. You *are* a fighter, Kara. We all are."

After she got her wits about her and was able to come to terms with her devastating illness, Kara decided that, yes, she would do battle against it, and not only that, but she'd win. She'd seen too much tragedy in her lifetime, she decided. "I refuse to allow myself to end up just another casualty of the so-called Kennedy curse," she said. Her adamant declaration to trusted friends was: "The Kennedy curse ends here, with me."

For Kara, survival meant coming up with a plan. "To that end she devised what she called her 'strategy for healing,' said Meghan Strayhorn, one of her closest friends at this time. "She told me she realized that in order for her to heal, she had to believe — and have no doubt, whatsoever — that her body was capable of doing so. Then, and only then, would she be able to manifest a true and complete healing. She combined a new age philosophy of self-healing with her own Catholic faith — thus, her 'strategy for healing.'

"She explained to me that Jesus Christ is quoted in the Bible as having said, 'Whatever you ask for in prayer, believe that you have it and it will be yours' [Mark 11:24]. He also said, 'It is done to you as you believe' [Matthew 8:13]. 'It's not as you *think* you believe or as you *want* to believe,' she said, 'it's *as you believe.*' To her, this scripture meant that the only way she could conquer cancer was to believe she'd already done so — and that in praying for a healing, it was already hers. 'It's the underlying belief that really shows up in your life,' she told me. That meant she couldn't allow herself to be infected by negativity."

In order to keep a clear mind about the outcome of her fight with such a deadly cancer, it was Kara's decision not to attend medical strategy sessions. She knew these appointments would do nothing but plant negative thoughts in her head, especially since it had already been decreed by most doctors that she was terminal. Therefore she asked her father to attend all such sessions, to sift through the "bad news" and just give her the information she needed: which was, basically, when to show up for her surgery. Though Ted didn't quite understand her reasoning, Vicki did. "Vicki got it right away," said Megan Strayhorn, "and told Ted not to think about, not to try to figure it out, not to debate it, to just do what Kara asked of him. And that's what he did."

After Kara explained her "strategy for healing" to her doctors, they were impressed. They'd actually wondered why she hadn't been to any of the medical conferences. Now it made sense to them, especially to Dr. Sugarbaker. He couldn't help but also notice that Joan had never attended any such meetings, either, and had never even been to the hospital. "So how's your mom handling things?" he asked.

Kara smiled. Then she changed the subject.

VICKI INTERCEDES WITH JOAN

For Kara Kennedy, dealing with her mother's precarious emotional state during this challenging time was complicated. When she would talk to her about her cancer, Joan would inevitably fall apart. She couldn't handle the anxiety and fear of her only daughter's battle with such a deadly illness. Kara would inevitably end up consoling Joan, not the other way around. In these, Kara's darkest moments, her mother couldn't give her hope — only more fear. Of course, this wasn't Joan's fault. No one blamed her. However, those in Kara's life who understood her philosophy about healing — such as her cousins Caroline and Maria and her stepmother, Vicki — suggested that she discontinue trying to enlist her mother in her recovery. Of course, this would be easier said than done.

Joan felt she had a right to be included in all decisions relating to Kara's health care and resented it that Ted seemed to have commandeered the process. She campaigned hard for inclusion, enlisting her sons to act on her behalf and make sure she was not shut out. However, every time Joan was given even the smallest bit of information, she went into a panic, spinning out of control and, consequently, becoming the focus of attention. It was a big distraction.

Ted's position was that Joan was being self-involved. "It's always about Joan," he said at this time. "How is she taking it? Is she drinking? What do we tell her? How do we tell her? Sure, she has had a tough time," he acknowledged, "and nobody is sorrier about it than I am. But it has to be about Kara right now, not about Joan." Ted said he would talk to his ex-wife and ask her to back off. However, everyone thought that was a terrible idea. After so many years of doing battle with each other, the former spouses knew how to push each other's buttons. No, Vicki said. She should be the one to speak to Joan. She had a rapport with her, she said, and felt she could reach her. "Now you're thinking just like a Kennedy," Ted told her proudly.

It had been ten years since Vicki married into the family. At almost twenty years younger than Joan, who was sixty-six at this time, she was as gorgeous as ever, still smart and in control. She had somehow managed to do the one thing Joan had never been able to do, which was to be a strong partner for

Ted on every level. Therefore, depending on her mood and what was going on in the family at any given time, Joan had mixed feelings about Vicki. Sometimes she had great respect for her. Other times she was more leery. Still, the two had shared many meaningful moments in the last decade, going all the way back to their first talk about the inherent lack of familial respect for women.

Vicki had done her research on Joan. As much as she loved Ted, she'd recently come to the conclusion that he had been guilty of using Joan's disease as a way to distract attention from his own misdeeds. Vicki couldn't help but note that during his marriage to Joan, almost every time Ted was seen with another woman his office diverted attention from it by suddenly addressing the matter of Joan and her battle with alcoholism. It was just another function of Kennedy culture patriarchy. One afternoon over lunch, when Vicki told Joan that she'd come to this conclusion, Joan almost cried. That was exactly right, she said.

"Joan had been saying this for years, yet no one would ever believe her," Marcia Chellis confirmed. " 'All the messages about me are being put out there by men,' she would complain. 'They have complete control over my image.' Sure, she had problems, she would always admit, but so much of what became known of them came from the Kennedy image-making machinery in an effort to protect Ted. Joan felt it also gave him license to cheat on her, because after all, what good was she? She *deserved* to be cheated on."

Joan told Vicki that eventually she had decided to start giving her own interviews to women's magazines so that she could get her point of view out there. Then, of course, everyone was upset, she said, because it had become clear that she didn't know how to keep the family's secrets. That didn't stop her, though. Once she realized people wanted to hear from her directly, she told Vicki, "I never stopped talking, and I didn't care what anyone thought of it, either."

These kinds of conversations helped seal a bond between the two Mrs. Kennedys. Therefore, Vicki felt certain she could reason with Joan.

"Vicki went to see Joan," recalled one source, "and from what I heard she sat down with her and said, 'Look, I understand how you feel. This is your daughter. You have a right to be involved in every aspect of her care. However, the selfless thing you can do right now is to let me and Ted handle things. I'm asking you this as a woman and as a mother. Can you please?'

"I think maybe Vicki had underestimated what Joan's reaction would be. She was upset. She felt disrespected, and she made sure Vicki knew it. There were a lot of 'How dare yous?' and 'Who do you think you ares?' Finally, though, she settled down. She took Vicki into her confidence by explaining that she was just trying to fix her mistakes of the past before it was too late. She feared Kara was dying and wanted the opportunity to be a real mom to her. She was also frightened of the unknown, whatever was to come. 'Please don't make me be alone in this,' she begged Vicki."

Vicki's heart went out to Joan; her concern for Kara's well-being was obviously genuine. She assured her that there would be many years ahead for the two of them. "Forget the past and don't worry about the future," she told her. *"Be here, now."* Vicki then promised to keep Joan posted every step along the way. She said that not one day would go by that Joan wouldn't know exactly what was happening. "I am on your side," Vicki told her. "I promise you that." Finally, Joan agreed to recede into the background, at least, she said, "for a few weeks."

"Vicki Kennedy was present every day, at every meeting, at the hospital, all of it," recalled Dr. David Sugarbaker. "If you had told me she was Kara's mother, I would have believed you. The way she treated her was as if Kara was her own. I never once saw Kara's real mother throughout the entire process. I supposed this was the result of an agreement that had been reached within the family, but

I certainly didn't ask too many questions about it."

In the end, Vicki kept her promise; she called Joan every day with an update. On those days when she couldn't immediately reach her, she became persistent in tracking her down. She didn't want there to be any doubt that she'd kept her word. Following the surgery, the two even had lunch so that Vicki could give Joan a full account of the doctors' prognosis.

After she was released from the hospital, Kara went to the Kennedy compound to recuperate at Ted and Vicki's. She would then undergo chemo in Washington and in Boston; Vicki accompanied her to most of her treatments. Throughout this time, Ted continued to visit and pray at the Basilica and Shrine of Our Lady of Perpetual Help. "It's not the biggest church, it's not the most beautiful church, and it's not in a good neighborhood," he said. "But it's my church now, because that's where I got my miracle." Seven years later, during another dark time for the family, when the Senator himself was battling cancer, he would make arrangements for his funeral be held at this same church. That final wish would be granted.

In time, it would be understood that Kara's surgery — and her "strategy for healing" — resulted in a complete success, one that was nothing less than miraculous; she would go into a full and total remission. Against all odds, this woman who most medical professionals thought was going to die would continue to raise her children and be able to enjoy a good and happy life.

■ ■ ■ ■

PART IV
THE SHRIVER WAY

■ ■ ■ ■

TRADITION

July 2003. A couple walked along the sandy shore of Hyannis Port, her head resting comfortably on his broad shoulder. It was a gorgeous Cape Cod summer day, the clear blue sky dotted with the occasional white puffball cloud. They were followed not only by three children but also a woman who appeared to be a nanny, dressed in a crisp white uniform. Walking behind her was a trio of photographers who'd been allowed entrée to the Kennedy enclave for a story about the clan in *Newsweek*. Clumsy, with all manner of equipment, they stumbled along the beach while endeavoring not to be distracting but failing miserably at it. White gulls with black-tipped wings swooped all around them, almost as if trying to protect the beach's serenity from their intrusion.

Tall and model-thin with dark hair framing an angular face, the young woman in large sunglasses would stop from time to time and glance over her shoulder to check on her children. Under her diaphanous white one-piece cover-up, she wore a sexy, formfitting red swimsuit. At one point, the man, donning only a knee-length checkered swimsuit, his muscles bulging over a ripped torso, walked to one of the little boys, tossed him into the air, and caught him in his arms. He squealed with delight. The cameramen smiled as they clicked away. "Arnold, please don't do that," exclaimed the woman. "You know that scares me." He flashed a toothy grin, nodded with confidence, and then leaned in and spoke to her, perhaps reassuring her that he had the situation under control. No doubt, he did. After all, he was Arnold Schwarzenegger, not just a famous actor but also one of the world's leading bodybuilders. The child, his five-year-old son, Christopher, was probably all of forty pounds. He gazed up at Daddy with adoration and demanded, "One more time. One more time." Again, Arnold popped him into the air as his wife, Maria Shriver, cringed and turned away.

Parents playing with their kids on this picturesque shore had been a time-honored family tradition for pretty much as long as Maria could remember. At this time, Maria had four children — Katherine, thirteen; Christina, about to turn twelve this month; Patrick, nine; and little Christopher. Back when she was a young girl, her own folks, Sargent Shriver and Eunice Kennedy Shriver,

620

would walk this same sandy span with their five offspring — Maria and brothers, Timothy, Anthony, Bobby, and Mark. Sometimes they would stop, lay out a blanket, and enjoy a little picnic. Eventually, though, they'd always end up in a game of touch football with Maria, her mother, and father on one team, all of her brothers on the other.

Somehow, even with the disparity in the number of team members, Maria's side would always end up the victors. That was mostly because Eunice had always been extremely athletic, as much so as any of her male siblings. In true Kennedy tradition, she was also unbelievably competitive. It was one of the first things Sargent realized about her when he started dating her in the fifties. "She would never allow any team on which she was playing to lose," he recalled. " 'You have to win. That's what Kennedys do. We win,' Eunice would say. The way we raised our kids, that spirit, that same tradition was passed to them, for better or worse."

"If we ever played a game, *someone* was going to win," Bobby Shriver confirmed in a joint interview with his sister, Maria. "Then, the first thing when you got home, you were going to be asked by Mummy, 'Okay. Who won? Did you win? You didn't win? Anything? *Nothing?* Goodbye, shut up.' That's the way we grew up. Today they don't teach competition. In school today, everyone on the soccer team gets a trophy. We didn't get a trophy: 'You didn't win? *No trophy?* See ya.' "

Maria noted, "I once said to my son Christopher, 'You always used to get so upset when you lost playing the board games Sorry or Trouble.' He said, 'But Mom, that's because you had to beat me. I was a three-year-old kid. What kind of mom always has to beat her three-year-old kid?' "

"You should have said, 'The one I had,' " Bobby told his sister, laughing.

"I *said* that," Maria exclaimed.

"That's the way we grew up, ladies and gentlemen," said Bobby, laughing, "Fifty years from now, we'll all be dead, but we'll want you to know something. *That's the way we grew up.* So, any psychotic things you think about us or have ever heard about us or have seen about us, it's all because of . . . *that.*"

Joseph P. Kennedy Sr. inspired all of the next generation of Kennedys. Here he celebrates his seventy-fifth birthday, on September 7, 1963, with his grandchildren in Hyannis Port. Left to right, as identified by the JFK Library: Kerry Kennedy, Caroline Kennedy (behind), Courtney Kennedy, Timothy Shriver (in front), Victoria Lawford (behind), Maria Shriver, Sydney Lawford, Christopher Lawford, Joseph P. Kennedy Sr. (seated), Kathleen Kennedy, John F. Kennedy Jr. (sits in front), Robert F. Kennedy Jr. (holding John Jr.), Michael Kennedy (right of Joseph P. Kennedy Sr.), David Kennedy (behind), Rose F. Kennedy, Robin Lawford, Robert Shriver III (behind Robin), Joseph P. Kennedy II (in back), Stephen Smith Jr., and William Smith (in front). (*Cecil W. Stoughton/John F. Kennedy Presidential Library and Museum*)

President Kennedy with his children, Caroline and John, in the Colonnade of the West Wing of the White House on March 28, 1963. (*Cecil W. Stoughton/ John F. Kennedy Presidential Library and Museum*)

Father-son time: President John Fitzgerald Kennedy and his namesake, John Jr. John's memory of his dad would always be a little foggy; he was about two and a half when this picture was taken on March 28, 1963. (*Cecil W. Stoughton/John F. Kennedy Presidential Library and Museum*)

Kirk LeMoyne (Lem) Billings would go on to mentor many of the next generation of Kennedys. Here he is (sitting in the back of the golf cart) in Atoka, Virginia, with his close friend the President, the First Lady, and John Jr., on October 27, 1963. (*Cecil W. Stoughton/ John F. Kennedy Presidential Library and Museum*)

Good-looking Kennedy cousins: John Kennedy Jr., sixteen, with Maria Shriver, twenty-one, in 1976. (*Globe Photos*)

Robert Kennedy Jr. and his first wife, Emily, in Virginia, 1981. Emily stuck by Bobby's side during the terrible, early days of his drug addiction. (*Frank Teti Collection/John Fitzgerald Kennedy Library and Museum*)

Arnold Schwarzenegger and Maria Shriver were married on April 26, 1986. Maria recalled wanting a husband outside of her family's expectations. "They wanted Washington, politician, Democrat," she explained, "so I picked Austrian, bodybuilder...*Republican.*" Of course, the laugh was on her: Arnold would one day become Governor of California! (*John Barrett/Globe Photos/Image Collect*)

Recalling the rift she had with her own mother over Aristotle Onassis, Jackie decided not to oppose her daughter, Caroline's, marriage to Edwin Schlossberg. Here are Caroline, Jackie, and Ed in June of 1986. (*Courtesy of Jamie Auchincloss*)

Caroline and Ed were married in Centerville, Massachusetts, on July 19, 1986. (*AP/Rex/Shutterstock*)

When Kerry Kennedy married Andrew Cuomo on June 9, 1990, the merger of the two powerful political families, the Kennedys and the Cuomos, was dubbed "Cuomo-lat." Left to right: Ethel Kennedy, Andrew, Kerry, Matilda Cuomo and her husband, Mario Cuomo, Governor of New York. (*John Barrett/Globe Photos/Image Collect*)

Ted Kennedy Jr. and his new bride, Katherine (Kiki) Gershman, wave to well-wishers after their wedding at St. Andrew's Church in New Shoreham, Rhode Island, on October 10, 1993. Left to right: Ted's sister, Kara; brother, Patrick; mother, Joan; and father, Ted. (*Susan Walsh/AP/Rex/Shutterstock*)

Patrick Kennedy celebrates at the Biltmore Hotel in Providence on November 5, 1996, after winning his second term in Congress. He's joined by his brother, Ted; sister-in-law, Kiki; and their two-year-old daughter, Kiley. (*Matt York/AP/Rex/Shutterstock*)

Patrick Kennedy, who always had a complex relationship with his father, Ted Kennedy, became a politician in part to gain his approval. Not only did it work, but Patrick served in Congress longer than any other politician in the family's storied history. Here they enjoy Thanksgiving at the Kennedy compound in 1998. (*Kevin Wisniewski/Rex/Shutterstock*)

"I'm not that pathetic Kennedy girl who'll stay home with the kids while her husband is out screwing around," said Carolyn Bessette. "No. I'm that pissed-off Kennedy girl in prison for taking matters into her own hands." Here she is with John and their dog, Friday, in January 1997. (*William Regan/Globe Photos*)

No matter the obstacles, John's love for Carolyn never wavered. "I never want to be that creepy Kennedy guy who doesn't care what his girl thinks," he said. "I hate those guys." Here is the couple at the White House Correspondents' Dinner in Washington on May 1, 1999. (*Tyler Mallory/Liaison*)

Kathleen Kennedy Townsend, the oldest of the Kennedy's third generation, became the first female political powerhouse in the family as Lieutenant Governor of Maryland under Governor Parris N. Glendening. Here she is, age forty-nine, in August 2000. (*Gail Burton/AP/REX/Shutterstock*)

Prince Anthony Stanislaw Albert Radziwill (Anthony) was not only John's cousin, he was his best friend for life. Anthony courageously fought cancer for years with John at his side. Here he is in a happy fishing moment on the Cape. (*Courtesy of Jamie Auchincloss*)

"Many are the plans in a person's heart," Eunice Kennedy Shriver told her daughter, Maria, when she had to abandon her own career for her husband's, "but it is *the Lord's* purpose that prevails." Here are the spouses after Arnold Schwarzenegger was sworn in as the thirty-eighth Governor of California in Sacramento on November 17, 2003. (*Rick Bowmer/AP/REX/ Shutterstock*)

The Kennedys pray at the gravesite of President John Fitzgerald Kennedy in Arlington National Cemetery to honor the fallen President on the fortieth anniversary of his death, November 22, 2003. Caroline (kneeling) places flowers. Behind her, left to right: her daughters, Tatiana and Rose; her husband, Ed; her son, Jack; Ethel; Ted; and Ted's wife, Vicki. (*J. Scott Applewhite/AP/Rex/ Shutterstock*)

Senator Ted Kennedy and his wife Vicki at the Democratic National Convention on August 25, 2008. "You may want to take the high road," Ted's daughter, Kara, had advised her stepmom during a quarrel. However, where the Kennedys were concerned, Vicki said, "the high road doesn't always take you where you want to go!" (*Photolink/Globe Photos/Image Collect*)

After Ted passed away, his daughter, Kara, accepted his Medal of Freedom award given by President Barack Obama on August 12, 2009. (*Rex/Shutterstock*)

Joseph P. Kennedy II couldn't be more proud of his son Joseph III, who remains one of the most influential congressmen in the family's storied history. Here they are at a campaign event in 2010. (*Elise Amendola/AP/REX/Shutterstock*)

In the summer of 2012, pop star Taylor Swift, twenty-one, helped Conor Kennedy, seventeen, cope with the tragic death of his mother. Here the couple shares a romantic moment at the fabled Kennedy Compound on August 17, 2012. (*WENN*)

Caroline Kennedy and her son, Jack, attend the Metropolitan Museum of Art's Costume Institute Gala on May 1, 2017. Caroline's colorful ensemble was a surprising choice for a woman not known to be particularly provocative when it comes to fashion. (*Carl Timpone/BFA/REX/ Shutterstock*)

THE KENNEDY TEST

Arnold Schwarzenegger first became acquainted with the Kennedys in August 1977 at the annual Robert F. Kennedy Celebrity Tennis Tournament in New York. Ethel was the first of the family members to introduce herself, followed by Ted. Since Arnold had come to the event alone, it was Ted's idea to have him meet his niece Maria Shriver. At twenty-one, Maria was young and gorgeous, with long dark hair, hugely expressive eyes, and an energetic personality; Arnold was immediately intrigued. Soon after meeting her, he was introduced to her mother. Since he was the kind of man who liked to take strangers by surprise and test their limits, the first words out of Arnold's mouth to Eunice were: "Wow. Your daughter sure has a great ass." Eunice came from a family of four brothers, so she wasn't easily shocked by anything any man ever had to say. "Yes, she certainly does," she told Arnold. "However, Mr. Schwarzenegger," she added with an arched eyebrow, "one might find inappropriate any commentary from *you* about it." Later, Arnold would recall of Eunice, "She had me at 'inappropriate.' I liked her immediately, and her daughter, too."

Maria was as taken by Arnold as he was by her. At eight years her senior, he was a muscular, good-looking guy with a contagious smile and a winning personality. Caroline Kennedy, nineteen at the time, was also present at the tournament. Thinking he was, as she put it, "a good prospect," Caroline soon became one of Maria's coconspirators — along with their cousin Kara, the seventeen-year-old daughter of Ted and Joan — in a plan to hustle Arnold back to Hyannis Port. They cornered him and asked if he might be interested in going to the compound. If so, they said, they had to leave *immediately.* Could he be that spontaneous? This would be Arnold's first test; the Kennedy girls knew he'd never fit into the family if he couldn't be as impulsive as the rest of them.

Arnold had never been to Hyannis Port; he didn't even know how to find it on a map. Of course, the Kennedys had a private jet at their disposal for the trip. There was no time to waste, he was told, not even time for him to return to his room and change out of his tennis clothes and put some money in his pocket. "No problem. You're staying at our house," Caroline told him. "You don't need money." The girls, by this time excited about their plot, also told Arnold that his room would be paid for by the Kennedy Foundation. They promised to have him back at his hotel by the next night.

Arnold wasn't sure if he should go, but something told him he was being tested, and, a competitor from way back, he liked nothing more than a good test. Plus, he'd been hearing about the Kennedys' hideaway his entire life, and he wanted to see it for himself. So he would throw caution to the wind. Kara would, many years later, recall, "It was kismet. There was something about this guy, and Caroline and I knew he was right for Maria. As usual, we were persuasive. Arnold didn't know what hit him."

"Arnold had always been fascinated with the Kennedys," recalled Janet Charlton, a popular gossip columnist who dated him in the 1970s. "He was intrigued by the way Joe Kennedy had a dream and saw it come to life with his sons' rise to power. Arnold was someone with his own dreams, someone who came to America from Austria in search of greater opportunity. To him, the Kennedys represented an America where anything was possible, where you could make all the money you needed, take care of yourself and your family, and even be of service to others. He told me he wanted to be President one day, even though he knew that was impossible because he wasn't born in the States. 'Things'll change by then,' he said. He was that kind of man, a dreamer like the Kennedys."

"First a planeload of the 'grown-ups' flew up," Arnold would recall. "Ethel, Teddy, and that older generation. Then, at nine o'clock, the younger generation went up and I tagged along. I remember landing at ten thirty or so at night, and we were soon at the so-called Big House. Now, Maria was really showing off. 'Let's go for a swim,' she said. 'What do you mean, go for a swim?' I asked. 'It's a beautiful night,' she told me. 'Let's go.' So we went out. We swam to a boat a long way out. She was a regular water rat, climbed on board to catch her breath then swam back in, racing me like an Olympic swimmer. I barely outswam her. Barely. I later figured out that all of this was part of the test," he would add. "The cousins dragged people up to the Kennedy compound all the time and then challenged them to see what they were made of and play tricks on them. That was how Kennedys gauged the measure of a man."

The next morning, the family was scheduled to attend Mass with the matriarch, Rose. Of course, Arnold only had with him his tennis shorts, T-shirt, and the sneakers he'd worn the previous day. Joe gave him a shirt to wear, which didn't fit and in which Arnold looked ridiculous. It was embarrassing — which, of course, was the whole point. Arnold remembered lots of Kennedys pointing and laughing at him: "This is hilarious. Look at his pants! Look at his shirt!" Could he handle being the butt of a joke? He'd better if he wanted to be accepted.

The rest of that day was spent with everyone huddled over hot bowls of the family's favorite Cape Cod clam chowder — a special recipe handed down over the years made of quahogs (which are large, hard-shelled clams) with salt pork and potatoes — and then competing in sports events, with Arnold proving his mettle. As an athlete, he was tough to beat, even for the Kennedys. The day culminated in a long walk with Rose, during which she spoke to Arnold in fluent German and asked him questions about physical fitness. Before he knew it, he was leading exercise classes on the beach at sundown — and showing sixty-nine-year-old Ena Bernard how to do better sit-ups.

In short, Arnold met each and every Kennedy challenge with great aplomb. Maria was sold. One last test would cinch the deal. Because he had no money to get back to New York, Maria offered him sixty dollars. Now, *that* was really humiliating. He had no choice, though; he took the money with a humble and gracious smile, which only ingratiated him even more to Maria. "He was game, for sure," she said of Arnold many years later.

A Shriver in a Kennedy World

Like so many Kennedys of her generation and those before it, Maria Shriver had the drive and determination to make sure she'd always get exactly what she wanted out of life. From an early age, she was clear about those goals, too. First of all, she wanted a husband who was *not* in politics. She'd seen so much disappointment in her family relating to the aspirations of her father, Sargent Shriver, she wanted nothing to do with Democratic politics.

"I wanted to make a name for myself way outside the family business," she recalled. "My goal was to be a network news anchor." She first became passionate about broadcast journalism back in 1972 when her father was running for Vice President. After volunteering to help with the effort, she found herself traveling in the back of the campaign plane with the press corp. "It was the best thing that ever happened to me," she would later say. "Soon after, I started my career in broadcasting at WJZ in Baltimore and KYW-TV in Philadelphia. So many people would come up to me and say, 'Which Kennedy are you?' At a very young age, I thought, You're going to know which one I am. I decided that I was going to be the Kennedy who makes her own name and finds her own job and works like a dog, but as far away from politics as possible."

Maria's disregard for politics was ironic considering that Eunice was the most politically minded of the three Kennedy daughters. Eunice's father once famously stated that if she were a male, she probably could have been President. She was a real character in her mismatched clothing — fashion definitely not her forte — her hair always in wild disarray while sucking on a fat cigar and going toe-to-toe with the men in the family in debates about cultural issues.

Eunice, who was eighty-two in 2003, was best known for founding the Special Olympics in honor of her developmentally disabled sister, Rosemary. Though she accomplished a lot in her life — her résumé includes many of our country's most important charitable foundations — some might argue that her contributions paled in comparison to her husband's.

Robert Sargent Shriver, eighty-eight in 2003 — "Sarge" — had a long and distinguished history. Not only was he pivotal in getting President Kennedy elected, he'd been chiefly responsible for staffing his cabinet. He'd also founded and served as the first director of the Peace Corps and launched Head Start, VISTA, and other programs directed at President Lyndon Johnson's so-called War on Poverty. He also served as Johnson's ambassador to France. "The problem was that Sarge had become a part of the LBJ administration after JFK's death, and if there was one person the Kennedys had animus for, it was LBJ," explained Hugh Sidey in 1999; Sidey covered the Kennedy administration — and that of many other Presidents — for *Time.* "When Sarge didn't give up his post as LBJ'S ambassador to come home and campaign for Bobby, that was pretty much it for him as far as a lot of Kennedys were concerned. It was as if they'd forgotten that when LBJ asked Sarge to be his Vice President, the first thing Sarge did was confer with Bobby — and then turn down the position."

"For most of his political career, the Kennedys went out of their way to stand in Sarge's way, his loyalty to the family rarely reciprocated," noted Jamie Auchincloss, Jackie's half brother. "History shows one incident after another of Sarge being over-looked, of being disrespected and not allowed to meet his goals. Why? Because of Kennedy pecking order," said Auchincloss. "Ted was next in line for the golden ring after Jack and Bobby — and no one else could seize it before Ted. Since Ted was never able to grab it either, it was denied Sarge.

"He stood his ground, though, and never stopped trying to serve. It's no surprise, then, that his children grew up feeling the sting of Kennedy recrimination. 'It wasn't easy being a Shriver in a Kennedy world,' Sarge's son Bobby would often state, and I daresay he was right about that."

"Somehow Sarge resisted becoming embittered by his difficult relationship with the Kennedys," recalled Hugh Sidey. "I found that remarkable. Maybe it was because he was such a deeply religious man who attended Mass daily, always carrying rosary beads in his pocket. He was the purest of men, someone who had real forgiveness in his heart, and he passed that on to his children."

Despite any closely held personal feelings about the Kennedys, Sarge always encouraged his children — Bobby, born in 1954; Maria, born in 1955; Timothy, born in 1959; Mark, born in 1964; and Anthony, born in 1965 — to campaign for the Kennedys whenever necessary, and they always did just as they were told. That said, the Shriver parents also made certain their offspring had their own family pride: they never thought of themselves as Kennedys, always as Shrivers.

Of course, not surprisingly, they also insisted that their brood find some way to be of service.

When Maria chose journalism as a profession and her way to give back, it was fine with her parents as long as she dedicated herself to being a "truth-teller," as Sarge put it. Maria promised him she would always work toward that ideal. Actually, though, the fact that her rejection of politics also informed her ideas about the kind of man she sought as a husband was a little more disconcerting to her parents than her chosen career. They believed she was limiting herself. After all, what was wrong with a respectable politician? However, Maria feared that if her spouse was in the family business she, too, would somehow end up getting dragged into it — and that wasn't what she wanted for herself or for any children she might one day bear. She said she wanted to "pick a husband way outside my family's expectations of me. They wanted Washington, politician, Democrat. So *I* picked Austrian, bodybuilder . . . *Republican.*"

AMERICAN DREAM

Arnold Alois Schwarzenegger was born in Thal, Styria (Austria), on July 30, 1947, to Gustav and Aurelia Jadrny Schwarzenegger. He had one brother, Meinhard, who died a young man, the victim of drunk driving. The Schwarzeneggers were practicing Roman Catholics.

As a kid, Arnold suffered through a distant and difficult relationship with his father, a police chief and a member of the Nazi party. In the past, Arnold has talked about the abuse he suffered at the hands of this strict father: "Many children were broken by their parents, which was the German-Austrian mentality. They didn't want to create an individual. But I was one who didn't conform, one whose will could not be broken. Every time I got hit — and every time someone said, 'You can't do this or that' — I said, 'This is not going to be for much longer, because I'm going to move out of here. I want to *be* somebody.' " When Gustav died in

1972, Arnold didn't attend his funeral.

Though the family had its financial struggles, they got by. However, Arnold wanted more than to just barely make it in the world. "I was never one to be satisfied with a mediocre lifestyle," he said. "I always knew that money was freedom and power. I wanted both."

At about the age of fourteen, Arnold, who excelled at several sports as a youngster, decided to become a bodybuilder. Within a few years, he began to compete, determined to emulate bodybuilding icons Reg Park and Johnny Weissmuller and especially Steve Reeves, the highly paid actor who'd starred in epic screen adventures such as *Hercules* and *Goliath*. Arnold cites his "need to be the best in the world, to be recognized and to feel unique and special" as the primary reason for his interest in bodybuilding.

In 1967, at the age of twenty, Arnold's dedication and tenacity paid off when he became the youngest ever Mr. Universe. At twenty-one, he fulfilled a dream he'd had since the age of ten, which was to move to the United States and settle in Los Angeles. Three years later, he won the Mr. Olympia title; he would go on to capture that title five more times. In 1977, his autobiography, *Arnold: The Education of a Bodybuilder,* became an international bestseller. He then attended Santa Monica College and later earned his

BA in business administration from the University of Wisconsin–Superior.

Arnold began his film career in 1970, parlaying his success as a bodybuilding champion into acting. For the next seven years, he appeared in a number of films before *Pumping Iron,* in 1977, brought him great international acclaim. "He was just so self-assured," recalled Janet Charlton, who was dating him at this time. "I was impressed with his German work ethic and discipline. He was highly organized and smart, not some dumb brute. He planned his every move, buying real estate early on, for instance, with his first money. He gave me money for business school at UCLA, but all I cared about was getting tires for my car. I wish I had listened to his guidance more closely."

When Arnold first started dating Maria, he found navigating terrain having to do with her ubiquitous family challenging. He was surprised, for instance, especially given how strong-minded and independent she was, that Maria was so dominated by familial duties and responsibilities. There was always a wedding, a birthday, a graduation, some family event at which her presence was required. "We practically don't have a private life," Arnold recalled complaining to Maria. However, no matter how much he protested, she — they — would still have to be present whenever called, house-hopping from one home on the compound to the next, breakfast here, lunch there . . . dinner somewhere else — rarely with outsiders, save a few weary guests.

As they got closer and shared their goals, Maria told Arnold that she wanted to be taken seriously as a TV anchor. He said he hoped to one day become a leading man in movies. That was fine with her, she told him — "anything other than a politician."

"In 1980, Maria moved to Los Angeles to work on my dad's [Ted Kennedy's] presidential campaign when he challenged Jimmy Carter within his own party," recalled Ted's son Patrick. "Of course, it was all hands on deck. Maria campaigned hard for her uncle, visiting Hollywood power brokers like Norman Lear to try to garner their support."

Unfortunately, Ted would have to drop out of that 1980 campaign when he failed to galvanize traction, in large part because people still hadn't gotten past his role in the tragedy of Chappaquiddick. When he did so, Arnold felt the decision was instructional. "It had to do with timing more than anything," he would say. "I watched and I thought, Okay, there is a time for these things. You have to know your time. I felt, at least back then even with the early films, that my time was still to be in competition. I also thought that maybe there were some other things in store."

Arnold chose this time to compete in the prestigious Mr. World contest. Maria was surprised; after all, he'd already proven himself in the bodybuilding world and had said he now wanted to be an actor. She felt his dreams and goals were all over the map, that he should have more focus. Typical Shriver. However, she supported him anyway, even accompanying him to Europe, learning the business behind muscle competition and practically managing his career. Or, as Arnold put it, "she was an animal for me over there."

In the early 1980s, Arnold and Maria moved in together in Los Angeles. Though Sarge and Eunice had reservations about them living together without the benefit of marriage, they actually liked Arnold from the start. He was a success in life as a result of good old-fashioned hard work, and that mattered to them. He was respectful, too; they didn't know if Maria had told him to do so or not, but he always stood up for them whenever they walked into the room.

By 1982, Arnold's acting career was on the rise as a result of his popular starring role in *Conan the Barbarian,* followed two years later by its sequel, *Conan the Destroyer.* Then, in 1984, he took on his biggest and maybe most familiar of his characters, the Terminator. Throughout the eighties, his star continued to rise as he became an international action star with *Commando, Raw Deal, The Running*

Man, Predator, and *Red Heat.* It was quite a streak, and Maria was proud of him. "I thought he was inspiring," she recalled. "People said he would never make it, that his body was too unusual for films, that his accent was too strong, that he couldn't act. But he never gave up. He had a dream and he went for it. That was very Kennedy/Shriver of him, wasn't it?"

Maria and Arnold married on April 26, 1986; Maria was thirty, Arnold, thirty-eight. Caroline Kennedy, twenty-eight, was Maria's maid of honor, just as Maria would be hers.

MAKING GOD LAUGH

Maria Shriver may not have wanted to marry a politician, but within a few years of being with Arnold it became clear that her specific vision might not have clarity. "You may not have wanted a husband who was political, but you got one," Sargent said, patting Arnold on the shoulder during one family meal; this was about two years after the Schwarzeneggers were married. It was around this time that Arnold had accompanied then–Vice President George H. W. Bush to a campaign rally, which marked the first time he was viewed in a political light by the public. "It's just a matter of time," Sarge told Maria with a wink. "Over my dead body" was her response.

Though Sarge and Eunice admired Arnold's determination to make it as an actor, they couldn't help but see something in him they thought suggested bigger and maybe more important ambitions. They'd had an actor in the family once, Peter Lawford, who'd been married to Pat. However, Peter was doing what he loved, and he had no interest in being a public servant. Arnold was different. He cared about the world around him and enjoyed lively conversations about politics when sitting around the Shriver dining room table.

All these years after his political life had ended, Sargent was determined to see the next generation stake its own rightful place, and he had a lot of enthusiasm about Arnold in that regard. The two men would always end up locked in deep conversation under an umbrella on the beach.

"Whatever those two are cooking up can't be good," Maria once said to Leah Mason.

"I'm sure your father is just offering some good political advice," Leah observed with a smile.

"Yeah, that's exactly what I'm afraid of," Maria said.

"I've always said this about you," Sargent told Arnold, again according to Leah's memory. "You have something special. Are you sure you don't want to go into the family business? Because I think you have it in you, my boy."

Shriver, whose hair was now white, always had a mischievous glint in his eye whenever he spoke to his son-in-law about politics. According to photographs taken on the day, he was wearing a white polo shirt and white shorts, his spindly-looking legs covered about a third of the way up in black socks, accompanied by sandals. Arnold, looking hot and uncomfortable in slacks and a long-sleeved striped shirt bursting at the seams, had to laugh. "Your daughter will kill me," he said, motioning to Maria. Shriver nodded. "Yeah, but don't let that hold you back," he said with a smile. "She'll get on board."

That Arnold was such a staunch Republican didn't bother Sarge or Eunice. "Even though they were Democrats in a powerful Democratic family, the Shrivers always felt like outsiders, anyway," noted Hugh Sidey. "Maybe Bobby [Kennedy] best encapsulated this pejorative feeling when he was once asked his opinion of Sarge. 'Yeah, well . . . he's a good Shriver' was his response. He'd completely underestimated the man, who was anything but a lightweight and certainly nobody's poor man's Kennedy. I'm actually not sure of the origins of this impression, because certainly Jack [JFK] loved and respected the guy."

Leave it to Sarge, though, to take such an unkind familial appraisal of him and turn it on its ear when asked about Arnold: "He's as much a Kennedy as any good Shriver," he joked.

Arnold's first political appointment was as chairman of the President's Council on Physical Fitness and Sports, where he served from 1990 to 1993 under George H. W. Bush. He would later serve as chairman of the California Governor's Council on Physical Fitness and Sports under Governor Pete Wilson. In 1999, he started talking publicly about politics, sounding much like a Kennedy (or maybe a Shriver) when he said he felt an urge to "do something bigger, to be of service."

Despite his growing interest in politics, Arnold's burgeoning film career continued unabated. He starred in *Twins* in 1988, followed by *Total Recall, Terminator 2: Judgment Day,* and *Batman & Robin.* In 2003, *Terminator 3: Rise of the Machines* grossed over $150 million domestically. That summer, Arnold proclaimed his candidacy in the recall election for governor of California. He would announce on August 6 on *The Tonight Show.* "I married into a political family," he would explain to Jay Leno. "You get together with them and you hear about policy, about reaching out to help people. I was exposed to the idea of being a public servant and Eunice and Sargent Shriver became my heroes."

Maria wasn't thrilled with this new plot twist in the story of a life she thought she'd planned so carefully. Of course she wanted to support her husband, but she had to wonder what his interest in politics would mean for her and for their family. "This is *so* not what I had planned," she told her mother.

IDENTITY CRISIS

In 2003, Maria Shriver found herself at an important crossroads. By this time, she was a highly successful television personality, having anchored the *CBS Morning News* with Forrest Sawyer from August 1985 until August 1986, co-anchored NBC News's *Sunday Today* from 1987 to 1990, and acted as a weekend anchor on NBC on Saturdays from 1989 to 1990 and on Sundays until 1993. Now, in 2003, she found herself working as a contributing anchor and correspondent for *Dateline NBC*. At forty-eight, she had a distinctive, Kennedy-esque look, one that translated well on television: an angular face, resembling her mother's, a gleaming white smile, penetrating dark eyes, and an abundance of well-styled brown hair. Her manner was authoritative, again like Eunice's. "Make a decision as to how you want people to perceive you," Eunice used to tell her, "and then be that woman."

Maria had achieved pretty much everything

she set out to do — marrying a smart, handsome man who wasn't in politics, bearing wonderful children, and working successfully in television. Though she had a good life, she was concerned about how Arnold's interest in politics would affect her own life. "I had to figure out a way to incorporate his new dream into my old one," she would later admit. "He had his acting career, and what a career it was. I never would have thought he would have given it up for anything in the world, he was that big a star and we had that good a life. Then, as often happens, things changed . . . and boy, did they ever."

Most people didn't think Arnold was a likely candidate for any kind of political office. Few even knew his views. Once he began to speak out, though, and make his positions known, his appeal became clear. He was an outsider, a little like Ronald Reagan and, later, Donald Trump. As sometimes occurs in politics, newcomers with fresh ideas who rarely or even never held public office can appeal to the disenfranchised in search of solutions to their problems. A staunch Republican who held the party's long-standing views, Arnold was tough on illegal immigration. He was also critical of too much government intervention in business. Some Californians began to appreciate his proposals, especially in how they might impact the state's declining economy by providing more jobs.

When Arnold announced his candidacy for governor to replace Gray Davis in a recall election, it became a big story. Schwarzenegger had quickly amassed a base, and it was vocal and powerful. His supporters viewed him as a man who'd come from nothing to become a huge success, and they believed his personal upward trajectory meant he could also be successful in government. He would shake things up, be "different." His strength of personality played a big part in his growing popularity. He *looked like* he knew what he was doing, even if, at times, maybe he didn't have a clue. It was thought by voters that "by his very Arnoldness, his very Terminatorness, he could cut through the self-serving culture of the governing class in Sacramento," according to former Reagan speechwriter Peggy Noonan.

Certainly, Arnold Schwarzenegger and Donald Trump had a lot in common as politicians, not the least of which was that Arnold was not very specific in describing his agenda. Voters wanted change, and as Joe Jr. had told Kerry when discussing her husband Andrew Cuomo's chances of becoming governor, "Pretty much always in politics, it comes down to one of two things: 'I hate that guy' or 'I don't hate that guy.' " With Cuomo, Joe said he was certain it would be "I hate that guy." He was right (at least at first; Cuomo would certainly later prove himself). With Arnold, it would turn out to be just the opposite.

Schwarzenegger's speechwriter, Landon Parvin, also known for his longtime work as the architect of Ronald Reagan's speeches, recalls, "It was the most amazing campaign. I had been around presidents, I was used to that kind of media chaos, but with Arnold, it was more than that. It wasn't just the mainstream American press, it was the entertainment press and also the foreign press. It was a fascinating fusion of politics and celebrity. There was just this incredible excitement. I can remember the morning of a senior staff meeting, I think it was after his first rally in Manhattan Beach. It was outside. There was this crush of people. Downtown guys in suits, surfer dudes, young people and old . . . you name it. There was just this incredible movement happening."

In October, the California recall election resulted in Governor Gray Davis being removed from office and Arnold being elected governor, defeating Democrat Cruz Bustamante. "This is a great day for California," he declared at a press event the next day. "This state is in trouble in many ways. I will fix it. I *can* fix it. I just need some time. I can change our economy, I can create jobs. Obviously, people believe that to be true, and I will not let them down." Maria sat on the sidelines as her husband spoke, along with their children, looking as if this was one of the happiest days of her life. Privately, though, she still had grave concerns. "My head did a three-sixty on my shoulders," she would recall. She would have to now accept that a huge life change was in the offing for her and her family.

Just as she had feared, Arnold's election would mean a redefining of Maria's life, in particular her beloved career. She'd taken a leave of absence from her duties at *Dateline* when he announced, but when she returned after the election it was clear that NBC had concerns. "NBC felt there could be a perception of a conflict of interest between my news job and Arnold's becoming governor," Maria later explained. She added, "It was uncharted water. The producers said, 'If we put you on the air while Arnold's campaigning, it'll look like we're endorsing him.' A lot of people were uncomfortable with that, so they took me off the air while he was running for office. I thought I'd return to reporting when the campaign was over. And then he won, and that was that."

After twenty-seven years of doing what she loved, leaving NBC wasn't easy. "I realized how much I had identified myself with Maria Shriver, newswoman," she recalled. "When that was gone, I had to really sit back and go,

'Well, actually, who am I now?' That sent me off on a process of really, for the first time in my life, looking deep within myself and asking myself, *Who do I want to be?*' "

Eunice sympathized with her daughter's conundrum, referring to it as being "locked in the horns of a dilemma." Some had assumed her position would be that Maria should do whatever she had to do to support her husband in the time-honored tradition of Kennedy women. Eunice was never a typical Kennedy woman, though. She'd always had a rewarding life separate and apart from Sarge's and had never walked in his shadow. Therefore, she appreciated that Maria had worked hard to forge her own identity and that turning away from it for the good of Arnold's ambition wasn't going to be easy. Mother and daughter spent many hours trying to unpack it all.

Eunice felt strongly that Maria should adapt to this big change in her life. She also advised Maria that doing so would be instructive for her children, acting as a life lesson that even when surprising curves come one's way, it's important to adapt. She also reminded her that in her new role she must never think of herself as a supplicant of her husband's. She had the opportunity to be a powerful woman in California, someone who could make valuable contributions. "In other words, it's time for you to take your seat at the table," Eunice told her. "Maybe it's time for you to stop running from your destiny. Maybe it's time for you to start embracing it." In the end, what Maria was left with was this memorable conclusion from her mother: "This isn't the end of your story. If anything, it's just the beginning."

In the years to come, Maria would work hard to find value in her work as California's First Lady. She began by leading the California Governor and First Lady's Conference on Women. Then she created the Minerva Awards, honoring "remarkable California women" who'd made an impact on the state with their "courage and bravery." Landon Parvin recalls her as being "incredibly smart, eager to make an impression. We had a few moments along the way where she would want to inject something into a speech that was perhaps a more Democratic spin on a subject. I remember that when Arnold gave a speech at the Republican National Convention, she kept trying to make it nonpartisan. I told her, 'Maria, you can't. It's a political party convention.' We would go back and forth on this a lot over time, and I began to understand that she'd been influenced by her uncle Teddy, who was known and lauded for always trying to cross party lines."

At one point, Maria Shriver called upon Nancy Reagan, a former First Lady of California, for advice. "What is it that I am supposed to do in this position?" she asked her. Nancy's response: "Do whatever you like, Maria. Because whatever you do, you'll be criticized." With that in mind, Maria just dug in. Eventually she would find her way through the mountains of red tape and political partisanship to learn how to get things done on a state level. "I figured it out," she said. "I just got in there and did what Shrivers do: we keep our heads down and we do the work."

GROWING UP SHRIVER

By 2004, the members of the Shriver family were all accomplished, each of Eunice and Sarge's adult children living rewarding, noteworthy lives committed to social change. "The Robert Kennedy family and the Senator Edward Kennedy family was always running for office," recalled Bobby Shriver. "In the Shriver house, though, most of us didn't run for office; we started programs. That energy of running for office, the street-fighting, partisan, competitive quality that existed in the other Kennedy households didn't exist in ours.

"Our childhood home in Maryland, which was called Timberlawn, was plenty competitive, but the competition and the questions were different: Did the Camp Shriver programs work? Did we need to get a new camp director? Where should we have more tennis or more swimming? Are the races being monitored correctly? We need some stopwatches; these stopwatches we have are no good and we can't time the races properly! *'What the hell? Who's in charge of stopwatches?'* In other words, the building of ideas and programs, and the people to work in them, was a more generative and creative process for us than asking, *How am I going to beat that guy in the next race?*"

It's been written in the past that the advantage the Shrivers had over most of their cousins was the solid upbringing from which they benefited as the offspring of two grounded parents, both of whom were ever present in their lives. That's true to an extent. However, Sarge and Eunice were definitely not sitting around waiting for the kids to get home from school. "They were *not* around," Bobby confirms. "They got up and went to the office in the morning, both of them."

Still, Bobby says, the Shriver parents did have a crucial impact on their offspring. "Kids know what their parents are like, whether they're around or not. It's the *story* of your parents that has the impact on you as a kid. As you get older, you begin to see that certain elements of the story aren't true, and you then get a more realistic view of who your parents are. It wasn't about them being around. It was about the intensity of their work."

It wasn't always easy being raised by such overachieving parents. "Yes — it drives you," Maria has said, "but if you're moving all the

654

time, you're not stopping to be or think or experience nature. A couple of years ago, a friend of mine who'd worked his whole life bought a loft in New York and fixed it up. It was serene and peaceful. He said, 'When I go there, I feel like I'm on a honeymoon with myself.' I mentioned this to my parents, and they said, 'What is the point of that? What are you doing to make the world a better place by going on a honeymoon with yourself?' They didn't get it. After I wrote my second book, I saw my father at the Cape. He said, 'What are you doing with yourself?' I said, 'I just wrote a book.' 'But you did the book already,' he said. '*That's over.* You need to do a new thing.' When you come from a family that has achieved so much, you're left with the challenge of either making peace with that or finding some way to do what you want to do. It's impossible to compete with that level of accomplishment."

By the beginning of 2004, Bobby Shriver, an attorney, was about to turn fifty. He'd had a colorful childhood, not missing out on much because he was determined to see it all, do it all; he lost his virginity at the age of fourteen while living in Paris with his family. He also attended Phillips Exeter Academy in New Hampshire, a difficult experience for him; he had such trouble with his studies he still experiences a surge of panic when recalling those days. In November, he would become a member of the Santa Monica City Council, a position he would hold for the next eight years. Later in 2004, Arnold reappointed him as chairman of the California State Park and Recreation Commission, a position he'd previously held under Governor Gray Davis. In a year's time — in 2005 — Bobby would marry Malissa Feruzzi and they would then raise two daughters, Natasha Hunt Lee and Rosemary Scarlett.

At the beginning of 2004, Maria Shriver — who would turn forty-nine that year — continued her work as California's First Lady while raising her four children with Arnold: Katherine, Christina, Patrick, and Christopher.

Timothy Shriver, who would turn forty-five in 2004, was devoted to children's issues, having been a former high school and college teacher. His interest was in developing programs for disadvantaged youth. Like his siblings, he was influenced as a kid by Camp Shriver, basically a daycare center for the intellectually disabled that his mother had established in the Shrivers' Maryland home. Eventually it was expanded into the Special Olympics. By the beginning of 2004, he had been married for eighteen years to Linda Potter, and they had five children: Sophia Rose, Timothy Jr., Samuel, Kathleen, and Caroline.

Mark Shriver would turn forty in February

2004. He'd already enjoyed a full and productive life of service as a member of the Maryland House of Delegates for two consecutive terms, from 1995 to 2003. He didn't seek reelection in 2002, instead running for a Congressional seat, which he lost at the primary stage. He was now senior vice president for U.S. Programs of the Save the Children charity. By 2004, he had two children of his own — Thomas and Mary Elizabeth — with his wife, Jeanne, whom he'd married in 1992.

Anthony Shriver would turn thirty-nine in 2004. Continuing the tradition of advocacy for children with intellectual disabilities, he created Best Buddies International, an international charity devoted to people with learning disabilities. (It has more than 1,500 chapters today.) Anthony had married the Cuban-born Alina Mojica, a former ballerina, back in 1993 and, by 2004, had four children, Teddy, Eunice, Francesca, and Carolina. They would have one more child, John, in 2009. They lived in Miami, where Best Buddies was headquartered.

"Faith. Not Hope. Faith."

In early 2004, much of the Shriver family was excited by an upcoming visit to the compound by Archbishop Sean Patrick O'Malley. A longtime friend of Eunice — and before her, Rose — O'Malley had earlier been stationed in Palm Beach, Florida, and was a regular guest of the family's when they were in residence at their estate there. Many of the Kennedys, Shrivers, Lawfords, and Smiths gathered at the Cape for Father O'Malley's visit in January 2004. According to the plan, he would celebrate Mass at ten sharp on his first Sunday there. After the service, another Mass would be said at Ted and Vicki's. Then there'd be a brunch at Eunice and Sarge's. Afterward, they would all converge on the Shrivers' veranda with Bloody Marys.

One plan for Father O'Malley's visit was for Ted and his sons — Patrick and Teddy — as well as Sargent and his sons — Bobby, Timothy, Mark, and Anthony — to take O'Malley out on the Senator's beloved schooner, *Mya,* to Nantucket. Maria and Arnold had already returned to Los Angeles after the holidays, and Kara — Ted's daughter — was in Boston with her children. However, since it was freezing cold, Eunice didn't want Sarge to go on the little jaunt. A small dispute regarding how many sweaters Sarge should wear ended up a loud, impassioned debate. O'Malley was so surprised by Sarge and Eunice's outburst, he had to ask if they were all right. No, Ethel said, things were definitely not okay with the Shrivers. She said Sarge had been slipping for the last few years.

At first it was difficult to be sure of what was happening to Sarge. He would forget people's names, repeat himself in conversation, and seem disoriented. Eunice blamed it on "old age," as did Ted and Ethel. Finally, in the middle of 2000, Sarge was diagnosed as being in the early stages of Alzheimer's disease. "You hear it but you don't really believe it," said Timothy. "Then you hear it again, and it sinks in a little, but still you don't get it. When you finally do accept it, it feels like the end of everything as you have known it."

Maria, in particular, wanted to know exactly what the diagnosis meant and how to handle it. Like her mother, she was ready to make lists, to have an agenda, to tackle it and make sense of it. She quickly realized it wasn't possible, though. "Once you see one case of Alz-heimer's, you've seen . . . one case of Alz-heimer's," a doctor told her. There was no way to predict how it would unfold for Sarge, and there was nothing anyone could do but pray.

True to his nature, Sarge wanted to maintain his schedule for as long as possible. A few weeks after his Alzheimer's diagnosis, he and Eunice were off to Ireland, the family's homeland, for the first Special Olympics World Summer Games ever to be held overseas. As Eunice stood onstage holding hands with Nelson Mandela, who officially opened the games, at historic Croke Park in front of sixty-five thousand cheering people, Sarge stood on the sidelines and beamed. It was as if nothing could slow these two down. The next day, Sarge gave a stirring speech to the Special Olympics board of directors at Dublin Castle. "It would be his last appearance at the Olympics, but he went out with a bang," said Mark Shriver. "We all marveled at his ability to rise above . . . to be the man he had always been even though there was this . . . *thing* . . . Alzheimer's going on in the background."

By the beginning of 2004, Sarge's condition had gotten much worse. At eighty-eight, he was older than all those in the old guard — seventeen years older than Ted, who was seventy-two. Now he had slowed down to the point where it had actually become heart-breaking for his children to watch. After all, Sarge had been one of the great minds of President Kennedy's New Frontier, well loved by almost everyone in government, regarded as "a good man," which is what President Bill Clinton would call him, in a world of politics where there weren't many left.

Determined not to let it all get to her, Eunice continued to insist on enlisting Sarge in dinner conversation when the children and their children came to visit. "What do *you* think, Sargie?" she would ask when someone made a point. "And how do *you* feel about that, Sargie?" she would wonder when someone else had an idea. She would not let the man she'd loved for more than fifty years slip away, not on her watch, anyway.

All four Shriver sons were present for the visit of Archbishop O'Malley, as were their wives and children. "After Mass, the boys — I call them boys, but they were all obviously grown men — sat down with the archbishop to pray privately," recalled a priest who had accompanied O'Malley on the trip. "Later I spoke to Mark, who was having a crisis of conscious about his father."

"I don't know how to do this," said Mark Shriver with tears in his eyes to the priest. "This isn't Dad," he said, pointing to Sarge sitting in front of the fireplace, vacancy in his eyes. "So many people say you end up becoming a parent to your parents," he observed. "That notion falls far short of the truth for me. A parent can control a five-year-old. But I can't control anything about my dad, least of all what's happening to him."

"But you must have faith," said the priest. "God is with your dad, wherever he is in his own mind in this moment. Look at him. He's safe and happy in his own world, Mark."

The two peered at Sarge, who smiled back at them from across the room.

Mark knew his cousins — Kara, Teddy, and Patrick — had been dealing with a failing parent, his aunt Joan, for many years. Now he, too, faced a different kind of debilitation in a beloved parent. "I know it's called growing up," he concluded, "but I have to confess, Father, it's been a long time since I had much hope."

The priest shook his head. "You need *faith*, Mark. Not hope. Faith." The rest of 2004 would remain challenging for the Shrivers as Sarge's disease continued to take its natural course. However, as Eunice liked to say, "The sun comes up every morning. No matter what, every morning it comes up."

At the beginning of the new year — on February 18, 2005 — the family grew just a tad bigger when Mark and Jeanne Shriver welcomed little Emma Rose Shriver to their fold. Pretty much nothing could compare to the moment when Mark handed Emma to her grandfather to hold for the first time. "*This* is life," Eunice said as she watched her husband gently cradle his new granddaughter. "It goes on, doesn't it, Sargie?" she asked him.

Gazing down at his granddaughter with tears in his eyes, Sarge nodded. "Change is the law of life," he said softly, almost trance-like. "And those who look only to the past or present are certain to miss the future." Eunice looked at her husband with amazement. It was just a line, but he had quoted her brother President Kennedy . . . and it was perfect.

■ ■ ■ ■

PART V
FAMILY AT WAR
AND PEACE

■ ■ ■ ■

"WELL DONE, MOMMY"

When he closed his eyes and called upon the moment, in the dark recesses of his mind Patrick Kennedy could always find his mother, Joan, on an expansive stage, sitting before a black Steinway piano in front of a mammoth orchestra. She would be playing for thousands of people, all formally dressed in tuxedos and gowns. Her flaxen hair was parted in the middle and cascading to her shoulders. Her skin was flawless; her occasional smile to the audience bright, engaging. A blue spotlight shimmered off her black-and-white lace Valentino gown with its sloping neckline and long sleeves; the image was somehow angelic. She played effortlessly, her fingers gliding over the keys. Sometimes she would soften her expression, seeming lost in the moment as the tempo slowed and then, with a slight change in her face, pick up again. Occasionally, she would tilt her head back, as if savoring the experience. She seemed to be loving her life, the music coming from a place deep within, setting her free and acting as medicine for her . . . healing her.

Once finished with her piece, Joan Kennedy would stand up and take her bows. The audience would rise in unison. Overwhelmed, she would walk to the wings in tears. There, Patrick would lock eyes with her for just a second. In that moment, he would feel such an abundance of affection for him, especially as she mouthed the words *I love you.* Then she would walk back out onto the stage, the sound of the audience's applause continuing to be thunderous.

Someone would come forth with a large bouquet of red roses.

The curtains then closed.

What a moment.

Did this really happen? Was it a genuine memory? Or was it just a story passed down in the Kennedy family about something Patrick hadn't actually witnessed but that felt real to him simply because he'd heard it so many times? As a grown man, he could never be quite sure. It was difficult to remember his troubled mother in such happy circumstances. Somehow, though, he could still recall her walking quickly toward him backstage while he and his father continued to applaud her. She was crying now, at least in Patrick's memory. She scooped him up in her arms and held him close as flashbulbs popped all around them. "It was a great success," he remembered his proud father saying while patting her on the shoulder. "Well done, Mommy. Well done."

Patrick was actually three on October 13, 1970, when Joan Kennedy performed Mozart's Piano Concerto no. 21 in the key of C and Debussy's Arabesque no. 1 for three thousand people while backed by the Philadelphia Orchestra at the Philadelphia Academy of Music. The event was a fund-raiser for the election campaign of Democratic politician Milton Shapp, who was running for governor. Thirty-four-year-old Joan — who'd lately been receiving rave reviews for her narration of such great orchestral pieces as *Peter and the Wolf* by the Russian composer Sergei Prokofiev — had been asked to appear as a guest pianist. Even though the marquee outside the theater read MRS. EDWARD (JOAN) KENNEDY — WORLD PIANO DEBUT, it really wasn't true. She'd been onstage not only narrating, but playing piano in public many times in the past, ever since she was a young girl in Bronxville. She started piano lessons when she was five and continued until she was twenty-one.

Patrick still isn't sure he was there. If so, where was Kara? Where was Teddy? With the passing of the years, no one seemed to remember if they were present or not, but Patrick felt sure he was there, snuggled in his

669

mother's arms. He would decide it had all happened just exactly as he remembered it. It was a memory that would sustain him, always. He'd never let it go.

When the Child Becomes the Parent

At about four a.m on the morning of March 29, 2005, Patrick Kennedy was awakened by the relentless ringing of the telephone on his bed stand. At thirty-seven, he had been a respected Rhode Island congressman for the past ten years, responsible for much important legislation having to do with health care, a cause he and his father had championed for years. Recently, he'd finished an intensive thirty-day rehab stay at the Mayo Clinic. Upon his release, he gave an impassioned speech at the National Press Club relating to a report called "The State of Depression in America," part of a larger effort to forge a public understanding of the mental-health parity bill to which he was dedicated. Patrick was still single, having thus far devoted his life completely to politics; he hadn't dated in two years and also had no children.

"Hello. What is it?" Patrick asked as he tried to force himself awake.

It was Teddy, calling from his home in Connecticut. "Mom's at Mass General," he said. "They found her sprawled out on the sidewalk on Beacon Street. Bleeding. In the rain."

"*Holy shit.* Who found her?"

"I don't know," Teddy answered. "Some Good Samaritan. You gotta go to her," he concluded. "She needs you, Pat."

After they spoke for a few more moments, Patrick agreed to go to Massachusetts General and see to Joan while Teddy promised to call Kara with the upsetting news.

Patrick hung up; he fell back onto his mattress, staring up at the ceiling for a long moment, his mind racing. At thirty-seven, he was now four years older than his mother had been back when she had her triumphant night at the Philadelphia Academy of Music. With the swift passing of the years, he had to wonder how things had gone so wrong.

"There had always been a special relationship between Patrick and Joan," once noted Dun Gifford, who had worked for Ted in the 1960s and remained a good friend until his death in 2009. "Kara and Teddy knew it, too, often joking that Patrick was 'Mom's favorite.' Joan would say he was the 'sweetest of the three' and would often recall a Christmas when he was about ten and felt badly that he didn't have a present for her under the tree. He went into his bedroom on Christmas morning and carefully did his best to wrap one of his scarves in colorful paper, and then came back out and handed the clumsy offering to his mother. 'It's not much, Mommy,' he said, 'but since you bought it for me, I know you like it, so . . .' It was a memory Joan cherished."

Once Patrick got to the hospital, he found a tangle of reporters already on the scene. Looking exhausted, his eyes glazed and red-rimmed, he told them, "You want to make sure there's someone there for her all the time, but at the same time you don't want to encroach on her privacy too much. When things like this happen, it makes you feel as though maybe you should have done more to make sure there's someone with her twenty-four/seven, and perhaps that might become necessary."

When he finally made his way to Joan's room, Patrick found her lying in bed with a bandage on her forehead and a sling on her arm. It was heartbreaking. She looked terrible, very thin, her usually bouffant hair plastered down, her makeup streaked. Patrick lay next to her and spent the rest of the morning curled up at her side. He would say he couldn't help but be reminded of all those times when he, as a little boy, was suffering from asthma and his mother would come into his room and slip under his sheets to comfort him.

In a few days, Patrick and his siblings would have to go to work to extend their guardianship over Joan. It was then that they would learn that she'd taken to secretly drinking again. Since, by court order, there was to be no liquor allowed in her household, apparently she was getting high on vanilla extract. It was just that bad. The Kennedys knew that something would have to be done, and soon.

THE INTERLOPER

One day at the end of April, Patrick, Kara, and Teddy found themselves in the conference room of a law firm in Boston meeting with one of the Kennedy family's attorneys. "It's a rite of passage," Kara was saying. "The young ones take care of the old ones, the same old ones who once took care of the young ones. So now we have to take care of Mom the way she took care of us." Kara looked well; it had been two years since her surgery, chemo, and radiation. Her hair had grown back, she was working out regularly at a gym, and had resumed her life. There was seldom a day when she wasn't filled with gratitude; she refused to accept anything other than joy in her life, not after all she'd been through. She was totally devoted to her children, Grace, eleven, and Max, nine. Two months prior, she had turned forty-five.

"We need to help Mom, whatever we can do," Patrick agreed.

By this time, Patrick was thirty-seven. He

had a doughy, round face and a haircut that was pretty much in the same style he'd had since he was ten — a shock of brown hair with bangs, short on the sides and long on the top. Like most of his relatives, he had that great Kennedy smile. He was good-looking, but in his own haphazard sort of way. Unlike many of his male cousins, he didn't care whether he appealed to the opposite sex. In his mind, he had important work to do in Congress and he was devoted to it. He always believed that when the right woman came along, he'd know it.

Teddy, now forty-three, actually looked more like what people thought the Kennedys were supposed to look like than did Patrick. He was squared-jawed like his father and always meticulously groomed and decked out in a finely tailored suit. He seemed more like a politician than his brother, who actually *was* a politician. "How in the world did we get here," Teddy asked, according to the attorney's memory, "with some guy we don't even know having so much power over Mom? We can't let this happen. We need to find this guy and we need to stop him."

Indeed, someone had been nosing around in Joan's affairs. Her children didn't know who he was or what he was after, only that his name was Webster Janssen and that he was sending letters to them and their lawyer announcing that he and Joan had reached an agreement. Under his advisement, she was selling property she owned, and he was going to be in charge of everything. *He* was going to be in charge? Someone they didn't even know? No. That wasn't going to happen.

After that terrible night Joan Kennedy was found on a Boston street in the rain, her children proposed an informal family contract to her under the advice of a therapist. It outlined her problems and stipulated that if she continued to drink alcohol, they'd be authorized to take over her financial affairs with Teddy as her temporary guardian.

Joan had, at this point, at least $9 million in holdings, including her condo in Boston and summer home on Squaw Island. Begrudgingly, she signed the deal, if only to show good faith with her children. She then went into a rehab treatment in Florida for a month. As soon as she got out and returned to Boston, she relapsed. The children then decided to obtain a statement from her doctor saying she was incapable of caring for her personal and financial affairs. They intended to enforce the informal contract; they wanted Joan placed under the restrictions of court-ordered care, with them responsible for her affairs, Teddy the overseer. This was a heart-breaking turn of events, but a necessary one. Kara, Teddy, and Patrick were torn between their desire to help their mother and their concern that she would never forgive them. A judge signed off on it.

Into the middle of this family quandary came Webster Janssen. As lawyers and accountants sifted through Joan's holdings while doing her taxes, they were thunderstruck to discover that prior to Teddy being named her guardian, she'd transferred the title of one of her homes into a trust that was controlled by Janssen. He was, apparently, encouraging Joan to sell the family's waterfront home on Squaw Island. (Even though Squaw Island was a five-minute walk along the beach to the other homes owned by the Kennedys — 0.9 miles, to be exact — it was still considered part of the Kennedy compound.)

When Joan's children confronted her to ask what was going on and who was Janssen, they were told in no uncertain terms to mind their own business. Yes, she had been working with Janssen, she said, and yes, she planned to make the sale, and her mind was made up about it. The siblings then asked their father about Janssen. He said he vaguely recalled the name but couldn't quite remember from where. It was strange, he agreed, a real mystery.

What the Kennedys didn't realize at that time was that Webster Janssen was actually Joan's second cousin. His mother, Belle, and Joan's mother, Virginia, were cousins. It was

Ethel who figured it all out once people in the family began asking around about him. She went into one of her dozens of scrapbooks and came to the conclusion that he'd been an usher at Ted and Joan's wedding back in 1958.

As it happened, Janssen, a trust investment officer at Citibank and Morgan Guaranty Trust, was not only a relative but a confidant of Joan's. According to what he would later recall, she had kept him from the family on purpose. "Why do they have to know everything?" she asked, according to Janssen. "She felt her privacy was constantly being invaded by Kennedys of every generation, and she wanted to compartmentalize some aspects of her life," he said. "I was one of those aspects. She was a woman trying desperately *not* to lose control."

As Janssen recalled it, he and Joan had been driving from her home to Boston to visit relatives in Maine when she told him she was worried about her finances. She said that all the stints she'd had in expensive rehabilitation centers had depleted her bank accounts. Because he was experienced in such matters, Janssen later reviewed Joan's portfolio and felt he could assist her. "She was in over her head," he recalled, "and it was a real mess. She's a nice person, and people were taking advantage of her," he said. "I didn't like what I saw. And then this family contract? Not even legal? Just written out and signed by Joan under duress, giving her kids control? No. She needed money; she had bills, mostly rehab bills not covered by insurance. She was worried."

When he asked how much time Joan spent at her home on the compound, she told him that it was no more than two months out of the year. "The New Wife is there," she said, referring to Vicki; she often also referred to herself as "the Old Wife." She said that while she got along with "the New Wife," "Ethel and Eunice and the rest of those old biddies are there, too, and I'm sick of being judged by them. Even my own housekeeper judges me."

"Really?" Janssen asked.

"Yes," Joan said, "you should see the way that woman looks at me."

"Fire her, then."

"I want to," Joan said, "but then I'd have to deal with my busybody kids about it, and God forbid I should make a decision of my own."

Webster suggested that Joan put the house on the market, saying he believed she could get about $7 million for it, which would be a sizable nest egg. He also told her that she needed to inform Ted and her children that he was advising her. Joan agreed to tell Ted about Janssen, but not the children. "She later told me that Ted approved of me and was just glad to have someone looking out for her," Janssen said. "I came to later understand, though, that this wasn't true. She hadn't told anyone."

In the opinion of Joan's children, there was no reason to sell the house, which had been in the family for decades. It was part of their cherished history; all three siblings had spent much of their youth there with their cousins and had many happy memories. "It's a piece of all of us," Kara said of the house. Joan had money in the bank, they said. She just needed to cash in some annuities; they'd figure it all out for her. Whatever happened, though, one thing was sure: they were not going to let her sell that house.

TESTING HER POWER

There was a lot of discussion about how to handle Webster Janssen. Teddy and Patrick simply wanted to strong-arm him and get him out of the picture. However, Kara had a different perspective. "What's the endgame here?" she kept asking. "Because it can't just be an escalation of a war with Mother." She realized that whatever they said to Janssen would likely get back to Joan and make things worse. Her brothers had to agree.

Kara said she wanted to handle Janssen on her own, or at least have the initial meeting with him. She wanted to take charge of the situation as much for herself as for her brothers. She *needed* to do it. It was important to her that she be allowed to continue in her effort to get her life back after her cancer. Though her brothers were concerned, ultimately it was decided to acquiesce to her wishes; they felt it would probably do her a lot of good.

The meeting with Janssen was set up in one

of the Kennedy lawyers' offices in Boston. "I got called in without much time to prepare," Webster Janssen recalled many years later. "When I told Joan about it, she said I should be careful. 'They're sharks,' she told me. 'Who, Joan?' I asked. 'Your children? Or their lawyers?' She looked at me and said, 'All of 'em.' "

When Janssen, who was seventy at the time, appeared at the office, he found Kara flanked by two attorneys, one male, one female. Also, Ted had asked two of the family's longtime business associates to sit in on the meeting. "It was in a conference room around a long table," recalled Janssen, "two people on each side at the end of it, and Kara seated at the head. She was thin. Short brown hair streaked with gray. As soon as she saw me, she rose, shook my hand, and offered me a beverage. She was nice, welcoming."

"Kara started by telling Janssen that she understood he was somehow related to her mother," recalled one of the business associates sent by Ted. "He confirmed it, saying his mom and her grandmother were cousins. Kara blinked several times. 'So what does that make you and me?' she asked. He said he wasn't certain, that he'd have to think about it. 'What does that make you and my mother?' she asked. Proudly, he quickly answered, 'Second cousins.' At this, Kara glanced over to me and shook her head in dismay. 'Certainly, you can't expect that the Kennedys would allow you authority over my mother given such a distant relationship?' she asked."

Janssen then, in an effort to buttress his case, confirmed that he'd not only been at her parents' wedding, he'd been at Kara's to Michael Allen. Kara said she most certainly didn't remember seeing him there. Fine. There were a lot of people at the wedding, she conceded. Janssen then noted that the fact that he'd been a licensed securities professional for the last forty-five years and that Joan had asked for his help should be enough for her children to just accept him. "Well, it's not," Kara declared. She then asked how much Janssen was being paid. Janssen answered by saying the terms of his financial arrangement with Joan were between the two of them, and he wouldn't disclose them without her permission. Kara studied him carefully. "Okay, look, the Kennedys want you to step aside," she said, getting to the point.

"But that's for *your mother* to decide," he protested.

"No," Kara said firmly. "That's for *me* to decide." She added that if he didn't turn over all documents relating to Joan by the end of the next day, "the Kennedys" would have no choice but to bring litigation against him. "The way she kept using the word 'Kennedys' sent a bit of a shiver down my spine," Webster Janssen recalled of the conversation. "I got it that she was referring to Kennedy power."

"Before the meeting ended, Kara laid it on the line. 'I'm very serious, Mr. Janssen. We don't require your services, and neither does my mother,' " recalled Ted's business associate. " '*I* advocate for Joan Kennedy,' she said. 'Not you. Not anyone else. And by the way,' she concluded, 'you can be sure that we'll be rescinding that trust. Won't we?' she asked, staring at me. I said, 'Oh, yes, absolutely.' "

Janssen said he would have to discuss all of it with Joan. He also proposed that he could perhaps be an ally to the Kennedys in helping to make good decisions for Joan, adding, "I am not the enemy. I am on your mother's side."

Kara stood up to signal that the meeting was over. "I actually don't know how I can make this any clearer to you, Mr. Janssen," she said, "but the bottom line is this: *We. Don't. Know. You,*" she concluded, deliberately punctuating each word to give it weight.

"I saw that we were at an impasse, so I stood up, as did the two attorneys," Webster Janssen recalled. "We all shook hands, and Kara thanked me for coming in. 'You never know, I may be able to help you,' I again stated. 'Who knows? Maybe we can even be friends one day.' I was just trying to be nice and keep the door open. 'Maybe one day,'

To Litigate Against Mother

"The one thing Webster Janssen didn't want was a prolonged, expensive legal battle with the Kennedys," recalled one of the observers at the conference with Janssen, "and the meeting he had with Kara suggested that this was exactly what was in store for him. I thought Kara was tough as nails and had done a stellar job in representing the family's interests. I told Ted, wow, your daughter is really something else. You should have been there to see her in action. She was stunning in the authority and power she wielded. I had known Kara since she was a little girl, so it was fantastic for me to see what kind of a woman she had become."

"I called Joan as soon as I got back to my office and told her what had happened," added Webster Janssen. "She was angry. 'How dare Kara say that?' she told me. 'No one advocates for me,' she said. *'I advocate for myself.'* "

Janssen was already taking a beating in the

media, and he knew it was because of the family. "There were statements in local newspapers impugning my professionalism and integrity," he recalled, "statements I could have sued them for, but I didn't want to go up against the Kennedy machine. It would have cost an arm and a leg and taken years to litigate, and, quite frankly, I didn't want to drag Joan through it. Therefore, I urged Joan to just let it go. She was incredibly angry, felt she was losing her freedom little by little to her kids."

Eventually, Joan decided to acquiesce to her children's wishes and stop working with Webster Janssen. Though upset, she dissolved the trust she'd set up with him relating to the house. She wasn't going to take the house off the market, though. "Too bad for my kids," she told Janssen. "It's *my* house, not theirs. They've lived like spoiled brats their entire lives, and enough is enough."

Disgruntled over their mother's decision to sell the property, Joan's children decided to fight the sale in court. A trial was set for June 2005.

"She's not happy with the fact we have sought guardianship," said Ted of his mother to *The Boston Globe.* "She's basically trying to retaliate against her own children by taking one of the things we love the most, which is Cape Cod. It's sad. This is the house we grew up in; this is our family home.

"The most important thing to understand is we're trying to save our mother's life, simply put," he added. "That's what's at stake. You can imagine how bad this situation has gotten for us to risk angering her and undertaking this legal action against our own mother. That's the situation. We tried to keep this private until the story broke a couple of weeks ago. She tripped and fell because she was intoxicated. That is just exactly what we're trying to stop. It's not easy for anyone who has faced a situation like this. I don't know if we're going to be successful but we have to try something. We're in a desperate situation."

It was really getting out of hand. Finally, Ted asked Vicki what she thought. "My opinion has no place in this," she said. When he asked if she might talk to Joan, she said she wasn't going to use her good relationship with his ex-wife as leverage. Obviously, she said, Joan was angry because she felt as if her wishes were being ignored. Ted would have to speak to her about it himself, she said. When he finally did, he told Joan that they must avoid a trial at all costs for the sake of the family. He was very persuasive. Eventually, Joan reluctantly agreed to what was called "an extension of the temporary guardianship," an arrangement which put her finances under the control of two court-appointed supervisors outside the family.

Still, the lawyer representing her children claimed she had no legal authority to sell the Cape Cod house. He even put the word out that prospective buyers could have a real fight with the Kennedys on their hands. "Just more of the same old Kennedy backstabbing," Joan said, upset. "Clearly, my children have learned from the worst offender of all, their father." Frustrated, Joan took the property off the market so that she could have time to figure out how to proceed.

After thinking about it, she became even more filled with rage and the sense that she shouldn't allow others to make decisions for her, even her kids, and especially her ex-husband. She'd done a lot for Ted over the years, even giving him an annulment so that he could marry Vicki in the Catholic Church, and *this* is how he repaid her? By helping their kids strip away her independence?

The inter-family legal battle continued and caused even more hurt feelings. It all finally ended with Joan securing her right to legally put the Squaw Island house back on the market. Kara then pleaded with her father, who had the right of first refusal as per the divorce settlement, to buy the property in order to keep it in the family. However, he declined. Though Ted was making about $165,000 a year as a senator, he was worth at least $50 million, so it does seem like he could have purchased the property if he had really wanted to do so. Since no one else seemed to be in a position to make the purchase either, the house was finally sold to a buyer with the best offer.

Why Joan had been so determined to see the house sold remained quite the mystery. She and Ted had spent their summers, and often other seasons, for almost twenty-five years as husband and wife there. After the divorce, Joan would continue to own it for almost another twenty-five years. That was fifty years of memories. Her children felt they were well versed on the state of Joan's finances and didn't feel money was really the motivation. Was it just because she wanted to win a big fight against them?

This Kennedy family war had taken a real toll. Soon after it was resolved, Patrick — by this time a sixth-term Democrat — announced that he wouldn't be doing that which his father and many of his supporters had hoped he'd do, which was to challenge Senator Lincoln Chafee, a Republican, in 2006. This was a tough decision to make for a guy who had spent his entire life looking for ways to be special, especially in the eyes of his father. "I had never actually wanted to run for the Senate — or, rather, whenever I considered it, I quickly realized that the additional media scrutiny could present an insurmountable challenge, and with my illness I was safer in the House," Patrick would later explain.

As expected, Ted was unhappy about Patrick's reluctance to move forward with a senatorial campaign. "My dad really wanted me to run for Senate," he recalled. "But while we were handling my mom's problems, I decided to finally burst the bubble and announce I wouldn't do it." Patrick said publicly that he believed he could best serve Rhode Island by retaining his seat on the House Appropriations Committee, where he delivered money for state projects. Now for sure Ted was disappointed in him — which was not unusual. "With my dad, happiness is a moving target, anyway," Patrick reasoned at the time. "He's angry today. Tomorrow he won't be. After that, who the heck knows?"

Without further clarification, everyone assumed Patrick wasn't running for Senate only because he was choosing his mother's care over his own political ambitions. There was more to it, though. "In fact," he recalled, "the life I needed to save at that moment was my own."

Weeks later, Patrick secretly checked into the Mayo Clinic in Minnesota with a new addiction to Percocet, which he had started taking for back pain and to relieve symptoms of his anxiety disorder and bipolar disorder. He'd been taking as many as twenty a day, yet somehow still managing to function as a congressman. "You can handle anything in the moment," he said at the time. "It's out of fear of what might happen in the future that undoes us. But I now see that the only way forward for me into my future is to take care of myself in the present," he said in a statement. "It remains my great challenge."

Breaking with the Past

Summer 2005. "There's just *so much* to do," Joan Kennedy was saying to Kara. "I don't know where to begin." Wringing her hands in despair, she seemed out of sorts as she gazed around at her surroundings. "So many memories," Kara said as she picked up a framed photograph of her parents on Ted's yacht.

According to pictures taken that day, Kara's short blond hair was parted on the right; she wore no makeup and was in a red blazer over a white T-shirt with jeans. Joan's hair was long, to her shoulders, and blond, in a style reminiscent of her 1960s ingénue look. Her face was plumper than usual and it looked as if she, perhaps, had undergone some sort of filler injections. Her lips seemed a little more cushiony than may be normal for a woman her age; they were painted a bright red. She was still thin and shapely, though, in her black velvet leggings and oversized white knit sweater.

Why Joan wanted to sell the large shingled home on Squaw Island was a question Kara and her brothers had been asking for months. Now it was gone for good, sold for about $4 million, far less than the $7 million Joan had hoped for as per Webster Janssen's evaluation. If her children hadn't gotten so bent out of shape about the sale, Joan maintained, buyers wouldn't have been scared off and she probably could have gotten full price, or more.

Given everything that had recently occurred, Joan's relationship with her children was more tense than ever. Still, Kara wasn't going to let her mother orchestrate the move on her own. She insisted upon helping. She'd actually wanted to hire a moving company to take all the home's contents and put them into storage. Most of the furnishings were to be sold with the house. However, Joan wanted to go through the smaller mementos herself and pack them safely.

It was agreed that Joan's caretaker and assistant would accompany her and Kara to the compound for the day of packing. Kara then called Ethel Kennedy's assistant, Leah Mason, to ask if she might also be able to help. Leah agreed to do so. Ten minutes later, she called back and said that Ethel wanted to also assist.

On the appointed day, Joan, sixty-eight, and Ethel, seventy-seven, stood in the living room of the enormous thirteen-room house and looked about it, both feeling sad and nostalgic. As two of the three women who had originally taken Kennedy brothers as wives — Jackie being the third — one can only imagine their memories of this place. While gazing around Joan's parlor, they would have seen lovely antique furniture all about them, which Joan had been collecting since she was young. There were also, of course, dozens of framed photographs of Kennedys throughout the years — pictures documenting Ted's many political campaigns, along with family vacations and photos of Jack and Bobby and all their relatives. It was virtually a shrine to the days of Camelot. When Kara said she didn't know why her mother wanted to sell the place, Ethel said, "That is *her* decision, Kara. Not yours."

Kara suggested that they all go through each room and take whatever pictures and other mementos they could find and put them into boxes. They figured it would take two days; Kara called it "the long goodbye."

"Oh, this was hard," recalled Leah Mason. "Thirteen rooms. And every room packed, and I mean *packed,* with little mementos, plaques, photos, trophies . . . every piece holding some important memory. It looked like a Kennedy museum. Joan's caretaker was no help at all. She kept pointing at pictures and saying, 'Oh my God. Look. It's Jackie!'

Meanwhile, Joan was weepy and upset. She had this habit of playing imaginary piano keys with her fingers when she was nervous. She kept saying things like, 'This stuff. Oh my God, it's all too much.' "

Patrick, looking distressed, showed up on the second day reserved for moving. Gazing about him at all the boxes, he said it felt to him like his mother was selling off his entire childhood. He had purposely avoided all details of the sale. His spokesman said he didn't know how much the property sold for, nor did he know anything about the new owners. Kara was aware of something about her brother that most people in the family didn't know, though: he'd just gotten out of the Mayo Clinic. He didn't even tell his parents or Teddy. Somehow his stay had also escaped media scrutiny. It wasn't successful, though. While it did handle Patrick's opiate addiction, there was a plethora of other prescription drugs he had in his medicine cabinet that hadn't been addressed, such as Ambien. Now, on this day, he seemed jittery, uneasy, and foggy. He rambled on about how he and his cousins used to love to catch Atlantic killifish in muddy marshes and grass flats with wire traps while here on the island.

Not surprisingly, being in the old house also brought up a lot of issues for Patrick. Leah Mason and Joan's caretaker both walked into the parlor in time to hear Joan angrily say to her son, "We all know how much I ruined your life, Patrick. But maybe *everything* doesn't *need* to be talked about." A few more statements were made by both mother and son having to do with whether keeping secrets was in the best interest of sobriety. "What in the world are you talking about?" Joan finally asked. "When have we Kennedys ever had any secrets? Please," she exclaimed as she rose and rushed off. From his demoralized appearance, Patrick felt terrible.

"Five minutes later, Joan reappeared," recalled her caretaker. "Standing in front of Patrick and Kara, she said, 'There's no escaping your father and no escaping my past with him as long as this house exists in my life. Why can't you two understand that?' They were surprised. We all were. Suddenly, Joan's urgency to rid herself of the old place made perfect sense. In her own way, she was actually taking care of herself, trying to break with a past that had been anything but kind to her."

"But Mother, why didn't you just *tell* us that?" Kara asked, bewildered. "We would have understood."

With hard eyes, Joan answered, "Because I do not have to explain myself to you. I get to have *my own thoughts* and *my own ideas* without having to ask for approval from you two, or your brother." With that, she rushed off once again. Kara ran after her while

Patrick just slumped into a chair.

Later, when almost all the packing work was done, Joan and Ethel decided to go down to the beach for a stroll. Kara and Patrick stayed behind in the kitchen, gazing sadly at the pen and pencil measurements on the wall in a corner that denoted how tall they and Teddy had grown every year of their childhood. "Look how little we were," Kara said sadly. Leah Mason joined them. "Can I get either one of you a drink?" she asked. Kara shook her head no. Patrick didn't respond; he just stared straight ahead at the scribbles.

"Kara said she should have realized the real reason her mother wanted to sell the house," recalled Leah Mason. "She felt so stupid. She said it was just obvious. 'We should be proud of her, Pat, not angry with her,' she told her brother. 'She feels she has to get rid of her old life, that it's the only chance she'll ever have of making a new one.' Patrick just seemed lost as he continued to look at the measurements on the wall."

Finally, seeming swamped by emotion, Patrick turned around, ran from the kitchen through the house and out the front door. He then trotted down to the beach where Joan and Ethel were standing, admiring the view. When he reached them, he said a few words to his mother and then took her into his arms. The two then held each other as a smiling Ethel turned around and slowly started making her way back up to the house. Halfway, she stopped and glanced over her shoulder to find mother and son still in an embrace that must have looked as if it would never end.

A DAUGHTER'S SURPRISE

Once everything was packed, the Squaw Island house sold, and all debates relating to it behind them, Kara Kennedy had a strong intuition about it. She couldn't shake the feeling that Joan would one day regret selling it. While she wanted to honor her mother's commitment to moving forward with her life, she knew her well. Without telling Joan or her brothers, Kara approached the new owners of the property with a proposal that had actually not been her idea but, ironically enough, originally that of the family's great nemesis, Joan's former representative, Webster Janssen.

"I had known when I was working with her that Joan wanted out of the house," Janssen recalled. "But I also felt that if she went through the process of selling, of truly letting go, maybe that might be enough for her to move on. Maybe then she would still want to stay there occasionally during the summer. So I had this idea to sell the house furnished,

701

and to have a provision in the sale that would allow Joan to lease the property during one or two of the summer months at the buyer's discretion," he recalled. It wouldn't always be possible, of course. The spring and summer months were the only reason to even own the property. But still, I was able to make that a part of the deal.

"I didn't tell Joan I was going to handle it that way. Then we stopped working together and I never thought about it again. I certainly didn't know Kara had gone back to my original idea. When I found out later through the grapevine, I was gratified. I felt I still had been able to have a hand in helping Joan, even with all the bad blood."

Like Janssen, Kara didn't tell Joan about the provision in the sale. Her reasoning was that if her mother never mentioned the house again she would simply assume that she'd moved on and that would be the end of it. However, in a year's time, Kara would find that she was absolutely right about her mother. When the summer season approached, Joan began to express deep longings for Squaw Island. "Tell me the truth, Mom," Kara said, according to one account, "do you regret selling it?" As difficult as it was for her to admit it, especially after all the family warfare, Joan had to say that yes, she *was* sorry she'd let the property go. "But it's too late now," she noted sadly.

One weekend shortly thereafter, Kara suggested that Joan join her and her two grandchildren — Grace and Max — for a weekend escape. After she helped Joan pack, the four got into Kara's vehicle and started driving to what Joan thought was to be a small resort near the Cape, "just a quick getaway," as Kara had put it. Much to Joan's amazement, though, Kara drove her to Squaw Island . . . and right up driveway to her beloved old house.

Joan was confused. "What's going on?"

That's when Kara told her mother that the house was still hers for this summer and for every summer thereafter if it was available, and if she wanted it. Overwhelmed, Joan simply couldn't believe it.

As mother and daughter walked into the house, followed by the children, they found the antique furniture still in place, exactly where Joan had left it. "Joan began to cry; she later told me," said her caretaker. "She told me that Kara took a big box from the trunk of her car and gave it to her. When Joan opened it, she found it filled with framed photographs of the Kennedys over the years, truly the crowning touch to making the home Joan's, once again."

Joan Kennedy would spend many of her summer months in the Squaw Island home from that time onward . . . and she still does today.

CRUCIBLE

At six o'clock on a May morning in 2006, Patrick Kennedy woke up, leapt from his bed, and went into the bathroom to shower. Glancing in the mirror, he suddenly realized he was wearing a suit — pants, shirt, tie, jacket . . . even his shoes. *What in the world?* Feeling groggy and disoriented, he peeled off the clothing and showered. He then dressed again, left his apartment, and went down to the garage. Once there, he saw that his automobile, a green Mustang, was missing. His mind racing, he couldn't figure out what was going on, but he knew it wasn't good. As he started walking to the Capitol, it all started coming back to him. He recalled that the night before, he'd taken a couple of Ambien and a few other drugs — he'd figure out which ones later — and then woke up within hours thinking he was late for a vote on the floor. He quickly got dressed, got into his car, and sped to work with his headlights off. He then smashed into a barricade in front of

704

the Capitol building. How was he not hurt? A sympathetic police officer helped him stash his car in the Congressional parking lot and drove him home. Hours later, he woke up in his suit, all of which brought him to this horrible moment of wondering just how long it might be before his misadventure was made public. Worse, what if he didn't remember all of what had occurred? What if he'd injured someone, or worse? At this point, it felt as if anything was possible.

Once he got to his office at the Capitol, Patrick sat at his desk and braced himself. Looking down at him from their oil portraits were his heroic uncles Jack and Bobby. There were also framed photographs of his father, Ted, all over the office. He stared at a picture of him and Joan at a campaign rally. He could feel himself buckle under the imposing weight of history.

Pulling himself together, Patrick then went into a meeting with Congressional leaders, one having to do with, of all things, mental health. His colleagues could tell that something was off with him, but then again, something was usually a little off with him. The meeting ended when Kennedy was called to the floor to vote on a port safety amendment. It was just one more day of an incredibly busy, stressful week during which he had tackled a dizzying amount of legislation on the House floor, from increased accountability of lobbyists to the cost of gasoline and other fuels to maritime and port security to complicated IRS tax codes and pension plan regulations, all of it demanding a great deal of study and preparation before he was able to vote. It seemed to never end.

After a couple of hours, Patrick's assistant came rushing over to him. "You need to get back to your office, immediately," he told him, seeming frantic. "Something big is happening."

Back at his office, Patrick came to understand that someone from the media had recognized his dented Mustang in the parking lot where it had been stashed. Photographs of the vehicle were already making the rounds in the press. Reporters were asking questions.

Patrick poured himself a Jack Daniel's and Coke, sat at his desk, and waited for the onslaught. It didn't take long before his secretary began fielding calls from the media, friends, family, and colleagues. Finally, she buzzed Patrick and told him that the one person he truly didn't want to hear from in that moment was on the line: the Senator.

"I saw the car in the press," Ted began, "and I don't know what the big deal is. It's just a fender bender." He didn't seem to grasp the gravity of the situation.

On one hand, Patrick was more than happy to downplay the accident for his father's benefit. He also wanted him to know how sick he was, and how dangerously close he'd come to not only hurting himself, but others. However, Ted had always insisted that there was nothing really wrong with Patrick that he couldn't just get over if he'd put his mind to it. He was tired of hearing about addictions in his family — his ex-wife, his children, his relatives — more Kennedys than he could count seemed to be hooked on one thing or another. "The problem with this family isn't disease," Ted always insisted, "it's lack of willpower. I'll tell you what you need," he would tell Patrick. "A swift kick in the ass, that's what you need. You want to be a better man?" he'd ask. "Fine. *Then be one.*"

It was ironic, given all his work in mental health care reform, that Ted still didn't really understand addiction. In some ways, his myopic view was reflected in a mental health equity act he championed and that had been signed into law back in 1998. It was designed to end prejudice against mental illness by making it illegal to treat brain diseases any differently than other diseases. However, the bill only covered mental illnesses considered the most serious, such as paranoid schizophrenia. It ignored more common conditions, such as alcohol addiction and bipolar disorder, both of which plagued his son. In fact, Patrick was in the middle of crafting a new bill that would cover *all* diseases and make it illegal to discriminate against any mental illness, no matter its root.

On this difficult morning, Patrick was in no mood to engage with his father. Instead, he told him he was tired and would talk to him later. Then, without much deliberation about it, he knew what he had to do: he made plans to check into the Mayo Clinic again — just five months after his last stint — to, once again, deal with his addictions.

For Patrick, this latest misfortune would mark another major defining moment in his troubled life. The time had come to admit the truth — *all of it* — after many years of either concealing it or letting bits of it slip through his perfected practice of obfuscating.

"I was an alcoholic; I was a drug addict; I had bipolar disorder and anxiety disorder, and I hadn't been properly admitting or treating them," he recalled. "And for the first time in my life, at the age of thirty-eight, I just wanted to stop lying about all of this." Patrick would express all of it in a press conference the next day; he would fess up to his decades-long battle with addiction and his recent stay at the Mayo Clinic and explain that he was going back in for more treatment. He would detail his problems with bipolar disorder, anxiety, and depression, courageously addressing it all and ridding himself of the shame, humiliation, and the deadly need for secrecy. He said he now wanted to not only be a better congressman but, as his father had suggested, a better man. He asked his constituency for the chance to do just that. "I hope that my openness today and in the past, and my acknowledgment that I need help, will give others the courage to get help if they need it. I am blessed to have a loving family who is in my corner every step of the way. And I'd like to call, once again, for passage of mental health parity."

Ted tried to act supportive; he released a public statement of encouragement, lauding the courage of his youngest child: "I have the rare and special honor of being able to serve with my son in the Congress, and I have enormous respect for the work Patrick has done. The people of the First District of Rhode Island have a tireless champion for the issues they care about, and today I hope they join me in feeling pride and respect for a courageous man who has admitted to a problem and taken bold action to correct it."

The next couple of months would be a blur. Patrick did his stint at Mayo as planned. He seemed better when he was released in August and joined his family on the Cape, as he had every summer for most of his life.

At the compound, it was as tense as ever between father and son. Now Ted was upset because a reporter from *The New York Times* had been pestering him to ask about his drinking habits. Apparently, the paper was preparing a piece on Patrick. Ted told the reporter he'd been "well" for the last fifteen years and that he only had an occasional glass of wine with dinner, which, at least according to most family accounts, wasn't exactly true. He'd definitely cut back thanks to Vicki, but he was still drinking a lot more than just the occasional glass of wine. Some friends had recently been alarmed when, before a meeting, he poured himself a healthy glass of vodka . . . and then dropped two Alka-Seltzers into it! As they fizzed, he smiled and said something about it being the latest cure for a hangover. "I can't stop this kind of transparency if that's what you want for yourself," Ted bellowed at Patrick. "But do not drag *me* into it. I am not compelled to discuss my private life with a reporter just so you can build yourself up in the court of public opinion. None of your relatives are."

That hurt.

"Well, Dad, you could've just said 'no comment,' " Patrick offered. While he didn't want to poke the so-called Lion of the Senate, what else could he say? In response, Ted glared at him. "People keep secrets for a reason," he said, "even from those they love. It's not your place to reveal them."

Now that Patrick was on the road to recovery, he decided he wanted to share his own story openly, thus his cooperation with that *New York Times* piece. "I wanted to aggressively tie my personal story to my ongoing legislative fight for mental health parity — an effort to outlaw the rampant discrimination in medical insurance coverage for mental illness and addiction treatment," he would explain. "Winning the parity fight would be the first step to overcoming all discrimination against people with these diseases, their families, and those who treated them. So I decided to go public exclusively to *The New York Times.*"

The article on Patrick's battle for sobriety and good mental health appeared on the *Times*'s front page on September 19, 2006. The timing couldn't have been worse. Two days earlier, Pat Kennedy Lawford died after a battle with throat cancer; she was eighty-two. Still reeling from the loss of his sister, Ted now also had Patrick's story with which to contend. "My God," he exclaimed to him during a dinner in his late sister's honor after the wake. "What have you done? What a disaster. When will you ever learn?"

Patrick tried to explain that he was just trying to be honest. "Okay," Ted said, angrily and loud enough for anyone to hear. "You want to take that dog for a walk? Fine. But if it bites me or one of your other loved ones on the ass . . . that's on you. *That's on you.*" Patrick then said, " 'Wait! Dad, I want to talk to you,' to which Ted very loudly said, 'No!' as he walked away."

711

Vicki went over to Ted and tried to calm him down. He didn't want to hear it, though. "This is none of your damn business," he snapped at her. His comment set her off. "Really?" she asked, irate. "None of my damn business? Really, Ted? *Really?*" While this brief exchange made a few people wonder about the state of Vicki's marriage to Ted, most recognized it for exactly what it was: spouses shooting off their mouths at each other in the heat of emotion. "Wow," quipped one of Ethel's sons, cocktail in hand. "Dinner *and* a show!"

For the most part, Patrick spent the rest of the evening staying out of the line of Ted's fire. Finally, though, he'd had enough of hearing him criticize him to anyone who would listen. He walked up to the Senator and, in front of witnesses, let him have it. "Better get used to it, Dad, because this is just the beginning. I want *all* the Kennedy secrets out, once and for all." This was unusual; Patrick was usually too cowed by Ted to go after him like that.

"That's your problem right there," Ted said, glaring at him.

"I don't think so, Dad," Patrick said, meeting his father with his own angry gaze. "I think it might be yours." He looked at Ted for a beat as if waiting for a reaction. Ted just stared at him. Patrick then patted him on the shoulder and walked away.

For Ted, this was a tough moment, even if Patrick did try to take the edge off it. He stood in place, stunned. Instantly, tears came to his eyes. Patrick had never spoken to him like that before, ever. Sure, maybe he deserved it. But still, from Ted's pained expression, it must have felt like a dagger in the heart. The next day, Patrick was filled with regret about it. He felt he'd let his emotions get the better of him. "You don't talk to your father like that," he told one person who had witnessed it. "Not in my family, anyway. It's just not right."

PATRICK PROVES HIMSELF

In November 2006, Patrick was reelected by the largest plurality of his career. He had shown real courage by facing up to his problems as opposed to trying to cover them up, and voters respected his bravery with an outpouring of sympathy, empathy, and support. When his son was reelected, Ted — who had just easily won his eighth term in the Senate — had to stop and think about what it was his own constituency wanted from him in terms of addressing mental health issues and how to best fill those needs — especially now that Democrats had control of the Senate and the House.

Trying to rise to the occasion of new public sentiment, Ted and his colleagues in the Senate continued working on their version of a new mental health parity bill at the same time that Patrick was working on one he felt was better legislation. Again, Ted's vision was narrower, not addressing coverage for any but the most dire of mental illnesses, and no parity for substance abuse disorder treatment. Patrick's was more sweeping, covering all mental illnesses and addictions. Father and son definitely disagreed. "In Patrick's view," recalled one lawmaker, "it was as if his father simply didn't want to recognize the generational challenge in his own family. He thought maybe that if Ted actually acknowledged these issues in his own bill he would perhaps feel compelled to speak about them in relation to the Kennedys."

"If I couldn't convince my father that he was not only backing the wrong bill but indulging in some strange form of legislative denial," Patrick would later recall, "then all I could do was try to beat him."

Patrick spent the first few months of 2007 canvassing the country, giving speeches to explain his bill, talking to people who had suffered the way he and his family had over the years with issues pertaining to mental health as well as substance abuse. He worked toward not only getting public sentiment on his side but also toward forging a deeper understanding of the issues and challenges that lay ahead.

In March, Patrick formally introduced his bill and all its specifics on the House floor. At this same time, Ted's bill was also slowly working its way through the channels of the Senate.

In May, Patrick got his chip for one year's

sobriety, a major personal victory. In July he turned forty. To celebrate the occasion, a party was hosted for him on the Cape that was attended by many of his family members, including his brother, sister, and both parents. During the festivities, Ted had too much to drink, as did Joan. While their three grown children watched sadly from the sidelines, it became painfully clear to them that their parents were still trapped by their diseases.

Both of his siblings were incredibly proud of Patrick. "You'll be remembered for so much more than just your relationship to Dad and the rest of us Kennedys," Teddy said in the company of other relatives. "You have a destiny all your own, Pat," he told him as he put his arm around his little brother. It was nice to hear; Patrick just hoped it was true.

Patrick Kennedy had seen his father command the Senate floor more times than he could count. It was always a privilege for him; he never took it for granted, that's how much respect and admiration he had for his father, no matter their differences. However, in all Patrick's years in Congress — thirteen by this time — Ted had only come to the House floor to watch his son debate a bill maybe three times. Therefore, when the Senator approached his youngest on the floor in March 2008, Patrick felt the gravity of the situation:

his most important bill finally the subject of heated debate for and against on the floor, so very close to actually becoming law . . . and his mostly disapproving father present for it. Ted smiled at Patrick, put his hand on his shoulder, and sat next to him at his desk as he watched one of the speeches. "I felt empowered and eight years old at the same time," Patrick would later recall.

As far as Patrick was concerned, Ted had come through for him when it mattered most. Though he'd had a different vision of mental health care, the Senator seemed genuinely proud of his boy for getting so far with his own version. It hadn't been easy, especially given all that Patrick had faced in his personal life at the same time he was working on this legislation. However, Ted's presence seemed to signal that he understood the fact that Patrick's personal odyssey was about to become the catalyst for great change in the way the country dealt with mental illness.

As one speaker followed the other, Ted whispered words of encouragement in Patrick's ear, especially whenever someone spoke well of the legislation. Finally, Patrick was recognized. He took the mic and, at first, was nervous. However, as father and son locked eyes, Patrick found the confidence and resolve he needed to give one of the most — if not *the* most — impassioned of arguments he'd ever put forth for any bill. "It was one of the best days of my life," he would later recall.

The votes came in, 268 to 148 — 47 Republicans joining 221 Democrats.

Victory.

That night Ted and Patrick went to dinner. The two ran into an old friend of the family's in the restaurant. Everyone shook hands. Then, putting his arm around his son's shoulders, Ted proudly stated, "This one, right here? This one really did me proud today." Patrick smiled. "He taught me everything I know," he said, gazing at his father. "Yes, but not everything *I* know," Ted added. There was a pause. Ted's rejoinder seemed maybe loaded with meaning . . . or maybe not. Whatever the case, Patrick decided to just ignore it and not let anything ruin the moment.

Patrick Kennedy's crowning achievement as a congressman, the Mental Health Parity and Addiction Equity Act of 2008, would soon be signed into law by President George W. Bush.

A PRESIDENT LIKE JACK

During the second week of January in 2008, members of the Kennedy family came together at Ted and Vicki's home on the Cape for discussions having to do with the upcoming presidential election. Who they threw their support behind in any election was still an important factor to any American campaign; a strong endorsement from a family as politically powerful as theirs could make all the difference between a win and a loss. The Kennedys, despite all their problems since the days of Jack and Bobby, still had a lot of persuasive power. Certainly, at the very least, Ted had the respect of millions, not to mention the value of what Patrick had contributed while in office. When it came to the presidency, obviously, the stakes were even greater. Certainly having Caroline or any of the other more high-profile Kennedys speaking at the Democratic convention in support of any hopeful pretty much guaranteed, if nothing else, a lot of media attention, a groundswell of base enthusiasm, and maybe even a history-making moment or two. Obviously, Joseph's progeny didn't take such decisions lightly. Up for discussion in January, then, were the merits for office of Democratic front-runners Hillary Clinton and Barack Obama. On this issue, as it would happen, the Kennedys would be divided.

Because former First Lady and New York senator Hillary Clinton was a close family friend, three of Ethel's children — Kathleen, Kerry, and Bobby — wanted to support her. They felt she had a strong platform having to do with human rights, especially women's issues, and she certainly had the experience. The first woman President? How could anyone resist such a proposition, especially when the woman in question had Hillary's experience in government? They were actually surprised anyone in the family would disagree. It wasn't so much that they took issue with Obama as much as he simply wasn't Clinton, and Kathleen, Kerry, and Bobby said they weren't going to abandon someone who not only was a personal friend but who was obviously best qualified for the job.

Ted wasn't sure about Hillary. He'd enjoyed a pleasant enough relationship with her over the years but found her, as he put it, "a bit prickly." For him, it wasn't so much about policy as it was about personality. Sure, Hillary shared Ted's and Patrick's passion for health care reform, which was a plus for her in their eyes. However, both father and son felt that she lacked something vital to winning any important election: personality.

Once, when asked about her uncle's views about politicians, Maria Shriver observed: "Teddy was on a perpetual campaign his whole life. He so enjoyed *people;* he was interested in their struggles because he had struggled himself. People admired his human frailties, and he saw that in those who came to him for help. He liked the crowd, he liked talking about his brothers, he liked talking about his parents. Of course, he liked legislating and he liked power. But he also liked parties . . . and he liked all the people who worked for him on the Hill . . . and he liked the people he served. He liked everything about it . . . the whole Irish thing. But it was about *people,* about communication. I think the thing about Teddy is that whether you agreed with him or didn't, on a personal level you had to at least *like* him, which is why he was always able to cross the aisle and be bipartisan."

Ted felt that, at least in the public arena, Hillary held back; she was reserved, maybe coming across as cold and detached. Also, she didn't seem like she'd ever struggled or that she could relate to a common man's challenges. She didn't appear to be empathetic. Of course, she actually did have empathy and was a smart woman who understood important issues that affected people of all cultures. However, for Ted, the problem was her image and how people perceived her. He felt that she seemed disengaged and over-rehearsed.

Many of Ted's views about Hillary would be voiced eight years later by other critics of hers when she ran unsuccessfully against Donald Trump for high office. The view of her surprising loss at that time was that it had been because she somehow lacked whatever was needed to galvanize a large swath of America that felt overlooked and disenfranchised. It was thought that Trump had been better able to appeal to that faction. Despite his wealth and the fact that he was a person who'd actually never struggled a day in his life, he was still able to convince millions of voters that he understood their concerns, that he cared about them, and that he, and only he, was the candidate who could provide the solution to their problems. He didn't have much policy in place, unlike Hillary, who had clear principles on many important issues. He was a bombastic personality, a shoot-from-the-hip kind of man who made a great many promises people weren't so sure he'd actually fulfill, but that was all he needed to win the presidency. One wonders what Ted would have thought of him. While he would no doubt vehemently disagree with most of his policies, certainly the man elected as the forty-fifth President would have at least been an example of Ted's notion that personality could sometimes be more important than platform.

Ted liked Barack Obama, the junior senator from Illinois. He said Obama reminded him of himself and, more important, of Jack and Bobby. Like those Kennedy brothers, Obama was a fiery and eloquent statesman. He had the kind of empathy Ted felt eluded Hillary. He knew how to express himself in a way that felt personal and meaningful. Also to his credit, Obama had important legislation planned having to do with human rights, which he said he fully intended to implement should he be elected.

Just a few weeks earlier, Obama had expressed to Ted his hesitation about running, saying he feared that he needed more seasoning in government before he could be an effective President. Of course, Ted had a long history of vacillating where the presidency was concerned. The job had been his for the taking a number of times along the way. He told Obama that what he'd learned from his own experiences was that timing was everything in politics, and no time was better than the present to make an important decision. "In four years, who knows what things will be like for you, your wife, and your kids?" he warned Obama.

Ethel agreed with Ted: Obama reminded her of Bobby, too; her son Max agreed. Jean Kennedy Smith also said she wanted to support Obama, a difficult decision for her because, after all, Bill Clinton had been the President to name her ambassador to Ireland. Patrick agreed, too; Obama was his man.

One person not present at Ted's home during the discussion was arguably the family's most influential tastemaker: Caroline. As the only daughter of the family's only President, the Kennedys knew that her opinion carried a lot of weight with donors as well as with voters. Unlike Ted, she had no political experience herself, but neither did she have scandals in her past.

Choosing between the two potential candidates put Caroline in a difficult spot because not only did she enjoy a good relationship with Hillary and Bill, but she was also quite friendly with their daughter, Chelsea. However, after careful consideration and a great deal of discussion with Ted, she came to the conclusion that she, too, wanted to stump for Obama. She felt he was an exciting new politician who promised great change from the über-conservative policies of eight dark years of President George W. Bush. Something about the excitement that he generated reminded her of what her father had done for the country back in 1960. Stories of Jack's appeal were the stuff of legend — this young senator, handsome and dashing but also incredibly articulate, who promised a new kind of America and who appealed to its youth with idealistic notions of personal responsibility and service. Barack was much like Jack, Caroline concluded.

Another reason for Caroline's interest in Obama was because her children had been telling her for some time that he was someone she should notice. They were young, but Tatiana, Rose, and Jack were Kennedys at heart and did pay attention to what was going on in the world.

With some of the Kennedys set on Hillary and others on Obama, they just had to agree to disagree; past experience had taught them that there was no point in trying to change anyone's mind, even though a good debate about the issues was not something from which any of them would ever shy away. Later, Maria Shriver would support Obama, whereas her husband, Arnold, would go with his party's candidate, John McCain. "We can be divided even in a marriage over these things," Maria would say. "It happens."

During the third week of January 2008, Caroline and Ted — in separate phone calls — officially informed the Clintons that they were throwing their full support behind Barack Obama. They were difficult conversations, of course.

Kicking off Caroline's commitment to

Obama was an editorial she authored for *The New York Times* on January 27, 2008, "A President Like My Father." She wrote: "I have never had a president who inspired me the way people tell me that my father inspired them. But for the first time, I believe I have found the man who could be that president — not just for me, but for a new generation of Americans." The next morning, Bobby Jr., Kathleen, and Kerry would author an editorial of their own in the *Los Angeles Times* explaining their endorsement of Hillary. In a separate statement, Kathleen said, "I respect Caroline and Teddy's decision, but I have made a different choice. At this moment, when so much is at stake at home and overseas, I urge our fellow Americans to support Hillary Clinton."

Later that day, Ted made the official announcement that he, too, was coming out for Obama. Then, Caroline and Patrick stood with him on stage at Bender Arena on the campus of American University in Washington, alongside their chosen candidate. To a cheering audience, Patrick started off by acknowledging that his father had just "shepherded the largest college tuition bill in our nation's history." He added, "One of my father's great achievements is that he lowered the voting age to eighteen." Applause. "And I can see that all of you are going to make good use of that in this election. Right?" More applause. He continued, "As President Kennedy said, 'Change is the law of life, and those who look only to the past or present are certain to miss the future.' " He then introduced his cousin, "a proven patriot and inspiration in her own right, Caroline Kennedy."

As she took the podium, Caroline never seemed more self-assured, more at ease. It was as if she was really coming into her own as a speaker. "Over the years I've been deeply moved by the people who told me they wished they could feel inspired and hopeful about America the way they did when my father was President," she said. "This longing is even more profound today. Fortunately, there is one candidate who offers that same sense of hope and inspiration, and I am proud to endorse Senator Barack Obama for President of the United States."

After a few more remarks, Caroline began to introduce her uncle. "For more than four decades in the Senate, Teddy has led the fight on the most important issues of our time, civil rights, social justice, and economic opportunity," she said while surrounded by cheering people holding red and blue placards that read STAND FOR CHANGE and CHANGE WE CAN BELIEVE IN. She continued, "Workers, families, the elderly, the disabled, immigrants, men and women in uniform all have no stronger champion. I know his brothers would be so proud of him. He's an inspiration to all members of our family . . ."

When Ted took the mic and started speaking, it was as if some sort of great political God had descended upon the stage; pretty much no one could deliver a speech like the Lion of the Senate. "I feel *chaaaaaaange* in the air," he intoned, drawing out the word with a glint in his eye. "What about you?" he asked the crowd, who responded thunderously. "Every time I've been asked over the past year who I would support in the Democratic primary," he continued, "my answer has always been the same. I'll support the candidate who inspires me, inspires all of us, who can lift our vision and summon our hopes and renew our belief that our country's best days are still to come. I've found that candidate. And I think you have, too. I'm proud to stand with him here today and offer my help, offer my voice, offer my energy, my commitment to make Barack Obama the next President of the United States."

For forty-six-year-old Barack Obama to follow Ted Kennedy on a podium was a big challenge, but he rose to it well. He looked deeply moved:

"I stand here today with a great deal of humility. I know what your support means. I know the cherished place the Kennedy family holds in the hearts of American people. And that is as it should be, because the Kennedy family, more than any other, has always stood for . . . what is best about America. They've stood by the idea that each of us can make a difference and that all of us ought to try, that no frontier is beyond our reach when we are united and not divided, and that those of us who are not content to settle for the world as it is can remake the world as it should be, that together we can seek a new world. No one embodies this proud legacy more than the people we've just heard from . . ."

Following his official announcement, Ted campaigned hard for Barack, using his considerable influence with the media and the public to extol the virtues of a man who, if elected, would be the nation's first African American president. His support encouraged fearful Democrats that it was worth the risk to come out for Obama, that the time was ripe for change . . . and that Obama was the man to bring about such change. It would turn out to be the last time Ted would ever be able to use his power and authority to convince his followers to support a candidate he felt most represented Kennedy values and ideals. Soon, everything would change for him, as it would for his entire family.

FAMILY EMERGENCY

On May 17, 2008, when the call came in to Patrick Kennedy that something had happened to his father, the problem wasn't immediately clear to him. Patrick was told that Ted had suffered a seizure at his home on the Cape and was being immediately airlifted from Hyannis Port to Massachusetts General. This was so unexpected. Ted had been just fine and working in the Senate and at home, as always. Alarmed, Patrick called Kara in Maryland and Teddy Jr. in Connecticut, and before long the three of them were flying to Boston to be with their father.

When the siblings got to the hospital, they found Vicki pacing back and forth in a waiting room. She looked drawn and anxious. Trying to maintain her composure, she explained that earlier Ted was walking his Portuguese water dogs, Splash and Sunny, when he collapsed on the beach. An aide helped him back to the house. Hearing someone urgently shouting out her name,

Vicki rushed into the dining room and found Ted slumped over in a chair, seeming disoriented. He had fallen to his knees on the beach. She called an ambulance to the house.

"Vicki knew in a split second that whatever was happening was grave," reported Lois Romano of *The Washington Post.* "She also knew it would play out in public. Knowing the media would be tipped off in minutes because of her 911 call, she worked her cell phone at her husband's side. Before the ambulance pulled up, she had already arranged for the Senator to be transported from the Cape to Massachusetts General Hospital, called his Senate staff to put in place a crisis management team, summoned family members, and notified his closest friends."

It was quickly determined at Cape Cod Hospital that the senator had suffered two small seizures. He was then, as per Vicki's prior arrangements, transported to Barnstable Municipal Airport and then by helicopter to Boston. When his family finally had a chance to see him, the senator actually looked pretty good. "I think my sugar just dipped," he explained with a shrug.

The next couple of days were difficult as the family waited for more news about Ted's test results. "Vicki spent a lot of time with Ethel, who was quiet," said one observer. "The idea of losing Ted nearly had her paralyzed. I don't think I'd ever seen her like that."

Of course, Ted had always been there for Ethel and her children. She'd never forget, for instance, the day she brought Rory home from the hospital after Bobby's murder; Ted was right at her side, joking to the media that since Ethel already had so many kids, he and Joan were going to take this one. They had so many memories, shared so much happiness and heartbreak, just the idea of Ted suffering in any way was quite upsetting to Ethel. "To me, she somehow seemed, I don't know . . . so much older, I guess," said the witness.

By Tuesday, test results were in and they were devastating. Ted had brain cancer, a malignant glioma of the left parietal lobe. It was incurable. One doctor predicted he had, maybe, four months to live; another guessed six.

Of course, Kara couldn't help but remember when she was given a death sentence. She also knew she was still alive, at least in part due to the fact that her father had refused to accept that diagnosis. She now said to him pretty much the same words he had once said to her: "We will fight this."

Kara immediately wanted to summon the best doctors in the world to see what could be done for her father, just as he had done for her. She wouldn't have to do so, though. Within days, doctors were contacting her, her brothers, and Vicki. One by one, they got in touch to offer their advice. "It worked backwards for my dad" is how Teddy put it. "Usually my dad had to go out and find the best doctors. But this time, *they* came to *him.*"

As he had been known to do in the past when his own children had cancer, Ted convened a meeting of medical experts. "The meeting on May 30 was extraordinary in at least two ways," wrote Lawrence K. Altman, M.D., the chief medical correspondent of *The New York Times.* "One was the ability of a powerful patient . . . to summon noted consultants to learn about the latest therapy and research findings. The second was his efficiency in quickly convening more than a dozen experts from at least six academic centers. Some flew to Boston. Others participated by telephone after receiving pertinent test results and other medical records."

Just as had been the case with Kara, everyone agreed that surgery was not an option — everyone but one doctor, Vivek Deshmukh, director of cerebrovascular and endovascular neurosurgery at George Washington University Medical Center. Unlike Kara, though, it was agreed that Ted could not be healed. The best that could be hoped for was a brief extension of his life. Ted felt it was worth it, as did Vicki. Therefore, Dr. Allan H. Friedman, codirector of the Preston Robert Tisch Brain Tumor Center at Duke University, was

733

summoned; he was known to be the best brain surgeon in the country.

The operation occurred on June 2, 2008, about a month after the seizure. After Ted survived it, everyone tried to do what Kennedys usually did under dire circumstances, which was to steel themselves for a good fight. In weeks to come, though, Ted's aggressive chemotherapy treatments took a toll even greater than any cancer. "Still, Ted had so much faith, he knew he would be fine, no matter what happened," said Vicki. "If his life was soon to be over, what did this mean? It meant spending time at the Cape, where he had so many good times, so much history. I think it also meant coming to terms with his children on certain things."

Vicki wasn't specific, but certainly there were any number of loose ends for Ted where Kara, Teddy, and Patrick were concerned. That summer, they spent as much time at the Cape with their father as possible, as did Joan, who also had her share of unresolved business with Ted. His family members wanted to have a more open relationship with Ted and dig down deep into subjects they'd shied away from in the past. However, it could be said that a man doesn't just change overnight, even when he knows he's dying; there were still a lot of issues Ted didn't want to discuss. He still believed he had done his best as a father and wasn't going to apologize for anything. It wasn't so much that his grown children needed admissions of guilt, though, as much as just a clearing of the air. "This was a tough time," Patrick would recall. "It was like chipping away at armor, trying to get to the heart of some important issues before it was too late. We felt that the clock was ticking."

These months would turn out to be important to everyone given Ted's reticence about opening up. In the summer, Patrick and Kara joined him and Vicki and some of their cousins at the compound for a few weeks, sailing every day on Ted's fifty-foot Concordia schooner, *Mya*. "Back at the house, my father made some time for us to speak privately — which we hadn't done in a while," recalled Patrick, "and while much of the conversation was about politics and legacy, it was warm and moving. I sent him a long letter afterward, thanking him for letting me come, letting him know I would always have his back, reinforcing that he had always been my 'emotional sustenance,' and saying, 'There is no one I know who could have endured more emotional heartache than you have in your life and yet you've managed to keep living and loving your family.' "

Patrick's entreaties to Ted couldn't help but affect him. He tried to forge a closer relationship not only with his youngest but with Teddy and Kara, too. Was everything straightened between them, all their grievances with one another at long last settled? Of course not. But they were family, and the bond they shared was undeniable. They knew their shared history would always endure. At the Fourth of July celebration that year, the Senator gave a toast to his children; his ex-wife, Joan; present wife, Vicki; as well as to the many extended family members who had gathered for the holiday: "When I'm not around, I want you all to remember this day. And I want you to remember how happy we are and what kind of family the Kennedys are. And I want you to take solace that we are Kennedys, each and every one of us, and that we are family and there is nothing more important than family. And I would want you to take that feeling and imprint it upon your own children, just as I would hope that they will then do with their children. Nothing is permanent. Nothing that is but the love."

A few days later, on July 9, Ted made a surprise visit to the floor of the Senate to vote on a Medicare bill that had fallen one vote shy of the sixty that were needed to break a Republican filibuster. Vicki definitely didn't want Ted to go, but she knew he had to do it; there was no way he would not cast that vote. With her and Caroline both watching from the gallery, Patrick helped his father onto the Senate floor, trailed by Barack Obama and John Kerry. The noted writer Leonard Fein wrote for the *Jewish Daily Forward:*

Enter Ted Kennedy, for the very first time since his diagnosis and surgery for a malignant brain tumor. Not only did all his colleagues, on realizing he'd entered the chamber, rise to applaud and whoop his presence; the gallery, too, where displays of this sort are proscribed, broke into sustained applause and was not gaveled to order.

"Yea," he said, and his "yea" carried enough Republicans to generate a veto-proof majority, preserving thereby (if it holds together) the core of a program that has dramatically improved the life circumstances of many millions of Americans.

■ ■ ■ ■

PART VI
A POLITICAL
GAMBLE

■ ■ ■ ■

TESTING THE WATERS

A year earlier, in 2007, Caroline Kennedy turned fifty. Throughout the next year, she often confided to friends and family members that she felt a little lost. Of course, a sense of not being fulfilled, of worrying that one is missing out on a true calling, is not unusual for a person of her age; a midlife crisis is how it might best be described. Caroline's children were now teenagers; she didn't feel they needed her as much. Her marriage to Ed was solid; they were happy together, and she would never complain about him. They had a shared history, which they cherished; they'd been through some sad times together and had survived them. She wondered, though, according to what she said in rare moments of openness, what would happen when the kids all went to college and just she and Ed remained at home? Would they be able to connect? He had his work and was invigorated by it, whereas Caroline just had what she called "the blahs" and felt that she needed . . . *something.* She kept telling her kids to hold fast to their dreams, but the question remained: What were hers?

This isn't to say that Caroline wasn't busy; she was still involved in a number of fulfilling charities. She was also still writing books; she'd written about the Bill of Rights and the right to privacy and had also compiled a series of anthologies, such as *The Best Loved Poems of Jacqueline Kennedy Onassis* as well as *A Family of Poems: My Favorite Poetry for Children* and *A Patriot's Handbook,* which included patriotic poems and speeches. She'd also edited *Profiles in Courage of Our Time,* a collection of essays about those who'd won the JFK Library's Profiles in Courage award. The books were bestsellers — but still, she had to admit she was bored. She had a yearning for something new.

A few years earlier, Caroline had taken a position in the New York City Department of Education as executive director of the Office for Strategic Partnerships, dedicated to raising money for education from private sectors. She'd been given the job by Joel Klein, the head of the department. During her time there, she'd begun to see how capable she was in influencing people and in convincing them to be committed to matters she felt important to children as well as to teachers. After a couple of years of feeling successful in that venue, she left that position to become a board member of the Fund for Public Schools. Throughout this time, she enjoyed working within the educational system; it stimulated her curiosity. She wondered if it was possible for her to extend her reach.

Of course, Caroline had always wanted to be of service. She'd been hearing her entire life that she had a responsibility to do so, and to a degree she felt she was satisfying the family mandate with her work in the education system and also by educating the public with her books. However, that wasn't the same as being a public servant. The more she thought of it, the more she realized that yes, this was what she wanted — *needed* — to do. "I want something more from my life," she told one trusted friend, "and I just can't pretend anymore that this isn't true."

It was shortly after these discussions with her cousins that Caroline began to campaign for Barack Obama. "She'd actually started watching his campaign in the fall of 2007, long before she threw her support behind him," said her friend Gary Ginsberg, who was an executive vice president of News Corporation, "and I could sense even then that she'd started to think of it in more practical terms for herself.

"She campaigned in places like Orlando and Indiana and Ohio, getting her hands dirty, doing real retail politics, and I think she was surprised by how much she enjoyed it. I think she found the whole political process more satisfying and engaging than she would have thought."

In stumping for Obama, Caroline came to a fuller realization that her opinions actually mattered. Her endorsement of the senator from Illinois had been vital to his campaign, and she knew it. Oprah Winfrey has this humorous story: "I was at Tina Turner's house over Christmas [2007], talking to her about Barack Obama. She paid no attention to me. But when Caroline Kennedy came out for Barack Obama, I got a phone call from Tina. She said, 'Oprah, I heard everything you said to me. But if *Caroline* says it — and because of what her whole family represents — then I'm for Barack, too.' I thought, 'I was sitting at your dinner table . . . and *you don't even know Caroline.*' "

David Axelrod, Obama's political strategist at the time, recalls Caroline as being "the purest brand in American public life." Of American royalty and untainted by scandal, she was greatly admired, and it felt good. A big problem for her, though, at least when it came to her public image, was that, despite everything she had going for her, Caroline could often appear somewhat cold and off-putting when being interviewed. For instance, after her speech at the Democratic National Convention, she seemed barely able to tolerate Katie Couric's on-camera questioning, especially when she started referencing Caroline's famous family. Treading cautiously, Katie asked Caroline if she felt "any pressure" given the prominence of the Kennedy dynasty. "I know you're very shy . . ." Katie began.

Oddly, Caroline took umbrage. "Are you going to ask me if I'm going to run for office, by any chance?" she asked, suddenly appearing combative. "Is that where you're going with this question?"

Katie was surprised at Caroline's touchiness: "Well, what do you think?"

Caroline shook her head in annoyance. "Well, you know, it's incredible," she said. "You're just so . . . *creative.*"

Undaunted, Katie pushed forward. "Maybe you have a renewed interest in going into political office," she offered, "since, I mean, you are already in public service. Because of Teddy's illness and because of the era sort of coming to a close, I'm just wondering if you feel any kind of responsibility."

One had to wonder why this line of questioning so bothered Caroline. Or, maybe more important, why wasn't she able to camouflage her annoyance. Instead, Caroline just completely shut down. Staring straight ahead, she said she didn't "make a lot of long-range plans" and left it there.

It wasn't a good moment. If anything, it

WHAT KENNEDYS DO

Everyone knew that Caroline was very different from her late brother, John. In many ways, she was just the opposite. She was an introvert who kept her own counsel, whereas John was always gregarious and outgoing. Because of these maybe superficial differences in their personalities, everyone believed John to be the sibling destined for public office, especially after he began publishing *George.* Now that he was gone, things were different, or at least they were for Caroline. She'd never been sure of her suitability as a politician — she once asked her grandmother Rose, "That's not really me? Is it?" To which Rose responded, "You bet it is." Caroline began to believe that *she* should be the one to throw her hat into the ring. She set her sights high, too: She wanted Hillary Clinton's seat in the Senate representing New York, a position that would be open for two years before the next election. New York's governor, David Paterson, would have to appoint

Clinton's successor in the interim, and his decision would be influenced by not only whoever was the most qualified for the job but also by who Paterson's constituency felt was the best fit. Caroline wanted it to be her.

Caroline had only a few vague ideas about policy having to do with education. She knew she would have her work cut out for her. After all, she had no experience in the political arena. However, what she did have going for her was her natural curiosity about things, her eagerness to learn, her desire to serve, and, of course, her name. She was a woman who could get anyone on the phone, anytime; she had Obama on speed dial. Certainly, she could use her influence to do a lot for New York. Even if she was rusty on the specifics of New York government, she was smart and well-read and could learn. She'd also become a pretty good speaker in front of an audience; she could definitely command a crowd.

Of course, if she was going to go for Clinton's seat, Caroline would need Ted's support. She feared that he would discourage her from pursuing it. If so, she knew she would be deflated; she had so much respect for him. Still, she needed to know. Therefore, she and Ed arranged to meet with him and Vicki at their home on the Cape, where he was staying while undergoing treatment. She was surprised at his reaction. Yes, he said, it was a good idea. She should do it. "I think you have what it takes," he told her.

Ed was surprised. He had fully expected Ted to veto Caroline's idea, and maybe he'd even hoped Ted's disapproval would be the end of it. He was actually perplexed by Caroline's sudden interest in politics. He wasn't sure she was made for it. He attempted to reason it out with her, warning her about the invasive nature of the game. After all, she was someone who could barely sit through an interview with *Ladies' Home Journal* without feeling attacked. Had she considered the kinds of probing questions she'd be asked by reporters if she was a candidate? They would certainly be a lot more difficult to address than whether she let her kids eat sugar. While Caroline listened to his concerns, she disagreed. That was fine with Ed; once he was sure that this was what she wanted, he would join Ted in supporting her.

The truth is that Caroline had caught Ted at his most vulnerable. After all, he was dying. He was also taking stock.

"The way Ted had been raised by his parents was to always consider the future of the Kennedy dynasty and to seek out the answer to the question: Who's next in line?" observed Dun Gifford, who had been his legislative assistant. "After all, there had been a Kennedy in the Senate for half a century. Ted thought it important that a Kennedy keep his seat after he was gone. He'd thought

Patrick could go all the way to the Senate just by virtue of the fact that he'd been such a credible Congressman. Though he could sometimes be critical of Pat, he had to admit that his boy was tenacious and a good fighter."

Lately, though, Patrick had been hinting about possibly quitting politics altogether. It had been tough on him, all those years in Congress. Also, despite his time in rehab, he was still misusing many drugs, mostly Adderall, which he called his "primary drug of abuse." He was now looking for a real solution to his life, a way to wrestle his bipolar disorder into submission. Recently, Vicki had even been working behind the scenes to keep Patrick away from his father because she feared if Ted knew how bad off he was, it would be too debilitating to him during an already difficult time. This strategy drove a wedge between son and stepmother. "*You* don't get to tell *me* when and if I can see my own father," Patrick told her in front of family members. He raised his voice at her, which she clearly didn't appreciate. She looked at him with hard eyes. "Oh really?' she said. "I beg to differ, Pat," she continued. "I think I *do* get to do that, and I think I *will* do that." She further said that her primary concern was for her husband, and that until she knew for sure that Patrick had his problems under control, she would closely monitor Ted's exposure to him, "for *both* your sakes."

"What is wrong with you?" he demanded to know.

"Funny," she answered, "I was just going to ask you that same question."

Patrick got it, though. He recognized that his problems were serious and he understood that Vicki was right to try to protect his father from them. Though his relationship with her would always be complex, deep down — as he would admit years later — he knew that she was almost always right in the tough decisions he'd all but forced her to make because of his illness.

Though Vicki tried to protect him, Ted knew what was going on; he knew his son well and could intuit that he was still in trouble. No, he finally decided. Even if Patrick didn't quit politics, he was clearly not cut out for it anymore. He needed a break — and Ted even told Patrick as much. He didn't want to die and have his son think he didn't care about his well-being. While the two were boating on Nantucket Sound, Ted leaned in so Patrick could hear him over the din and said, "You know, you don't have to do this if you don't want to. I don't want you to feel forced to continue in public office. You should do what makes you happy."

Patrick would recall being so stunned by Ted's advice, he didn't even know how to respond. He had spent his entire life trying to get his father's approval, which was why he'd gone into government in the first place. It had been hard. He barely got through some days, and lately, his addictions seemed more out of control than ever. Ted's words came as a great relief to Patrick; he really *did* want out. Now it would just be a matter of time.

With Patrick out of the running, who was left? Teddy Jr. wasn't a politician at the time, and neither was Kara. There were a couple of Shrivers who maybe could go far, but as much as he loved them, Ted never felt that the Shrivers were taken seriously when it came to running for office. Ted had more faith in Bobby's kids. Bobby Jr., though, was an environmentalist, so he was out of the political game. Joe was always a good bet, and probably he would have been able to reenter politics. After all, who even remembered who Sheila Rauch was after all these years? However, Joe was completely content at Citizens Energy, far from the scrutiny of public life. Kathleen? She didn't want anything to do with it anymore, either. She was happy with her own lot just as it was, working in tandem with several charities. There were a few others in the family who sometimes spoke of running, but none seriously. Some of the younger fourth generation, the grandkids of the old guard, like Joe's son Joe III, had lately been expressing interest; maybe one day he would be a contender for some office. However, for now, it looked like Patrick's quitting would mean there would be no Kennedy in office for the first time in fifty years. That proposition was something Ted simply couldn't accept.

Another persistent narrative about the Kennedys of the younger generation was that they had done little to nothing to change the world. It was always about Jack and Bobby whenever historians examined the storied history of the family and its impact on the world, and to a lesser extent, Ted. "But how could any person compare with JFK's achievements of dealing with the Cuban Missile Crisis or even his stunning failure of the Bay of Pigs?" asked Dun Gifford. "What could ever be compared to the way Bobby took on the underworld as attorney general? The history-making achievements of him and Jack and even Ted could never be matched by their kids unless they found themselves in similar positions of government . . ."

Ted, especially since 1980, had achieved even more than his brothers in terms of governmental accomplishments — of course, he had had more time to do so — but even he remained in their shadow. It certainly wasn't true, though, that the next generation had done nothing. It was just a way for critics to be reductive of them. "Think of Patrick's many years in Congress alone and of all the legislation for which he was responsible," pointed out Dun Gifford. "Outside of government, look at what Bobby Jr. had done for the environment, and consider everything Joe had done for the underprivileged with Citizens Energy. Most of the generation, in fact, was made up of political activists of one sort or another. I mean, look at what the Shrivers had all achieved. Still, the perception that the next generation lacked accomplishment was persistent, and I know for a fact that Ted absolutely hated it."

Ted wanted to prove the skeptics wrong. Caroline joining him in the Senate? That just might do it. Therefore, when she came to him with her proposition, he was intrigued. If anything, this was a bit of a Hail Mary strategy on the Senator's part, though, and he had to have known it. After all, this was the same man who felt that Hillary wasn't cut out for President because of her personality. He had to have known his niece's chances were slim, if just based on how she acted in the public eye alone. It was rather like expecting the ever-so-private Jackie to wake up one day and suddenly decide she was going to be a politician.

One of Ted's aides has this story to tell:

Ted, Vicki, Ethel, and a few other Kennedys, including Kathleen, along with some of their acolytes, were at the Cape together after Caroline's visit. They were talking about her news. Bobby thought yes, Caroline should go for it, as did Patrick and Teddy. Joe wasn't so sure; he'd been burned by politics in the past and wondered if his cousin could handle it.

Ethel thought it was a terrible idea. Caroline was not a politician — "not yet, anyway," Ethel said. The fact that Ethel would challenge Ted at this time when she was so worried about his health and scared to lose him said a lot about how strongly she felt about the matter at hand. She said she felt it was his responsibility to talk some sense into Caroline, that he owed it to her late father to protect her. Invoking the name of the slain President was a dramatic move for Ethel; she never did so lightly. However, she seemed truly worried that Caroline would take Ted's encouragement too far and would actually run for office. "You know, that was once Bobby's seat," Ethel added. It was a sacred trust, she reminded everyone; Caroline was not ready for it.

Kathleen was perplexed. "You were so encouraging of me when I wanted to run for office back in '86," she noted. "Why are you not of Caroline?" Ethel answered, "Isn't it obvious?" Of course, Ethel was referencing the stark difference in the cousins' personalities. Maybe she was the more outgoing, Kathleen agreed, but she also warned her mother not to underestimate Caroline. She noted her recent electrifying performance at the Obama rally. Not only that, Caroline was a constitutional scholar and had authored some good books. She'd also raised millions for the New York City school system. Kathleen had long been involved in the scholastic system; after becoming the first Kennedy to ever lose an election when she lost that Congressional seat back in 1986, she took a post in the state's department of education. She knew it was hard work. "She definitely knows how to reach people," Kathleen said of Caroline. "Besides, Mummy, she's very smart and very curious about things."

Ethel wasn't convinced. "*I'm* very smart and *I'm* very curious about things," she countered. "You think I should run for the Senate, too? Fine, then," she said. "Sign me up. Let's see how far *I* get." Her sarcasm belied her cold, calculating objectivity. After all, Ethel had been immersed in politics as long as Ted. She felt that the position of senator held immense power and that Caroline simply wasn't ready for it. *Of course* Ethel wanted her niece to serve. However, she felt Caroline would be better off serving in the state legislature first, and then thinking about the Senate. Starting out slow, she said, made a lot more sense. "Don't forget about what happened to Max," she said. There was silence for a moment; no one could ever forget what had happened to Max.

Matthew Maxwell Taylor Kennedy — Max

— is the ninth of Ethel's children and a graduate of Harvard and of the University of Virginia Law School; he was named after Maxwell Taylor, chairman of the Joint Chiefs under JFK. Back in 2001, he had his own foray into politics when he decided to run for a Massachusetts Congressional seat. A former assistant district attorney of Philadelphia, he'd long been a human rights and environmental activist, making many philanthropic missions through Central and Latin America. As well as writing the bestselling book *Make Gentle the Life of This World: The Vision of Robert F. Kennedy,* Max also worked on the campaigns of his uncle Teddy, Michael Dukakis, Al Gore, and John Kerry. He would travel a rough road, though, once he began campaigning for himself. He seemed ill-prepared to give speeches, his demeanor reminding some of his cousin Patrick before he put the work into becoming a good orator. Poor responses to Max's public persona chipped away at his self-confidence until, finally, he just dropped out of the race. Though she was proud of him for at least trying, Ethel felt her son hadn't really thought his candidacy through all the way. Now Ethel felt that Caroline was doing the same thing.

Vicki disagreed. She and Caroline had always had a frigid rapport; they'd never hit it off. Still, Vicki felt Caroline should be given a chance. Whether it was a good fit for her or not, in Vicki's mind, as a woman in the family reaching for something as big as senator, how could they not support her?

Vicki had to credit herself at least in part for Ted's open-mindedness toward the idea. He seemed to have more respect for the opposite sex ever since they married and Vicki began insisting he treat the women in his life a certain way. She had definitely changed Kennedy culture for the better when it came to its well-known misogyny. Rarely, if ever, did the men in the family dare to make a sexist comment in her presence. They knew better. One of the younger Kennedy women put it this way: "Vicki gave a big 'fuck you' to the patriarchy around here."

Once, in frustration about something, Bobby repeated the old cliché "Women — can't live with 'em, can't live without 'em." Vicki took it as an opportunity to enlighten him. "Exactly what do you mean by that?" she asked, challenging Bobby. She got very close to him, probably less than two inches between them. "I . . . um . . . I . . . um . . . it's nothing, Vicki," he said, stammering. "It's just one of those old sayings." Vicki told him it was precisely because of those kinds of "old sayings" that sexism still persisted. "Words have meaning," she told Bobby. "So I would invite you to examine your vocabulary." Poor Bobby left the room with his head hanging so low, he looked like a student who'd been chastised by his second-grade teacher. Later, according to one reliable source, Bobby had to admit to his brother Joe that maybe Vicki had a point. "Bobby said, 'You know what? She's right,' " recalled the source. " 'Maybe we need to check ourselves, Joe. How do we want to raise our boys?' Joe said, 'No. I'm good. We're fine. And my boys are just fine, too, thank you.' "

Despite Joe's predictable attitude, some in the family did feel that Vicki was changing the way people viewed the potential that women in the family had in politics. Others disagreed, pointing out that Kathleen, whose career as a politician predated Vicki, was the true pioneer in that regard. Vicki's influence could still be felt, though, even if just in small ways such as her reprimand of Bobby. Now she was solidly behind Caroline.

Ethel then brought up what was perhaps the sorest subject of all for Ted, his interview with Roger Mudd, back in 1979, which was, in many ways, the reason he decided not to challenge President Jimmy Carter for the Democratic nomination. When Mudd asked Ted why he wanted to be President, Ted froze; he seemed to not have a good answer or, if he had one, didn't know how to articulate it. "Why would we push Caroline into this thing when she also doesn't really have an answer to that kind of question?" Ethel asked.

It was actually unusual for Ethel to remind anyone of this failure. In fact, six weeks after this Mudd interview was broadcast, the Kennedys celebrated Christmas together at the Cape, as always. The family was posing for a photo shoot for a magazine when the writer asked Joan Kennedy for a comment about the interview. Joan was about to say something when Ethel clapped her hand three times in front of her face and said, *"No! No! No!"* — one "no!" for each clap. "We don't talk about that, Joan."

Now, nearly thirty years later, Ethel was the one bringing it up. Ted definitely didn't want to remember it, though. He brushed it off and said he believed Caroline was ready, and he also thought they owed it to Jack and to Bobby to encourage her. She was someone who could get things done, he said. People pay attention to her. She can be an influencer. "You'd be surprised at how much that means," he said. "Being persuasive is all that matters when you're trying to get something done." If Caroline wanted to pursue politics, he said he wanted to support her and he felt the family should as well. "After all," he concluded, "this is what Kennedys do, isn't it? This is what family is all about."

THROWING HER HAT
INTO THE RING

In November 2008, Barack Hussein Obama II was elected forty-fourth President of the United States. Caroline Kennedy felt strongly that Ted's and her endorsement of him went a long way toward getting him in office; the family was both proud and happy, even those who had opposed his presidency. At least a Democrat had won.

On December 3, Caroline telephoned New York's governor, David Paterson, to tell him of her intentions to be considered as a candidate for Hillary Clinton's Senate seat. He wasn't thrilled. It sounded like a stunt to him. Though Paterson would eventually need to appoint someone to that senatorial seat, he felt that Caroline just wanted it if it could be handed to her, which, in his mind, wasn't fair to those he felt really deserved it — contenders like her cousin by marriage Andrew Cuomo, married to Kerry, a seasoned politician who had been an attorney general, a cabinet secretary, and a governor's adviser.

Also, in two years, Caroline would have to actually run in an election for that seat if she was now appointed to it, and Paterson didn't think she would have it in her to wage a full-out campaign.

Still, she was *Caroline Kennedy,* so he wasn't going to be completely dismissive of her. He told her to talk to people in local office, maybe go visit the mayor of New York City and other elected officials. He also suggested a tour of New York to put herself in public view. He hastened to add that she should stay away from answering too many questions from the media. That's where he felt she would be at her most vulnerable.

As soon as Caroline made that call to Paterson, the story was leaked. Before she knew it, she had to mobilize a staff of advisers because people were now asking questions, they were getting excited, and her new interest in politics had become headline news overnight. As the frenzy continued to build, Caroline did the exact opposite of what most politicians might do under such circumstances. Instead of capitalizing on the moment, she retreated from it.

A good example: On December 5, Caroline attended a birthday party for a friend. After years of doing so, Caroline knew how to read a room. She could scope out a party and, as if she had some sort of radar, immediately figure out who she thought was an enemy, or at the very least, a skeptic. On this night, she sensed everyone as being against her. The subject of her running for Senate came up, of course. Rather than talk about a possible platform, she clammed up as if she were being asked a personal question about one of her kids or, worse yet, one of her parents. Such reticence wasn't a good sign. Politicians who have fire in their bellies love to talk policy any chance they get, and that didn't seem to be Caroline.

Despite any misgivings building within her, the groundswell for her possible campaign continued to mount. New York's Mayor Michael Bloomberg even told the press it was a fait accompli that Caroline would run, and that people should just begin to get used to the idea. However, local politicians, like Gary Ackerman of New York's Fifth District, disagreed. "One of the things we have to observe is that DNA in this business can take you just so far," he said on television's *Face the Nation.* "You know, Rembrandt was a great artist. His brother, Murray, on the other hand — well, Murray Rembrandt couldn't paint a house."

Very quickly, the knives came out for Caroline among more than a few Democrats who felt that they, not she, were better suited. New York politicians such as Carolyn Maloney, Steve Israel, and Tom Suozzi began to weigh in, but in subtle ways. They didn't speak

negatively about Caroline, but their sur-
rogates spread the word that she was deeply
unqualified. Governor Paterson, meanwhile,
made it clear he wouldn't support anyone,
even Caroline, until after Hillary Clinton was
officially confirmed as Secretary of State. It
would be all about whoever could galvanize
the most attention as a possible candidate.

Despite skepticism, after just a couple of
weeks, by the middle of December, it appeared that people might actually accept
Caroline Kennedy as a senator; in one poll,
voters preferred her to Andrew Cuomo 33
percent to 29 percent. However, on the
seventeenth when Caroline was asked during
an impromptu interview exactly why she
wanted to be a senator, she balked and didn't
seem to have an answer. Her aides rushed
her from the room, which was duly reported
by the press the next day.

That same week, Caroline went on to
Rochester and Buffalo to give it her best shot
in another interview, but something was
definitely off. She was so ill at ease, it looked
as if she was hiding something. Of course,
the only thing she was trying to hide was just
how much she hated answering questions.

"Whereas she was used to being on a
pedestal, now she was always being shouted
and screamed at," observed her uncle Jamie
Auchincloss. "She was naturally taken aback
to be thrust into this carnival atmosphere.

When she got out of Manhattan and got to know the folks in Rochester, Albany — the union halls and the PTAs — she realized how insulating her fame had been. Instead of cocktails in the homes of the top Democratic influencers in those areas as she may have expected, she was really in the trenches with the people ... in hotels with hallways blocked off and amid heavy security as photographers climbed up the sides of walls and sneaked in windows. Advance men for her looked more like a presidential detail than the team of a state's senatorial race. Because of all the security, she didn't get to have those conversations with the people that were so necessary. Ultimately, she looked like a product instead of a person."

The next week or so found Caroline dodging questions while her camp issued carefully written answers to media inquiries. Meanwhile, she spent her time boning up on policy. It had quickly become a real pressure cooker for her as she struggled with learning all there was to know in crash courses about New York politics, immigration, the economy, gay rights, and whatever her strategists felt she could handle. She began to realize that she was in over her head, as did everyone around her. However, she wasn't raised to be a quitter; therefore, she would persevere. "We're in the business of politics," she knew her grandfather used to say. "We're not here to lose.

We're here to win."

On December 26, Caroline gave an interview to the Associated Press and managed to get through it, as well as a TV interview with NY1's *Inside City Hall.* She went home that night feeling that maybe she'd done a fairly decent job in addressing immigration and education concerns. Some were impressed. "You always get a sense of entitlement or a sense of royalty, whether it's the Rockefellers or the Kennedys, and she never came off like that," said Al Sharpton, who had a lunch with her in Harlem. "It was never like she felt like you were honored to meet her. She came off very studious, very sober, very serious. And I had that impression of her way before she ever thought about politics."

The next morning, though, things began to deteriorate when Caroline sat down with reporters Nicholas Confessore and David M. Halbfinger from *The New York Times.* They didn't want to know her position on policy as much as they wanted a clear-cut answer, once and for all, to a simple question: Why did she want to be a senator? Her simple interest in the job wasn't enough for her to deserve it. What was her motivation? What would be her platform? She was now being asked basically the same obvious question that had ruined her uncle's chances almost thirty years earlier when he didn't know how to explain his desire to be President.

The question as to why a person wants to lead is not a difficult one if that person has deeply considered and held ideals and beliefs. It can and should be answered with strength, clarity, and determination. However, if a person is unsure or even faking it, things can take a dramatic turn for the worst — which is what happened with Ted and what now happened to Caroline. She gave a weak response rife with "you knows" and "ums." As was later oft-reported, she said "you know" almost two hundred times in the course of about an hour:

I think that what we've seen over the last year, and particularly and even up to the last — is that there's a lot of different ways that people are coming into public life now, and it's not only the traditional path. Even in the New York delegation, you know, some of our great senators — Hillary Clinton, Pat Moynihan — came from, you know, other walks of life. So, I don't think that that is, uh — so I think in many ways, you know, we want to have all kinds of different voices, you know, representing us, and I think what I bring to it is, you know, my experiences as a mother, as a woman, as a lawyer, you know, I've been an education activist for the last six years and, you know, I've written seven books — two on the Constitution and

767

two on American politics. So, obviously, you know . . .

When asked why she hadn't given Hillary Clinton an earlier heads-up when she planned to support Barack Obama, Caroline became flustered and refused to answer.

I think this is about the future, and, um, you know, that's what I want to talk about, which is, what's going on in our state, you know, why I would be the best person to help deliver for New York. We're facing, you know, an economic crisis, the paper this morning said there's, you know, five billion dollars of construction projects which just stopped, you know, that's, you know — conversations a year ago, that — besides, that, I don't, as I said, I have conversations with a lot of people, and those are confidential.

None of what she said made Caroline sound particularly articulate or informed, which was a shame because she had a better grasp of the issues than her rambling monologue would suggest. The problem for Caroline wasn't a lack of knowledge as much as it was an inability to convey it effectively. Like a lot of politicians, she was better with practiced talking points than she was with shooting from the hip.

Things got even worse when, in an effort to try to get Caroline to recount what happened when she told Ed that she wanted to be a senator, the reporters asked, "for the sake of storytelling, could you tell us a little about that moment?" Her answer? "Have you guys ever thought about writing for, like, a woman's magazine, or something?" Of course, the next question was, "What do you have against women's magazines?" She snapped back, "Nothing at all, but I thought you were the crack political team here."

Apparently, the final straw for Caroline came when the writers pushed her about how much she lived on a year: "Is it $2 million? Is it less than $2 million? Is it more than $5 million?" Now she was really peeved, and she couldn't hide it; she refused to answer.

"If I can just throw one more question out there," David Halbfinger suggested.

"I think we're done," Caroline announced.

When the article was published on December 27, 2008, it was devastating. Unfortunately, the publication's editors opted not only for a feature but also a word-by-word transcript in which they published every "you know" and every "um" she'd muttered. It made her appear to be inarticulate. It probably never would have happened, though, if she had not insulted the writers. She was hurt, embarrassed, and, ultimately, outraged.

"They made me look like a complete idiot,"

she raged to one member of her campaign staff. She took the newspaper, rolled it up, and slapped it hard on a desk. "See? *This* is why I don't give interviews," she said angrily. "These jerks knifed me right in the back." This kind of emotional display was unusual for Caroline; she'd never been an emotive person. It looked to some as if the stress of the last couple of weeks was really getting to her. She also blamed the PR company she had hired to roll out her campaign; clearly, in her mind at least, its publicists had totally miscalculated her preparation — or lack thereof — for such an important interview.

"She's not glib in the way that predictable politicians are glib," Richard Plepler, who was a copresident at HBO and a friend of Caroline's, noted after the article was published. "She is thoughtful, articulate, and fundamentally decent, and if you discussed any number of complicated issues with her that are currently part of the political dialogue, she would be both informed and deeply thoughtful."

Plepler's particular view of Caroline didn't appear to be borne out by her many stammering responses to questions from those *New York Times* reporters. History shows that this particular interview Caroline Kennedy gave to the so-called Old Gray Lady pretty much marked the end of the line for her.

"A Kennedy Always Has the Final Word"

On January 10, 2009, trying to act undaunted by the disappointment of the *New York Times* debacle, Caroline Kennedy met with Governor Paterson to more formally discuss her aspirations for the Senate. She'd now had some time to take his advice and work her way through the New York boroughs, meeting people, shaking hands, and doing her share of interviews even if to mixed results. All accounts of this meeting confirm that he came forth with a warning that, in weeks to come, he'd be talking to other candidates who also wanted the position, and that Caroline shouldn't be upset to hear that he'd done so. That's just how the game is played, he cautioned her, and "I don't want this intrigue about Hillary's Senate seat to be viewed as a fait accompli for you. That wouldn't be fair to you." On one level, Kennedy agreed, but on another she had to wonder if maybe the Governor had some secret agenda. Was he

771

really trying to tell her not to get her hopes up?

On January 20, Barack Obama was inaugurated as President of the United States. It was a big moment for the country, and, of course, for the Kennedys, who had supported him. Ted and Vicki, along with Kara, Teddy, and Patrick, were all present for the swearing-in, as were Caroline and Ed; most of the Shrivers, including Maria; and an assortment of other Kennedys and Smiths, even those who hadn't supported Obama, such as Kathleen and Bobby Jr.

After the swearing-in, Governor Paterson had a conversation with Caroline's cousin Kerry during which he suggested strongly that Caroline would be his pick. In the days to come, the governor then became the go-to guest for many talk shows, and for one reason: to talk about Caroline. Was he going to appoint her, or not? On some shows he said he was sure he would and on others he suggested he wasn't, all of which just served to keep the story alive. He had a reputation for being mercurial, anyway.

Then what some felt was the inevitable finally happened: Caroline lost her steam. One friend of hers reported meeting her for lunch at her home in New York. There were photographers staked outside her estate's front gates, her children were scared, their lives turned completely upside down. All the chaos was stressing her marriage, Caroline admitted. "Ed is unhappy," she told her friend. "He said it's up to me but he thinks I should quit this thing. We had such a nice, quiet life and now we have *this,*" she said as phones rang all over the house and aides dashed about, talking to one another about this story in a newspaper, or that one in a magazine.

"She was disgusted with the whole thing," said Caroline's intimate. "She said she wished she could change her mind. I told her it was not too late. 'Just say you're done,' I told her. But she said that quitting wasn't an option. She said she wished she'd just released a simple statement, a letter to the governor saying she was interested in the seat. Then giving a few reasons why and let that be the end of it. The tour of New York and all of the interviews and photo ops and interaction with this naysayer and that one, she now believed, hadn't been in her best interest. When I left her, I embraced her and could feel the bones in her spine. She was thin and seemed somehow frail and I thought, No, if she continues with this thing, it will for sure be the end of her. I said, 'Caroline, get your old life back. This is not good for you.' She looked at me and nodded."

At this same time, a new controversy began to build relating to Caroline's spotty voting record and rumors that some members of her household staff were in the country illegally. Who knew if it was true or not? By the end of January, though, there would be a few more mediocre interviews and weak personal appearances, and Caroline looked as though she was finished. It was as if one day she was in, and the next she was out — a lot like her cousin Max Kennedy years earlier. "Politics will do that to a person," said Maria Shriver. "It can be life-ruining. I have seen it in my own family. I have seen it in others'."

Complicating things further was a strong rumor that Caroline's operatives traced back to the governor's office that he really wasn't going to name her to the position, anyway. "Are you kidding me?" Caroline asked one of her team members. She was irate. After everything she'd been through, the governor might name someone else? Of course, this had always been a possibility; there was never a single moment during which she or anyone on her team felt her to be an absolute shoo-in for the appointment. However, combined with everything else going on, the possibility that she might be passed over pushed Caroline closer to the edge.

She knew who she had to call: Uncle Teddy. When Caroline finally reached him, he was weak, barely able to talk. It was a bad day for him. However, he spoke to her in depth and, ultimately, suggested she drop out. If she felt strongly that Paterson would not name her,

Ted didn't even want her in the race. Being overlooked by the governor would look bad for her and the family, he said.

Ted had a caveat to his advice, though: he wanted Caroline to spend the next two years studying in order to get a firmer grasp on all the pertinent issues affecting her state. He wanted her to learn the ropes of being a politician, he said, because he still believed she had it in her. Running for the seat in two years would be difficult, he reminded her, because a real competitor would have it in for her and do whatever he or she could do to make her look bad in the eyes of the voting public. Therefore, she should steel herself. "It's New York," he reminded her, according to one account, "and, as is New York's way, they're going to come at you hard. They love scandal there, and as you've seen, if they can find a hint of it, they thrive on it." Still, he felt she could handle it if she took the time to really prepare for it. For now, though, he felt she should drop out. He urged her not to let Paterson have the final word. *She* should have the final word, he told her: "A Kennedy always has the final word." Caroline thought Ted's advice was good. She thanked him for it.

Two days went by. There was more waffling. It was still a tough decision and, as it would happen, one that would ultimately be made by her children. "The way I heard it," recalled one of the Kennedys' intimates, "the kids felt their mom was changing, and not for the better. They asked their mom to please bow out. That was it; that was all she needed to hear. She would never disregard the opinion of her children. So she talked to Ed about it, and he agreed that she should let it go. And that was the end of it."

On January 22, an email was sent to the media from Caroline's team that announced that she was dropping out of consideration, with no reason given other than "personal reasons." In the end, governor Paterson would end up appointing Kirsten Gillibrand, a congresswoman from Hudson, New York, to fill Hillary Clinton's vacated seat.

Caroline's entire senatorial gambit had lasted for just seven weeks. However, it had taken everything out of her. It would be some time before she'd be able to come to terms with it. In many ways, it felt to her as if she'd been living someone else's life. She felt exposed for the first time, unable to shape public opinion about herself. None of it was familiar terrain. In the end, she had to wonder if it had all been a big mistake.

TRANSITIONS

By the summer of 2009, Caroline Kennedy had put her senatorial gambit behind her and her life had returned to normal. However, now she and the rest of her many relatives would have to cope with the passing of two of the most important members of the Kennedy hierarchy. Or, as Mark Shriver put it, "the last lions were staging their exit from the arena."

First, Mark's mother, the indomitable Eunice Kennedy Shriver, passed away on August 11 at the age of eighty-eight. Her death was tough on her children, of course, but particularly difficult for Sarge, who was by this time deep in the throes of Alzheimer's.

The day after Eunice died, Kara Kennedy stood in for her ailing father, Ted, at the White House as President Barack Obama presented him with the nation's highest civilian honor, the Presidential Medal of Freedom. Twenty-five years earlier, this same award was bestowed to Eunice by President

Ronald Reagan for her work with the mentally disabled. Now, all these years later, it was Ted's turn. Teddy and Patrick were present for the ceremony, as were Vicki and her two children, Caroline and Curran Raclin.

Kara looked elegant and classically understated in a white silk top with dolman sleeves and black cigarette slacks with heels. Her spiky, short brown hair was smartly tinged with blond streaks. As Obama put the medal around her neck, she smiled proudly.

Though gravely ill, Ted was somehow able to attend Eunice's viewing and prayer service; for many of the Kennedys, this would mark the last time they would ever be in his company. He was too ill to make the later church service. With Ethel and Vicki both flanking him and trying to steady him, he bent over to kiss Eunice on the forehead and then broke down in tears. Two weeks later, on August 25, 2009, the Senator followed his beloved sister in death.

The finality of Ted's passing seemed unfathomable to his family, as it did much of the country. He had been a senator for almost forty-seven years. With the help of Vicki, over the last twenty, at least, he'd turned his life around to become one of the great liberal legislators of all time, "the Lion of the Senate," as he was so well known.

For Ted, there would be a vigil at the compound in the sunroom of the Big House, where his body would lie in state. Then there would be a two-day public viewing at the JFK Presidential Library preceding a private memorial service there. The funeral Mass would take place in Boston at Our Lady of Perpetual Help, the same church in which Ted had prayed for the miracle that had been granted to Kara after her cancer diagnosis. President Barack Obama was set to deliver a eulogy while three past Presidents would all attend. Once upon a time, Ethel would have been the one trying to boost everyone's spirits during such a sad time. Now she was subdued and seemed overwhelmed. Everyone knew how hard it would be on her losing Ted, especially so soon after Eunice.

By this time, Leah Mason had been employed by Ethel for almost thirty years. She'd taken some time off, moved to Europe for a while, and then returned. A day or two after Ted's death, she found Ethel sitting in front of her vanity, gazing sadly at herself in the mirror. She walked behind her and gently placed one hand on her shoulder. "Is there something I can do for you, Mrs. Kennedy?" she asked. Looking at their reflection, Ethel shook her head. She then said she'd known the precise moment Ted passed because she'd been sleeping and had been jolted awake, "as if someone walked on my grave." The same thing had happened with her nephew John, she said. She'd been asleep and sprung up in bed and somehow knew that he and Carolyn were gone, though she didn't want to admit it to anyone. Leah looked at her with sympathy. She'd long admired Ethel's invincible strength in the face of adversity. The two shared a moment before Ethel shook it off and visibly steeled herself. "Okay. Enough of this," she said as she rose from her chair.

With the "old guard" dying off one by one, it was as if a torch was now being passed. It fell to Vicki to help make for a smooth transition, no small feat considering all the details of Ted's service for which she was responsible. In a surprising and upsetting turn of events, she decided that she didn't want Patrick to speak at the service. "This is a big deal," she told Kara and Teddy, according to one account. "How can we be sure Pat isn't going to show up completely out of it?" He would never do such a thing, his siblings said. Vicki wasn't so sure; this was a tense, emotional time in his life, she noted. Patrick was grieving his beloved father. If ever he was going to turn to drugs, she feared it would be now. "He's going to embarrass us all," she said, "and I'm not going to allow it." Of course, Vicki was in an emotional state. In fact, though, she did have a point. Could they really trust Patrick?

Deep down, Patrick would later say, he understood Vicki's concern. After all, he'd be the first to admit that he still hadn't conquered his addictions. His stepmother was right: his grief could be a trigger. Still, he felt that for Vicki to rob him of such an important moment was cruel. It was also devastating. Because they'd never had an easy rapport, he feared there was no way he would ever be able to change her mind. When he went to talk to her about it, he couldn't even find the words. While he tried his best to defend himself, she cut him off before he had a chance to finish the speech he'd probably spent hours practicing. She said she was sorry, but her mind was made up about it. She wasn't willing to take a chance. Vicki was right; if Patrick was ever going to relapse it would be now, but maybe it wouldn't be because of his father's death as much as it might be because of her decision relating to the funeral.

When Patrick talked to Kara about the problem, she suggested they bring their mother into the conversation. Though Joan understood Vicki's concern, she was also worried about her son. She believed he should be given an opportunity to prove himself. So she felt she and Kara should appeal to Vicki. Therefore they arranged a meeting with her.

One always had to wonder how Joan felt whenever she pulled up to Ted and Vicki's enormous Federal-style home in Northwest Washington. The house in McLean, Virginia, in which she and Ted had spent most of their marriage, was certainly nothing like this. Richard Burke, Ted's former aide, once described that home as "an average, gray-shingled ranch house." Ted's home with Vicki was anything but average. Standing in the front entryway, with its large white columns and other stately influences reminiscent of White House design — such as the semi-elliptical fan transom over the black-lacquered front door and the large suspended lantern swinging above it — must have been difficult for Joan. While she was content in her present small but well-appointed apartment on Beacon Street in Boston, it's likely that this sprawling residence took her breath away. It had to make her wonder, *If only . . .*

After a servant answered the door, Joan and Kara were escorted through the grand marble-and-wood foyer, where they would have seen hanging on one of its walls Ted's impressive oil painting of the Kennedys' Cape Cod compound; it was inscribed "To Mother, always happy days at the Cape." In a parlor filled with French antique furniture with striped fabrics hung a 1926 oil painting of the patriarch, Joseph P. Kennedy. On the grand piano in the corner was a collection of family photographs assembled with enormous displays of fresh roses in oversized vases of Baccarat crystal. Joan and Kara followed the servant as he took a sharp left through the enormous kitchen, past the morning room, and out French doors that led to a well-manicured terrace that extended along the entire length of the house. There they found Vicki in a sunlit corner, as if posed for an *Architectural Digest* photo shoot. She was sitting in one of the elegant seating areas on green wicker furniture centered between two enormous pink blooming hibiscus plants. She was alone; an abundant breakfast arranged on the large round table before her. In the middle of the table was another crystal vase overflowing with dozens of white peonies. "Thank you," she told a maid who had brought out even more food. "That will be all for the moment." For just one person, everything seemed . . . *big.* And lonely. Kara and Joan joined her.

"Kara told me she didn't say much to Vicki," said Meghan Strayhorn, one of Kara's closest friends at this time. "Joan took control. 'Do you remember when you came to me a few years ago and asked me to back off where Kara's caretaking was concerned?' she asked Vicki. 'You told me that out of love for Kara, I should let you and Teddy be in charge of the big decisions having to do with her cancer. Now,' she said, '*I* am coming to *you* with a favor.' " Joan told Vicki that it would "kill Patrick" if he wasn't allowed to speak at his father's service. She said that he'd been preparing his eulogy for weeks. He loved his father so much, Joan said, it would crush him not to be able to eulogize him.

Vicki was usually a strong, stoic person. However, with Ted's loss weighing so heavily on her, it seemed that Joan's plea was more than she could handle. She broke down in tears. Joan reached across the table and took both her hands into her own. "Kara told me it was an incredibly moving moment: her mom, the so-called Old Wife comforting the New Wife," said Meghan Strayhorn. "Joan promised Vicki that Patrick would not embarrass them, that he would never let them down. Vicki said she would take Joan at her word; so, yes, Patrick would be permitted to speak at the service."

What's most interesting is that, at least from all available evidence, Joan and Kara elected not to tell Patrick that they'd intervened on his behalf. Apparently, to this day, Patrick thinks that his making it clear to Vicki and to the executor of his father's estate, Ted's longtime friend Paul Kirk, that he would be speaking was what did the trick. Who knows why mother and daughter kept their involvement from him? Maybe they just didn't want to embarrass him with the knowledge that they'd intervened. All we know for sure is that after Paul Kirk informed him that he could speak, Joan told her elated son, "I'm counting on you. *You are Patrick Joseph Kennedy.* I believe in you. Do us all proud."

Happily, Patrick did not disappoint. In his

stirring tribute to his father, he spoke of a childhood during which he suffered "chronic and crippling asthma attacks," saying his father was always at his side, "holding a cold wet towel on my forehead until I fell asleep again" after debilitating headaches caused by his medication. He recalled that because he always required a no-smoking, non-allergic room during family trips, that meant he would end up with the nicest accommodations, and his father as his roommate. "I couldn't have seen it at the time, but having asthma was like hitting the jackpot for a child who craved his father's love and attention," he said. "When his light shined on me alone, there was no better feeling in all of the world." He also spoke of the fun of boating expeditions and shared many sentimental memories as well as mentioning that father and son had been the primary sponsors of the Mental Health Parity and Addiction Equity Law. He closed by saying, "Now it's time for you to rest in peace. May your spirit live forever in our hearts, and as you challenged us so many times before, may your dream for a better, more just America never die. I love you, Dad, and you will always live in my heart forever."

When he was finished, an emotional Patrick left the lectern and walked back down to the first row of pews, where a tearful Vicki stood to greet him, her eyes full of warmth. She embraced him. That's when he knew he'd done his father and her proud. He then looked at his mother; she smiled and blew him a kiss.

Senator Edward Moore Kennedy would be buried at Arlington with his brothers John and Robert and his sister-in-law Jacqueline.

With Ted Kennedy now gone, his niece Caroline felt even more of a desire to be a public servant, if only because she knew how much it would mean to him. There were many reports in magazines such as *Time* and *Newsweek* that speculated about the line of succession in the Kennedy family, and there seemed no clear answer as to which Kennedy might take the family into a new age, especially with rumblings that Patrick would be giving up his Congressional seat. Eight months earlier, when she withdraw from consideration for the open Senate seat, Caroline had felt she let her uncle down. He assured her that this was not the case; she took him at his word. However, about a month before he died, she and Ed went to see him at the compound. "She just needed to be sure that he was not disappointed in her. It meant so much to her," said one of her cousins. "Of course, Uncle Teddy put her mind at ease." Ted told his niece it was never easy to push oneself out of a comfort zone as she had during her brief political gambit. It took real courage for her to put herself out there. He was proud of her, he said, and he believed that her parents and brother would have been as well. Caroline couldn't have appreciated her uncle's words more; he always knew exactly what to say to her to make any difficult situation in her life feel just a little better.

What happened in New York had been brutal for Caroline; there was no denying it. However, she had to admit that there had also been something incredibly enlivening about it. It had felt . . . *worthwhile.* She now knew she needed to tailor any future role in politics in a way that would mesh with her own personality. She was more certain than ever that she wouldn't abandon the family mandate to serve. She'd just put it on hold for the time being.

As Caroline mulled over her future as a public servant, her cousin Patrick was preparing to walk away from his own role in government. In March 2010, his father's and his own greatest cause, the Affordable Care Act, was passed into law. Patrick was at the signing ceremony, proud to finally see the legislation he and his father and colleagues had spent years developing made official by President Obama's signature. With this work now done and his father now gone, Patrick felt that the time had come for him to make a new life for himself.

On February 12, 2010, Patrick Kennedy announced that he would not be running for a ninth House term. At just forty-two, he'd been in Congress for sixteen years, the senior member of the Rhode Island delegation. Things just weren't the same after his father was gone, he explained, and he'd been thinking about stepping down. He'd even discussed it with Ted. "For me, I had an audience of one," he said. "That was my dad. As exciting and as meaningful as work is and as my career is, ultimately something clicked inside of me that there was something that was missing," he concluded. "I want a fuller life."

Patrick said he was finished once and for all with politics. He would now advocate for mental health and addiction issues privately. It felt good. It felt right. He would make this decision about his life not based on what was best for anyone else. He had served at the public's pleasure for many years. Now it was time to serve at his own and to be the one to make the decision about it. It would turn out that his father's advice to his cousin Caroline had resonated for him as well: "A Kennedy always has the final word."

■ ■ ■ ■

PART VII
BETRAYAL OF
THE HEART

■ ■ ■ ■

BRED TO LOOK THE OTHER WAY?

As is well known by now, becoming a Kennedy wife can be fraught with certain challenges, going all the way back to Rose Fitzgerald's flawed marriage to the chronically unfaithful Joseph P. Kennedy and then her daughters-in-law Jackie's and Joan's troubled marriages to Jack and Teddy. Where Bobby was concerned, maybe he cheated on Ethel, but we don't know for sure and, based on what we do know of his character, it's doubtful.

In terms of the third generation, the experience of each woman who married into the family has been, of course, particular to her upbringing and personality, as well as specific to the character of the man she took as a husband. Just surveying the RFK branch of the family, many of the women who took Ethel's sons as husbands have actually had good marriages, especially worth noting considering the misogynistic leanings of Kennedy men. Sheila Sinclair-Berner has been married to Christopher since 1987; Victoria Anne Strauss to Max since 1991; Anne Elizabeth "Beth" Kelly to Joe since 1993; and Molly Stark to Douglas since 1998. It's worth remembering that Sheila Rauch, Joe's first wife, was no milquetoast; she found a way to fight back after Joe insisted on an annulment in the 1990s by writing her devastating memoir. Victoria Gifford made an empowered decision to divorce Michael after the Marisa Verrochi scandal. Unfortunately, Mary Richardson, Bobby's second wife, would find herself in a torturous marriage to a man who seemed completely incapable of fidelity.

While women who married into the family no doubt have interesting stories should they ever decide to tell them, so do those who were actually born Kennedy. After all, these young women were raised in a culture that generally accepted infidelity. Sometimes they were fortunate and never had to deal with it: Kathleen Kennedy Townsend, for instance, has been happily married (as of this writing) for forty-five years (since 1973) to a husband who, from all accounts, has always been good to her. The same holds true for her cousin Caroline Kennedy, married for thirty-two years (since 1986). Maria Shriver, though, wasn't as fortunate.

Despite sweeping changes over the years relating to feminism and women's rights, Maria would somehow find herself stuck in the same kind of troubled marriage as some of her female relatives of the fifties and sixties. Her union with Arnold Schwarzenegger seemed to suggest that no matter the country's climate, men of a certain character and sense of entitlement will still misbehave. It has to do with wealth and prestige and a sense of power. Maybe it has to do with politics, too. In Maria's case, add show business to the mix and the result was truly toxic.

Shortly before the 2003 gubernatorial election, Arnold's political career was rocked by multiple allegations of sexual misconduct. The *Los Angeles Times* published a series of scathing articles in which sixteen women accused him of sexual harassment and humiliation over a thirty-year period. Arnold admitted to having "behaved badly" but insisted that most of the allegations were false. He waffled, though. "Some of it probably happened," he said, "and some of it probably didn't. But I apologize in any case to anyone I offended." Considering all the women who'd been profiled, as well as later testimony from many people in the entertainment industry who claimed to have caught Arnold in compromising positions, it's difficult to escape the conclusion that he was probably unfaithful to his wife. There's simply too much evidence to believe otherwise.

History shows that it didn't matter to voters that Arnold might have been a sexual predator, no matter how many egregious complaints were lodged against him. Again, the Schwarzenegger trajectory reminds one of Donald Trump's thirteen years later. During Trump's presidential run and even after he was in office, complaints of sexual harassment were made against him with, again, as many as sixteen women coming forward. However, his base decided that even if these allegations were true, they had no bearing on whether he would be a successful leader.

A big difference between Schwarzenegger and Trump would be the degree of their wives' support. Of course, Melania Trump backed her husband. However, to say she was vociferous about it would be untrue, especially after she kept quiet when Trump was accused of having sex with both an adult film star and a *Playboy* playmate and then paying them both off to keep quiet. Unlike Melania, Maria didn't just issue a few supportive comments about her husband and then smile mysteriously, causing people to wonder what was truly in her heart. To the contrary, she supported Arnold with everything she had, even putting her personal integrity and professional credibility on the line.

Of the reams of newspaper articles about the subject, Myriam Marquez of the *Orlando Sentinel* put it best: "There was Maria, in stop after stop, never wavering, never once showing any sign that there could be an ounce of doubt in her mind about her husband's ethical core. She asked voters: Whom are you going to trust? Anonymous women who are saying bad things or even those who give their names and talk about Arnold's raunchy side, or this woman, the gal who has pledged to love him for better or worse? Trust me, she told voters. I'm his wife, the mother of his four children, the woman who knows him best."

Ultimately, of course, Arnold was elected, and, as we have seen, in the Shrivers' world winning was everything, so in that respect, maybe everyone got what he or she wanted out of the deal. Still, outside of the political arena, in her private moments when she wasn't trying to sway voters, one has to wonder how Maria was able to square it all.

Maria's mother, Eunice, never had to contend with infidelity from the deeply religious Sarge. With his strong moral compass, he wouldn't have been able to live with himself if he ever strayed. He and Eunice were happily married for fifty-six years.

Given her family history, one can understand that, at least at the start, Maria didn't have the coping skills to grapple with her marriage to the cheating Arnold. According to her intimates, she had to figure it out on her own without Eunice's help. As one person close to her put it, "she wouldn't have discussed this kind of thing with her mother since she knew it would have broken Eunice's heart. Eunice adored Arnold. In the end, Maria was pretty much on her own when it came to dealing with him."

Also, it's worth remembering that Maria was a woman who'd become a terrific success in the male-dominated television industry. She *had* to be tough. She could probably write a book about the many indignities she'd suffered along the way in television, or, at the very least, the demonstrations of disrespect from male colleagues in positions of power. In other words, she wasn't a delicate, overly sensitive, or emotional person. She brought that toughness into her marriage. Though it obviously wouldn't inure her from heartbreak, it would definitely imbue her with the resolve she needed to focus on the positive and have a good, quality life despite any marital adversities. She once told a friend, "I am well aware of Arnold's limitations." She'd created a happy world for herself as California's First Lady, was respected and revered by many people. She also had her children.

At one point, Maria appeared on her close friend Oprah Winfrey's show to deny that she, like some of her Kennedy predecessors, "always look the other way." She said, "Well, you know, that ticks me off. I am my own woman. I have not been, quote, 'bred' to look the other way. I look at that man [Schwarzenegger] back there in the green room straight on, eyes wide open, and I look at him with an open heart." Reading between the lines, though, Maria suggested she knew the character of the man she'd married and had made a conscious decision to accept him and his flaws. In other words, she looked the other way — just like Rose . . . just like Jackie . . . just like Joan . . . and just like so many others.

Where Arnold was concerned, he had his own way of viewing things. One person who worked with him closely in government recalled a conversation the two had about his behavior. "It was during the period when the *Los Angeles Times* was doing its greatest damage," he recalled. "I sat down with Arnold and had a frank conversation with him about the women who had come forward."

The associate asked Arnold if he was worried about how the news might affect Maria. No, Arnold said. He said that Maria knew what she had signed up for when she married him. He'd never been a saint, he admitted, but he treated his wife and children well and that would have to be enough for them. In his view, they were all happy, so what was the problem? Was he afraid Maria might one day also stray? Arnold made a face and chuckled as if that was the most ridiculous thing he'd ever heard. If she was unhappy, she would tell him so and, because he loves her, he would probably do something about it. "Like?" the associate asked. Arnold shrugged. Maybe he would divorce her, he theorized, if she said it would make her happy. However, he hastened to add, he didn't think that this was what she wanted.

"What *does* she want?" the associate asked.

"To be married to me, obviously, and to give our children a nice life," Arnold answered, getting testy.

"And what do *you* want, Arnold?"

"For this conversation to end."

A SECRET FINALLY REVEALED

It's likely that accepting her marriage for what it was made Maria Shriver feel somewhat in control of her own destiny. However, there was one aspect of her life that was not in alignment, and it had to do with the son of her longtime live-in housekeeper, a youngster named Joseph. With the passing of time, the resemblance between him and Arnold had become startling. This situation had been troubling Maria for years. When she'd least expect it, little Joseph would walk into the room with the same face as her husband's — the eyes set wide apart, the strong chin, even the shape of his mouth — and it would stop her dead in her tracks. By 2010, she wanted — *needed* — to know the truth about this boy. Was he Arnold's son? However, Maria had long ago gotten used to a certain way of being in her marriage with her husband; true candor was never their forte. In fact, when she'd asked Arnold a few years earlier if he was Joseph's father, he hotly denied it. She didn't quite believe him, but she decided to let it go. She was busy, anyway, and it was just easier to be avoidant.

Maria, who would turn fifty-five in 2010, remained an extremely popular First Lady of California as she continued to promote the ideals of service and volunteerism passed on to her by her parents. She was deeply committed to many philanthropic organizations devoted to feeding the poor and finding ways to assist the disadvantaged. Meanwhile, at home, her children were growing up fast: Katherine was about to turn twenty-one; Christina nineteen; Patrick seventeen, and Christopher thirteen. Arnold was now sixty-three.

Generally, Maria was content with her busy life, as complicated as it was; she was also dealing with her aging parents, which was not easy. Someone had said something to her recently, though, that hit her hard. She and some friends had been talking about a person's bad marriage when one of them observed, "Unfortunately, women can get used to anything." Maria immediately objected, saying not only was that an untrue statement, it was insulting. However, later it gave her pause: Was she guilty of doing just that? Had she just gotten used to a bad situation not only in her marriage but also where Joseph was concerned? It certainly seemed like the case.

Though she was angry at herself for having waited so long to address the immediate concern of the housekeeper's son, she knew there was still time to claim her power over it. To that end, she'd begun hinting to the household employee, a woman named Mildred Baena, from Guatemala, that she suspected something was amiss by offering ostensibly supportive statements such as "I'm here if you need to talk." According to what Mildred would later remember, these entreaties made her feel uncomfortable and caused her to wonder if, as she later put it, "something was up." Something *was* up.

One day in the summer of 2010, Maria finally just cornered Mildred. "Tell me the truth," she insisted, "is Joseph Arnold's son?"

For a second, Mildred didn't know how to respond. Then the floodgates opened and the tears began to flow. "Yes, yes, yes," she said as she fell to her knees in a dramatic moment that, when described by people with knowledge of it, sounds like something right out of a soap opera. "It's true. He is. I'm so sorry."

Seeing this woman who'd worked for her as a loyal servant for twenty years on her knees, combined with the truth of Arnold's deception, caused Maria to also begin to cry. So this is what it had come to? The same old worn-out story: a cheating husband whose actions now claimed two victims, the wife he cheated on and the other woman with whom he had cheated. It was nothing if not a tired cliché — especially as it related to Kennedy women. However, the emotional scene also provided a seminal moment for Maria, at least according to what she would later confide in certain of her friends. Recalled one of them, "It was the moment when she finally said, 'You know what? *Goddamn it, that's enough.* I am finished. Finally, I am truly finished with this bullshit.' "

"Please get up," Maria told Mildred through her tears. "You should never be on your knees, ever." After the woman rose, she then promptly collapsed in Maria's arms. "It's not just Arnie's fault," she cried. "It's mine, too. It takes two." Maria then tried to comfort her.

One has to marvel at the character of a person who is able to put her own feelings aside long enough to console someone guilty of such a betrayal. It says something about the way Eunice and Sargent raised Maria that her first response was to comfort Mildred rather than to lash out at her. It makes sense, though. The Shriver children had all been taught the virtue of selflessness; it was an important part of their Catholic upbringing. Of course, it's one thing to be instructed to consider others first when one is a child and the situation is hypothetical; it's quite another when one is an adult and the crisis is real. Maria, even in such a terrible moment for her, was able to remember who she was at her core: a Shriver, through and through.

As it turned out, Mildred's son, Joseph, had been born back on October 2, 1997, after she had a brief affair with Arnold. Her relationship with Arnold began one afternoon in 1996, as Arnold later explained, "when Maria and the kids were away on holiday and I was in town finishing *Batman and Robin.* Mildred had been working in our household for five years, and all of a sudden we were alone in the guesthouse."

A friend of Mildred's picks up the story:

"Patty [Mildred's nickname] had a crush on Arnold. When he expressed interest in her, she was swept away by him. It wasn't just one night. It went on for a while under Maria's nose. Then, when Patty became pregnant, she didn't know what to do. She felt terrible. She actually loved Maria and knew that the bad choices she'd made with Arnold could ruin her [Maria's] family. 'Haven't you ever done something you regret?' she asked me when I challenged her. She also knew Arnold would never choose her; not only did she feel she had fewer advantages than Maria Shriver, she also knew he'd never break up his family for her. She was just the housekeeper. What was she supposed to do? So she decided to have the baby and keep quiet."

"At the time I was intimate with Arnold, I thought I loved him," Mildred confirms. "But

I knew he was married and had a family who I cared very much about, too. So, I decided I would just go on with my life and not hurt anyone."

"After Mildred gave birth" Arnold later recounted, "she named the baby Joseph and listed her husband as the father. That is what I wanted to believe and what I did believe for years. Joseph came to our house and played with our kids many times. But the resemblance hit me only when he was school-age, when I was governor and Mildred was showing her latest photos of him. The resemblance was so strong I realized there was little doubt he was my son."

Arnold finally confronted Mildred in 2000, when Joseph was three. (By this time, she and her husband had split up.) It was then that she broke down in tears and told him the truth. "From then on I paid for his schooling and helped financially with him," said Arnold.

Once he knew the truth, Arnold asked Mildred to keep Joseph's paternity a secret . . . from Maria and from everyone else. She agreed. The fact that he was able to run for governor with such a scandal looming is astonishing in retrospect, especially considering that there had been so much controversy with women coming forward to allege sexual harassment. Maria had, of course, vigilantly supported him during that turbulent time, standing up for his character and insisting that all the stories about him were completely untrue.

Now Maria knew the truth about Arnold, Mildred, and Joseph. Making it all the more painful, when doing the math in her head she quickly realized that she'd been pregnant at the same time as Mildred; she and Arnold welcomed Christopher into the world shortly before Joseph's birth.

"Does Arnold know?" Maria asked Mildred.

"Yes."

"Of course he does," Maria said, shaking her head. "For how long?"

"Ten years."

The timing of such a devastating revelation couldn't have been worse. Soon after her mother's death, Maria and her siblings moved Sarge into an assisted-living residence in Bethesda called Fox Hill, close to where her siblings Mark and Timothy lived with their families. It was torturous watching Sarge slowly slip away; soon he didn't even remember his daughter's name. She needed to marshal all her strength and resolve to get through it. Therefore, whatever Arnold had done ten years earlier couldn't matter, at least not at this time. No, Maria decided; she would deal with it later.

Mildred Baena was ready to quit, too ashamed to stay on as the family's housekeeper. Maria said it wasn't necessary. Instead, she suggested that Mildred stay on for the rest of the year. "Oh, and by the way, don't let Arnold know that I know," she told her. She agreed.

Apparently, Arnold wasn't the only one who could keep a secret.

THE TRUTH HURTS

In January 2011, after seven years of governing California, Arnold Schwarzenegger's second term was over. He had come into office with no experience, just an abundance of ambition and personality, which, as it would turn out, wasn't really enough to get things done — especially with a Democratic Senate blocking him every step along the way. He started out tough and adversarial, not understanding that he would need Democrats to see any agenda through. As a result, he made many enemies early in the game and was never able to successfully reach across the aisle. Instead of balancing the budget as he'd promised voters, the deficit rose from $6 billion in 2003 to more than $25 billion by the end of 2010. He did see to landmark climate change legislation, though, and certain infrastructure advancements as well. However, when it came to fully understanding fiscal and budgetary matters, he was in way over his head. Back in 2003, when he first got into office, he was so popular there'd been talk of a constitutional amendment so that, though he had been born in Austria, he could run for President. By the time his second term was over, his approval rating was only 22 percent. His political life was probably over, or at least that was the popular consensus. What people didn't know, though, was that there was also about to be a real sea change in his personal life.

On Arnold's second day out of office, the morning of January 4, Maria decided it was finally time to get a complete airing of his relationship with Mildred Baena and the child born of it. She started the new year by setting an appointment with the marriage counselor the two had been seeing of late. Maybe Maria didn't feel she could get the truth out of Arnold on her own. Arnold had always been so secretive, as Maria knew after thirty years with him. Once, years earlier, he was scheduled to have open-heart surgery and had decided not to tell her about it because, as he put it, "she had a tendency to blow things up into high drama." He informed his doctor that he was going to tell Maria he was going to go on a one-week vacation to Mexico. Then he would have the surgery and afterward check into a hotel for a week. His physician thought he was out of his mind and urged Arnold to tell his wife what was going on — which he finally did.

There were so many stories like this over the course of her marriage, Maria didn't want to try to have it out with him about Mildred without someone present to referee the exchange and prevent him from just outright lying to her. "We're here today because Maria wants to know the truth," the therapist began as the couple sat before her. "Your governess's thirteen-year-old son, Joseph. Is he yours?" she asked Arnold. "Are you the father?"

With his mind probably racing, Arnold looked as if he didn't quite know what to say. Finally, he just blurted it out: "Yes, it's true." Of course, Maria already knew it was true, as she then explained, and had known it for some time.

"You knew and didn't tell me you knew?" Arnold asked, trying to turn the tables on her.

"That's not really the issue," Maria said, barely able to look at him.

Arnold then filled in some details; he explained that he and Mildred had gotten together back in December 1996 when Maria and the kids were out of town and he was completing *Batman and Robin*. The two found themselves in the guesthouse one day, and nine months later, Joseph was born.

Mildred — who must have had her reasons — said the baby was her husband's, and Arnold believed it, or at least he wanted to believe it. He then allowed the growing boy to play with his own children; everyone got along well. However, by the time Joseph was three, Arnold couldn't ignore the strong resemblance. He then demanded the truth from Mildred, and she gave it to him. He decided not to tell Maria, even when she had her own suspicions, for many reasons. He recalled that the first time Maria asked about Joseph's paternity, he denied being the boy's father because he wasn't sure. He didn't want to hurt her and "blow up" their marriage. He also admitted having reservations about whether she would keep the secret since, as he put it, "you share everything with your family." He finally concluded that she was already going through such a difficult time because of her parents' illnesses; he didn't want to add to her load. "There are a lot of reasons," he said. He felt "horrible" about all of it.

"And so you decided to just let her continue living in the house and working for us, all right under my nose?" Maria asked.

"Yes." He explained that he thought he could "control the situation better" if she was still under their employ. Also, he felt as if it would be punishing Mildred if he let her go. "I fucked up," he said, all this according to his memory of the therapy session.

Arnold had been a good father, Maria would have to admit, and a strong leader, too, but in terms of being a faithful husband? Obviously, he'd fallen short of the mark. Prior to this therapy session, she'd had time to acknowledge her own complicity in their bad marriage. She'd already owned it. Now she was done with it. Maria said she wanted out of the marriage; she just needed time to figure out "how that will look."

Arnold didn't even try to talk her out of it. What could he say? "The truth hurts," he said pitifully. Maria had to agree.

"I asked myself what had motivated me to be unfaithful, and how I could have failed to tell Maria about Joseph for so many years," Arnold would later recall. "As I told the therapist, secrecy is part of me. Much as I love and seek company, part of me feels that I am going to ride out life's big waves by myself."

Maria Shriver didn't know exactly how the future would play out for her and Arnold after this therapy session, but she did know one thing for sure: he would definitely be riding out the rest of "life's big waves" without her at his side.

On January 11, a week after Maria confronted Arnold, her father, Sargent Shriver, died quietly in Bethesda, Maryland. The funeral Mass would be at Our Lady of Mercy, the home parish where Sarge had attended Mass almost every morning. He was buried next to his wife of fifty-six years, Eunice, at

St. Francis Xavier Cemetery in Centerville, Massachusetts.

Four months later, in April, Maria and Arnold sat down with their children to tell them that their mother and father needed "a break" in their marriage while offering no details about Arnold's having fathered a child outside of it. Maria then moved into a nearby hotel.

In May, word got out about the separation; it wasn't long then before the revelation of Joseph's paternity was headline news in the *Los Angeles Times.* The day before the story broke, Arnold was forced to tell his children about the deception. "I asked them for forgiveness," Arnold later said. "They cried. It tears your heart out."

As of this writing — 2018 — Maria and Arnold are still not officially divorced, seven years after Maria's filing. They haven't explained why they've not moved forward, either, choosing to keep their privacy. Though they don't live together, the couple seems to have found a way to be friends as they co-parent their children.

Sometimes family dynamics are too complex for outsiders to completely fathom the ebb and flow as people change their opinions of one another while grappling with matters of the heart. According to their intimates, though, credit has to be given to Maria, for she is the one who set the standard as to how she wants her children to treat Arnold. They respect him, just as she and her brothers had always respected Sarge. Apparently, they no longer question his bad choices; they just love him despite them.

■ ■ ■ ■

PART VIII
A MIRACULOUS LIFE

■ ■ ■ ■

JUST PERFECT

By July 2011, Kara Kennedy's cancer had been in remission for eight years. Doctors now considered her cured, as did she and her family. It was a true miracle, and no one in the family would ever take it for granted.

Though Kara had dated a few men after her divorce from Michael Allen, she'd never really been romantically interested in any of them. Was it because of the way she saw her father treat her mother? The suggestion was often made by friends. She didn't know if she'd been affected by her parents' bad marriage, and she didn't feel compelled to figure it out, either. Instead, in addition to raising her children, she spent time addressing some of the root problems in her relationship with Joan. Feeling blessed to even draw breath, she couldn't imagine holding on to old grudges about the past, especially relating to the way she was raised. As a mother herself, Kara had come to understand that Joan had done the best she could under the circumstances of her life at the time. In recent years, Kara had spent many of her summers with her children and Joan at Squaw Island. Mother and daughter would take daily long walks on the beach and try to deepen their understanding of each other, especially now that Ted was gone. "I was so mad at her for so many years," Kara said at the time, "for me to continue to try to rescue my relationship with my mom is so important to me."

Joan was actually a lot better; she wasn't drinking, anyway. She had her good days and her bad. Her bipolar medication tended to make her unpredictable; Kara knew she had to give her latitude and not take anything she said in a moment of anger too personally. Ted's death had been particularly hard on Joan. She'd never been able to reconcile their relationship; there'd just been too much history. In a perfect world, they would have had that one great talk that would have helped them come to terms with all their bad history. However, Joan knew that Ted had lost patience with her a long time ago, and it broke her heart. "But all of your other relatives are just as screwed up as I am," she once told him. "How come you're okay with them, but not with me?"

On July 15, the Kennedys came together for the wedding of Kara's brother Patrick to a thirty-six-year-old sixth-grade history teacher named Amy Petitgout. Finally, he was getting married; everyone in his life was elated. Now that he was out of public office, Patrick's story had taken a decidedly better turn, especially when he met and fell in love with Amy. Married previously, she had a daughter, Harper, who was three. The couple met back in March 2010 at a fund-raiser in Atlantic City. "He was tired," Amy says of Patrick of the time they first encountered each other, "and really emotional. Not a regular guy. He didn't sleep well, and he talked a lot about his dad. It was a big departure for me, because, well, my last relationship was not very much about feelings. I liked that kind of openness."

With his addictions now at long last under control, Patrick was a completely different man. "We're relying on AA and a totally different lifestyle," Amy told the writer Stephen Fried. "And," she said, smiling, "I'm nice to him all the time."

The couple was wed on the beach at the compound. It was sad, though, that relatives didn't show up as they once had for big events such as a Kennedy wedding. Caroline, who was never really one for these sorts of family events anyway, wasn't present and neither was Maria Shriver. Kara admitted to being a little disappointed; she missed her best friends, but she understood that things had changed and that people had moved on with their own lives. Still, plenty of family members were present, such as Ethel's off-spring: Kerry, Chris, and Max, as well as Bobby Jr. and Cheryl Hines, and Rory Kennedy and her husband, Mark Bailey. There were also Anthony, Tim, and Bobby Shriver. Vicki, Ted's widow, was present, of course, as well as her two children.

"My mother, Joan, and my aunts, Ethel and Jean, are spending a lot of time playing with their great-grandchildren all around them," Patrick — tall as ever, still red-haired and still freckled — told the media that had assembled just outside the gates. "I feel like my dad's orchestrating everything from up above and that he's doing a great job and he's telling us to get out on his sailboat and enjoy the ocean like he always did. My brother, Teddy, is my best man, which makes the day even better for me."

"Okay. See you in September, kid," Patrick told Kara as he kissed her goodbye at the end of a long, memorable day. He noted that he and Amy would soon visit her in Washington, "and, who knows? We may even have some good news," he added, winking. Kara knew that her brother and his new wife were trying to get pregnant. "You can do it, Pat," she told him as she playfully chucked him under the chin. "I have faith in you."

A week after the wedding, Joan and Kara were spotted browsing a village antique shop in the center of town. "She's my best friend,"

Joan said of her daughter to this reporter, who happened upon them while on a research mission in Hyannis Port. Though Joan, at seventy-three, appeared small and frail, she still had the great smile of her youth. Her blond hair was piled under a baseball cap and she was wearing large aviator sunglasses. "We do everything together," she added, beaming at Kara.

Gazing at her mother, Kara handed her a small trinket. "Mom, look at this little diamond elf," she said. "What does this remind you of?"

Joan examined Kara's offering. "Oh my gosh," she exclaimed. She said it looked exactly like a doll she and Ted had given Kara for Christmas years ago when Kara was about ten. "I always called you my little elf," Joan said. "Daddy found that doll in Alaska."

Kara smiled at the memory. "Oh, how I loved that doll," she told me. "I've always wondered what happened to it."

Joan smiled. "It's in the attic at home," she told Kara. "I still have it. I'd never throw it out. Never."

Turning to her mother, Kara made a decision: "You know what? I'm going to buy this for you," she said. She then handed the piece of jewelry to the store clerk to ring it up. "Would you like a box?" the cashier asked. No, Kara said. She then took the trinket and carefully pinned it to Joan's lapel.

A GREAT LOSS

On Friday morning, September 16, 2011, Patrick Kennedy wolfed down a big breakfast of eggs, pancakes, and bacon in his hotel room at the Four Seasons in Washington while speaking to Amy on the telephone. He was in town for a political rally, and he and his wife were making plans for the next day; Amy would be arriving in the morning and they would have dinner with Kara at about five. "Cool," Patrick said, "see you then."

Patrick was looking forward to seeing his sister especially since he and Amy were expecting, just as he hoped they'd be by this time. He planned to break the news to Kara over dinner. Amy thought it was maybe a little too early, though. After all, she was just six weeks along and was worried about jinxing things. No, Patrick decided, he was too happy to keep the news to himself. Because Kara had been the first Kennedy to whom he'd introduced Amy, he felt she had a vested interested in their happiness; he wanted her to be the first to hear the good news. "And besides," he said, "I don't believe in jinxes."

A couple of hours later, Patrick was sitting at a desk in his room and preparing a speech when the phone rang. It was his former chief of staff, Sean Richardson. He said that Kelly O'Donnell from NBC News had just called him to ask him to confirm some terrible news. "They found Kara," Richardson said, his voice shaking. "She was in a steam room at her health club. They think she'd just done some laps, and . . . I don't know . . . they found her, Pat! They found her."

Patrick didn't understand. "What do you mean, *they found her*?" he asked, his panic rising.

"I don't know how to tell you this," Sean said. He didn't have to finish.

All Patrick could manage to ask was: *"How?"*

Kara was only fifty-one. It was sudden. She'd had a heart attack after working out. Later it would be thought that unbeknownst to them all, the chemotherapy she'd undergone to treat her cancer had damaged her heart. It was hard to believe. No one even had a chance to say goodbye to her, but as the Kennedys well knew, life doesn't always provide the perfect cinematic goodbye.

Sobbing, Patrick hung up and called Amy to give her the terrible news. He also called Teddy, who said he would call Joan. Then quick calls were made to as many of Kara's loved ones as could be reached: Caroline in New York, Maria in Los Angeles, Kennedys, Shrivers, Smiths, and Lawfords all over the country. "After everything she'd been through, it seemed impossible," Patrick recalled. "She was in such great shape and always had an amazing attitude about life. You just couldn't imagine that this could happen."

Patrick knew what he had to do: he had to go to Kara's home to be with Grace, who was about to turn seventeen, and Max, fourteen. He'd spend the afternoon with them and the hours into the night, telling them heartwarming stories about their courageous mother and who she'd been in his life and in the lives of everyone she'd touched. Her bravery, her spirit . . . her love of family; he wanted to remind Kara's children of all of it. He understood from his own personal experience with loss that it would be these precious memories that would sustain them during the dark days ahead. "I had this profound sense that I had to honor Kara in the way I acted during those first twelve hours," Patrick would recall. "And I just kept thinking, I can't do what was often done with us — talk about other things and ignore all the elephants in the room. I had to tell them the truth. Kara would have wanted me to do that for her, and for them."

Of course, losing Kara so suddenly was

devastating to everyone. For her part, Ethel thanked God Ted wasn't alive to have to bear it; she didn't think he would have been able to do so. Sister Pauline Joseph recalled, "I was actually in the room with Mrs. Kennedy at Hickory Hill when she heard about Kara the day after it happened. I'm not positive, but I think it was Teddy Jr. who called with the news. I heard her chastise him and ask, 'But why didn't you tell me sooner?' And from what she later told me, he said he didn't know why, he just wanted to wait. He thought maybe it was because he envied the fact that she didn't know about it, and he wanted that to remain the case for a little while longer. As soon as she hung up, she looked at me and said, 'I have to call Joansie.' I thought to myself, How terrible is it that these two women of Camelot had to come together again in the face of yet another great and sudden tragedy?"

Just imagine the trials Ethel had watched her bear since the day Joan Bennett joined the Kennedy family more than fifty years earlier: her difficult marriage to Ted, through her alcoholism, her miscarriages (one suffered immediately after the ordeal of Chappaquiddick), her bipolar disorder, and everything else she endured, all of it winding toward this terrible time in her life that would find her burying her only daughter. "I also heard Mrs. Kennedy's side of that conversation," recalled the nun. "After she expressed her condolences, she told Joan, 'We were given eight more years with Kara. How blessed we all were, Joansie. How truly blessed.' She noted that Max was just six when Kara was diagnosed [with cancer], and Grace was eight. Now Max was fourteen and Grace sixteen. 'Thank God Kara had those eight years to raise them,' Mrs. Kennedy said, 'and thank God those kids now have those precious memories with their mom.' "

Observing Joan at Kara's funeral at Holy Trinity Church in Washington — so small and weak in her black turtleneck sweater and pantsuit, her hair still long and golden — most people did have to wonder how she would ever survive Kara's death. She was so shattered and numb, Patrick and Teddy had to help her as she slowly made her way into the church.

As Kara's best friends, Caroline Kennedy and Maria Shriver, sat with their families during the service, Teddy recalled that he and his sister had collaborated on their father's reelection campaign back in 1988. Kara's responsibility, he said, was public relations. He said that when poll numbers began to drop, some urged the senator to "go negative." However, Kara strongly disagreed. "She implored Dad to emphasize instead his primary strengths, which were his compassion and his willingness to fight for what he believed in, things that even his political opponents would agree with," Teddy said. "She reminded him why he was in political life." Their father would end up winning that election by his largest-ever margin and, said Teddy, "our father always credited Kara for that win."

After the Mass, on the way out while following the casket, Max and Grace literally had to hold their grandmother up; she was too weak and overwrought to stand on her own. True to her nature, though, Joan would somehow rebound. About a half hour later, she would hold court in the parking lot while surrounded by people who just wanted to be near her, to comfort her, and to express their sorrow. Their love seemed to lift her. Soon, she was reminiscing, talking about Kara's wedding to Michael Allen back in 1990.

Joan recalled that as she and Kara planned the big day, Kara told her she wanted a black gospel choir to sing during the ceremony. This was dismaying, she said, because she'd always imagined a lovely string quartet playing Mozart at her daughter's wedding. However, Kara's mind was made up about it; she wanted gospel music. "I was so determined that she have the wedding of her dreams, I spent months going to black churches all over the city trying to understand gospel," Joan recalled in an animated way; she seemed to be relishing the telling of the story. "Finally, I found just the right choir at the Twelfth Baptist Church in Roxbury, one of the oldest Baptist churches in the country," she said. "They were thirteen of the best gospel singers ever and, believe you me, when Kara got married nothing like this had ever been heard at Our Lady of Victory. *Are you kidding me?* This was something for the ages."

As Joan Kennedy smiled, she concluded, "Kara was so proud of me that day. She really was. And I was proud of her, too."

■ ■ ■ ■

PART IX
DEMONS

■ ■ ■ ■

GASOLINE TO A FIRE

Back in the spring of 2008, Mary Richardson Kennedy was lying on a couch in Ethel's home on the Cape. Sister Pauline Joseph was kneeling at her side, holding her hand and praying with her. Ethel walked into the room and gently placed a cool folded towel over her daughter-in-law's head. Mary had a hangover, a usual occurrence these days. "I think I need a lot more than just prayers right now," she said, looking up at the nun.

"What is it you need, dear?" the nun asked her.

"A new life," she answered.

Ethel knelt down next to the nun and looked at Mary with steely determination. "No, Mary," she said. "I'll tell you what you need. You need to look in the mirror and you need to figure out just who you are, and it's not this." She reminded Mary that she'd warned her not to marry Bobby but that she'd decided to do it anyway. Now she needed to make the marriage work. She said that whatever he did in his private life shouldn't have such a debilitating effect on her. "That's what men do, Mary," she exclaimed. "You always wanted to be a Kennedy? Fine," Ethel said. "You got your wish. *Now figure it out.*"

After she got all that off her chest, Ethel looked up at the nun and noticed her subtly shaking her head. Ethel's face then softened. After all, she'd known Mary for almost thirty-five years, since 1974, when she and Kerry were roommates at Putney.

Taking a gentler tone, Ethel reminded her daughter-in-law that when she was a freshman, an art history teacher had accused her of cheating on a term paper and gave her an F. It was the first time she'd ever received a failing grade. "And you wouldn't stand for it, would you?" Ethel asked. "You fought back!" When Mary defiantly confronted the teacher, he defended himself by saying he'd been teaching at Putney for thirty years and that he'd never read a freshman term paper quite like Mary's. Obviously, he said, she'd copied it from someone else. "I told him he was full of shit," Mary said, "and asked him to name any work of art, and I'd sit down and write him a paper about it." When he named the Sistine Chapel, Mary wrote in longhand an excellent analysis of Michelangelo's work off the top of her head in thirty minutes. "He was amazed," Mary remembered, "and he said, 'I'm so sorry, I stand corrected.' Then he gave me an A-plus." Ethel nodded with satisfaction. " 'See! *That's* who you are, Mary,' she said. 'You're a fighter. Right now, you're being tested. That's what this is — a test.' " Then, according to Sister Pauline Joseph, who witnessed the conversation, Ethel said she worried about Mary all the time. "I think of you as a daughter," she told her. "We're not a family without you, kiddo." Before she took her leave, she added, "Come find me later and we can talk."

As Mary sat up, the nun handed her an Alka-Seltzer. She stared hard at it as it fizzled in the glass and said that Ethel was right. She needed to pull it together. She just didn't know how to do it. "You have to pray," the nun told her. Mary nodded; she was still deeply Catholic. "I know I have to keep fighting," she said as she tried to clear her head. "I can do it."

"You *can* do it," said the nun.

"She would go into a kind of altered state, which we came to call her 'episodes,' " Bobby remembered of Mary. "Her features would change with her jaw set forward, her face paled, her eyes notably darkened, her voice alternatively breathy or hard. Mary's mood vacillated between rage and self-pity. Her behavior often became violent and destructive."

One night, Mary attacked Bobby in the

bathtub with a pair of scissors. During another evening, Bobby woke up to find her standing at his bedside, staring down at him with menacing eyes. Without warning, she pounced. She began to pummel him with her fists, beating him hard. His nose and mouth bleeding, he struggled to get her off him. Finally, after a few minutes, he was able to get away. He opened a window — they were on the second floor of their home — and jumped to safety.

It could be argued that Mary's emotional problems didn't have a lot to do with being a Kennedy. Certainly, she was ill before she married Bobby. The fact that he had his own issues made things much worse for her, though. Bobby's challenges were connected to his sense of Kennedy entitlement and predilection for misogyny and sexism. In that regard, he'd always known that something wasn't quite right about his pathological need for sexual gratification. When he was diagnosed as being a sex addict sometime in the early 2000s, it made sense. His brother Michael had once been given that same diagnosis, though at that time some people wondered if it was really just a good excuse for him to be with Marisa Verrochi. However, with the passing of time, more became understood about this addiction, though there are still psychiatrists today who don't believe in it.

Bobby kept incredibly detailed journals about not only his sexual conquests but about those times when he was able to resist. If one peruses these diaries, it's evident that he lived a life of guilt and shame throughout the 1990s and into the 2000s as he was intimate with as many as fifty different women a year and found the strength to avoid doing so with about another fifty. He called it his "greatest defect, my lust demons. It's not misogyny," he explained. "It's the opposite. I love them [women] too much." He also reflected in one entry that after his father's murder, "I felt he was watching me from heaven. Every time I was afflicted with sexual thoughts, I felt like a failure. I hated myself."

"The havoc his addiction played on his life and on the lives of everyone in his midst was as real as real gets," said one of his relatives. "It required years of serious treatment. I remember he once told me, 'I wouldn't wish this on my worst enemy.' The fact that infidelity was also a trigger for Mary's illness was like adding gasoline to an already raging fire."

"THE MEN ARE DOGS. THE WOMEN, FOOLS."

Since marrying Bobby, Mary Richardson Kennedy had borne four children — John Conor in 1994, Kyra LeMoyne in 1995, William "Fin" Finbar in 1997, and Aidan Caohman Vieques in 2001. She loved being a mother, and she was a good one, too; she'd even taken courses in parenting and then started teaching classes herself. However, in her role as a mother, Mary began to feel stagnant, especially as compared to Bobby, whose life as an activist was so fulfilling.

At this time, Bobby became dedicated to educating people about the dangers of children's vaccines and childhood autism. He was also still involved in the protection of New York's drinking water. Moreover, he and his associates had formed a bottled water company, Keeper Springs Natural Spring Water.

For her part, Mary seemed to be not invested in much other than obsessing over her fear that Bobby might leave her. Certainly, there was a lot she could have devoted herself to as a woman married to a Kennedy, any number of charities to which she could have lent her name. Years earlier, when she was working with Kerry at the Robert F. Kennedy Center for Justice and Human Rights, she was tasked with putting together food, clothes, and medical supplies for a mission to El Salvador. The goal was to fill just one truck. Within about six weeks, she had accumulated ten tractor trailers full of supplies worth tens of millions of dollars. Now, though, she couldn't seem to focus on anything other than her marriage.

"How's it going with Bobby in the boudoir?" her friend Alyssa Chapman asked Mary, according to her memory of "just girl talk between friends."

"It's okay," Mary said glumly, "but Bobby gets mad because I want the lights out."

"Why would you want that?" Alyssa asked.

"Why do you think?" Mary shot back.

"It took me a second to get it," recalled Alyssa Chapman, "but I suddenly understood that Mary didn't feel attractive anymore and she didn't want Bobby to see her clearly when they were making love. She started making sad statements, such as 'You know, a lot of people find me interesting. Why doesn't he?' She hadn't been raised to accept this kind of treatment from a man, she told me. 'I was raised to be *admired,*' she said. 'You've heard about this Kennedy curse?' she asked me. 'I finally figured out what it is: The men are dogs. The women, fools.' "

Lately, Mary had also begun threatening suicide, and Bobby believed she'd actually do it. After his brother David died of an overdose, everyone in the family felt tremendous guilt about it, but none more than Bobby. He now felt a real responsibility to Mary and said he'd never be able to live with himself if she ended her life. He wrote to her brother, Thomas Richardson, to express his deep concern and ask for help. "I know you think Mary's going to kill herself," Richardson responded in an email of his own, "but I guarantee she won't. I may regret those words one day, but that's how I feel."

Worn out from all the drama, Bobby tried to end it with Mary on Father's Day in June 2006. He moved out of the house. "But Mary told me she would never allow a divorce," said her friend Victoria Michaelis; the two had been close since attending Brown University together. "She loved her husband and wanted to save her family," said Victoria. "Also, she was very Catholic. Divorce was against her faith, a worst-case scenario not just for herself but for any woman. 'I just will not allow it,' she told me. 'I have to find a way to make my marriage work. It's the only way.' "

GIVING SICKNESS A NAME

At the end of the summer of 2008, Mary's illness was, at long last, diagnosed. "You're married to a woman who has borderline personality disorder," her psychotherapist told Bobby. Like most people, he knew little about BPD. Of Bobby's research into it, the writer Laurence Leamer would later note for *Newsweek,* "When he opened *I Hate You, Don't Leave Me* by Jerold J. Kreisman and Hal Straus, he finally felt he had an understanding of what was happening with his wife. Bobby read that the *Diagnostic and Statistical Manual* of the American Psychiatric Association lists nine criteria for BPD, five of which must be present for a diagnosis. Mary seemed to have every one of the nine, including a perceived sense of abandonment, a lack of identity, recklessness, suicidal threats, intense feelings of emptiness, and inappropriate displays of anger."

Finally, there was an explanation for Mary's behavior, and one that actually made sense.

"We'd all been trying for so long to understand," said Alyssa Chapman. "There was a great sense of relief. My God, we thought, this is it. Even though it sounded daunting — *borderline personality disorder* — we were so happy to have this . . . *thing* be named."

Despite the diagnosis, Mary's family to this day doesn't believe that she suffered from BPD. They have called the diagnosis "a vindictive lie" and "an insult to those who do struggle with this very serious illness." They would always maintain that Mary's problems were a direct response to continued psychological abuse by an unfeeling, insensitive husband. Kerry just tried to keep the peace with them and act as a buffer between them and her brother while everyone tried to find new ways to help Mary.

By this time, Kerry Kennedy had made a good and productive life for herself, built around activism and philanthropy. She and Andrew Cuomo divorced in 2005. A year later, he went on to a stunning comeback after his 2002 political embarrassment by being elected New York State attorney general in a race against Republican nominee Jeanine Pirro (who is presently a noted Fox News commentator). In 2010, Andrew would be elected the fifty-sixth governor of New York. Meanwhile, Kerry would continue to raise their children, co-parenting with her former spouse, with whom she remained close, as well as continuing her work as a social activist.

Despite how busy she was, Mary's problems were always foremost on Kerry's mind. While she sometimes felt torn in her allegiances to her brother and her best friend, she still believed she knew what was best for Mary, and that was to *not* be with Bobby. The fact that he wanted out of the marriage gave Kerry even more confidence that her advice to Mary to let him go was good for both of them. Then Bobby suddenly changed course.

For Bobby, Mary's BPD diagnosis answered a lot of questions. At least now he knew what he was dealing with. In the fall of 2008, he decided to recommit himself to the marriage.

One friend of his recalled that being at the Kennedys' home for dinner in October 2008, he found Mary in a good mood. As she prepared a salad in the kitchen with the chef, she spoke of a vacation she and Bobby planned to take now that things seemed a bit calmer. They were thinking of a cruise, she said. The way she glanced over at Bobby and caught his eye made it clear that the two still had something strong. As Mary spoke in an animated manner, Bobby stared at her with a small, loving smile. Despite everything they'd been through, she remained beautiful in his eyes. "You could see the adoration he had for her," said the witness to the scene. "As I watched, I thought, My God, he loves her so much. I had no doubt that he could make it work. I later said to him, 'You're doing a good job with her, Bobby. Whatever you're doing, keep it up.' He looked at me and said, 'Can I let you in on a secret?' I said sure. He said, 'I actually don't know what the hell I'm doing.' "

The calm didn't last long. A couple of nights later, Kerry and some other friends were at Mary's home when she came completely undone and started talking about killing herself. "Mary! You need to keep your shit together," Kerry told her, grabbing her by the shoulders and shaking her. Everyone was startled by Kerry's outburst. "You have to fight this thing in you," Kerry said as she started crying. "At least for your kids, don't you dare stop fighting it." Kerry warned her that every time she threatened suicide, she risked having her children taken from her.

Kerry really was at her wits' end. "The system is Kafka-esque," she would later explain. "Here's Mary, teetering, possibly suicidal. If she admits that she is, the court takes her kids away and her therapist has to commit her, calling police if she won't go voluntarily. So she was stuck. If she saved herself, she risked losing her children — her greatest fear."

In the winter of 2010, Bobby met a woman who apparently helped him understand just how destructive his marriage was not only to him but to Mary as well as their children. She was the television actress Cheryl Hines, who played Larry David's wife on the popular sitcom *Curb Your Enthusiasm* and was presently in a role on TV's popular series *Brothers & Sisters.* Her own marriage was ending; she had one child. In his darkest moments, Cheryl gave Bobby hope. Her love for him provided the trigger he needed to finally make his move: He filed for divorce after sixteen turbulent years of marriage to Mary.

Of course, Mary didn't take it well and neither did her and Bobby's children, especially their oldest boy, seventeen-year-old Conor. Of the four kids, Conor had always been the most attached to his mother. He was protective of her, hated seeing her so unhappy, and couldn't help but blame his father. For a time, he didn't even want to speak to him.

Conor (and his brother, Fin) had long suffered from severe asthma and anaphylaxis allergies. In addition to peanuts, Conor was particularly allergic to almost thirty other substances. "Mary had to take him to the emergency room twenty-five times in the first three or four years of his life," Kerry Kennedy would recall. "Back in 1998, she helped Bobby raise more than $30 million to establish the Food Allergy Initiative, a nonprofit organization to fund research. She would

Bringing Her Home

When the sun rose on Wednesday, May 16, 2012, Mary Richardson Kennedy was nowhere to be found. Though the housekeeper and her husband had thoroughly searched the premises, they couldn't find her. They found her driver's license, cell phone, glasses, and car keys, but not Mary. Searching her bedroom, the couple was disturbed to find a short span of rope tossed haphazardly onto the bed. They then remembered that, two weeks earlier, Mary had asked them to purchase it for what she said was a sofa repair. They didn't think much of it then, but they certainly did now. At about one o'clock in the afternoon, after searching the outdoors, they decided they had no choice but to call Bobby.

This call was one Bobby had feared for the better part of the last ten years. He knew instantly that Mary had done something to herself. When he arrived at the estate he, too, searched the premises. Not knowing what to think, he got into his car and drove to the nearby town of Armonk to ask around about Mary; the answers back were all the same — no one had seen her. He then located her AA sponsor, who said she hadn't seen her since Monday at her meeting, where she seemed just fine.

By this time, thirty minutes had passed since Bobby had gotten the call; that's how fast things were moving. He said he was going back to the house; the sponsor followed him. Once they returned to the property, the two searched a wooded area around the estate. As Bobby continued looking in the forest, the sponsor joined the caretakers as they checked an old barn. "Wait, what's that over there?" the housekeeper's husband asked when something caught his eye.

In a corner was a terrible sight: a woman suspended by a rope from a beam, slightly above eye level. The rope appeared to have been wrapped at least a half dozen times around her neck and then carefully knotted. Her face was a mask of terror, her eyes bulging, her skin gray. Her hands were gripping the rope at her neck as if in a futile attempt to pull it away. It was Mary. At the sight, the housekeeper became hysterical, falling to the ground and curling into a fetal position while crying. Her husband stood in place, horrified. Meanwhile, the AA sponsor ran out to her car and began to frantically press on its horn to summon Bobby. He arrived within minutes. "No, no, *no, Bobby,*" she pleaded as he rushed by her. *"Don't go in there."* Not heeding her advice, Bobby raced toward his wife and enveloped her with his arms. He struggled to pull her down. He couldn't do it. Bursting into tears, he fell to his knees. "Cut her down! Cut her down!" he screamed out as he looked up at Mary's corpse swinging at the end of the rope. "Somebody get a knife and cut her down!"

"No, Bobby," said the sponsor, now also sobbing. "It's too late. She's gone."

Bobby called 911. He then began to pray while standing in place and staring at Mary as if mesmerized, his eyes not blinking as tears splashed his face. Somehow he'd always known it would end like this, with Mary taking her own life. The sight of it, though, transfixed him. He couldn't believe his eyes. He also couldn't look away.

No one could believe that Mary would actually take her life, if only because they knew how much she loved her children. Obviously, Bobby, Kerry, and all of the family were devastated, but Ethel took it particularly hard, having long thought of Mary as a daughter. She said at the funeral that she'd tried to convince Mary that if she got help and was able to save her marriage, perhaps one day she'd end up running a household on the Cape at the Kennedy compound in her old age. Of course, this idea was in direct conflict to what Bobby wanted, but Ethel said she was just trying to give her daughter-in-law a little hope.

Not surprisingly, Mary's children — Conor, seventeen; Kyra, sixteen; Fin, fifteen; and Aidan, eleven — were all left deeply traumatized. It must have seemed to them that they never had a chance at happiness. After all, their mother had been ill for their entire lifetimes. Of course, Bobby tried to be present for them, as did their half siblings — Bobby III, twenty-eight; and Kathleen, twenty-four — but there remained a troubling sense of foreboding. Everyone Mary left behind seemed to be suffering from some form of post-traumatic stress disorder, not sleeping well, appearing either jittery or withdrawn.

In the weeks to come, Bobby took the kids to visit the family's former governess, Ena Bernard, in Florida, where she now lived. Ena, who was now 104, had always been there for him after his father died, and he sensed that maybe she could help his children come to terms with the tragedy in their own lives. They'd always loved her; anytime she came to visit from Florida was special for them and their half siblings. When Fin saw Ena, he hugged her tightly and began to sob, causing Fina to express concern about the boy's overwrought emotion. "It's just that he loves your mother so much," Bobby told Fina. Everyone knew, though, it was more than just missing Ena.

"Like millions of Americans, Mary suffered from mental illness," Kerry Kennedy would say after the death of her best friend. "She fought it as hard as she knew how. But that disease was not Mary herself. She was deeply Catholic, and she was an angel, a beam of light calling us all to our better angels. And like the archangel Michael, who battled Satan when he tried to take over Heaven, Mary fought back the demons who were trying to invade the Paradise of her very being. She fought it with dignity and with love, but in the end the demons won. I think God said to her, 'Mary, you have been my warrior on the front lines for too long, you have fought valiantly and now I'm bringing you home.' "

■ ■ ■ ■

Part X
The Family
Endures

■ ■ ■ ■

KENNEDY FASCINATION

In the summer of 2012, the Kennedys would do what they'd done throughout their storied history after the occurrence of great tragedy: by the grace of their God, they would pull together and get through it as a family. This healing would occur, as it always did, in their coming together at the compound on the Cape. Different this year, though, was the emergence of an unlikely character. She was a young woman who would provide not only much-needed distraction for all who were still grieving Mary's death, but even a bit of romance for the teenaged son she'd left behind, Conor. This new player was the young, doe-eyed pop star Taylor Swift.

By the summer of 2012, Taylor Swift was twenty-two and incredibly successful, with millions of records sold and seven Grammys won. As it happened, she was also quite the Kennedy aficionado. Not only had she read numerous books about the family, she'd also seen a number of TV documentaries and miniseries about them. An avid collector of memorabilia, Ethel was her favorite, she explained, "because when you look back at the pictures of her and Bobby, they always look like they are having the most fun." After seeing one photograph of the two at a dance in the 1940s, she said, "I kind of wrote a song from that place. I just was so in love with them."

In the summer of 2011, upon reading that Taylor was a fan of her mother's, Rory Kennedy reached out to her office to ask for concert tickets for her and her daughters — nine-year-old Georgia and seven-year-old Bridget. (She and Mark Bailey also had a four-year-old son, Zachary.) Swift's office happily granted the request. After the show, the Kennedys went backstage to meet the pop star. An excited Taylor then told Rory about the song she'd written in honor of her parents. "I asked Rory if it would ever be possible for me to meet her mother," Taylor recalled. "She said, 'Sure. Here's her number.' Ethel was kind enough to have lunch and spend a few hours talking with me, and ever since then I've been so inspired by how full of life she is and the way she tells her story."

A few months later, Rory invited Taylor to the Sundance Film Festival to see the documentary *Ethel,* which she had directed about her mother. So exuberant was Taylor on the red carpet posing with Ethel, a bemused

Teddy Kennedy referred to her as "a Kennedy groupie." Afterward, Ethel, who was eighty-three by this time, offered to host her in her home over the Fourth of July weekend. Taylor eagerly accepted.

Taylor then had what she thought was a great idea. She is known for her big Fourth of July soirées; they're usually celebrations held on a sun-drenched beach, a splashy affair that is greatly anticipated by her friends. In all her reading about the Kennedys, Taylor had always been fascinated by Joe and Rose's legendary Big House; she wondered if she could host her annual party there. She called Rory to ask, promising that this year she'd make sure it was a low-key affair. Understanding that staying at the legendary property would be thrilling for a young woman so fascinated by the Kennedys, Rory said she'd look into it.

By this time the deaths of Ted, Eunice, and Sarge had precipitated a sea change in Kennedy culture; life at the compound wasn't quite the same. Ted had promised his mother, Rose, that when he died the Big House would be repurposed for charitable and educational programs. Therefore, in his will, he stipulated that the home be absorbed as a holding of the newly created Edward M. Kennedy Institute. "This is what Mrs. Rose Kennedy and Senator Kennedy wanted," explained institute trustee Nick Littlefield, "that the house would continue to serve public purposes and be preserved for the American people."

Ostensibly, the Big House would eventually be open to the public, though that seems unlikely for many years since there are still Kennedys living at the compound. For instance, Teddy Jr. now owns Jack and Jackie's former residence — the President's House — and lives there with his wife and family. Meanwhile, the Senator had bequeathed Patrick a structure akin to an apartment attached to the Big House. It's small but functional, and Patrick had always loved it. He would remodel it beautifully in 2018 so that he and his family would be able to enjoy the summer months there. Other family members are scattered here and there; Ethel's son Christopher — for instance — and his wife, Sheila, have a summer home on Squaw Island near where Joan Kennedy often summers.

Of course, Ethel still lives next door to the Big House in the home she's owned for decades. In 2011, much to the surprise of many, she reluctantly sold Hickory Hill. She'd actually put the estate on the market in 2004 for $25 million, but it took seven years to unload it and not until she reduced the price to about $8 million. Leaving was incredibly emotional for Ethel given her cherished memories of her marriage to Bobby and the raising of their children together.

Ethel telephoned Ena Bernard to com-
miserate about the sale with someone she felt
would truly understand. "She told my mother
she had a lot of anxiety about letting the old
place go, but that it was just too expensive to
keep up and too big for her to stay in now
that everyone had their own lives," recalled
Fina Harvin. "My mother understood. She
loved Hickory Hill, too. 'It will be with us,
always,' she told Mrs. Kennedy. 'Everything
that happened in that great big house is
stitched into our hearts forever. So you can
let it go now, Mrs. Kennedy. You can let it
go.' "

Ethel also told Ena that one of the many
heartbreaks connected to selling the family's
beloved homestead was knowing that it would
probably be demolished due to its age and
outdated amenities. She was correct. The new
owners completely gutted the place. Now
Ethel would split her time between the
compound in Massachusetts and her home
in Florida.

When Rory checked with Vicki about the
possibility of Taylor Swift hosting a party at
the Big House, she was told that it wasn't
possible because doing so would jeopardize
the property's tax-exempt nonprofit status.
Though Taylor was disappointed, she still
wanted to take Ethel up on her invitation to

BLESSED TO BE ALIVE

On Sunday night, July 1, 2012, Taylor Swift arrived at the Kennedy compound for her promised visit. She could not have been more excited; she and some of the younger Kennedys, including Patrick (Maria and Arnold's son) and Conor (son of the late Mary and Bobby), both of whom were eighteen, spent the night on the beach, drinking, swimming, and having a good time playing flashlight tag — a favorite Kennedy pastime, basically "tag" in the dark. She and Patrick seemed to have instant chemistry, which was not so surprising. He was slim, good-looking with a smile like his mother's, and apparently difficult for Taylor — who'd had a wide array of boyfriends in the public eye, such as Joe Jonas, John Mayer, and Jake Gyllenhaal — to resist.

On her first morning at the compound, Taylor was treated to a little taste of the Kennedys' summer lifestyle, which in many ways hadn't changed in the last fifty years. One thing that was different, though, was the absence of sign-up sheets for meal shifts. Now there was one meal prepared in the morning, one in the afternoon, and one for the evening.

The day started with a huge breakfast in the nook of Ethel's enormous kitchen, prepared by her chef and served by her waitstaff. According to the menu (one was provided to guests every day), Ethel had the cook prepare his Palm Beach crab stack with poached eggs — basically, crab cakes on English muffins with eggs, tomatoes, cheese, and hollandaise sauce. There was also a side of Irish potato cakes — topped with Irish smoked salmon — as well as homemade blueberry-orange bread with marmalade butter.

The atmosphere was boisterous as always, much less formal than it would be at dinner, with Kennedy youngsters, teenagers, and young adults coming and going in their swimsuits and the older adults — on this day, including Patrick, Teddy, and Rory with their spouses and, of course, Ethel — properly seated. "Elbows off the table," Ethel kept telling the kids; it had always been a pet peeve of hers and remains so. There was no serious discussion about politics or world affairs, though. Rather, the conversation had to do with which yacht was going to be taken out for sailing that day . . . who was going to be on which touch football team . . . where the volleyball game would be taking place . . . all the usual Kennedy summer concerns. As a diehard fan coming into this rarified world, Taylor Swift had to have found it all pretty exciting.

Lunch was served on Ethel's patio — grilled lobster *or* mushroom gorgonzola and bacon burgers *or* hardwood-grilled New York sirloin steak. Joe told the chef to take the day off so that he and his twin sons, Matthew and Joseph III, could man the barbecue. They had a lot of fun serving up food for everyone.

After lunch, the entire family gathered on Ethel's patio, where Taylor — in red shorts and a black T-shirt with white polka dots and a red polka-dotted scarf folded around her head — played guitar and performed an acoustic rendition of the tune she'd written in honor of Ethel and Bobby. It was called "Starlight," with lyrics such as: "I met Bobby on the boardwalk, summer of '45/Picked me up late one night at the window/We were seventeen and crazy, running wild." (Ethel actually did meet Bobby in 1945 when she was seventeen.) Ethel was moved, her smile genuine. She said the impromptu performance took her right back to her youth and reminded her of that lovely time in her life. When Taylor then asked Ethel what her reaction had been to seeing Bobby for the first time, her eyes twinkled and she answered with one word: "Wow."

Definitely, after hearing the moving tribute, everyone was completely taken with Taylor Swift. As far as they were concerned, she was now pretty much an honorary Kennedy.

Dinner, as formal as ever with Ethel seated at the head of the table, started with a first course of baked brie wrapped in filo with walnut glaze; the second course, barbecued cajun shrimp with melon and Midori sauce and, for the main course, Mediterranean-style halibut with clams and mussels. Afterward, there was a generous sampling of desserts, including Kara's chocolate cake — so named because it was served at her wedding back in 1990.

Three days later, Taylor's Fourth of July at the Kennedy compound would be a fun and memorable holiday, even sans the big party she'd hoped to host at the Big House. She and Patrick definitely seemed like an instant item; paparazzi caught them embracing throughout the day. "Had such an amazing day. Best 4th of July I could ask for," young Schwarzenegger tweeted. "Hope everyone had a great day!"

Happily, Taylor managed to pass with flying colors the historic Kennedy tradition of being tested to gauge her mettle. Over the years, Jackie Bouvier, Arnold Schwarzenegger, Carolyn Bessette, and countless others had been forced to at least *try* to rise to the occasion of being able to compete with the Kennedys in their athletic and competitive world. "You know what she really is?" Ethel later said of Taylor. "She's game. She had never sailed before; she sailed. She had never dragged before. She dragged. She played everything else everyone else was doing and she was good at it, and no fuss."

The "dragging" Ethel referred to happened on the morning of the holiday. Taylor, wearing a frilly polka-dotted bathing suit with a white bow at the décolletage, was on a boat with a gaggle of young, athletic Kennedy girls when a couple of them jumped into the water to grab a rope that would then be dragged by the yacht — "dragging." Taylor was reluctant. Hanging on to a rope while being pulled through the waves? "No, that's not for me," she said. Ethel wouldn't hear of it, though. "If you don't do this," she told her, according to Taylor's memory, "you run the risk of being boring. *Now, get in the water.*" (It reminded some of a needlepoint Ethel has had in her home for years, which reads: IF YOU OBEY ALL THE RULES, YOU MISS ALL THE FUN.) In the end, Taylor did as the matriarch commanded and had a great time. In some ways, she says, it was even a teachable moment. "Ever since then, I decided that to really live, you have to jump in, you have to take chances," she would later say. "You have to embrace the unpredictability of life instead

MEMORY

It turned out to be a happy and relaxed Independence Day for the Kennedys, with much of the family present for the festivities, including Joan. Having her present was a real treat because she'd not been well, her advancing age (she was seventy-five) as well as bipolar issues making things tough on her. On this day, wearing red-white-and-blue slacks and a white blouse with a red baseball cap, she seemed much better. At one point, she, her son Teddy and his wife, Kiki, along with Ethel and her son Bobby and his girlfriend, Cheryl, found themselves in a little huddle with a few friends like Sister Pauline Joseph, who, after all these years, was still always present at Kennedy family functions. They all sat on the hot sand in white Adirondack chairs and watched as the kids played on the beach before them, waves frothing and churning all about them. Patrick was there, too, along with his wife, Amy, and their infant, Owen, who'd been born back in April.

"It's such a beautiful life, isn't it?" Ethel said, taking it all in.

"As relaxed as we all were, Mrs. Kennedy was still worried about Bobby," the nun recalled. "It had just been two months [since Mary's suicide]. I remember Cheryl asking her, 'Do you think he will ever find closure?' And she snapped, 'Oh, Cheryl. Please. Closure is just a myth,' which was very much like Mrs. Kennedy.

"Bobby was definitely quiet, seeming to be in his own little world while talking to Cheryl and watching the young ones frolic. He seemed peaceful to me, though, not troubled, as if maybe he really was beginning to reconcile things. He's such a man of faith, I knew he'd find his way. 'Trust in the Lord with all your heart and lean not on your own understanding,' I told him, quoting Proverbs. He nodded and said, 'I do. Every day, I do.' "

As well as his deep faith, Bobby's work also kept him from completely falling apart during this darkest of times. Lately, he was calling on environmentalists to blame Congress, not Obama, for the fact that so many of the President's promises about further studies and legislation relating to climate control had not yet come to pass. Republicans had blocked each and every move Obama tried to make, causing Patrick to say, "We haven't seen a Congress like this before in American history." Bobby, who had been named one of

Time's "Heroes of the Planet," kept up the good fight, though, especially with the 2012 presidential election just a few months away. He couldn't be as fiery a speaker as he'd once been, though, because he now suffered from a vocal disorder called spasmodic dysphonia — involuntary muscle spasms in his larynx that made it difficult for him to speak. It had been a problem for some time but lately, with stress, had become much worse. He still suffers from it today; it's a permanent condition.

At one point, according to Sister Pauline Joseph, Bobby's son Conor came up to his father, walked behind him, knelt down, and wrapped his arms around him tightly. Bobby leaned his head on Conor's arm, and the two remained in that position, talking softly to each other. As they whispered, Conor would kiss his father on the side of his face. After maybe fifteen minutes, the teenager stood up and then ran back down to the beach to be with the others his age.

Meanwhile, a gaggle of excited little girls in bathing suits followed Taylor Swift on the shoreline as if she were some sort of modern-day pied piper. Occasionally, Taylor and Patrick would hold hands and walk off on their own, she with her head on his shoulder. He would lean in and kiss her on the lips. It was sweet — maybe young love or maybe not, but definitely sweet. It felt hopeful, as if the

SUMMER FLING

Taylor Swift was only eleven in 2000, when K. D. Lang released her popular song "Summer Fling" with the lyrics: "The smell of Sunday in our hair/We ran on the beach with Kennedy flair . . . my new fun thing . . . my summer fling." It was one of Taylor's favorite songs. Twelve years later, she would have the opportunity to actually live the experience with her own summer fling — and not with the wiry Patrick Schwarzenegger, to whose beguiling charm she'd originally been attracted. As it happened, Patrick, who's an actor, had to leave for work. After he was gone, Taylor set her sights on his more strapping cousin, the brown-eyed, square-jawed, and shaggy-haired Conor Kennedy. She then spent a week (of July 23) with him at his family's home at Mount Kisco, which is where she got to know him and his story.

Of course, Conor was still deeply grieving his mother; this was an especially dark time for him. Taylor was saddened when she heard the details of how Mary Kennedy had died. She was close to her own mother and couldn't imagine how Conor was able to go on after facing such tragedy. She admired his strength, his resolve. Then, while getting to know him, she began to understand just how his many life-threatening allergies had impacted his young life. He didn't confide in her to elicit sympathy, but Taylor's heart went out to him just the same. She also recognized his vulnerability. "I'm not as crazy about sunsets as the rest of my relatives," he told her as they sat on the beach and watched vivid colors splash in the sky. "Sunsets feel sad, like maybe the end of things," he said. "I like the beginnings of things better."

Though he was four years her junior, she couldn't help but recognize his quiet maturity. When she asked about the dark history of tragedy in his family and what he may have learned from it, he said he'd come to a simple conclusion: "Life's messy." It sounded like the observation of a kid who'd seen a lot, been through a lot, and had stopped trying to make sense of it. Rather, he'd just decided to accept what he couldn't control and move forward despite it, much like so many of his Kennedy forebearers who'd seen the worst life had to offer yet persevered despite it. Also, he hated being alone, he said. The idea filled him with terror. "I've been surrounded by family from the time I can remember," he told her, according to one account. "That's how it is with the Kennedys. You're always with Kennedys. You grow up constantly surrounded by Kennedys. So when you're alone and there are no Kennedys, it's terrifying. I don't know how to do it." He wondered if his mother felt the same way, if maybe this was one of the problems that had plagued her.

On the twenty-fifth, the couple had dinner at Marcella's Pizza in Mount Kisco; on the twenty-seventh, they were seen kissing on the beach; on the twenty-ninth, they went sailing on the Cape after going to church in Hyannis Port. By August, Conor and Taylor were being followed everywhere by paparazzi and, in that great, time-honored tradition of Kennedys, attempting to duck them at every turn. At one point, they were photographed making out on one of the piers and frolicking in the ocean, Taylor in a polka-dotted two-piece. They were a gorgeous, sexy young couple. "Wait. I thought she was with Patrick," Ethel told her son Bobby. He shrugged. "Kids," he said. He actually approved of the little romance, though. Bobby had been worried about Conor, as he was all his children. He thought it was probably a good idea for him to have some sort of distraction, and certainly Taylor Swift was a pretty good one.

As some Kennedys sat around wondering about Conor and Taylor, matters of greater magnitude were also being discussed on the premises. Typical of the historical juxtaposition of events when it came to culture at the compound, men and women with serious concerns had converged in the Big House in meetings designed to find ways to change the world, while at the same time, just yards away, people frolicked on the beach, seeming to not have a care in the world.

Since leaving office, Patrick Kennedy had become one of the founders of an organization called One Mind, dedicated to the research and exploration of brain studies and mental illnesses. One Mind's first conference took place in May 2011 in Boston, where leading scientists, researchers, and business leaders from across the country converged to collaborate and share philosophies about neuroscience and strategies for more comprehensive research. As well as Ted Jr. and Caroline Kennedy, Joan made an appearance, the only time she'd been seen in public since Ted's funeral.

In May 2012, the second One Mind conference was held in Los Angeles at UCLA. Now, a few months later, Patrick was already planning the third. However, because One Mind dealt primarily with the future of research, he felt the need to establish a new organization that would concern itself with present-day issues, such as insurance coverage for those suffering from mental illnesses. He wanted to call it the Kennedy Forum and, to that end, invited some of the country's leading scientists, researchers, and human rights activists to the compound in August. Their meetings would be the first to take place in the Big House since it had been taken over by the Ted Kennedy Institute. Even Joan attended, saying that she wanted to contribute in any way she could and making it clear that she wanted to continue to be as open as possible about her own mental health issues if it would mean helping others. On that same day, Patrick recalled, "I couldn't resist pointing out to the group, during a brief lull in the dialogue, that the girl in the bathing suit walking down the path to the docks was Taylor Swift, who was then dating my nephew and probably already composing the song about their breakup."

In a week or two, it became pretty clear that Taylor was moving fast; she'd become serious about Conor in what some felt was record time. She became so consumed by him, and maybe by the Kennedy lifestyle, that in mid-August she actually decided to buy property on Cape Cod to be close to him. While her decision seemed surprising to some observers, maybe it just showed how easy it was to get swept away by the Kennedys. Taylor spent $4.9 million on a thirteen-room (seven-bedroom) home overlooking Nantucket Sound, with its own private beach and guesthouse. She owned several other homes across the country and considered her manse in Nashville to be her primary residence. Therefore, these new digs near the compound would be strictly for summer use.

"Conor liked Taylor, don't get me wrong," said his friend, "but this business of her buying the house on the Cape made him nervous. After all, it was just one property away from the compound. It seemed as if she was getting a little too attached, spending five million bucks on a house just to be near the guy."

On August 17, a bit of a wrinkle would present itself in this new Kennedy romance when Conor's cousin Kyle — daughter of Vicki Gifford Kennedy, Michael Kennedy's widow — married a fellow named Liam Kerr. According to Vicki, who had gone on to a quiet, unassuming life while raising her children after her husband's death, Conor sent her a text an hour before the wedding reception at the Fairmont Copley Plaza to say he'd forgotten to RSVP. He wondered if he and Taylor could still attend. Vicki said no, absolutely not. Later she would explain that she feared Taylor's presence would detract from the attention rightly due her daughter on her special day.

Conor and Taylor showed up anyway. As soon as everyone present realized who Conor's date was, focus shifted from the bride to the Grammy Award–winning pop star, just as Vicki had feared. Upset, Vicki went up to Taylor, introduced herself, and asked her "as nicely as I could" to leave. In return, Taylor gave her a long stare. "It was like talking to a ghost," Vicki said. "She seemed to look right past me." She and Conor then just breezed right by Vicki and went on to enjoy the festivities. "Vicki told me that was complete bullshit," said the reporter Gayle Fee. "While a lot of women might have been like, 'Oh wow, *Taylor Swift,*' not Vicki. Eventually, one of Conor's cousins came up to him and warned him, 'Dude, you'd better check yourself. Aunt Vicki is pissed. I think she's gonna drag Taylor Swift out of here by her ponytail.' That's when the couple left the party."

That night, Taylor and Conor had a disagreement. Apparently, Conor had misrepresented the situation and told her that they'd been invited to the reception. She said she never would have gone had she known they were crashing the party. *How could you do that to me?* They apparently got past it, though; the next day they visited the gravesite of Conor's mom, Mary, at St. Francis Xavier Cemetery in Centerville, Massachusetts. Wearing large celebrity sunglasses, Taylor, with her head bowed, seemed to be praying while holding Conor's hand.

In the days to come, word of the wedding reception misunderstanding was leaked to the media. Kathie Lee Gifford — Vicki Kennedy's stepmother and the stepgrandmother of the bride — decided to confirm on television that Taylor had been kicked out of the reception. Taylor was, as she put it, "mortified" by the revelation. She immediately had her spokeswoman deny the whole thing and say that the bride was actually "thrilled" that she was present.

She then called Ethel to make sure there were no hard feelings. She explained that when Vicki asked her to leave, there was so much pandemonium going on around her she had completely misunderstood her. Chaos always happens, she said, whenever she walks into a room full of strangers, and that's why she appeared to be so blank-eyed. It's also why she stayed. While Ethel was sorry about it, she couldn't take it seriously. "There are so many more important things to worry about in the world," she said, spoken like a woman who's known real problems. "Don't worry, kiddo," she reportedly told Taylor. "There will plenty more days in the sunshine."

Not many more for Taylor and Conor, though. In September, Conor ended it with Taylor. She was disappointed. Thinking they'd have a future together, she'd actually started doodling "Taylor Swift Kennedy" on a notepad just to see how it looked — and it looked pretty good. Luckily for her, though, she had new music being released and wouldn't have much time to lament the end of her "fun thing," her "summer fling." She had to begin promoting the album, which was called *Red* and which, incidentally, included her tribute to Conor's grandparents, "Starlight."

In a couple of months, Taylor would sell the house she bought near the Kennedy compound. Purchasing it had just been a lark. It seemed like a good idea at the time, anyway. It actually paid off for her, though: She made a million-dollar profit. This sale would not mean, however, an end to her friendship with the Kennedys.

In December, Taylor Swift would be honored at the 2012 Ripple of Hope gala in New York for her philanthropic efforts; since the start of her career, she has donated millions of dollars to charity. The annual star-studded event is organized each year by Kerry Kennedy to pay tribute to those committed to social change. Past honorees have included President Bill Clinton, George Clooney, Hillary Clinton, and Vice President Al Gore. It's named after Bobby Kennedy's "Ripple of Hope" speech (also known as his "Day of Affirmation" address), which was given in June 1966 in South Africa when Bobby was a New York senator.★

★ In 2018, Kerry Kennedy would write a book about her father called *Robert F. Kennedy: Ripples of Hope,*

"Taylor is getting the award because my father believed in the power of youth," Kerry said of the pop star. "Here's a young woman — twenty-two years old — who has put herself out in the world, and in an incredibly powerful and strong way."

Today, when Conor looks back on the first summer after his mother's death, he's grateful to Taylor Swift. She helped him through a tough time by bringing to it a little bit of romance and just a touch of Kennedy melodrama, which, he had to admit, was actually fun. For her part, Taylor looks back on it as that special time in her life when she got to experience, at least in some small way, getting to know members of the fabled Kennedy family she'd so idolized. "It was one of the best times of my life," she has said.

---

which was composed of essays about influential men and women whose lives had in some way been impacted by Bobby.

OLD FRIENDS
OF HICKORY HILL

On July 23, 2013, Ethel Kennedy walked outside onto her porch at the Cape facing the sea and eased her aged, eighty-five-year-old frame into a wicker chair. She was lost in thought. Moments earlier, she'd gotten the news that Ena Bernard had passed away at the age of 105.

Where had the time gone?

Ethel was just twenty-three when she hired Ena to help with baby Kathleen. That was sixty-two years ago. Ena had been with Ethel through so much over the span of forty-four years, a calming presence in the face of most of the tragedies that had visited the family. Of course, they also went up against each other quite often. When remembering their skirmishes, Ethel couldn't help but smile. Since Ena retired in 1995, the Kennedys paid for all her medical expenses; the family had also provided her with a pension plan.

It had been five years since Ethel last saw Ena, the occasion being the celebration of her one-hundredth birthday in June of 2008. Ethel and most of her children, as well as their spouses and offspring, flew down south for the party, which was held in a banquet room at the Signature Grand hotel in Davie, Florida. The fragile, white-haired Ena, who was now confined to a wheelchair, was overwhelmed that the Kennedys would show up for her party. They also had a chance to reconnect with Ena's daughter, Fina. Each Kennedy sibling gave a heartfelt speech, paying tribute to a woman who'd helped raise them. They then gave Ena an award: a small trophy that said "For Ena, who captured the hearts of the whole family, and whose 50 years of giving pow-pow has made us all better."

Now Ena was gone, having died at her home in Sunrise, Florida. Ethel and eight of her grown children would attend the funeral at All Saints Catholic Church: Joe, Bobby, Kathleen, Kerry, Christopher, Maxwell, Douglas, and Rory.

After the service, Ethel walked up to Ena's casket and knelt before it, making the sign of the cross, and then prayed for at least five minutes. Then, in greeting Ena's many friends and family, Ethel held court as she spoke of Ena. "She didn't work for me," Ethel said. "*I* worked for *her*," she joked. "If it wasn't for her, I don't know what I would have done after Bobby died." She admitted that she really didn't know what to do with so many kids, saying, "I figured I'd just make it up as I went along, but I found out it was tougher than I thought it would be." She smiled as she recalled how her children sometimes ribbed Ena, even as adults. For instance, when Ena went through menopause, she gained some weight, which inspired a new nickname for her from the Kennedys she'd raised: "Costa Rica Fats." Ethel cringed at the memory. "Ena would say to me, 'How did you raise such awful kids?' " she recalled. "And I would laugh and say, 'I didn't raise them. *You did.*' "

Of course, Ena Bernard wasn't the only trusted caretaker of Ethel's children at Hickory Hill during its halcyon days. There had been many others. One of the most valuable of her staff was her estate manager, Noelle Bombardier, someone Ethel hadn't seen in more than twenty years. The end of their relationship wasn't as amicable as Ethel and Ena's because it had involved a truly frightening incident at the Kennedy compound.

Noelle had gone to Hyannis Port to prepare the estate for Ethel's summer stay. Other than house painters who were putting a fresh white coat on the home's exterior, Noelle was alone there with her ten-year-old daughter, Danielle. One afternoon, the little girl was gone for about thirty minutes before her mother realized it. No one knew where she'd gone. One of the painters said he thought he saw her walking hand in hand with a woman he didn't recognize, away from the compound and across the shoreline. Frantic, Noelle called the police. She then got into her car and drove along the beach at a breakneck speed until finally finding Danielle and the stranger, already surrounded by a SWAT team with guns drawn. After Noelle tore Danielle from the woman's arms and demanded an explanation, the abductor said, "Oh, this is your child? I thought this was Ethel Kennedy's daughter Rory." Noelle was flabbergasted. "Were you trying to kidnap Rory?" she asked. "Yes," admitted the woman. An hour later, after she composed herself, Noelle called Ethel to report the attempted kidnapping. She told her not to worry; the perpetrator was in custody and she was pressing charges against her. "No, absolutely not," Ethel said. "You'll do no such thing." She then explained that if Noelle filed a police report, news of it might inspire copycat kidnappings of Kennedy children. "But if this was *your* child, I'm sure you would feel very differently," Noelle said, crying. "No," Ethel responded with icy reserve. "I assure you, Noelle, I would not."

"This incident put a real wedge between me and Mrs. Kennedy," Noelle Bombardier would recall many years later. "I simply couldn't understand how she would not want to press charges. 'In fact, I want you to just forget it ever happened,' she told me. Of course I couldn't do that. 'I'm sorry, Mrs. Kennedy,' I said, 'but I don't think I can work for you any longer under these circumstances. I'm going to have to quit.' She remained calm and told me to sleep on it. The next morning, I called and said I was driving back to Hickory Hill. 'But if you leave now, who will let the maids in to clean the house for my arrival?' she asked. 'I don't care about the maids,' I told her. 'I'm upset.' So I drove back and we really had it out. 'You are totally overreacting,' she told me. 'After all of these years, I can't believe you want to leave Hickory Hill over this one little incident. I don't want to lose you, Noelle.' I told her I just didn't feel safe, and the fact that she didn't care about what could have been a true disaster in my life really affected me. So, shortly after that, I left Hickory Hill. It was very painful to me. I loved Mrs. Kennedy and the entire Kennedy family."

Noelle and Ethel didn't see each other for more than twenty years. Then, at around the time of Ena Bernard's death, Noelle attended a benefit for the Daughters of the American Revolution in Washington, D.C. She happened to see Andy Williams's manager and went up to him to say that she knew the vocalist from her Hickory Hill days. "Why,

Mrs. Kennedy is here, too," he told her. "Why don't you come back after the show and say hello to Andy, and see Mrs. Kennedy as well?"

"Of course, my heart jumped a little," recalled Noelle. "It had been so many years and I still had so much emotion attached to Mrs. Kennedy. But I wasn't sure what her reaction would be to seeing me, considering the way we parted."

Following the show, Noelle went backstage. After greeting Ted Kennedy, she looked around and spotted Andy Williams, whose back was to her. She noticed he was speaking to someone, but she couldn't see who because he was blocking her vision. When he moved just slightly, Noelle saw that it was Ethel. As Andy continued to speak, Ethel stared over his shoulder at Noelle with a look of disbelief on her face. She patted Andy on the arm, said a few parting words to him, and then made a beeline to Noelle. "Oh my God, it can't be true," she said with tears in her eyes. "Is that you, Noelle? Is that really you?" Noelle smiled. "It's me," she said. "How are you, Mrs. Kennedy?" Ethel grabbed Noelle and pulled her into an embrace.

Noelle later recalled of the touching moment: "What can two people say when they know they'll probably have just a few moments together and there's so much rich history between them? We held each other tightly. I guess we didn't really need words."

"Just look at you," Ethel said as she pulled away. "My God. I can't believe it."

"The years sure have passed," Noelle said, "but tell me the truth," she added with a smile. "We still look pretty good, don't you think, Mrs. Kennedy?"

Ethel took in her old friend from head to toe and smiled. "Heck, yeah, we do, kid," she said, laughing. "You bet we do."

WHAT BINDS US

The Edward M. Kennedy Institute for the United States Senate — a facility to educate the public, students, and anyone interested in the work and duties of the United States Senate — was formally dedicated on March 30, 2015. The ceremony featured speeches by President Barack Obama (who was accompanied by First Lady Michelle Obama) and Vice President Joe Biden. Other speakers included Massachusetts governor Charlie Baker; Boston mayor Martin J. Walsh; and Senators Elizabeth Warren, Ed Markey, and John McCain — introduced by Ted Kennedy Jr., who noted that "my father so enjoyed his collaboration with you for many, many years." A year earlier, Ted Jr. had surprised his friends and family by announcing his candidacy for a seat in the Connecticut state senate. He was elected in November 2014 and then reelected in 2016. Certainly his father, who never viewed his namesake as a political animal, would have been overjoyed.

Before introducing Joe Biden, Patrick Kennedy had a few words. Still looking youthful with his mop of reddish brown hair and in a suit that seemed a little too big for him, he said, "As I see this crowd here, I see my father, because all of you are a part of his life. And seeing you brings back great memories for me and my entire family." With tears in his eyes, he continued, "I want to take this moment before I have the honor of introducing the Vice President to acknowledge my mother . . . Joan Bennett Kennedy."

At the mention of Joan — who was now seventy-eight — the entire place erupted into applause. Then, within seconds, everyone — including family members such as Caroline Kennedy and Ed Schlossberg; Ted's widow, Victoria Reggie Kennedy; and his sister Jean Kennedy Smith; as well as the many dignitaries and officials present — all rose to their feet. Looking a bit frail, Joan — in a cream-colored coat, her blond hair falling to her slim shoulders — stood up from her seat in the front row to acknowledge the reception. Once everyone was reseated, Patrick noted, "Of course, my dad would be saying, 'Make sure you remember your mother.' " Then, pointing to the sky, he said, "So I did, Dad. I did."

After a number of speeches, Vicki was introduced. Looking elegant with her dark hair parted on the side and wearing a magenta-colored outfit with large pearls around her neck, she didn't appear to be a day older than she had been twenty years before when she married Ted. "Teddy loved the United States Senate," she said. "He hoped that everybody who came to this institute would know that politics — and he called it politics — is a noble profession, even if it's messy. Even if it's hard. We are Americans, he said, this is what we do. We reach the moon. We scale the heights. I know it. I've seen it. I've lived it." After much applause, she then introduced President Barack Obama.

It could be said that President Obama's eloquent words that day said as much about the many generations of Kennedys — what they've endured as a family and what they've tried to teach by their example, the good and the bad — as it did about the inspiring life and enduring legacy of the man of honor, Senator Edward M. Kennedy. Yes, terrible things have happened to the Kennedys, sometimes by fate and circumstance, sometimes by their own volition. But there have also been moments of . . . *greatness* and, who knows? Perhaps some of those moments inspired a few generations of Americans to do with their lives that which they might not have otherwise thought possible. Or, as President Obama noted:

"What binds us together across our differences in religion or politics or economic theory," Ted wrote in his memoir, "[is] . . . the capacity to reach across our differences to offer a hand of healing." For all the challenges of a changing world, for all the imperfections of our democracy, the capacity to reach across our differences is something that's entirely up to us.

May we all, in our own lives, set an example for the kids who enter these doors, and exit with higher expectations for their country. May we all remember the times this American family, the Kennedys, has challenged us to ask what we can do; to dream and say why not; to seek a cause that endures; and sail against the wind in its pursuit . . . and live our lives with that heightened sense of purpose.

EPILOGUE:
AMERICAN PROMISE

It was January 29, 2018. There he stood, looking robust behind a podium, like so many of his ancestors and relatives, in front of a nation of millions, the virtual embodiment of the hopes and dreams of not only a new generation of Kennedys but of those who still believed in the dream and in a family that had always personified that dream. He was Joseph Patrick Kennedy III, Democratic representative of Massachusetts' Fourth Congressional District — the thirty-seven-year-old grandson of Bobby and great-nephew of Jack. Though he'd been serving for five years, this was the first time many people in America had ever laid eyes on Joe. As he stood before America in a light purple shirt and maroon tie with no jacket, his demeanor and personality shone through loud and clear. He was pure Kennedy — the artful connection with his audience, the eyes alert and sincere, the cadence of his language reminding some of his father, Joe, during his

892

political heyday. He also displayed a quality many critics of Donald J. Trump, the President who'd just given his State of the Union address, felt was perhaps lacking in him: empathy. Most politicians will tell you that it can't be faked. Either you care about people or you don't. Of Trump's White House, he said:

This administration is not just targeting the laws that protect us, they are targeting the very idea that we are all worthy of protection. For them, dignity is not something you are born with, but something you measure by your net worth, your celebrity, your headlines, your crowd size. Not to mention the gender of your spouse, the country of your birth, the color of your skin, the God of your prayers. Their record has rebuked our highest American ideals, the belief that we are all equal, that we all count in the eyes of our laws, our leaders, our God, and our government. That is the American promise.

As he spoke, Joe Kennedy exuded self-assurance and power; in every way, he was a Kennedy mastering his moment and reminding some of the way President John F. Kennedy had handled himself in the historic televised presidential debate with Richard M. Nixon in 1960. The response to him the next day would be overwhelmingly positive. Most media outlets agreed that he was a real up-and-comer, someone to keep an eye on, which, of course, is what the Kennedy family had been saying about him for years.

Joe III is one of twin boys born in 1980 to Joseph P. Kennedy II and Sheila Rauch. He was born just two months after his uncle Teddy abandoned his presidential aspirations in 1980. He was six when his father was elected to Congress, eleven when his parents divorced, seventeen when his mother's book, *Shattered Faith,* was published, which helped ignite the fire that eventually consumed his father's political career.

At twenty-three, after graduating from Stanford in 2003, Joe joined the Peace Corps, an important foundation of the family's legacy established so long ago by his great-uncles Jack and Sarge. At twenty-six in 2006, he and his brother, Matthew, worked for their uncle Ted's reelection campaign before he enrolled in Harvard Law School. He graduated at twenty-nine and went on to work at the Cape and Islands office as an assistant district attorney. In 2011, he joined the Middlesex County district attorney's office. A year later, he officially entered politics, running in the Fourth Congressional District for the newly vacated seat of the retiring Barney Frank. Others had considered opposing him, but there was no point; he was a shoo-in not only because of his family's popularity in the state but because he just seemed to have "it" — again, that ineffable quality that makes a politician. He won against Republican Sean Bielat with 61 percent of the vote. He won again in 2014 and then again in 2016.

Despite the disappointing end to his father's political career, Joe refused to be discouraged when it came to public service. Paying heed to his grandmother Ethel's admonitions, he always knew he would serve in some capacity. He inherited the burden of expectation and didn't mind it; he embraced it. "I grew up around politics," he told *Boston* magazine. "But I think politics is a unique field in that you have to put yourself out there in a very public way for the entire world to see. People think my family pushed me into running for office. The person who pushed me most *not* to run for office was my father. He said, 'If you don't want to do this, it is going to be an absolutely brutal experience for you. So make sure that this is something that you yourself want to do and not some sort of invented idea of obligation.' And that's some of the best advice I've ever gotten."

Joe married Lauren Anne Birchfield, an attorney, in December 2012; they met in Harvard Law School, students of future senator Elizabeth Warren. They have had a happy marriage and are now the parents of a daughter, Eleanor "Ellie," born on December 29,

2015, and a son, James Matthew, born on December 20, 2017.

Joe's twin brother, Matthew, who studied business at Stanford and Harvard, is a partner at InfraLinx Capital, an international project development and finance company. He's the oldest of the twins by eight minutes, which he jokes were the "greatest eight minutes of my life. It's all been downhill from there." He has been married to Katherine Lee Manning since 2012, their wedding having taken place at the Kennedy compound, of course.

Many of the Kennedy men of Joe's generation have not had the kinds of troubled personal relationships that characterized their parents' experiences. As this fourth generation of Kennedys steps into the light of public scrutiny, it would seem they've learned some important lessons about fidelity and commitment by watching their mothers and fathers duke it out over the years. Also, to their great advantage, this new generation doesn't have to deal with the same kind of trauma suffered by their parents; after all, they're one generation removed from the murders that so deeply affected their older relatives.

"Joe III and [his brother] Matt were raised by a mom [Sheila Rauch] who taught them to respect women," said Gayle Fee, who covered the Kennedys for thirty years for the *Boston Herald.* "It was a different generation in many ways. Many of the boys of that era

— and these would be the grandkids of Ethel and the rest — were raised by strong women like Sheila and like Michael's widow, Vicki. These were women who didn't put up with a lot of nonsense for long. When Sheila was unhappy in her marriage, she did something about it; she divorced Joe and then fought the annulment he sought. Then she wrote that book. So her sons saw a strong, determined woman they could respect. It was a new day, all right. Sheila raised those boys on her own and kept them away from any bad influences."

Joseph Patrick Kennedy III wants nothing more than to continue the legacy of his great American dynasty, the Kennedys. Named after his great-grandfather, the family patron and architect of all their dreams and ambitions, Joe is proud of what his ancestors have achieved. It doesn't seem as if he feels he's surrounded by, as Lem Billings once put it, "footprints, all of them deeper than his own." Rather, one has a sense that Joe walks in tandem with his forebearers while charting his own political course with his own special brand of big-hearted liberalism. Especially given Ted Kennedy Jr.'s announcement in February 2018 that he would not run for a third term in the state senate, all eyes have been on Joe to continue to carry the torch for the family.

Joe serves because he wants to, though, not

because he feels he must. Things have definitely changed in that regard in the Kennedy family. The pressure to be a public servant has dissipated with time, and maybe that's for the best. Some of the new generation is involved in philanthropy, while some have no interest in it. For instance, Ethel's granddaughter Michaela Cuomo, daughter of Kerry Kennedy and Andrew Cuomo, is an activist intent on raising money for sexual assault awareness. Kyra LeMoyne Kennedy — Bobby Kennedy Jr.'s daughter with the late Mary Richardson Kennedy — seems a little less invested in social activism. Unfortunately for her, at least for the time being, she'll probably be best known for her great comeback to a bouncer after being refused entry into a club because she was nineteen in 2015: "I'm a Kennedy," she screamed at him. *"Google me."* She followed that classic line with a threat for the ages: "If you don't let me in, the governor will be calling." A year later, her father insisted she shut down all her social media when she fought back at a blogger who had criticized her and her friends. "I can play games, too, bitch!" she posted. Kyra is twenty-three as of this writing. "She'll learn," Bobby Jr. said of his daughter. "Give her time. You should've seen *me* at that age." Two years later, her twenty-two-year-old cousin, Caroline Summer Rose Kennedy — one of Max Kennedy's three kids

— would make a few headlines with her own memorable line when she and her father were arrested for disturbing the peace during a house party in Hyannis Port: "You don't know who you're messing with," she exclaimed. "I went to Brown and I'm a teacher, *sweetheart.*" The charges against father and daughter were eventually dismissed.

Despite the personal tumult her venture into politics had caused her back in 2008, Caroline Kennedy still knew she wanted to serve her country in some way. She knew it was what her uncle Teddy had wanted, too. What she didn't know was how she might satisfy the family's mandate while at the same time maintaining her privacy and also staying out of the line of fire of partisan politics. In early 2013, the right opportunity presented itself when President Barack Obama, grateful for her support during his campaign, asked her to be his nominee for the job of United States ambassador to Japan, succeeding Ambassador John Roos.

In September 2013, Caroline sat before the Senate Foreign Relations Committee to answer myriad questions from Democratic and Republican senators about possible platforms and ideas. She'd come a long way in just a few years' time. Now she presented herself as a completely different woman from the one five years earlier, who'd seemed unable to answer a simple question without becoming defensive. On this day, she was confident and calm, eager to put forth her ideas, anxious to impress and to be approved. If given the opportunity, she said, she wanted to focus on student exchange programs as well as military concerns and trade relations. In October, she was approved by unanimous vote as the first female United States ambassador to Japan.

For the next three years, Caroline would spend most of her time in Japan, though she and her family would also reside as much as possible in the States. Though her job was, for the most part, ceremonial, as are the duties of most ambassadors, it was the perfect fit for her in that it satisfied her desire to serve yet didn't expose her to much controversy. When she resigned from the position in 2017 it was only because political appointees of one administration generally don't stay on for the next one; President Donald J. Trump had ordered all Obama appointees to resign before his inauguration without giving them the customary extension to get their affairs in order.

Caroline moved back to the United States full-time, and she and Ed live in New York today.

Besides Joseph P. Kennedy III, another young Kennedy in whom people seem intensely interested is the only grandson of President Kennedy — Caroline and Ed's son, John Bouvier Kennedy Schlossberg, better known as Jack. Born in 1993, as he reached adulthood and became more high profile, it was clear that Jack was well-spoken and ready for the attention.

Jack, a member of the John F. Kennedy Library New Frontier Award Committee, has become a confident speaker with the passing of time. In November 2013, he introduced Barack Obama at the Medal of Freedom award dinner commemorating the fiftieth anniversary of his grandfather's assassination. A member of the committee for the Profile in Courage Awards, he also hosted the ceremony in 2014. He's often involved in high-profile Kennedy honors and makes numerous television appearances to talk about them.

A Yale graduate (2015) with a history degree focused on Japanese history, Jack is presently attending Harvard Law School.

Though she appears to take the public's growing fascination with her son in her stride, people with knowledge of the situation say that Caroline is keenly interested in seeing him pursue politics. "Caroline is a kingmaker," said family friend R. Couri Hay, "a *Kennedy* kingmaker. The family is always looking to see who amongst them will rise to the pinnacle of power. All eyes are on Jack. Some of the other Kennedys, with the excep-

901

tion of Joe III, will likely fade away while Caroline anoints Jack as, forgive me for saying it, the crown prince of Camelot. It's Caroline, with her vision and her ability to look back in history with moral judgment, who gets to decide when he's ready to assume the mantle of her father and his grandfather."

One character trait Jack — who is now twenty-six — has in common with his uncle John Kennedy Jr. is his openness; he seems to have no fear of public scrutiny. Maybe that's ironic given that ever since he was a child, his mother has cautioned him to be leery of others. He has rejected that advice, as have his sisters, Rose, thirty-one, and Tatiana, twenty-nine.

Rose is a Harvard graduate with a degree in English who got her master's in the Interactive Telecommunications Program at NYU's Tisch School of the Arts. She's also a comedian who wrote a digital web series called *End Times Girls Club*. Tatiana is a Yale graduate whose internship with *The New York Times* led to a job as an environmental reporter for that newspaper.

Robert Kennedy Jr. married Cheryl Hines in 2014. From all accounts, the two have had a happy union, with Bobby's rabble-rousing days long behind him. He has also apparently conquered his sexual addiction. He and his mother, Ethel, with whom he'd long had a contentious relationship, have had a détente for many years now. "I was also able to recognize that my mother's passing storms of nettlesome temper were mainly the fruit of her own personal miseries, and I began to see the extraordinary qualities in her character," he wrote in his memoir, *American Values.* "She always put her children first, while understanding that 'I love you' and 'No' could be part of the same sentence."

Bobby has continued his tireless advocacy for environmental issues. He continues to argue, for instance, that vaccines containing mercury are unsafe for children. While he's not opposed to all vaccines, he does seek to make them safer.

Recently, Bobby set his sights on unraveling the mystery of his father's murder. He's long suspected that Sirhan Sirhan didn't act alone and was possibly not even the shooter. As he points out, the autopsy report indicates that Kennedy was shot at point-blank range from behind, including a fatal shot behind his ear. Sirhan was standing in front of him.

In December 2017, Bobby had what must have been an incredible experience of visiting Sirhan Sirhan at the Richard J. Donovan Correctional Facility outside San Diego, where he has been imprisoned for nearly fifty years. "I went there because I was curious and disturbed by what I had seen in the evidence," said Bobby, who was sixty-three at the time. "I was disturbed that the wrong person might have been convicted of killing my father. My father was the chief law enforcement officer in this country. I think it would have disturbed him if somebody was put in jail for a crime they didn't commit."

With Cheryl waiting in the car outside the facility, Bobby spoke to Sirhan Sirhan for about three hours. As of this writing, he hasn't yet revealed what he learned, but he's now more convinced than ever that, while somehow likely involved, Sirhan Sirhan didn't kill his father. It's been reported that he plans to examine all angles in a book that he's writing about the subject.

POSTSCRIPT: PERMISSION TO SPEAK FREELY

On April 11, 2018, Ethel Kennedy turned ninety. All her children and many of her grandchildren celebrated the milestone with a party a month later in Palm Beach, Florida, where she resides for about half the year (the other half being spent at her home at the Kennedy compound). As expected, during the festivities there was no shortage of robust, Kennedy-esque speeches from some of Ethel's grown children, such as Kathleen, Joe, and Bobby Jr. The grandchildren — more than thirty — also came forth with home-made cards and other demonstrations of great affection for "Grandma."

Ethel's life has been a long and incredible journey full of breathtaking highs and crushing lows, so much of it entwined with rich and important American history. She remains, even at her advanced age, a vital woman, still eager to serve. "In recent years, my mother has made more than a dozen human rights pilgrimages to deliver food and medical supplies, repatriate refugees, afflict the tyrannical, and comfort the afflicted," Bobby Kennedy wrote in 2018. "By standing up to bigotry, corporate misbehavior, and confronting cowardly or venal public officials, whether on the left or the right, she has won freedom for prisoners of conscience all over the world." Her daughter Kerry has noted of her mother's most recent humanitarian efforts: "She's gone on human rights delegations to Namibia, Albania, Czechoslovakia, Haiti, Hungary, Kenya, Mexico, Northern Ireland, Poland, and South Africa."

In June, Ethel took part in a symbolic one-day hunger strike organized by the RFK Human Rights Center protesting the Trump administration's policy of separating families at the border to Mexico. Almost fifty other members of the Kennedy family participated, including Ethel's daughter Kerry and her grandson Massachusetts Representative Joe Kennedy III. "Generations of Americans did not toil and sacrifice to build a country where children and their parents are placed in cages to advance a cynical political agenda," she said.

"So many people in our family are involved in social justice work, and it's always attributed to my father, which he deserves," Kerry notes. "But the truth is he died when we were very, very young, so that really comes from my mother. Those are *her* values. Those are the aspects of Daddy that she chose to have us remember and think about."

Even though Ethel remains an activist for social justice and human rights, it's her influence over the entire Kennedy family that best defines her. She remains the head of the dynasty with more than one hundred family members. She once called Ted the "keeper of the castle," a title that most certainly now defines her. President Barack Obama was sure to point out as much back in 2014, when he awarded her the Presidential Medal of Freedom:

. . . we give thanks to a person whose love for her family is matched by her devotion to her nation. To most Americans, Ethel Kennedy is known as a wife, mother, and grandma. And in many ways, it's through these roles that she's made her mark on history. As Bobby Kennedy's partner in life, she shared his commitment to justice. After his death, she continued their work through the center she created in his name, celebrating activists and journalists and educating people around the world about threats to human liberty. On urgent human rights issues of our time — from juvenile justice to environmental destruction — Ethel has been a force for change in her quiet, flashy — unflashy, unstoppable way. As her family will tell you, and they basically occupy this half of the room, you don't mess with Ethel.

That same year, Ethel went on camera, along with her son Max and many young members of the Kennedy's fourth generation, to take the ALS Ice Bucket Challenge. Probably nothing demonstrates more how much things have changed in her world than seeing the family's redoubtable matriarch — a woman for whom people would jump to their feet when she entered a room — raise a plastic bucket over her head and drench herself with freezing-cold water.

The day after her birthday, Ethel's old friend Sister Pauline Joseph called to extend her congratulations. Though she'd been retired for the last twenty years, she'd stayed in touch with Ethel. She found her in an unusually contemplative mood.

Ethel noted that even though she has few of the infirmities of the aged, she does use a wheelchair from time to time. She couldn't help but remember when Joseph and Rose Kennedy were similarly confined. Joe lived to be eighty-one, his storied life interrupted by and ultimately ended by a stroke. Rose, despite her own strokes, lived to be 104. "I'm sure that's not for me, though," Ethel said of Rose's longevity. "I'll be ready to go sooner than that."

In a long-ranging conversation that seemed

like a meditation on her life, Ethel had to admit to certain regrets. This was unusual for her; she's definitely not a woman given to much introspection, preferring to live her life in the moment. "While I've accepted who I was as a mother," Ethel told the nun, "it's sometimes harder to accept who I *wasn't.*"

She said that she still struggles with the reasons she wasn't more equipped to handle David's and Michael's problems. However, she now understands how uninformed she and everyone else in the family were about the realities of addiction. She grapples with the senselessness of John's airplane crash, too. "However, she's comforted knowing he's with Jack and Jackie in heaven," said the nun. "She feels the same about David and Michael being with Bobby."

"I do think about the girls a lot," Ethel said. She then spoke a little about Carolyn Bessette-Kennedy and Mary Richardson Kennedy. Both young women had come into the family with such excitement and hope for the future but then found themselves so completely disillusioned because, as Ethel aptly put it, "being a Kennedy isn't for the faint of heart." The one question that still haunts her about Carolyn all these years later, she said, was "*Why* in the world did she have to get on that plane?"

In the end, Ethel said, she now understood that almost everything that had happened to her generation of Kennedys as well as to the next one was in one way or the other intrinsically tied to the murders of Bobby and Jack. She'd spent years believing that blaming their deaths for subsequent misfortunes was a way to excuse bad behavior. Now, at ninety, she said she finally understood that "you just don't get over something like that. People think you move on, but guess what? You don't. Then again," she said, "nobody gets a free ride in this world. Pain is a part of life. You can't escape it." She also said that not a day goes by when she doesn't think about all Bobby and Jack missed of seeing the generation that followed their own, and even the one after that. She still prays on her knees every day for both brothers, as well as for Ted, Jackie, Eunice, Sarge, and everyone else who has passed. "Maybe they're all sitting around in heaven agreeing that I could've handled a few things differently, though," Ethel concluded.

"Permission to speak freely?" Sister Pauline Joseph asked, just as she'd always done over the years before becoming candid. Ethel said, of course. The nun began, "Please have no regrets about —" But Ethel interrupted her, saying she didn't have any, "not a one."

"You were a good mother, Mrs. Kennedy," continued her friend. "You loved your children with everything you —"

Ethel cut her off again. *"I know that,"* she

said, seeming a little annoyed. Irascible as ever, she would never change.

"She then asked how long we've known each other," recalled Sister Pauline Joseph. "I had to really think about that one. 'Gosh,' I said. 'Going on sixty years, I would imagine. Can you believe it, Mrs. Kennedy?' "

According to the nun, Ethel was quiet for a moment, maybe pondering the passing of so much shared history. "We sure have had our moments, haven't we?" she finally asked. "And with that being the case," she continued, "don't you think it's time to start calling me . . . *Ethel*? After all, we're not getting any younger, are we?"

"*That's* certainly food for thought," said Sister Pauline Joseph, surprised. Then, after a moment's hesitation, she thought better of it: "Okay, well, goodbye for now . . . *Mrs. Kennedy.*"

Ethel had to laugh. "Yes, Sister," she said as she hung up. "Goodbye for now."

AUTHOR'S NOTE

It has been my great honor to write about the Kennedys for the last twenty years. I completed the manuscript for my first book about them, *Jackie, Ethel, Joan,* in 1999. It was published a year later. I immediately began working on the next one, *The Kennedys: After Camelot.* Though I became sidetracked by a number of other biographies, *The Kennedys: After Camelot* was always a chief concern of mine; the research for it continued for ten years. It was finally published in 2012. Six years later, in 2018, I wrote *Jackie, Janet & Lee,* a history of the *other* side of Jackie's family, the Bouviers and the Auchinclosses, and, of course, their relationships to the Kennedys.

Jackie, Ethel, Joan and *After Camelot* were both produced as successful television miniseries, and *Jackie, Janet & Lee* is in production as I write this note.

You now hold in your hands my fourth Kennedy book, *The Kennedy Heirs.*

913

I've always been fascinated by the third generation of Kennedys, who are the primary subjects of this book, having met and interviewed many of them over the years. For instance, I have a memory of Michael Kennedy that stands out for me. In the spring of 1997, when I was researching *Jackie, Ethel, Joan,* I sought access to certain oral histories in the John Fitzgerald Kennedy Library and Museum. (Today most of them are online, but back then one actually had to go to the library and get permission to view the transcripts or hear the tapes.) I had met Michael at a fund-raiser for his brother Joe in Boston and asked if he could help me access what I needed. He was hesitant. Still, we exchanged numbers. A week later, he called me at my home in Los Angeles and said he would accompany me to the library and help me pull the material I needed for my book.

As I noted in the text of this book, Michael sat behind me for six hours and watched me as I attempted to do my research. "Michael, I'm okay here, really," I told him. "You can go." He shook his head. "No. Not until you do." He was protective of his family's legacy, and I had to respect as much. He even asked to see my notes when I finished. He had taken his own and wanted to compare. With nothing to hide, I agreed. He sat and reviewed everything, nodding his head and smiling. He even crossed out a few lines.

Afterward, seeking to break the ice with him, I suggested a cup of coffee. He agreed, though, again, he seemed reluctant. We then spent about ninety minutes talking about our childhoods, mine lived anonymously in the suburbs in Philadelphia, his as a public person, a Kennedy, at Hickory Hill, his mother's estate in Virginia, and also at the Kennedy compound on Cape Cod. "I was always on the outside looking in," he said, "but it was okay. I didn't mind it." I asked him to elaborate, but he wouldn't. When I asked what his mother was like, he smiled and said: "Depends on the day." I didn't ask about the recent scandal relating to Marisa Verrochi, but he brought it up if just by suggestion. "I'm rebuilding my life," he told me. "When I finish the reconstruction I'll give you a real interview." I asked if he saw a future for himself in politics. He laughed and said, "Not now I don't." Then he added that it was okay; "Some people have a taste for blood. Some don't."

Months later, when I was writing the acknowledgments to *Jackie, Ethel, Joan,* I wanted to acknowledge Michael's assistance. I sent him the brief mention I wanted to publish, a couple of sentences thanking him. He called me a few days later and asked me not to acknowledge him. He said he didn't know what the tone of the book would be and didn't want to be seen as condoning it.

That was fair. Six months after that, he was gone.

I had met John Kennedy Jr. several times prior to meeting Michael, the first time many years earlier. I couldn't help but be struck by the differences in their personalities: Michael so removed and cautious, John so available and easy to know.

The first time I met John and his sister, Caroline, was back in 1977 at the famous Studio 54 nightclub in New York. My friend Michael Jackson was filming *The Wiz* in New York at the time; I was there writing a story about the movie for a magazine. It was a private party in a back room at Studio 54 for some of the cast and crew. John and Caroline were surrounded by press, as was Michael. I was sitting at a back booth with his sister La Toya. Occasionally, Michael would come over and say a few words to us and then drift back into the crowd. At one point, La Toya got up to go to the restroom. Someone took her place, slipping into the booth. He leaned over to me, put out his hand, and introduced himself: "I'm John Kennedy." Then he said, "Can I ask you a favor?" JFK Jr. wants a favor? From me? "My sister and I want to meet Michael Jackson," he said with a bashful grin. "Can you make that happen?" It was the kind of surreal moment that, looking back on it all these years later, is hard to believe. "Sure thing," I said. He called Caroline over, we went over to Michael, and I introduced them. Michael seemed a little weak in the knees, I remember; just being in the presence of Kennedy royalty seemed to throw him.

After a few moments of chitchat, I took a couple of pictures of Michael with John and Caroline using John's camera. Afterward, I sat at the bar and talked to John for about an hour. He was seventeen, and I wasn't much older. I don't even remember what we talked about, I just remember his incredible smile and his open spirit. I also remember thinking to myself that this guy could be anyone's best friend, he was just that nice. I guess I was a little swept away by him. His sister? Not so much. I'm pretty sure she didn't say a word to me that night, or if she did I don't recall it. I just remember her eyeing me with suspicion. "She doesn't trust reporters," John said with a laugh.

Years later, John's mother would go on to edit Michael's book *Moonwalk.* In the mid-1980s, I had the chance to know Jackie Onassis while she was at Doubleday, where I published my first two books. Years after that, a few of the pictures of Michael, John, and Caroline that I took somehow leaked out, and anyone can find them today on the internet.

Both Kennedys — Michael and John — were raised by traumatized mothers, but in different ways. It's of course their differences that make them so compelling, their stories that make them so unique. Both are gone now, and missed by so many.

General Comment

The vast majority of material in this book was culled from more than four hundred interviews conducted by myself and my researchers over the last twenty years. When an author specializes in a subject as I have the Kennedys, he collects a massive amount of firsthand interviews with principal players in American history. Many of those sources find their way into more than one book; some interviews conducted many years ago for one book find their way into other works as they become relevant to stories being told. I make sure that the vast majority of my interviews are on tape. Occasionally, though, a source is squeamish about being recorded, and in that case I or the researcher will take copious notes.

From traveling the world and talking about my work, I know that readers are always interested in the interview process. I can state that in almost all cases my interview subjects are pressed for answers not just in a single session but in many encounters over the course of years. I've spent as many as forty hours with a single source, going back to confirm information, to ask for details that would never be thought of as relevant but, for me, are important elements of storytelling. It's not unusual for me to have a source scour an attic for months to find a picture of a Kennedy just so that I could state without question that he or she was at a certain event at a certain time. Many of my sources will tell you that I have driven them out of their minds, but I do it for the sake of accuracy.

I've been in the business of documenting Kennedy history for more than twenty years, long enough to have made significant contacts inside the family. Specifically for this book, I conducted a number of important interviews with not only members of the Kennedy family but with others involved in their history on a "deep background" basis, which means I've agreed to use all their information but to not identify them as sources. This method is crucial sometimes in achieving the kind of candor required by a book like this one. Nearly all these interviews were conducted on tape, allowing me to be precise in my reporting.

Note also that most of the secondary sources utilized in this book — texts of speeches, transcriptions of television shows, and other videos — have been cited in the text and, with some exceptions allowing for a little more detail, will not be repeated here. Obviously, I also referred to countless books and newspaper accounts; I've only listed here the ones I thought might inspire further inter-

RESEARCH

The Kennedy Heirs would not have been possible without the assistance of many organizations that provided me with articles, documents, audio and video interviews, transcripts, and other material that was either utilized directly in this book or just for purposes of background, especially the John F. Kennedy Presidential Library and Museum. I want to especially thank Maryrose Grossman for her assistance over the years in accessing the library's archives. I would also like to thank Megan Woods at the library for her help. As I do with all of my Kennedy-related books, I must also acknowledge David Powers, former special assistant to President John F. Kennedy and the first curator of the JFK Library. I was lucky enough to interview him back on January 11, 1990, and a lot of that material is used in this book, if only for background. Certainly, no mention of the JFK Library is complete without a nod to Mr. Powers, who died on

921

March 28, 1998, at the age of eighty-five.

The Edward M. Kennedy Institute for the United States Senate in Boston was a great resource for me. Thank you to Natalie Boyle there for her assistance.

I want to especially thank Noelle Bombardier, who was the estate manager at Hickory Hill. She gave us numerous interviews for this book and shared many memories of her life with Ethel Kennedy, and I am deeply indebted to her. She's a wonderful woman who has great respect for Ethel as she does for all of the Kennedys; she always looks back with fondness on her years with the family, and I so value her contribution to all of my books about the Kennedys.

I also want to make special mention of Josefina "Fina" Harvin, Ena Bernard's daughter. Ena worked for Ethel Kennedy for more than forty years, and Josefina was all but raised at Hickory Hill and the Kennedy compound during much of that time. I want to thank her for all her assistance with this book.

In the hopes of meeting Rosemary (Rose Marie) Kennedy, I visited St. Coletta's in Wisconsin in 1998, the nursing home in which she was cared for, during my research for *Jackie, Ethel, Joan.* While I was able to meet and speak to her, I was, unfortunately, unable to formally interview her. However, it was at this time that I met one of the Roman

Catholic nuns who had cared for Rosemary and who, as it would happen, would become a primary source for this book, *The Kennedy Heirs*. Because she asked not to be identified, in these pages, she and I agreed on giving her the pseudonym "Sister Pauline Joseph." This is the first time in the writing of twenty books — based on easily more than two thousand interviews — that I've ever employed the use of a pseudonym for a source. However, I felt it necessary in this case to grant the request because the source still has close ties with the Kennedy family and felt that her memories might compromise some of those relationships. I want to thank her for the many interviews she granted me for this work. I conducted six interviews with her in 2017 and three more in 2018.

I want to especially thank Cathy Griffin for all her hard work on this book. This one presented a real challenge in that there are so many moving parts. As always, Cathy found just the right people for us to interview and was present for them and supportive as they told stories that were sometimes sensitive. She has been my primary researcher since 1990 and I am eternally grateful to her.

I had to hit the ground running with this book, doing the vast majority of interviews for it myself in Boston, Washington, New York, and Los Angeles. It was an amazing and worthwhile two years on the road, and I have to say I enjoyed it tremendously. Thanks to all the many people I met in the process who gave me insight into one of the most powerful and influential family dynasties of our time.

In Memoriam

Many of the stories I have told over the years are as much about my sources and their life experiences as they are about the subjects of my book, in this case the Kennedys. Often I am trusted to be a messenger for precious memories shared with me for the first time. Because I am always conscious of the fact that these stories will remain indelible in my books long after the storytellers are gone from this world, I take very seriously my obligation to be accurate, fair, and as *caring* as possible in my writing about their thoughts, feelings, and recollections. Since, sadly, some of my most trusted sources have passed away, I would like to remember them here.

I would like to acknowledge Leah Mason, who gave me more than a dozen interviews over the years relating to her life and time at Hickory Hill. I could never have written this book or my others about the Kennedys without her assistance. She also allowed me access to her unpublished manuscript, *Ethel Kennedy and Life at Hickory Hill,* which was of tremendous help to me. Sadly, Leah passed away in October 2018 at the age of ninety. She will be greatly missed.

John Perry-Barlow was a valuable source of mine for all of my Kennedy books, including this one. John had many vocations in his lifetime — lyricist for the Grateful Dead among them — but what most impressed me was his work in helping us understand the responsibility of the internet, which he once described in an essay for the Electronic Frontier Foundation as "a world that all may enter without privilege or prejudice accorded by race, economic power, military force, or station of birth . . . a world where anyone, anywhere may express his or her beliefs, no matter how singular, without fear of being coerced into silence or conformity." John was a cattle rancher, which is how he met and befriended John Kennedy Jr.; Jackie sent her son, who was seventeen at the time, to intern on his ranch. He had so many fascinating moments with Kennedy over the years, all the way up to John's untimely death, many of which are told in this book for the first time. He was a singularly unique person. John Perry Barlow died on February 7, 2018. He was seventy.

I would also like to acknowledge Christopher Lawford, whom I interviewed several times over the years. The first time I met Christopher was back in 1996 when I was working on my book about Frank Sinatra. As

Peter Lawford's son, of course Christopher had his fair share of amazing Sinatra tales as passed down to him by his father. His mom, Pat Kennedy-Lawford, was one of Marilyn Monroe's best friends, and Christopher shared with me many stories of knowing Marilyn as a child, which I used in my book about Monroe. Over the years as I began to write about the Kennedys, Christopher could be counted on to tell a new story, verify an old one, or provide context or understanding to an anecdote that would only make sense to someone born a Kennedy. He was also an inspiring motivational speaker and wrote several wonderful books, which are acknowledged in my Source Notes. He will be greatly missed by so many people. Christopher left us on September 4, 2018. He was sixty-three.

Webster Janssen was an important source of mine not only for this book but also for *The Kennedys: After Camelot.* Though they were distantly related, he and Joan Kennedy were close, and I so appreciated his stories of how he tried to help her. In the process, of course, he found himself in opposition to her grown children who were also looking out for her best interests. It's a complicated story and I remain grateful to him that he trusted me with it. Mr. Janssen died on May 29, 2012.

I would also like to remember Dr. David Sugarbaker, professor and chief, Division of

Thoracic Surgery at the Baylor College of Medicine, Houston, Texas. I so appreciated his time and patience in helping me tell the story of his time with Kara Kennedy when he was chief of thoracic surgery at Dana-Farber/Brigham and she was his patient. "Her courage and the way she approached her illness has never been explored," he said, "and I think it's maybe an example of how to deal with adversity, a story which maybe can inspire and encourage others in similar situations." Through the telling of his memories here for the first time, I do think Kara's bravery comes into clear focus for us, and for that we owe a debt of gratitude to Dr. Sugarbaker. Sadly, he died on August 29, 2018, at the age of sixty-five.

Another wonderful woman who gave so much of her time to me was Adora Rule, who worked for Jackie's mother, Janet Auchincloss, as an assistant for many years; she started with Janet when she was just eighteen, right before Jackie married Jack in September 1953. They remained friends until Janet's death in 1989. Adora was a valuable source not only for this book but for my previous one, *Jackie, Janet & Lee.* I was so sorry to learn that she passed away in October 2018, at the age of eighty-three.

I would like to acknowledge the late Kennedy historian Lester David. For a while, we were with the same publisher, Carol Publish-

SOURCES AND OTHER NOTES

John Kennedy Jr. and Carolyn Bessette-Kennedy

Interviews: Ariel Paredes (August 1, 2017); R. Couri Hay (July 2, 2010, September 16, 2017, September 18, 2017); Hugh "Yusha" Auchincloss III (October 12, 1998, November 1, 1999); Nini Auchincloss Strait (October 11, 1998); George Smathers (October 5, 1998, December 12, 1998); John Perry Barlow (February 1, 1999, April 15, 2015, August 28, 2017, September 10, 2017); Sister Pauline Joseph (March 1, 2011, March 1, 2017); Gustavo Paredes (August 20, 2016, October 7, 2016, July 21, 2017); Stephen Styles-Cooper (May 1, 1998, April 15, 2005, May 11, 2010, June 18, 2015); Stewart Price (July 12, 2013, September 1, 2016, February 1, 2018); Tammy Holloway (May 31, 2010, June 2, 2010); Bryan Holloway (June 1, 2010); Richard Bradley (June 5, 2010, September 14, 2017, October 1, 2017); Holly Safford (May 15, 2010); Phillip Bloch (May

20, 2010); Virgil McLyn (May 31, 2010); Christopher Lawford (May 5, 1998, August 3, 2009, September 2, 2017, January 23, 2018).

Jacqueline Kennedy Onassis's commentary about celebrity biographies — "what would be the point of writing about a celebrity if you weren't going to reveal his or her secrets," etc. — was made to the author in 1985 at Doubleday Publishing Company.

John Kennedy Jr.'s commentary about the responsibility of media was to the author after the announcement of his *George* magazine enterprise on September 7, 1995, in New York's Federal Hall.

"Slightly more frightening . . ." Madonna to the author, June 1989.

The man at the center of Carolyn's "emotional affair" asked to not be identified.

Max Kennedy's commentary relating to his family's view of the press (". . . there's a perception that we Kennedys are opposed to the public having a fuller understanding of who we are, of what makes us tick") was to the author in 1998 at a book party celebrating the release of his work, *Make Gentle the Life of This World: The Vision of Robert F. Kennedy.*

President John F. Kennedy's speech ("The hour of decision has arrived. We cannot afford to wait and see what happens while the tide of events sweeps over and beyond us . . .") was given to the National Association of Manufacturers at the Waldorf-Astoria on December 6, 1961.

Articles: "Story of JFK Jr.: A Profile of Courage" by Michael Kilian, *Chicago Tribune,* July 22, 1999; "How Caroline and John Remember Their Father" by David E. Powers, *McCall's,* November 1973; "Ted Kennedy's Memories of JFK" by Theodore Sorensen, *McCall's,* November 1973; "Crazy for Carolyn" by Tessa Namuth et. al., *Newsweek,* October 20, 1996; "JFK Jr.'s Final Journey" by Evan Thomas, *Newsweek,* August 1, 1999. I also drew from my extensive research for the two-part series I authored, "The Life and Loves of the Prince of Camelot," *Woman's Day,* July 26, 1999, as well as my three-part series, "JFK Jr. — Golden Child," *Star,* August 1999. Also, I started researching a book about JFK Jr. in 1998 and, upon his death, decided to switch to my book about the Kennedy wives, *Jackie, Ethel, Joan.* I've drawn from that original research for this volume.

Volumes: *Fairytale Interrupted: A Memoir of Life, Love, and Loss* by RoseMarie Terenzio; *What Remains: A Memoir of Fate, Friendship, and Love* by Carole Radziwill; *The Men We Became: My Friendship with John F. Kennedy, Jr.* by Robert T. Littell; *Jacqueline Kennedy Bouvier Onassis: A Life* by Donald Spoto; *The*

Bouviers: From Waterloo to the Kennedys and Beyond by John H. Davis; *Times to Remember* by Rose Fitzgerald Kennedy; *Mother American Night: My Life in Crazy Times* by John Perry Barlow.

Speeches: "Mud Wrestling with History: Snapshots of My Life as a Brother-in-Law to John F. Kennedy" by James Auchincloss.

Oral Histories: Dun Gifford/RFK Oral History Project; Roswell Gilpatric/JFK Library; Luella Hennessey/JFK Library; Robert Francis Kennedy/JFK Library.

Television: I drew from my research and report "JFK Jr.'s Argument with Carolyn," *Day & Date,* March 4, 1996.

Ethel Kennedy
Interviews: Noelle Bombardier (September 5, 2017, September 29, 2017, as well as all interviews conducted for *After Camelot* in 2012); James Skakel (January 3, 1997); Josefina "Fina" Harvin (January 9, 2017); Joseph Gargan (March 17, 1999 and follow-up email questionnaire, April 1, 1999, October 3, 2002, December 1, 2016); Andy Williams (August 1998, May 2002, January 2011); Gore Vidal (April 8, 1998, June 2, 1998, May 1, 2010); Jamie Auchincloss (November 7, 1999, May 2, 2008, May 3, 2008); Barry Davis (October 15, 2016); Danine Barber (November 11, 2016, November 12, 2016); Ann Skakel McCooey (September 12, 2017);

Leah Mason; Christopher Lawford.

Articles: "A Gift from Long Ago" by Bob Herbert, *The New York Times,* November 22, 2010; "The Kennedy of Hickory Hill" by Hays Gory, *Time,* August 25, 1969 (Note: This is Ethel Kennedy's only cover story in *Time*).

Volumes: I referred to my extensive research for my books *Jackie, Ethel, Joan* and *The Kennedys: After Camelot.* I also referenced *The Nine of Us: Growing Up Kennedy* by Jean Kennedy Smith; *The Kennedy Legacy* by Theodore C. Sorensen; *With Kennedy* by Pierre Salinger; *Rose Kennedy and Her Family: The Best and Worst of Their Lives and Times* by Barbara Gibson and Ted Schwarz; *Ethel Kennedy and Life at Hickory Hill* by Leah Mason (unpublished manuscript); *Life with Rose Kennedy: An Intimate Account* by Barbara Gibson and Caroline Latham; *Rose: A Biography of Rose Fitzgerald Kennedy* by Gail Cameron; *Moon River and Me: A Memoir* by Andy Williams.

Documentaries: *Ethel,* the 2012 HBO documentary directed by her daughter Rory Kennedy and written by her son-in-law Mark Bailey, from which I culled quotes from Christopher, Maxwell, and Courtney Kennedy.

The note from Jackie to Ethel ("My Ethel, I stayed up . . .") was put up for auction by

Heritage Auction Galleries in 2006. It has since been returned to the Kennedy family.

Kennedy Family History

Interviews: Eunice Kennedy Shriver (2002); Hugh Sidey; Neil Connolly (December 2, 1998, April 2, 2007); Theresa Lichtman (February 2, 2018); Christopher Lawford (October 20, 2009); Frank Mankiewicz (August 25, 1998); Dun Gifford; Ted Sorensen (April 1998; May 2008, in conjunction with the publication of his book *Counselor: A Life at the Edge of History;* March 2009); Patricia Seaton Lawford (June 1, 2017); Lois Aldrech (August 5, 2016, August 6, 2016); Arthur Schlesinger (March 1, 1997, March 28, 2003, April 18, 2006); Robert McNamara (June 2008); Jacques Lowe (December 15, 1998, July 11, 1999, November 7, 1999, October 12, 2000).

I also referenced the transcript of Mr. Sorensen's speech at the Charleston School of Law on February 23, 2010.

Eunice Kennedy Shriver's comment "I've come to believe that it's not what happened to our family . . ." is from the author's personal interview, 2002.

Kerry Kennedy's comment "It's difficult when your most private moments . . ." is from the author's interview with her after the symposium on Kennedy women at the JFK Library, October 1996.

Articles: "Oprah Talks to Maria Shriver," *O: The Oprah Magazine,* June 2008; "The Fall of the House of Kennedy" by Daniel Henninger, *The Wall Street Journal,* January 21, 2010.

Volumes: *In the Kennedy Kitchen: Recipes and Recollections of a Great American Family* by Neil Connolly and Elizabeth Benedict; *Symptoms of Withdrawal: A Memoir of Snapshots and Redemption* by Christopher Kennedy Lawford; *Moments of Clarity: Voices from the Front Lines of Addiction and Recovery* by Christopher Kennedy Lawford; *Fully Alive: Discovering What Matters Most* by Timothy Shriver; *A Good Man: Rediscovering My Father, Sargent Shriver* by Mark K. Shriver; *American Values: Lessons I Learned from My Family* by Robert F. Kennedy Jr.; *Jacqueline Kennedy: Historic Conversations on Life with John Kennedy* by Michael Beschloss; *Hostage to Fortune: The Letters of Joseph P. Kennedy* by Amanda Smith.

Documentaries: Note that throughout this book, I referenced the CNN documentary series *American Dynasties: The Kennedys,* from which I culled quotes by Robert Kennedy Jr., Patrick Kennedy, and Kathleen Kennedy Townsend. I, too, was a commentator on each of the six episodes of that CNN series.

Forum: "The Kennedy Women" at the John

Fitzgerald Kennedy Library and Museum, October 4, 1996 (after which I had the opportunity to meet and question Kerry Kennedy, Kathleen Kennedy Townsend, Rory Kennedy, and Victoria Reggie Kennedy).

Oral Histories: From the Edward M. Kennedy Institute: Robert Shriver III and Maria Shriver, January 29, 2019; Victoria R. Kennedy, April 8, 2010; Caroline Raclin (daughter of Victoria Reggie Kennedy), November 11, 2008.

Lectures: Kerry Kennedy book signing and lecture, Cape Codder Resort & Spa, July 2, 2018; Robert Kennedy Jr. book signing and lecture, Cape Codder Resort and Spa, August 23, 2018.

Kennedy Wealth

Interview: Benedict F. Fitzgerald Jr. (April 11, 2004, March 30, 2014).

Articles: "The Kennedy Clan Decides to Cash in Last Big Business" by Mitchell Pacelle, David D. Kirkpatrick, and Calmetta Y. Coleman, *The Wall Street Journal,* January 26, 1998; "Merchandise Mart Sold" by J. Linn Allen, *Chicago Tribune,* January 27, 1998; "How the $1 Billion Kennedy Family Fortune Defies Death and Taxes" by Carl O'Donnell, *Forbes,* July 8, 2014; "Size of Billionaire-Bashing Chris Kennedy's Fortune a Mystery, Still" by Kim Janssen, *Chicago Tribune,* June 1, 2017; "State's

Longest-Practicing Lawyer Looks Back on Drama-Filled Career," by David E. Frank, *Massachusetts Lawyers Weekly,* March 13, 2014.

Television: "Kennedy's Wealth Exceeded Tens of Millions," CBS News, August 31, 2009.

Kara, Teddy Jr., and Patrick Kennedy

Interviews: Kara Kennedy (January 3, 1998, April 4, 2011); Dun Gifford (2005); David Burke (1999, 2008); Richard Burke (August 23, 1999); Ted Sorensen (2008); Thomas Franken (May 12, 2018); Pat Bruno (January 23, 2018); Megan Strayhorn (April 11, 2018, April 12, 2018); Marcia Chellis; Sister Pauline Joseph; Dr. David Sugarbaker (January 5, 2017, January 15, 2017); Webster Janssen (November 14, 2011, November 16, 2011, December 1, 2011, and a follow-up telephone conversation on January 12, 2012, based on new information relating to Joan's being able to lease the Squaw Island home in summer months).

Note that Joan's court-appointed caretaker who witnessed the packing of the Squaw Island home asked for anonymity. Leah Mason was also present and corroborated her memories in interviews for my book *The Kennedys: After Camelot.*

I would also like to thank Mary Gillan, who was Dr. Sugarbaker's assistant at Dana-

Farber/Brigham. Her interviews were conducted on January 19, 2017, and January 26, 2017.

I would to thank the late author James Spada for providing me with a wealth of material on Ted, Joan, and their children, Kara, Teddy Jr., and Patrick, which he compiled during the process of developing a book about the senator. His in-depth research — including his interviews with many of their intimates — proved invaluable to this book, and I would like to gratefully acknowledge him. He was a good friend. He passed away in May 2017.

Joan's comment about the difference between stumping for Patrick as opposed to the years she spent doing the same thing for Ted ("Well, for one thing, Patrick says thank you") was to the author, November 1992.

The writer who happened upon Kara and Joan in an antique store in Hyannis Port in August 2011 (". . . my little elf") was the author.

Articles: "The Dream Lives On" by Kara Kennedy, *Globe Magazine,* April 3, 2011; "Kennedy, His Children, and Cancer: He Helped Them Beat It, but Now the Fight Is His" by Sally Jacobs, *The Boston Globe,* May 25, 2008; "Untimely Death Shocks Kennedy Family" by K. C. Myers, *Cape Cod Times,* September 18, 2011; "Funeral Mass Held for Kara Kennedy" by Jessica Gresko, *Cape Cod*

Times, September 22, 2011; "Kennedys Disagree on Sale of Cape House" by Andrea Estes, *The Boston Globe,* April 12, 2005; "Kennedy Clan Clashes over Sale of Cape Cod Mansion" by Francis Harris, *The Telegraph,* April 13, 2005; "Democrat, Republican and a Bond of Addiction" by Mark Leibovich, *The New York Times,* September 19, 2006; "Patrick Kennedy Admits Addiction After Car Crash" by David Stout and John Holusha, *The New York Times,* May 5, 2006; "Patrick Kennedy Packs Up 63 Years of Family History" by Abby Goodnough, *The New York Times,* December 16, 2010.

Volumes: *A Common Struggle: A Personal Journey Through the Past and Future of Mental Illness and Addiction* by Patrick J. Kennedy and Stephen Fried; *The Senator: My Ten Years with Ted Kennedy* by Richard E. Burke, William Hoffer, and Marilyn Hoffer.

Senator Edward Kennedy

Interviews: Joan Kennedy (2001, 2013); Richard Burke (August 23, 1999); Dominick Dunne (June 3, 2007, June 8, 2007); Webster Janssen; Pat Bruno; Dr. David Sugarbaker; Mary Gillan.

Articles: "Kennedy's Battle in the Nation's War Against Cancer" by Gina Kolata and Lawrence K. Altman, *The New York Times,* August 27, 2009; "The Story Behind Ted

Kennedy's Surgery" by Lawrence K. Altman, *The New York Times,* July 29, 2008; "A Drum Major for Righteous Indignation" by Leonard Fein, *Jewish Daily Forward,* July 12, 2008; "A Left Coast Kennedy" by Susan Salter Reynolds, *Los Angeles Times Magazine,* March 14, 1999; "Ted Kennedy on the Rocks" by Michael Kelly, *GQ,* February 1990.

Volumes: *True Compass: A Memoir* by Edward M. Kennedy; *Last Lion: The Fall and Rise of Ted Kennedy* by the Team at *The Boston Globe,* edited by Peter S. Canellos; *Ted Kennedy: The Dream That Never Died* by Edward Klein; *The Kennedy Men: 1901–1963* by Laurence Leamer.

Oral Histories: Charles L. Bartlett/JFK library; Rose Fitzgerald Kennedy/Herbert Hoover Library Foundation; Frank Mankiewicz/RFK Oral History Project; Joan Braden/JFK Library; Maud Shaw/JFK Library; Nancy Tuckerman/JFK Library; Kenneth O'Donnell/Lyndon Baines Johnson Library; Pierre Salinger/RFK Oral History Project; George Smathers/U.S. Senate Historical Office; Charles Spalding/JFK Library. From the Edward M. Kennedy Institute: Edward M. Kennedy, June 3, 2005, June 17, 2005, October 13, 2005, March 20, 2006, May 8, 2006, August 15, 2006, November 29, 2006, January 6, 2007, February 12,

2007, February 27, 2007, April 3, 2007, May 7, 2007, May 30, 2007, August 7, 2007, October 8, 2007, December 8, 2007, January 7, 2008; David Axelrod, 2012; Melody Barnes (staffer for Edward Kennedy), undated; David Burke (chief of staff to Edward Kennedy), April 9, 2008.

Speech: Senator Ted Kennedy at Harvard John F. Kennedy School of Government, October 26, 1991.

Victoria Reggie Kennedy

Interviews: Dun Gifford (2005); Edmund M. Reggie (August 4, 1998). I interviewed a caretaker who has worked at the Kennedy compound for thirty years and who asked for anonymity.

Articles: "Victoria Reggie Kennedy Provided Stability for Ted Kennedy When He Needed It Most" by Lois Romano, *The Washington Post,* August 28, 2009; "Death of Edward 'Ted' Kennedy Raises Questions About Political Dynasties" by Lois Romano, *The Washington Post,* August 27, 2009; "How the Tragic Death of Ted Kennedy's Only Daughter Brought His Widow and Ex-Wife Closer Together" by Meghan Keneally, *Daily Mail,* April 23, 2014.

Forum: "The Kennedy Women" at the John Fitzgerald Kennedy Library and Museum, October 4, 1996.

Oral Histories: From the Edward M. Kennedy Institute: Victoria R. Kennedy, April 8, 2010; Caroline Raclin (daughter of Victoria Reggie Kennedy), November 11, 2016.

Transcript: "Text: Interviews with Vicki Kennedy," June 28, 1995, and May 13, 1999.

Video: "Dedication of the Edward M. Kennedy Institute for the United States Senate," March 30, 2015 (entire event); "Oprah Winfrey Interviews Victoria Reggie Kennedy," *The Oprah Winfrey Show,* November 25, 2009.

Joan Kennedy

Interviews: Joan Kennedy (November 1992/ *Joy of Classical Music* book tour, March 2001, September 12, 2011, as well as a personal letter, November 19, 1998: "Fortunately, I am well and happy in this present stage of my life — the joy of spending a lot of time with my four grand children and enjoying my part time job as Chairperson of Boston's Cultural Council and serving on the Board of Directors of four great Boston institutions. I am blessed with many dear friends whom, I have known since my college days, and I still play the piano or narrate with orchestras for a favorite charity"); Leah Mason; Dun Gifford; Dr. Gerald Aronoff; Webster Janssen; Marcia Chellis (January 14, 1998, March 1, 1998, and also I drew from Ms. Chellis's comments on the television program "People Are Talking," San Francisco, 1985).

I also relied heavily on my interviews with Joan Braden, originally conducted for my book *Jackie, Ethel, Joan.* Joan was married to CIA official and journalist Tom Braden, whose book *Eight Is Enough* was adapted by ABC as a TV series in 1977.

Articles: "The Fall of Joan" by Michelle McPhee and David Wedge, *Boston* magazine, May 15, 2006; "An Intimate Portrait of Joan Kennedy" by Barbara Kevles, *Good House-keeping,* September 1969; "Joan Kennedy's Story" by Betty Hannah Hoffman, *Ladies' Home Journal,* July 1970; "Joan Had to Learn to Live with Heartache" by Eleanor Roberts, *Herald American,* December 7, 1982; "Prime Time with Joan Kennedy" by Sally Jacobs, *Globe Magazine,* July 9, 2000; "Joan Kennedy Treated for Alcoholism," Associated Press, October 9, 2001; "After 24 Years, Joan Kennedy Ends Marriage" by Gail Jennes and Gioia Diliberto, *People,* December 20, 1982; "Joan Kennedy Surveys Her Sober Life" by Gail Jennes, *People,* April 7, 1978; "Joan Kennedy Finds Solace in Memories of Daughter, Kara" by Liz McNeil, *People,* September 20, 2011; "Kennedy, His Children and Cancer" by Sally Jacobs, *The Boston Globe,* May 25, 2008.

Volumes: *The Joy of Classical Music: A Guide*

for You and Your Family by Joan Kennedy; *Joan: The Reluctant Kennedy* by Lester David; *The Joan Kennedy Story: Living with the Kennedys* by Marcia Chellis; *Jackie, Ethel, Joan: Women of Camelot* by J. Randy Taraborrelli.

I also referenced extensive research for my report "Joan Kennedy" on *Entertainment Tonight,* November 2000.

Anthony Radziwill

Interviews: Gustavo Paredes; John Perry Barlow; Stephen Styles-Cooper; Carole Radziwill (September 2005); Christopher Lawford.

Volume: *On What Remains: A Memoir of Fate, Friendship, and Love* by Carole Radziwill.

Michael and Victoria Kennedy (and the Verrochis)

Interviews: Josefina "Fina" Harvin; Noelle Bombardier; Leah Mason; Joseph Gargan; Theresa Lichtman; Tim Robbins (May 1, 2018); Jamie Auchincloss (December 1, 2016, October 11, 2017, November 2, 2017); Rose Burgunder Styron (February 21, 2013); Thomas Davis (March 2, 2018); Ben Bradlee (October 1, 1995); Linda DelVechio (June 8, 2017, June 10, 2017, August 11, 2017); (Police Chief) Brian Noonan (August 29, 2017, August 30, 2017); Ren Ayers (August

22, 2017); Philip Geyelin (March 1, 1998); Astrid Gifford (September 3, 2017); Gayle Fee (May 22, 2018); Bryan Holloway; Robert DuPont (June 15, 2017, July 5, 2017).

I drew from the lengthy conversation I had with Michael Kennedy in 1997, as described earlier in these notes.

I interviewed several people close to the family of Marisa Verrochi, including relatives of hers, all of whom asked for anonymity. I am granting them that request.

Articles: "Subpoena Eyed in Sex Scandal: Baby-Sitter Keeping Mum on Kennedy" by Helen Kennedy and Michele McPhee, *New York Daily News,* April 27, 1997; "Sitter's Father to Talk to Cops" by Michele McPhee and Helen Kennedy, *New York Daily News,* April 28, 1997; "Kennedy Took Baby Sitter on Excursions: Maine Records Show Teenager Joined Family on Rafting Trips" by Scot Lehigh and Stephen Kurkjian, *The Boston Globe,* May 24, 1997; "A Betrayal in the Family" by Pam Lambert, *People,* May 12, 1997; "Controversy Surrounds a Kennedy's Alleged Affair with a Baby-sitter," *The Boston Globe,* April 25, 1997; "They're at It Again! RFK Son 'Slept with Schoolgirl, 14!' " *New York Post,* April 25, 1997; "The Kennedys in Aspen: A New Year's Tragedy" by Matthew Malone, *Modern Luxury,* November 27, 2017; "Kennedy Family, Friends Say Farewell to

Michael" by Elizabeth Mehren, *Los Angeles Times,* January 4, 1998; "Tragedy Strikes Again" by Nancy Gibbs, *Time,* January 12, 1998; "Death in Aspen" by Patrick Rogers, *People,* January 19, 1998.

Volumes: *American Values* by Robert F. Kennedy Jr.; *Symptoms of Withdrawal* by Christopher Kennedy Lawford; *Moments of Clarity* by Christopher Kennedy Lawford; *Fully Alive* by Timothy Shriver; *A Good Man* by Mark K. Shriver; *The Whole Ten Yards* by Frank Gifford and Harry Waters.

The "Brain Trust" meeting was described to me by a source present who asked to not be named.

Television: "Kennedy Tragedy on the Slopes," *The Geraldo Rivera Show,* January 8, 1998; "The Deadly Games the Kennedys Play," *The Geraldo Rivera Show,* June 18, 1998.

Throughout, I also drew from the text of Robert F. Kennedy Jr.'s eulogy of his brother Michael Kennedy, 1997.

Michael Skakel

Interviews: Noelle Bombardier; Leah Mason; Mickey Sherman (March 11, 2005); James Skakel (1994); Benedict F. Fitzgerald Jr. (April 11, 2004, March 30, 2014); Stephen Styles-Cooper; Randy Beattie (October 17, 2017).

Articles: "Michael Skakel Renounces Kennedys" by Neil Vigdor, *Stamford Advocate,* April 25, 2013; "Michael Skakel Was Convicted of Murdering Martha Moxley, So Why Is He Free?" by Leonard Levitt, *The Daily Beast,* April 22, 2017; "Opinion: Little Doubt That Michael Skakel Was Wrongly Convicted in the Martha Moxley Case" by David R. Cameron, *New Haven Register,* January 1, 2017; "Kennedy Cousin Michael Skakel Seeks to Suppress Audiotape in Upcoming Murder Retrial Where He Says He Pleasured Himself Outside Victim's Window the Night She Died," Associated Press, July 23, 2014; "It's All in the Family" by Richard Lacayo, *Time,* July 26, 1999.

Volumes: *Dead Man Talking* (an unpublished manuscript by Michael Skakel); *Framed: Why Michael Skakel Spent over a Decade in Prison for a Murder He Didn't Commit* by Robert F. Kennedy Jr.; *The Mysterious Murder of Martha Moxley: Did the Political and Financial Power of the Kennedy/Skakel Families Trump the Truth?* by Joe Bruno; *Murder in Greenwich: Who Killed Martha Moxley?* by Mark Fuhrman; *Justice: Crimes, Trials, and Punishments* by Dominick Dunne; "Dead Man Talking: A Kennedy Cousin Comes Clean" by Michael Skakel and Richard Hoffman (unpublished book proposal).

Correspondence: Robert F. Kennedy "Impact Letter," August 8, 2002.

Note: For more on this topic, go to www
.marthamoxley.com.

Ena Bernard

Interviews: Josefina "Fina" Harvin; Noelle
Bombardier; Leah Mason; Christopher Lawford.

Articles: "A Kennedy Nanny, 100, Has
Tales to Tell" by Georgia East, *Los Angeles
Times,* December 29, 2008; "Ethel Kennedy
Clan Attends Sunrise Funeral of Beloved
Nanny Ena 'Mimi' Bernard" by Susannah
Bryan, *Sun Sentinel,* August 8, 2013.

Volumes: *American Values* by Robert F.
Kennedy Jr.

Kirk LeMoyne "Lem" Billings

Interviews: Allan Burke (March 10, 2018,
March 11, 2018, April 5, 2018); Ben Bradlee; Andy Williams.

Volumes: *Jack and Lem: John F. Kennedy
and Lem Billings: The Untold Story of an
Extraordinary Friendship* by David Pitts; *Symp-
toms of Withdrawal* by Christopher Kennedy
Lawford; *American Values* by Robert F. Ken-
nedy Jr.; *The Kennedys: An American Drama*
by Peter Collier and David Horowitz; *The
Kennedys: America's Emerald Kings: A Five-
Generation History of the Ultimate Irish-Catholic
Family* by Thomas Maier.

Kirk LeMoyne Billings's Oral Histories:
From the JFK Library: March 25, 1964, June

19, 1964, June 24, 1964, July 7, 1964, July 22, 1964, January 15, 1965, February 20, 1965, June 11, 1965, June 18, 1965, January 9, 1966.

Robert F. Kennedy Jr., Emily Black Kennedy, and Mary Richardson Kennedy
Interviews: Josefina "Fina" Harvin; Andy Williams; Sister Pauline Joseph; Joseph Gargan; Joseph Fricke; Bob Galland (January 4, 2000); Allan Burke; Marjorie Dougherty (January 2, 2018, March 3, 2018, April 11, 2018); Alyssa Chapman (May 1, 2018); Noelle Bombardier; Christopher Lawford; Victoria Michaelis (September 27, 2017).

Articles: "Alcoholism Runs in Kennedy Clan, Son of RFK Tells Interviewers," Associated Press, October 17, 1997; "RFK's Sex Diary: His Secret Journal of Affairs," by Isabel Vincent and Melissa Klein, *New York Post,* September 8, 2013; "RFK, Jr.'s Diaries Reveal Intense Family Drama after JFK Jr. Death," by Josh Duboff, *Vanity Fair,* November 4, 2013; "Robert Kennedy Jr.'s Sex Diary Sounds like a Real Bodice-Ripper" by Juggalo Law, *Above the Law,* September 9, 2013; "Robert F. Kennedy Jr. Diary Talks 'Lust Demons,' Slams Al Sharpton, Jesse Jackson: Reports" by Paige Lavender, *Huffington Post,* September 9, 2013; "The Last Days of Mary Kennedy" by Laurence Leamer, *Newsweek,* June 11, 2012; "Mary and Robert F. Kennedy Jr.'s Tragic Marriage Detailed" by Matt Pearce, *Los Angeles Times,* June 10, 2012; "Mary Richardson Kennedy, Wife of RFK Jr., Found Dead in New York," by Tina Susman, *Los Angeles Times,* May 16, 2012; "Autopsy: Mary R. Kennedy Died of Asphyxiation from Hanging" by Michael Muskal, *Los Angeles Times,* May 17, 2012; "Ode to My Best Friend — Mary Richardson Kennedy" by Kerry Kennedy, *Huffington Post,* May 22, 2012; "Autopsy of RFK Jr.'s Wife Finds Antidepressants but No Alcohol" by Lily Kuo, Reuters, July 7, 2012; "Mary Richardson Kennedy, Stepmonster?" by Wednesday Martin, *Psychology Today,* June 13, 2012.

Volumes: *American Values* by Robert F. Kennedy Jr.; *The Riverkeepers: Two Activists Fight to Reclaim Our Environment as a Basic Human Right* by John Cronin and Robert F. Kennedy Jr.; *Jack and Lem* by David Pitts; *Ethel: The Story of Mrs. Robert F. Kennedy* by David Lester; *The Kennedy Women: The Saga of an American Family* by Laurence Leamer.

Television: "Kerry Kennedy Press Conference Relating to Mary Richardson Kennedy's Death," YouTube; "Mary Kennedy's Family Blasts Stories on Her Death," CNN, May 18, 2012; "Kerry Kennedy Acquitted in DWI Trial," CNN, February 28, 2014.

David Kennedy

Interviews: Noelle Bombardier; Leah Mason; James Skakel.

Articles: "Ethel Kennedy Today" by Adele Whitely Fletcher, *Lady's Circle,* September 1969; "David Kennedy — 1955–1984" by Peter Carlson, *People,* May 14, 1984.

Volumes: *American Values* by Robert F. Kennedy Jr.; *Bobby Kennedy: The Making of a Liberal Icon* by Larry Tye; *Symptoms of Withdrawal* by Christopher Kennedy Lawford; *The Kennedys: An American Drama* by Peter Collier and David Horowitz; *Behind Blue Eyes: The Biography of David Anthony Kennedy* by Grahame Robert Bedford; *The Senator* by Richard Burke; *RFK* by Dick Schaap; *Ethel* by Lester David; *Robert Kennedy and His Times* by Arthur M. Schlesinger Jr.

Kathleen Kennedy Townsend and David Townsend

Interviews: Kathleen Kennedy Townsend (after "The Kennedy Women," seminar at the John Fitzgerald Kennedy Library and Museum, October 1996; dressing room, *Oprah Winfrey Show* taping, November 1997); Noelle Bombardier; Leah Mason; Jamie Auchincloss, Josefina "Fina" Harvin; James Skakel; David Burke (2000).

Articles: "The Daughter Also Rises" by Daniel LeDuc, *The Washington Post,* November 28, 1999; "Watching as a Race She Can't Lose Slips Away" by Johanna Neuman, *Los Angeles Times,* September 1, 2002; "Kennedy Townsend Enters Race for Governor," Times Wire Reports, *Los Angeles Times,* May 6, 2002; "Robert Kennedy's Eldest Child to Run for Office," United Press International, *Los Angeles Times,* January 27, 1986; "Daughter of RFK Opens House Campaign," United Press International, *Los Angeles Times,* May 30, 1986; "Kathleen Kennedy Townsend: Just Like Her Father?" by Sally B. Donnelly, *Time,* August 2, 1999.

Documentary: *Ethel.*

Video: "The Young Kennedys: Interview with Joseph Kennedy II, Max Kennedy, Christopher Kennedy, Kathleen Kennedy Townsend, and Kerry Kennedy Cuomo," *The Oprah Winfrey Show.* (As part of my research for my book *Jackie, Ethel, Joan,* I attended this taping in November 1997 in Chicago, where I had the opportunity to meet Christopher Lawford, Bobby Kennedy Jr., and Kathleen Kennedy Townsend. Some of their quotes in this book are from that show, and also from questions I was able to ask them after the taping); "Kennedys of the Third Generation," *60 Minutes,* October 19, 1997.

Joseph Kennedy II, Sheila Rauch Kennedy, and Anne Elizabeth "Beth" Kelly Kennedy

Interviews: Sheila Rauch Kennedy (June 1998); Barbara Gibson (October 1, 1998, October 10, 1998, November 10, 1998, December 15, 1998, March 10, 1999, April 15, 1999, January 4, 2000); Ben Bradlee, Pamela Kelley Burkley (August 24, 2017); Josefina "Fina" Harvin; Noelle Bombardier; Senator John Tunney (1998); Amy Thompson-Huttel (August 25, 2017, October 3, 2017).

As indicated in the text, the meetings between the Kennedys relating to Sheila Rauch's book were described to me by sources who were present for them and who asked for anonymity.

Articles: "Political Progeny Makes Tracks to Follow in Famous Footsteps," Associated Press, *Los Angeles Times,* November 6, 1986; "A Kennedy Faces the Fallout from a Scandal" by Sara Rimer, *The New York Times,* July 10, 1997; "Another Kennedy Accident Victim Remains a Friend" by Cynthia McCormick, *Cape Cod Times,* July 25, 1999 (updated January 4, 2011).

Volumes: *Shattered Faith: A Woman's Struggle to Stop the Catholic Church from Annulling Her Marriage* by Sheila Rauch Kennedy; *Robert Kennedy and His Times* by Arthur M. Schlesinger Jr.; *A Thousand Days:*

John F. Kennedy in the White House by Arthur M. Schlesinger.

Kerry Kennedy and Andrew Cuomo

Interviews: Helen Thomas (September 25, 1998), Alyssa Chapman; David Axelrod (2012).

I interviewed a number of people presently associated with Governor Andrew Cuomo for purposes of deep background only since they felt unauthorized to speak about their experiences with him.

Articles: "The Making of Andrew Cuomo" by Jonathan Mahler, *The New York Times Magazine,* August 11, 2010; "Andrew Cuomo and Kerry Kennedy," *People,* June 25, 1990; "Kennedy-Cuomo Union Appears to Be Ending" by Jennifer Steinhauer, *The New York Times,* July 1, 2003; "How Andrew Cuomo Gets His Way" by Jeffrey Toobin, *The New Yorker,* February 16, 2015; "The Cuomo Daughters' Key Dual Role" by Erica Orden, *The Wall Street Journal,* August 7, 2010.

Volumes: *All Things Possible: Setbacks and Success in Politics and Life* by Andrew M. Cuomo; *Crossroads: The Future of American Politics* by Andrew Cuomo; *The Contender: Andrew Cuomo, a Biography* by Michael Shnayerson.

Caroline Kennedy, Ed Schlossberg, and Family

Interviews: Matthew Johnston (April 11, 2017); Letitia Baldrige (2005); Benedict F. Fitzgerald Jr.; Marta Sgubin (October 22, 1998); Gustavo Paredes; Ariel Paredes; John Perry Barlow; Stephen Styles-Cooper; Joan Braden (1998); Lisa McClintock (2011); Olga Price (September 3, 2010); Adora Rule (April 1, 2015, May 1, 2016, August 1, 2016); Eleanor Doyle (1998); Rebecca Abelman (January 5, 2018, March 2, 2018, April 4, 2018); Sister Pauline Joseph (March 1, 2010, March 2, 2018); David Axelrod (2012); Dun Gifford; Oleg Cassini (June 5, 1998, March 5, 2004); Clint Hill (January 4, 1998, March 5, 2010, June 4, 2010, April 3, 2011); Jack Walsh (March 9, 1998); Joseph Paolella (September 11, 1998, September 17, 1998); Virginia Guest Valentine (July 22, 2016); Winthrop Rutherfurd III (October 14, 2016, November 19, 2016); Delores Goodwin (June 5, 2016, July 10, 2016, August 8, 2016); Mary Tyler Freeman Cheek McClenahan (January 11, 1998); Nancy Tuckerman (March 10, 2007); Mona Latham (May 4, 2009, April 3, 2010, January 11, 2011); Margaret Kearney (March 11, 1998); Marie-Hélène de Rothschild (May 15, 2016); Kiki Feroudi Moutsatsos (July 12, 2016); Jonathan Tapper (April 25, 2016, April 27, 2016, May 3, 2016); Michael Dupree (September

27, 2016, January 3, 2017); Lenny Holtzman (February 1, 2018, March 6, 2018); Richard Bradley (June 5, 2010, September 14, 2017, October 1, 2017); Christopher Lawford.

As well as the above, I interviewed a number of people presently associated with Caroline Kennedy Schlossberg for purposes of deep background only since they felt unauthorized to speak about their experiences with her. I also drew from my extensive research for my article "Caroline Kennedy," *Star,* November 15, 1999, and my two-part series "Caroline Kennedy" for *Woman's Day,* March 2000.

Articles: "Caroline in the Spotlight" by William Wright, *Ladies' Home Journal,* August 2001; "Love and Loss" by Ellen O'Hara, *Ladies' Home Journal,* August 1994; "Caroline Kennedy: You Just Keep Going" by Elizabeth Kastor, *Good Housekeeping,* October 2001; "Caroline Kennedy Schlossberg: Champion of Civility" by Romesh Ratnesar, *Time,* August 2, 1999; "A Kennedy Romance" by David Van Biema, *People,* March 17, 1986; "A President Like My Father" by Caroline Kennedy, *The New York Times,* January 27, 2008; "Kennedys for Clinton" by Kathleen Kennedy Townsend, Robert F. Kennedy Jr., and Kerry Kennedy, *Los Angeles Times,* January 29, 2008; "Younger Kennedys Continue Service to the Country" by Robin Abcarian, *Los Angeles Times,* August 27,

2009; "Caroline Kennedy Busts on *New York Times* Reporter in Interview" Fox News, December 28, 2008; "Transcript of the Caroline Kennedy Interview," *The New York Times,* December 27, 2008; "Daddy Didn't Want His Little Girl to Be a Kennedy" by Harriman Janus, *Photoplay,* May 1969.

Details of the meeting of Kennedys relating to the pros and cons of Caroline's run for the Senate were relayed to me by an anonymous source.

Volumes: *Symptoms of Addiction* by Christopher Kennedy Lawford; *Kennedy Weddings: A Family Album* by Jay Mulvaney; *The Kennedys* by Peter Collier and David Horowitz; *First Ladies: The Saga of Presidents' Wives and Their Power, 1961–1990* by Carl Sferrazza Anthony; *Just Enough Rope: An Intimate Memoir* by Joan Braden; *Death of a President: November 20–November 25, 1963* by William Manchester; *As We Remember Her: Jacqueline Kennedy Onassis in the Words of Her Family and Friends* by Carl Sferrazza Anthony; *Jackie, Ethel, Joan* by J. Randy Taraborrelli; *After Camelot* by J. Randy Taraborrelli; *Jackie, Janet & Lee* by J. Randy Taraborrelli.

I also utilized my research for "Caroline Kennedy," an *Entertainment Tonight* report that I produced, November 22, 2000.

Oral Histories: Janet Auchincloss/JFK

Library, September 5, 1964, September 6, 1964; Letitia Baldrige/JFK Library; Luella Hennessey/JFK Library; Maud Shaw/JFK Library; Charles Bartlett/JFK Library; Jacqueline Kennedy Onassis/LBJ Library, 1974, as well as the newly released oral histories for the JFK Library in 2011; Rose Fitzgerald Kennedy/Herbert Hoover Library Foundation; Dun Gifford/RFK Oral History Project; Roswell Gilpatric/JFK Library; Frank Mankiewicz/RFK Oral History Project; Nancy Tuckerman/JFK Library; Kenneth O'Donnell/LBJ Library; Pierre Salinger/RFK Oral History Project; George Smathers/ U.S. Senate Historical Office; Charles Spalding/ JFK Library.

Television: "Meet Marta: The Nanny Who Cared for the Kennedys" by Max Barbakow and Cristina Costantini, ABC News, March 12, 2013; Clint Hill interview with C-SPAN, https://www.c-span.org/about/history/, May 2012.

Maria Shriver, Arnold Schwarzenegger, and the Shriver Family
Interviews: Eunice Kennedy Shriver (April 2002); Sargent Shriver (April 2002); Mark Shriver (April 2002); Timothy Shriver (April 2002); Maria Shriver (2002); Arnold Schwarzenegger (1994, 1999, 2002, 2003); Randy Beattie (October 16, 2017); Janet Charlton (October 30, 2017); Jamie Auchincloss; Leah Mason; Hugh Sidey; Landon Parvin (October

9, 2017); Lenny Holtzman.

I also drew from informal conversations I had with Maria Shriver in April 1994 — during a period of time when we were working on a segment about Michael Jackson for *Dateline NBC* — for this and other sections of the book.

Regarding my interview with Eunice Kennedy Shriver: it took place in the spring of 2002 for an article I was writing at the time on the Special Olympics for *Redbook*. I drew from that interview for this part and other sections of this book.

I also met Sargent Shriver at that time and drew from my conversation with him in this section of the book, as well as in others. I have always had a lot of admiration for Mr. Shriver, and I hope that much is clear in my writings about him. "I have a story about pretty much everything, don't I?" he asked me. And that he did. (I also referenced the Sargent Shriver files from the LBJ Library for this section of *The Kennedy Heirs*.)

The Roman Catholic priest referenced in the chapter "Faith. Not Hope. Faith." asked not to be identified by name.

Articles: "Mildred Baena, the Housekeeper Who Had a Child with Arnold Schwarzenegger Speaks Out for the First Time," *Hello!*, June 14, 2011; "Mark Shriver Talks About His Family, the Kennedys, and Writing About His Dad's Decline" by Lloyd Grove, *Daily*

Beast, June 7, 2012; "Oprah Talks to Maria Shriver," *O: The Oprah Magazine,* June 2008; "Mr. and Mrs. California" by Marie Brenner, *Vanity Fair,* May 18, 2011; "Arnold in Office" by Connie Bruck, *The New Yorker,* June 28, 2004; "Women Say Schwarzenegger Groped, Humiliated Them" by Gary Cohn, Carla Hall, and Robert W. Welkos, *Los Angeles Times,* October 2, 2003; "Schwarzenegger Fathered a Child with Longtime Member of Household Staff" by Mark Z. Barabak and Victoria Kim, *Los Angeles Times,* May 17, 2011; "Schwarzenegger Plans Inquiry into Groping Allegations" by Nancy Vogel, Peter Nicholas, and Henry Weinstein, *Los Angeles Times,* November 7, 2003; "Schwarzenegger Whispers Become an Admission" by Adam Nagourney and Jennifer Steinhauer, *The New York Times,* May 17, 2011.

Volumes: *The Kennedy Family and the Story of Mental Retardation* by Edward Shorter; *Total Recall: My Unbelievably True Life Story* by Arnold Schwarzenegger; *Fantastic: The Life of Arnold Schwarzenegger* by Laurence Leamer; *And One More Thing Before You Go . . .* by Maria Shriver; *I've Been Thinking . . . : Reflections, Prayers, and Meditations for a Meaningful Life* by Maria Shriver; *What's Heaven?* by Maria Shriver; *Ten Things I Wish I'd Known — Before I Went Out into the Real World . . .* by Maria Shriver; *Just Who Will You Be?* by Maria Shriver; *The Shriver Report: A Study* by Maria Shriver and the Center for American Progress (various reports); *Fully Alive* by Timothy Shriver; *A Good Man* by Mark K. Shriver; *Sarge: The Life and Times of Sargent Shriver* by Scott Stossel; *Point of the Lance* by Sargent Shriver.

Oral History: From the Edward M. Kennedy Institute: Robert Shriver III and Maria Shriver, January 29, 2019.

Video: Arnold Schwarzenegger interview with George Stephanopoulos, *Good Morning America,* ABC News, October 1, 2012; Arnold Schwarzenegger interview with Lesley Stahl, *60 Minutes,* CBS News, October 1, 2012; Bobby Shriver interview, *The Larry Elder Show,* January 28, 2014; Maria Shriver interview with Diane Sawyer, *Good Morning America,* May 11, 2009; "Maria Shriver–Arnold Schwarzenegger Scandal Exposes a Familiar Kennedy Flaw" by Susan Donaldson James, *ABC News,* May 20, 2011; "Schwarzenegger's Lawyer Slams Latest Double Whammy: Alleged Cover-Up and Mistress No. 2," by Gina Serpe, E! News, May 25, 2011.

I also referenced videotapes of Maria Shriver's testimony before Congress about Alzheimer's as well as Ms. Shriver's *The Alzheimer's Project* for HBO and the eulogy for her mother, Eunice Kennedy Shriver; also,

American Experience: The Kennedys, PBS, 1992.

I interviewed several people in the family of Mildred Baena, all of whom asked for anonymity.

For much more on the Shrivers, go to www.EuniceKennedyShriver.org.

Conor Kennedy and Taylor Swift

I interviewed several people close to both Conor and Taylor in 2017 and 2018, all of whom asked for anonymity. Also: Gayle Fee; Leah Mason; Barry Thomas Sterling (May 12, 2018); Barbara Lewis (May 15, 2018); and Sister Pauline Joseph.

Articles: "Ethel Kennedy Explains the Taylor Swift Je Ne Sais Quoi" by Julie Miller, *Vanity Fair,* October 15, 2012; "Ethel Kennedy May Approve of Taylor Swift Marrying Her 18-Year-Old Grandson" by Julie Miller, *Vanity Fair,* September 25, 2012; "We're Neighbours! Taylor Swift Moves Next Door to the Kennedy Compound as She 'Buys $5m Cape Cod Mansion' " by Lizzie Smith, *Daily Mail,* August 13, 2012; "Taylor Swift Buys $4.9 Million Cape Cod Beach Home Near Boyfriend Conor Kennedy's Family Estate" by Gina Pace, *New York Daily News,* March 6, 2013; "Taylor Swift made $1 Million Profit After Selling Hyannis Port House Near Ex Conor Kennedy's Family Compound: Report" by Zayda Rivera, *New York*

Daily News, March 7, 2013.

Volume: *A Common Struggle* by Patrick J. Kennedy and Stephen Fried.

Videos: "Taylor Swift New Hyannisport Neighbor Says Ethel Kennedy," Capecast, YouTube, October 12, 2012; "Ethel & Rory Talk Taylor Swift and 'Ethel' at the Celebs .com Studio at Sundance," Celebs.com, YouTube, January 31, 2012; "2012 Ripple of Hope Awards Ceremony" (entire gala).

Joseph Patrick Kennedy III and Lauren Anne Birchfield Kennedy

Interviews: Joseph Patrick Kennedy III (March 1998; February 2011); Noelle Bombardier; Leah Mason.

Articles: "Meet Joe Kennedy, the Democrat Taking on Trump" by Tessa Stewart, *Rolling Stone,* January 30, 2018; "Joe Kennedy III Carries the Kennedy Legacy into Fight Against Trump" by Jon Ward, Yahoo! News, January 30, 2018; "Joe Kennedy III Reacts to Trump: 'Bullies May Land a Punch,' Don't Win," Associated Press, January 30, 2018; "A Life of Challenge" by Maxwell Kennedy, Inside Borders, June 1998; "Meet the Next President Kennedy" by Matt Viser, *Town and Country,* July 6, 2017.

Oral History: Frank Mankiewicz–RFK #3. August 12, 1969 (JFK Library).

Video: "Full Transcript and Video: Joe Kennedy Delivers Democratic Response to State of the Union," *The New York Times,* January 31, 2018; "Rep. Joe Kennedy Weighs In on Trump," *The Daily Show,* August 2, 2017.

Audio: "Representative Joe Kennedy III Reflects on Great-Uncle JFK's Legacy," JFK Library, May 29, 2017.

Miscellaneous

"Kennedy Makes Campaign Stop in Sterling" by Pam Eggemeier, Saukvalley.com, September 18, 2017; "For the Democrats, Chris Kennedy" by the editorial board, *Chicago Tribune,* February 21, 2018; " 'Untouchable' Kennedys Boast About Bad Behavior All Over Hyannis Port," by Gabrielle Fonrouge, *New York Post,* August 30, 2017; "How a Kennedy Family Party Devolved into an 'Angry Mob,' According to Cape Cod Police" by Kenzie Bryant, *Vanity Fair,* August 23, 2017; "Kennedys Are Hyannisport Hypocrites When It Comes to Racial, Ethnic Diversity" by Howie Carr, *Boston Herald,* July 8, 2018.

PERSONAL ACKNOWLEDGMENTS

I want to thank my editor, Charles Spicer, for all his encouragement and also for his interest in following up our *New York Times* bestseller together, *Jackie, Janet & Lee,* with this work, *The Kennedy Heirs.* I'm so honored to be edited by Charles and published by St. Martin's Press. Thanks also to Charles's assistant, Sarah Grill. My appreciation, as well, to Bethany Reis, who did a wonderful job copyediting this manuscript.

I would also like to acknowledge my domestic literary agent, Mitch Douglas, for the last twenty years of his terrific representation. Mitch is a good friend as well as my agent, and I am eternally grateful to him.

And I would like to acknowledge my foreign agent, Dorie Simmonds of the Dorie Simmonds Agency in London, who has not only represented me for more than twenty years but is a trusted friend.

I would like to thank my amazing attorney, Stephen Breimer of Bloom, Hergott, Diemer,

Rosenthal & LaViolette, for his dedication to my career. Special thanks also to Candice Hanson.

Thanks also to Laurie Pozmantier at WME.

Special thanks also to Jo Ann McMahon and Felinda Adlawan of Horowitz Zaron McMahon.

I also want to acknowledge my television producing partner and good friend, Keri Selig, who has been in the trenches with me now for more than six years. We're a great team. Thanks also to her chief assistant, Kimberly Current of Intuition Productions.

I would also like to acknowledge my good friend Andy Hirsch for reading this book before publication and for his point of view. Jillian DeVaney also read it in manuscript stage and offered invaluable insight, and so I thank her as well. Barb Mueller read it in its infancy, as well, and I appreciate her, too. Thanks also to Linda DiStefano for her work as proofreader, not an easy job.

My thanks to Jonathan Hahn, my trusted friend of nearly twenty years.

Thanks to: Andy Steinlen, George Solomon, Jeff Hare, Samuel Munoz, Brandon Schmook, Richard Tyler Jordan, John Passantino, Hazel and Rob Kragulac, Andy Skurow, Brian Newman, Scherrie Payne, Freda Payne, Susaye Greene, Barbara Ormsby, Marlene Morris, Kac Young, Yvette Jarecki, Mary Downey, Laura Fagin, Corey Sheppard, Rita

Bosico, Deb Armstrong, Susan Kayaoglu, Sal Pinto, Michael Coleman, Rob Kesselring, Howard Field, Stephen Kronish, Gordon Reid Wallack, Esq., and Lindsay Brie Mathers.

I have always been so blessed to have a family as supportive as mine. My thanks and love go out to: Roslyn and Bill Barnett and Jessica and Zachary; Rocco and Rosemaria Taraborrelli and Rocco and Vincent; and Arnold Taraborrelli. A big smile, also, for Spencer Douglas Taraborrelli.

I must also acknowledge those readers of mine who have followed my career over the years. I am indebted to each and every reader who has stuck by me. I am eternally grateful to anyone who takes the time to pick up one of my books and read it. Thank you so much.

All my books are written with my late parents, Rocco and Rose Marie Taraborrelli, in mind at all times. I miss them.

J. Randy Taraborrelli
January 2019

ABOUT THE AUTHOR

J. Randy Taraborrelli is the author of 20 biographies, most of which have become *New York Times* bestsellers, including: *Jackie, Ethel, Joan: Women of Camelot; After Camelot: A Personal History of the Kennedy Family 1968 to the Present,* which was adapted as a miniseries for Reelz; and *Jackie, Janet & Lee: The Secret Lives of Janet Auchincloss and Her Daughters, Jacqueline Kennedy Onassis and Lee Radziwill,* currently being adapted as a television series by Tomorrow Studios. Visit the author's website at www.jrandytaraborrelli .com.

The employees of Thorndike Press hope you have enjoyed this Large Print book. All our Thorndike, Wheeler, and Kennebec Large Print titles are designed for easy reading, and all our books are made to last. Other Thorndike Press Large Print books are available at your library, through selected bookstores, or directly from us.

For information about titles, please call:
(800) 223-1244

or visit our website at:
gale.com/thorndike

To share your comments, please write:
Publisher
Thorndike Press
10 Water St., Suite 310
Waterville, ME 04901